Advance Praise for *A Breath of Freedom*

With this book, Höhn and Klimke make an enormous contribution to African American History, German History, Military History—and how they intersect. It is beautifully written, persuasively argued, and expertly researched.

Gerald Horne, University of Houston, author of
*Black and Brown: African-Americans and
the Mexican Revolution, 1910–1920*

Nearly three million African American soldiers served in West Germany in the years from the end of World War II to the end of the Cold War. In this vital and riveting book, Höhn and Klimke trace how black GIs' encounters abroad offered both a space to experience the freedom denied them in the United States and a chance to build an internationalized civil rights movement in concert with German activists. A story of transnational alliances grounded in complex local realities, *A Breath of Freedom* is a stellar work of international history.

Adriane Lentz-Smith, Duke University, author of
Freedom Struggles: African Americans and World War I

This book profoundly enhances our understanding not only of the history of the civil rights movement but also of the history of the Cold War. With a clear and undogmatic style, Höhn and Klimke convey the fruits of an impressive amount of research in German and American archives. They provide a compelling narrative that is essential reading for anyone interested in the ways in which transnational connections reshape national histories.

Akira Iriye, Harvard University, former president of the American Historical Association and author of *The Globalization of America*

As a young GI in Germany in 1945 and 1946, I discovered that the early American occupation was a microcosm of the racial and civil rights struggle that would emerge later in my life. My own experience thus anticipates and validates the main thesis of Höhn and Klimke's *A Breath of Freedom*.

David Brion Davis, Yale University, author of
Inhuman Bondage: The Rise and Fall of Slavery in the New World

A fascinating exploration of an important but previously ignored topic. Through their rich history of black GIs in Germany, Höhn and Klimke have demonstrated that the American story of race was indeed a transnational one.

Stephen Tuck, Oxford University, author of *We Ain't What We Ought to Be: The Black Freedom Struggle from Emancipation to Obama*

Höhn and Klimke's carefully researched and lucid book stands for a paradigm shift in our reading of the civil rights movement and deserves to become a classic in the field: not only does it invite the movement's relocation in a transnational context; it also succeeds in illustrating the innovative potential of this global perspective with its in-depth case study of the specific intersectionality of post-World War II Germany and African America.

Maria Diedrich, University of Münster, founding president of the Collegium for African American Research (CAAR), author of *Love across Color Lines: Ottilie Assing and Frederick Douglass*

Despite the countless books that have been written about the Cold War, the story of black GIs and their civil rights struggle outside of the United States remained untold—until now. In *A Breath of Freedom*, Höhn and Klimke make a signature addition across a number of scholarly fields including Black Diaspora, Military, Civil Rights, and Comparative Studies, to name a few. There simply is no comparable work on this subject. With its solid research, incisive analysis, and broad historical reach, this book should become a fundamental text for anyone curious about the cross-section of African American History and International Relations.

Clarence Lusane, American University, Washington, DC, author of *Hitler's Black Victims: The Historical Experiences of European Blacks, Africans and African Americans during the Nazi Era*

A Breath of Freedom is a fresh breath of air in the field of African American history, blowing captivating new insights into the transnational dimensions of the black freedom struggle and the role that soldiers' experiences abroad played in it. With its historical precision and engaging storytelling, this book is sure to appeal to general audiences and scholars alike.

Simon Wendt, University of Frankfurt, author of *The Spirit and the Shotgun: Armed Resistance and the Struggle for Civil Rights*

This beautifully written book eloquently illustrates how people and cultures work in tandem, sometimes struggling against, sometimes inspiring one another, and how, in the case of Germans and African Americans, this historical entanglement inevitably helped both societies move toward the North Star of greater freedom for all. Höhn and Klimke's account thus encourages you to believe again in the possibilities of Martin Luther King's "World House."

Joy Ford Austin, Executive Director, Humanities Council
of Washington, DC, and former president of the African
American Museums Association

Depicting the African American GI as the unheralded keystone of the civil rights movement in America during the post-WWII era, this book exhilaratingly exposes the two-facedness of America denazifying Germany while practicing Jim Crow segregation in its own military. With a thorough analysis of the African American press's role in disclosing this hypocrisy, it reveals the many ways in which subsequent civil rights leaders owe their success to the groundwork laid by African American GIs. Together, they forged the space to launch a civil rights revolution in America.

Calvin Robinson, President, NAACP,
Rhein-Neckar Branch (Heidelberg, Germany)

By honoring the service of African American soldiers and their families, this powerful and comprehensive book successfully shines a spotlight on the historic intersection between the struggle against Nazism and the emergence of the civil rights movement in the United States. Honest and straightforward in describing the circumstances under which these GIs volunteered to serve, Höhn and Klimke meticulously document their sacrifices and contributions at a pivotal time in history. Acknowledging the present day challenges that remain with respect to racial prejudice and discrimination on both sides of the Atlantic, the book is an important reference and required reading for students, scholars, and the many veterans and families who share their personal experiences.

Rosemarie Peña, President, Black German Cultural Society

This important study amends Cold War history by delineating the substantial, though very different, roles that African Americans played in East and West Germany before the fall of the Wall. The volume makes a significant contribution to the expanding fields of Black Diaspora and Transnational Studies.

Sara Lennox, University of Massachusetts, Amherst,
former president of the German Studies Association

The first study of its kind, *A Breath of Freedom* explores German inter-actions with the African American civil rights movement both from the Western and Eastern side of Iron Curtain. Of special significance is Höhn and Klimke's incorporation of the East German perspective, including groundbreaking accounts of Martin Luther King's 1964 visit to the divided city of Berlin, East Germany's celebration of Angela Davis as a communist superstar, and the fate of black U.S. soldiers who defected to the GDR. With vital new insights on the interrelatedness of African American and German history at the height of the Cold War, this book unquestionably makes a major contribution to the emerging scholarship on the interna-tional dimension of the black freedom struggle.

> Britta Waldschmidt-Nelson, University of Munich, author of
> *Dreams and Nightmares: Martin Luther King, Malcolm X,*
> *and the Struggle for Black Equality in America*

This engaging and well-researched book is a must-read for scholars and students of military history, civil rights history, political science, as well as the social sciences. Combining different strands of African American history and honoring the individual contributions of numerous veterans and black activists, it provides valuable historical and cultural context to illustrate the range and depth of the civil rights movement.

> Jerome Long, Wesleyan University, served in the U.S. Army
> in Austria and Germany in 1952–54

With an abundance of eyewitness accounts, contemporary news reports, and other historical materials, Höhn and Klimke demonstrate the irony of black American soldiers experiencing a true breath of freedom in the land of the former Nazi racial state. They reveal how these GIs and returning veterans, flanked by their segregated military units and their newfound freedom abroad, were motivated to call for justice in the army and at home. Thus, this book provides the definitive link between black American sol-diers and the civil rights movement and places the freedom struggle on the worldwide stage of history.

> Maggi M. Morehouse, University of South Carolina, Aiken,
> author of *Fighting in the Jim Crow Army: Black Men*
> *and Women Remember World War II*

With this most important volume, Höhn and Klimke render a novel view-point on the captivating history of African American freedom fighters by recounting the manifold ways in which black men serving in the military advanced the process of liberating Americans, as well as Germans, from the traps of racism.

> Pellom McDaniels III, University of Missouri, Kansas City, curator of
> *They Came to Fight: African Americans and the Great World War*

A Breath of Freedom

The Civil Rights Struggle, African American GIs, and Germany

Maria Höhn

and

Martin Klimke

First published in 2010 by
PALGRAVE MACMILLAN®
in the United States—a division of St. Martin's Press LLC,
175 Fifth Avenue, New York, NY 10010.

Where this book is distributed in the UK, Europe and the rest of the world,
this is by Palgrave Macmillan, a division of Macmillan Publishers Limited,
registered in England, company number 785998, of Houndmills,
Basingstoke, Hampshire RG21 6XS.

Palgrave Macmillan is the global academic imprint of the above companies
and has companies and representatives throughout the world.

Palgrave® and Macmillan® are registered trademarks in the United States,
the United Kingdom, Europe and other countries.

ISBN: 978–0–230–10473–0

Library of Congress Cataloging-in-Publication Data

Höhn, Maria, 1955–
    A breath of freedom : the civil rights struggle, African American GIs, and
Germany / Maria Höhn and Martin Klimke.
       p. cm.—(Culture, politics, and the Cold War)
    ISBN 978–0–230–10472–3 (alk. paper)—
    ISBN 978–0–230–10473–0 (alk. paper)
       1. African American soldiers—Germany (West)—History. 2. African
American soldiers—Germany (West)—Social conditions. 3. African
American soldiers—Social conditions—20th century. 4. African
Americans—Social conditions—20th century. 5. Germany (West)—Race
relations—History. 6. United States—Race relations—History—20th
century. 7. Civil rights movements—United States—History—20th century.
8. United States. Army—African American troops—History—20th century.
9. World War, 1939–1945—Participation, African American. I. Klimke,
Martin. II. Title.

E185.63.H64 2010
940.54'03—dc22   2010019156

A catalogue record of the book is available from the British Library.

Design by Newgen Imaging Systems (P) Ltd., Chennai, India.

First edition: October 2010

10 9 8 7 6 5 4 3 2 1

Printed in the United States of America.

Contents

Illustrations

Foreword

In many ways, discussion of Dr. W. E. B. Du Bois, a preeminent scholar of the twentieth century, historian, and founding member of the National Association for the Advancement of Colored People (NAACP), constitutes a remarkable opening frame for this book, as well as a bastion of inspiration for the ideas and ideals it expounds upon. His biography makes him a chronological precursor to the black GIs the book is about: like them, he lived in and was transformed by his experiences (1892–1894) as a student in imperial Germany, prior to becoming the first African American to receive a PhD in History from Harvard University in 1895. Du Bois's early experiences in Germany, beyond the color line he knew in the United States, gave him a new sense of freedom. No doubt, this European sojourn contributed to the formulation of his ideas about the transformative effects of a higher education for blacks, which he believed would allow them to see themselves through their own eyes rather than through the eyes of whites. This idea as well as Du Bois's early inter- and transnational approach to history—he was among other things, the father of "Pan-Africanism," aimed at cultivating unity among black people throughout the world—inform the contours of this study, which explores the impact of African American GIs living and serving their tours of duty in Germany. In the same way that Du Bois's time in Germany transformed his perspectives, African American GIs' experiences outside the United States and especially the Jim Crow South had a tremendous influence, not only on the soldiers' perceptions of themselves, but also on their host nation and upon the United States after they returned home.

The presidency of Barack Hussein Obama, a Harvard alumnus like Du Bois, provides an equally remarkable closing frame and an appropriate context for the publication of this book because his election made the impossible possible in my lifetime. As the Executive Director of the Congressional Black Caucus Veterans Braintrust, I am honored to write this preface for numerous reasons. First, advances in information technology, and especially the Internet, make this work especially valuable as an access point to this important history for everyone. This book, of course, is a companion volume to the web site and digital archive "The Civil Rights Struggle, African American GIs, and Germany" (www.aacvr-germany.org), which hosts a myriad of primary materials, including historical documents, images, and eyewitness testimonies that make this history come alive not only for students and scholars but for the general public and civil rights activists alike. Second, supporting this endeavor helps me to fulfill my role, as emphasized by my involvement in the World Veterans Federation (WVF) in Paris, as a citizen of the world in terms of sharing memories, facilitating access to memory, and interpreting historical facts, thereby promoting greater understanding among people. The WVF has offered me a unique window to the world of veterans affairs outside of the American context. The WVF Standing Committee on African Affairs (SCAA), in particular, through its examination of the unequal treatment of African veterans, shows that their experience often mirrors that of their African American counterparts. Similarly, both the SCAA and the Veterans Braintrust face major challenges finding hosts and sponsors (i.e., countries, groups, or individuals) and resources to support future research, meetings, and national forums. Their meetings have brought forth many scholarly research questions about the contributions and connections between African American and African veterans' experiences in war and peace.

After World War I, Du Bois and others noted the transformative effects that serving overseas had had on black GIs. With World War II and the creation of the worldwide web of U.S. military bases after 1945, millions of black servicemen had similar life-changing, cross-cultural experiences. This book focuses on Germany in particular, not least because of America's postwar occupation and mission of denazification and reeducation, which made Germany the European country that hosted the largest number of African American GIs over the longest period. But Germany is also especially suited as a case study because of its salient role in the history of the twentieth century on the whole: as a colonial power in Africa, the aggressor in World War I, the home of the Nazi Party beginning in the 1930s with its ideology of Aryan supremacy, and as the aggressor again in World War II, which left a divided country on the frontline of the Cold War struggle; and finally, as a focal point in the collapse of the Eastern bloc with the fall of the Berlin Wall in 1989. As this powerful book makes amply clear, throughout the long twentieth century, German history was intertwined with African and African American history in many ways that bear careful future study. While the civil rights struggles of the 1960s and 1970s within the United States have received wide scholarly attention, the postwar periods of the 1920s, 1930s, and 1950s, along with black GIs' roles and contributions to the civil rights movement, are not documented or understood as well. This book helps to raise awareness of the activities and rippling effects of the African American Freedom Movement in these decades. Moreover, Germany provides a unique prism offering new perspectives on the civil rights struggles of the 1960s and 1970s, too, especially when the encounters between African Americans and Germans on both sides of the Iron Curtain are viewed within the broader context of the Cold War and the challenges the United States was facing on its bases around the world.

Altogether, the transnational geographic and broad chronological scope of this project promises to heighten awareness of the importance of these interactions among a wider audience of Americans, African Americans, Europeans, Africans, and veterans.

It is my sincere hope, too, that, through the explication of the African American experience in Germany, this important book will shed further light on the Africa Diaspora and the prominent role Africa itself played in World War I and II and throughout the history of the twentieth century. As Du Bois proclaimed in 1903, the problem of the twentieth century was the problem of the color line, or the relationship of the darker to the lighter races of men in Asia and Africa, in America, and the islands of the sea. This was certainly true in the American military in Europe, as this book so richly demonstrates. But it was also true of the African colonies. In fact, Du Bois argued that World War I was primarily a competition for Africa's resources, an inevitable war for empire that the Berlin Conference of 1884/1885 had managed only to postpone. This seems a highly plausible proposition given that all of sub-Saharan Africa, with the exception of Ethiopia and Liberia, was in European hands when the war broke out, parceled out as colonies or so-called protectorates. Within the new perspective of the African Diaspora, wherein black people around the globe perceive themselves as part of a larger community related to Africa, telling the story of African American soldiers and their experiences overseas thus reflects on the broader African experience as well. The greater freedom black GIs enjoyed in Germany gave them ideas of freedom that American Southerners found to be "new-fangled," contributing directly to the civil rights movement and fueling momentum for the African independence movements. Hence, by shifting the focus to the high number of black servicemen and women who completed their tours of duty stationed abroad throughout the twentieth century, this book expands our understanding of the African Diaspora, revealing that it is a much broader, deeper, and complex phenomenon than is tradition-ally assumed. The intersection of all these experiences is more appropriately studied within the framework of world history, which investigates the inter-woven threads of peoples and nations that became increasingly intertwined over the course of the past century. Along these lines, it can be hoped that the type of transnational historical research this volume represents can be of benefit not only to historians but also to future planners and decision makers as a tool for developing educational initiatives, public policies, and programs both nationally and internationally.

This coincides with the goals and objective, or task-orientation, of the Congressional Black Caucus Veterans Braintrust. Since first convening in 1988, it has been dedicated to improving the lives of black veterans, their families, and communities nationwide. It does this by giving national voice and visibility to black veterans' collective concerns to bring about social change and enhance social policy, as well as national memory. Finally, as a chronicler of the history of blacks in and out of the military, the Veterans Braintrust continues to encourage and support new research and the publication of journal and mass media articles. For example, I recently penned "Black Veterans in the Fight for Equal Rights: From the Civil War to Today," which Congressman Larry Kissell (D-NC) then introduced to the House to be adapted into House Concurrent Resolution 238 to recognize black veterans as an integral part of the civil rights movement and the fight for equal rights in America. It was passed by the House of Representatives, 111th Congress, 2nd Session, February 26, 2010, with the support of Chairman Bob Filner of the House Veterans Affairs Committee. Consequently, now seems to be an especially auspicious and fitting moment—within the larger context of Obama's presidency—for this book to appear, telling the story of black GIs in Germany and their impact on the civil rights movement at home, and for me as the executive director of the Congressional Black Caucus Veterans Braintrust to proudly support this publication.

RON E. ARMSTEAD
Executive Director,
Congressional Black Caucus Veterans Braintrust

Acknowledgments

This book represents the fruits of a collaborative effort dating back to 2004, when we as future coauthors first corresponded regarding our overlapping research interests before meeting at a 2005 conference in Heidelberg. In addition to our firm belief that the story of this book was worth telling and had been neglected for far too long, chance, opportunity, as well as the trust and help of many people converged fortuitously to make this volume possible.

Our book presents the first findings of a larger research project that explores the connection between the U.S. military presence abroad and the advancement of civil rights in the United States, paying particular attention to the relationship between African Americans and Germans. At the heart of this project is a digital archive (www.aacvr-germany.org), which makes available a wealth of sources and scholarly material on this important but little known chapter in American and African American history, as well as transatlantic relations after World War II. The archive, "The Civil Rights Struggle, African American GIs, and Germany," contains a wide range of American and German sources from federal, state, local, as well as newspaper, university, and private archives. Also featured are oral histories from African American GIs who served in Germany, an extensive collection of photographs (some of which are reprinted in this volume), and a selection of historical documentaries. *A Breath of Freedom* is rooted in this digital archive and a related photography exhibition that provides a rich sampling of the many ways in which the actors in African American and German history crossed paths, interacted, and even collaborated. In order to share this exciting history, we have written this book with a general audience in mind, but we also intend for it to speak to scholars, teachers, and students who are interested in the reverberations of the African American freedom struggle outside the United States.

Without the unflagging support of our three cooperating institutions— which form a transatlantic triangle that has been the structural and moral support for our work—we would not have been able to undertake this endeavor. Our appreciation, therefore, goes to the German Historical Institute (GHI) of Washington, DC, and its director Hartmut Berghoff, for believing in this work from the very beginning, guiding it along the way, and supporting it by, among many other things, establishing a research focus at the institute on the relationship between African Americans and Germany. Along the same lines, we are grateful to the GHI's deputy director Uwe Spiekermann, administrative director Sabine Fix, former deputy director Philipp Gassert, as well as our colleague Anke Ortlepp, for facilitating various facets of the project, thereby underlining the institute's firm commitment to this new focus.

At Vassar College, President Cappy Hill and Dean of the Faculty Jon Chenette have been excited about this project since we first brought it to their attention. Their generous support has allowed us to continue with our work at crucial junctures. Both President Hill and Dean Chenette recognized how a research project such as this one not only offered exciting new perspectives to scholars but also presented unprecedented opportunities to involve undergraduate students in primary research. We thank them for thinking "big" and making it possible for Vassar College to be part of this ambitious transnational project.

At the University of Heidelberg, Detlef Junker, founding director of the Heidelberg Center for American Studies (HCA), and its executive director Wilfried Mausbach, both unequivocally committed to the project, have been equally forthcoming with their personal and institutional support. Together with the HCA, which has served as a platform for bringing our research to German audiences, they have been dedicated facilitators as well as organizational and intellectual pillars for our project on the other side of the Atlantic, for which we are extremely thankful.

We are grateful to Ron E. Armstead, the executive director of the Congressional Black Caucus Veterans Braintrust, for his tireless engagement in promoting the neglected history of African American veterans and with it, our project. His admirable enthusiasm, stamina, and resolve have done a great deal to bring that history to public awareness and made it possible for many veterans to share their stories with us.

We are, likewise, thankful for the support we have enjoyed from several other key institutions. In July 2009, the NAACP surprised us by presenting us with the Julius E. Williams Distinguished Community Service Award during its centennial convention in New York City in recognition of our work. The award, named after the first national director of the NAACP Department of Armed Services and Veterans' Affairs who joined the civil rights organization in 1966 and organized the Veterans' Affairs Department in 1969, was a great honor, obliging us to continue to illuminate the manifold, but often underacknowledged contributions of black veterans to American and German history.

Throughout the course of the project, the Humanities Council of Washington, DC, has been a wonderful partner, cooperating with us to host several events and initiatives. The council's symposium on the global legacy of Dr. Martin Luther King Jr. in the fall of 2008, forty years after his murder, prompted us to create our photography exhibition on "African American Civil Rights and Germany"—an exhibition that continues to tour cities on both sides of the Atlantic. We are thus grateful to executive director Joy Ford Austin and the former program director Tyra Fenell, as well as Donald Murray, Lisa Alfred, Eva Lucero, and Albert Shaheen for their consistent support and suggestions. The Black German Cultural Society and its director Rosemarie Peña have been similarly generous in supporting our research project. Its members have shared their biographies with us, thus enriching our findings with a crucial Afro-German perspective. We look forward to collaborating and deepening our relationship with both organizations in the years to come.

Additional thanks go to Jeff Whatley, Ashtan Moore, and Adam Rast at the National Geographic Society for skillfully working on the restoration of some of our photographic material; to the Collegium for African American Research (CAAR) and its current president Sabine Broeck from the University of Bremen; as well as CAAR's founder and first president Maria Diedrich from the University of Münster; to Mark Donfried, director of the Institute for Cultural Diplomacy and coorganizer of the Black History Month in Berlin; and to the director of the Goethe Institute Washington, DC, Ulrich Braess, and the cultural programs coordinator Sylvia Blume, for helping to support our work in a transatlantic context.

The patience and energy of many archivists, private collectors, and photographers have been key to the success of this project. We would like to express our particular gratitude to the archives that have formed an institutional partnership with us, and the archivists who have been steadfast in assisting us: Oliver Sander and Martina Caspers (Bundesarchiv Koblenz), Kerstin Risse and Peter Vier (Bundesarchiv Berlin), Michael Geib (Docu Center Ramstein), and Roland Stolte (St. Mary's Church, Berlin), whose passion and dedication in researching the visits of Martin Luther King Jr. and Ralph Abernathy to East Germany have been invaluable to our project and this book. Furthermore, we would like to thank Romana Berg (Bildarchiv Preußischer Kulturbesitz), Barbara Schäche (Landesarchiv Berlin), Eva Herms (Berliner Verlag), Siegward Lönnendonker (APO-Archiv, Freie Universität Berlin), Reinhart Schwarz (Hamburger Institut für Sozialforschung), Klaus Rheinfurth (Institut für Stadtgeschichte, Frankfurt/Main), Katrin Merbach (akg-images), Ines Wetterer (dpa), Jörg Lampertius (ullstein bild), Sabine Kokkelink (Picture Press), Sven Riepe (SZ-Photo), Florian Fottner (Stadtarchiv Zweibrücken), Silka Quintero (The Granger Collection, NY), Lynn Slawson (NAACP), Diana Lee (*The Philadelphia Tribune*), John Gartrell (*The Baltimore Afro-American*), Caroline Waddell (United States Holocaust Memorial Museum), and Lisa Marine (Wisconsin State Historical Society) for making these rare photographic materials available to us. Our special thanks go to Helma Harrington and Christine Krüger, widows of cartoonist Ollie Harrington and photographer Siegfried Krüger, respectively, as well as to the wonderfully gifted photographers Barbara Klemm, Matt Herron, Perry Kretz, and Manfred Tripp. They were excited about this project, and we are most grateful for their generosity in sharing their photos and cartoons with us.

Two cooperation partners deserve particular mention. Award-winning documentary filmmaker Hans-Jürgen Hilgert produced several oral history interviews for our web site and filmed a conference on the civil rights struggle and twentieth-century Germany we convened at Vassar College in October 2009. The director of the Archive of Soldiers' Rights, e.V., in Berlin, Dieter Brünn, had been a supporter of our individual research for many years, even before we began our collaboration. Both of these individuals exhibited exceptional passion, energy, and generosity in working with us. Tragically, both of them passed away suddenly and unexpectedly during the final stages of producing this book. We are tremendously saddened by these losses.

Our sincerest thanks also go to all of our interview partners for their trust and time in imparting honest and often very moving insights into their personal experiences, particularly Leon Bass, Angela Davis, Joe McPhee, Walter Patrice, Alcyone Scott, Thomas P. Stoney, Debra Tanner Abell, Thomas Ward, Garland Core, Felix Goodwin, Harold Montgomery, Spencer Moore, A. William Perry, Reuben Horner, Fred Hurns, Denette Harrod, Lawrence Johnson, Charles Hanson, Jim Williams, Joe Stephenson, Joseph Hairston, Ogelsby Barrett, and Karl Dietrich Wolff. We will also be forever grateful to Maggi Morehouse, who so generously agreed to have the interviews she conducted with a number of World War II veterans in the early 1990s included in our digital archive.

We would also like to acknowledge the help, feedback, and comments we have received from many colleagues along the way: Uta Balbier, Manfred Berg, Philipp Gassert, Leroy Hopkins, Sara Lennox, Wilfried Mausbach, Maggi Morehouse, Anke Ortlepp, Peggy Piesche, Harvard Sitkoff, Judith Weisenfeld, and Simon Wendt. Marina Jones and Natalia King, visiting fellows at the GHI in 2009/2010, have been similarly gracious in sharing their knowledge.

This book would not have been possible without our first-class research team in Washington, Poughkeepsie, Heidelberg, and Berlin. Above all, Laura Stapane, our project coordinator, deserves major credit for her good cheer and masterly organizational and administrative skills, with which she has kept us on track, procured the copyright permissions for the images in this book, and supervised the digitization effort. In short, she has helped us complete this project according to schedule and with great proficiency. Alexander Holmig and Elisabeth Piller have tirelessly located and unearthed many treasures from archives in Germany and the United States, providing indispensable help in putting together the material for this book and our archive. Sylvia Landau has been a great investigator for the visit of Dr. Martin Luther King. Furthermore, Thea Brophy, Betsy Hauck, and Sophie Lorenz have been skilled and self-motivated research assistants on both sides of the Atlantic, as have Vassar students Matthew Blair, Michael Ilardi, Merema Ahmed, Molly Kumar, Jessica Regunberg, Katie Paul, Duane Bailey-Castro, Emma Woellk, and the American Cultures Senior

Colloquia of Spring 2008 and 2010, who repeatedly stunned us with their findings and stimulating insights.

At Palgrave, we are grateful to our editor Chris Chappell for his trust and dedication, as well as Sarah Whalen and Heather Faulls for skillfully guiding the book through its production process. Thanks are also due to Patricia Sutcliffe at the German Historical Institute, Washington, DC, not only for her careful and thoughtful copyediting, but also for her optimism and inexhaustible commitment to the project. Her tough questions impelled us to clarify and sharpen our ideas and prose, and the book is a better one for it.

Finally, we would like to dedicate this book to the African American veterans who served in Germany, and especially those of the World War II generation whose service and heroism have for so long been ignored. They helped to liberate Germany from the evil of Nazism, and secured for Germans, born after the war, the freedom, and democracy that African Americans were still denied in their own country. We are humbled by their sacrifice and are grateful for all they have done in advancing the struggle for freedom and civil rights at home and abroad.

MARIA HÖHN AND MARTIN KLIMKE
POUGHKEEPSIE AND WASHINGTON
May 2010

Abbreviations

AAA	Archiv des Auswärtigen Amtes, Berlin (Archive of the Ministry of Foreign Affairs, Berlin)
ACLU	American Civil Liberties Union
AFRC	Armed Forces Recreation Center
AKG	Archiv für Kunst und Geschichte (Archive for Arts and History)
APOB	APO-Archive, Free University of Berlin
AStA	Allgemeiner Studierendenausschuss (General Student Board)
ASWAD	Association of the Study of the Worldwide African Diaspora
BArch-Berlin	Bundesarchiv, Berlin (Federal Archive, Berlin)
BArch-Koblenz	Bundesarchiv, Koblenz (Federal Archive, Koblenz)
BEST	Black European Studies Program, University of Mainz
BPP	Black Panther Party
BRD	Bundesrepublik Deutschland (Federal Republic of Germany, West Germany)
BStU	Bundesbeauftragte für die Unterlagen des Staatssicherheitsdienstes (Federal Archive of the Commissioner for Stasi Records)
BZ	*Berliner Zeitung*
CAAR	Collegium for African American Research
CAD	Civil Affairs Division of HICOG
CBC	Congressional Black Caucus
CDU	Christlich Demokratische Union (Christian Democratic Union)
CORE	Congress of Racial Equality
CPUSA	Communist Party USA
DDR	Deutsche Demokratische Republik (German Democratic Republic, East Germany)
DOD	Department of Defense
DPA	Deutsche Presse Agentur (German Press Agency)
EJAS	*European Journal of American Studies*

EM	Enlisted Man (Men)
ETO	European Theater of Operations
EUCOM	European Command
FAZ	*Frankfurter Allgemeine Zeitung*
FDJ	Freie Deutsche Jugend (Free German Youth)
FEPC	Fair Employment Practices Commission
FR	*Frankfurter Rundschau*
FRG	Federal Republic of Germany (West Germany)
GDR	German Democratic Republic (East Germany)
GI	Government Issue (term describing members of the U.S. armed forces)
GStA PK	Geheimes Staatsarchiv Preussischer Kulturbesitz, Berlin (Secret State Archives Prussian Cultural Heritage Foundation, Berlin)
GYA	German Youth Activity clubs
HICOG	Office of the High Commissioner
HIS	Hamburger Institut für Sozialforschung (Hamburg Institute for Social Research, Hamburg)
HUAB	Humboldt University Archive, Berlin
HQ	Headquarters
IANAS	Interdisziplinärer Arbeitskreis für Nordamerikastudien (Interdisciplinary Research Group for North American Studies)
INFI	Internationales Nachrichten- und Forschungsinstitut (International News and Research Instititue)
ISD	Initiative Schwarze Menschen in Deutschland (Initiative for Black People in Germany)
JAG	Judge Advocate General Corps
KCA	The King Center, Atlanta
KKK	Ku Klux Klan
LOC	Library of Congress, Washington, DC
LRO	Land Relations Officer
MESEA	The Society for Multi-Ethnic Studies: Europe and the Americas
MFDP	Mississippi Freedom Democratic Party
MP	Military Police
NAACP	National Association for the Advancement of Colored People
NARA	National Archives and Records Administration, Washington, DC/College Park, MD
NATO	North Atlantic Treaty Organization
NCO	Noncommissioned Officer
OWI	Office of War Information
PRA	Paul Robeson Archive, Academy of Arts, Berlin
PV	*Pfälzische Volkszeitung*
QM	Quartermaster Company
RAF	Rote Armee Fraktion (Red Army Faction)
RZ	*Rhein-Zeitung*

SAPMO	Stiftung Archiv der Parteien und Massenorganisationen der DDR im Bundesarchiv, Berlin (Foundation Archives of Parties and Mass Organizations of the GDR in the Federal Archives, Berlin)
SCAA	Standing Committee on African Affairs, WVF
SCLC	Southern Christian Leadership Conference
SDS	Sozialistischer Deutscher Studentenbund (German Socialist Student League)
SED	Sozialistische Einheitspartei Deutschlands (Socialist Unity Party of Germany)
SNCC	Student Nonviolent Coordinating Committee
SS	Schutzstaffel (Elite Nazi Formation)
STO	Southern Theater of Operations
SZ	*Süddeutsche Zeitung*
UCLA	University of California at Los Angeles
UCMJ	Uniform Code of Military Justice
UNRRA	United Nations Relief and Rehabilitation Administration
USAAF	United States Army Air Forces
USAREUR	U.S. Army Europe, 7th Army
USHMM	United States Holocaust Memorial Museum, Washington, DC
VEB	Volkseigener Betrieb (People-owned enterprise, i.e., national corporation in the GDR)
VE-Day	Victory in Europe Day (May 8, 1945)
VOL	*Voice of the Lumpen*
WAC	Women's Army Corps
WBA	Willy-Brandt-Archiv im Archiv der Sozialen Demokratie der Friedrich-Ebert-Stiftung (Willy Brandt Archive in the Friedrich Ebert Foundation's Archives of Social Democracy, Bonn)
WVF	World Veterans Federation
ZK	Zentralkomitee (Central Committee of the Socialist Unity Party of the GDR)

Introduction

While serving in occupied Berlin in 1947, the distinguished African American writer William Gardner Smith realized that, after being treated as social equals in postwar Germany, African American GIs would "never go back to the old way again."[1] Germany retained its reputation as a special place for black soldiers even after the American occupation ended in 1949 and the U.S. military took on the task of protector for the young Federal Republic. Former U.S. Secretary of State Colin Powell was a newly commissioned second lieutenant when he arrived in Gelnhausen in 1958 and discovered, as he would later write in his autobiography, that "[f]or black GIs, especially those out of the South, Germany was a breath of freedom."[2] Their encounter with a society free of Jim Crow–era segregation prompted many of these soldiers not only to demand equal rights while stationed in Germany but also to join the civil rights movement once they returned home to the United States. Their experiences in postwar and Cold War West Germany thus proved pivotal in the struggle against racial discrimination in America.

Since the fall of the Berlin Wall in 1989, historians have shown how American foreign policy concerns and U.S. competition with the Soviet Union in the non-Western world from the 1950s through the 1970s forced policymakers in Washington to support the civil rights agenda.[3] What has received scant attention in these interpretations is America's military presence in postwar Europe and the role played by the expanding U.S. military base system in the unfolding drama of the civil rights struggle. By bringing a segregated army to bases across Western Europe and other parts of the globe, the United States literally transported its racial conflict and the actors in that conflict onto foreign soil.[4] Astonishingly, there has been almost no discussion of how the experiences of black troops overseas helped to advance the cause of civil rights at home during the twentieth century, in particular during the Cold War.[5]

To help launch this discussion, we have chosen to look at West Germany, not least because it hosted the largest deployment of American troops outside the United States following World War II. Until the drawdown that followed the collapse of the Soviet Union in 1991, some 250,000 American soldiers were stationed in West Germany every year, accompanied by their families and tens of thousands of civilian employees of the Department of Defense. Altogether, almost twenty million Americans have lived in West Germany since the end of World War II, with approximately three million of them African American. Furthermore, because of the postwar military occupation, and America's ambitious efforts to reshape German society after the defeat of Nazism, West Germany was more widely exposed to American political and social developments than other countries with U.S. bases.

West Germany is also a logical choice because American policymakers saw the country as the linchpin of Western defense during the Cold War. Given Germany's central role in the North Atlantic Treaty Organization (NATO) defense strategies and its symbolic importance as the likely European battleground in a military conflict between the two superpowers, the politicization of black soldiers over civil rights took on particular significance. Thus, while the civil rights movement made itself felt wherever U.S. troops were stationed, West Germany was the country that was most intimately intertwined with this important chapter of American history.[6]

The civil rights battle of African American GIs in West Germany was not just a side effect of the larger contest taking place in the United States. On the contrary: it was during the postwar occupation of defeated Nazi Germany and in Cold War West Germany that the contradictions between America's claim to be the leader of the "Free World" and its own institutionalized racism became most painfully apparent to the global community. Indeed, when historian David Brion Davis later reflected on his military service as an eighteen-year-old in Mannheim, he recalled the Germany of 1946 as "a microcosm of the racial and civil rights struggle that would dominate America in the 1950s and 1960s." Germany was the place where he first "glimpsed the contours of the United States into which [he] would mature."[7] In the context of America's mission to democratize German politics, the pursuit of civil rights by African American GIs took on geopolitical dimensions that became an integral part of the larger movement.

While President Truman had effected the de jure integration of the military when he issued Executive Order 9981 on July 26, 1948, de facto integration would not come about until the Korean War. It was not achieved in the European Command until late 1954.[8] To a significant degree, that milestone decision resulted directly from the unrelenting pressure exerted by American civil rights organizations and the black press.[9] Their reports on the army's progress and setbacks in democratizing post-Nazi Germany convinced white liberals in the United States, as well as officials in the State Department, that the continued segregation of the military was unacceptable. Not only did it undermine America's political mission in Germany, but it also made the United States an easy target for Soviet and East German propagandists, who used the military's racist policies to expose American hypocrisy.

During the closing years of World War II and increasingly thereafter, African American GIs complained about the military's discriminatory practices, the brutality of the overwhelmingly white military police force, and the lack of black officers. They protested loudly when military commanders, in order to preserve "racial peace," instructed local pub owners to observe American-style racial boundaries, thus bringing Jim Crow segregation into German communities that bordered on military bases. Once the civil rights movement gained momentum in the 1950s, black GIs deployed overseas proved to be crucial actors in that struggle. By 1960, sit-down strikes to integrate lunch counters were taking place not only in Greensboro, North Carolina, but also on and around U.S. military bases in Germany.

As early as the late 1950s, African American GIs had urged civil rights leaders and American media representatives to come to Germany to investigate the widespread discrimination within the military and the system of "informal" segregation that defined American garrison towns across Germany. These protest activities, in turn, led to high-level government investigations, such as the one that in 1964 produced *The President's Committee on Equal Opportunity in the Armed Forces, Final Report: Military Personnel Stationed Overseas*, which constituted the government's first concerted effort to tackle entrenched racism and discrimination in the military.

Unlike black GIs elsewhere in the world, those stationed in Germany found allies among local civilians, who supported them in their fight for racial equality.[10] Because military deployments to Germany usually lasted two to three years, African American GIs came to know and in many cases form friendships with local residents. Such associations were especially prevalent in German university towns that also hosted U.S. military bases. Shared interests in African American musical forms, such as jazz and blues, and the burgeoning civil rights movement in the United States, encouraged such relationships. In the early 1960s, for example, black GIs began to collaborate with German students who had spent time in the United States and with African American students studying at German universities to propagate the goals of the movement. Often students of color from non-Western countries who were enrolled at German universities joined in this unusual partnership. In university centers like Frankfurt, Heidelberg, and Berlin, soldiers and students united to publicly protest racism and voice support for civil rights in the United States.

After the emergence of the Black Power movement in the mid-1960s and the assassination of Martin Luther King Jr. in April 1968, African American GIs in Germany intensified their collaboration with local university students to fight racism both in the U.S. military and in German communities. Among the most important events was the "Call for Justice" meeting held on July 4, 1970, in the auditorium of Heidelberg University. This event was also endorsed by the president of Heidelberg University, who provided a venue for the meeting and would make university buildings available when the U.S. military prohibited demonstrations on its bases. Similar protests took place in smaller garrison towns like Kaiserslautern (with a population of 80,000), where more than 40,000 U.S. troops were

posted. Frankfurt University was the site of several large solidarity protests, which were carried out on behalf of Angela Davis—an activist who
had been a student there between 1965 and 1966—that brought together
African American servicemen, exchange students, and German students.

In East Germany, solidarity with the African American cause even took on
the form of a government-funded domestic and international campaign based
on the state's ideological commitment to combat imperialism, colonialism,
and racism. The East German government hailed civil rights activists as the
heroes of the "other America"—the America of the oppressed. Despite the
lack of diplomatic relations between East Berlin and Washington, the German
Democratic Republic welcomed African American deserters as well as representatives of the civil rights struggle with open arms. The regime hosted
extensive receptions for W. E. B. Du Bois in 1958 as well as singer and intellectual Paul Robeson in 1960. It produced a flood of literature on the black
freedom struggle in the decades after World War II and allowed Dr. Martin
Luther King Jr. in 1964 and Dr. Ralph Abernathy in 1971 to deliver sermons
in East Berlin churches. At the beginning of the 1970s, East German officials
also engineered a comprehensive solidarity campaign for Angela Davis, which
involved all segments of society, turning her into a communist pop star.

Despite these propaganda efforts, it was the collaboration between
Black Panther GIs and radical students in the Federal Republic that most
provoked the American and West German governments to implement the
unfulfilled civil rights agenda. The radicalization of black GIs, and the
support they received from students throughout Germany, led to comprehensive investigations by the Pentagon (the "Render Report"), the
National Association for the Advancement of Colored People (NAACP),
and the Congressional Black Caucus.[11] To address the U.S. military's racist policies, as well as the individual grievances of black GIs, the Federal
Republic initiated a wide-ranging project to improve housing and repair
barracks for U.S. military personnel and their families. It also began a
broad educational program designed to deter discriminatory practices by
West German landlords, restaurateurs, and bar owners. Significantly, the
NAACP established a branch office in Frankfurt in 1971 to deal with the
complaints of black soldiers, both on base and off.

*   *   *

African American GIs and their activism in Germany played a vital role in
the broader struggle against racism and for civil rights. Their experiences
abroad convinced many of them to join the struggle once they returned
home, and others continued their protests in Cold War Germany. Their
deployment in racially segregated units, at a time when the United States
claimed to be the leader of the "Free World," gave rise to Truman's 1948
Executive Order, and by the late 1960s and early 1970s, their activities in
West Germany had led to substantial reform that had reverberations in
other military commands abroad as well as in the continental United States.
To a considerable extent, it was the protest activities of African American

GI activists stationed in Germany that transformed the U.S. military into the most integrated institution of the United States by the mid-1970s.

Given the centrality of black soldiers' experience overseas—and especially in West Germany—to the larger history of the American civil rights movement, it is puzzling that we know relatively little about this important chapter of American and African American history. One reason for this neglect may be reluctance on the part of scholars not trained as military historians to do research on military topics. By the same token, those who do focus on military history often gloss over its social and cultural dimensions, concentrating on strategy and efficiency rather than the complaints of low-ranking GIs. Furthermore, because historians have traditionally worked within narrowly defined disciplines or geographical and chronological boundaries, the transnational character of many aspects of American history, and especially African American history, have only begun to fully emerge within the past decade.[12] For similar reasons, the American military presence has failed to attract the attention of many German historians. While dozens of volumes have been produced on America's impact on German society, the deployment of more than two million African American GIs and their families to Germany since 1945 has remained, for the most part, an untold story.

Leaders and participants in the civil rights struggle, on the other hand, were very much aware of this international impact, which they repeatedly used as leverage in their efforts to bring about domestic reform.[13] Few people saw this interconnectedness of American history more clearly than Dr. Martin Luther King Jr. In a lecture delivered in Oslo on December 11, 1964, after accepting the Nobel Peace Prize, King sought to place America's journey toward racial justice in a global context:

> In one sense the civil rights movement in the United States is a special American phenomenon which must be understood in the light of American history and dealt with in terms of the American situation. But on another and more important level, what is happening in the United States today is a relatively small part of a world development.[14]

In the same lecture, King asserted that all human beings are united in a "worldwide fellowship," a belief that had undoubtedly been reinforced during his visit to Berlin three months earlier. Invited by Mayor Willy Brandt to come to the city that just a year before had so enthusiastically welcomed President John F. Kennedy, King toured numerous sites during his two and a half days there and, most importantly, held a sermon at the Waldbühne, a large outdoor amphitheater, before 20,000 people. King used this sermon to connect his spiritual message of brotherhood to the situation in Berlin: "[This city] stands as a symbol of the divisions of men on the face of the earth. For here on either side of the wall are God's children, and no man-made barrier can obliterate that fact." He went a step further and compared the civil rights struggle in the United States to the political struggle of the divided city, arguing that just as the United States was proving to be "the testing ground of races living together in spite of their differences," the people of Berlin were "testing the possibility of co-existence for the two ideologies" then competing for world dominance.[15]

Regrettably, historical memory has largely ignored Dr. King's visit to Cold War Berlin. Even when more than 200,000 Berliners turned out to hear then-presidential candidate Barack Obama speak in Berlin's Tiergarten on July 24, 2008, few commentators in the United States or Germany noted the connection. This is particularly astonishing given the prominence of Dr. King and the civil rights movement in Obama's campaign rhetoric, which he invoked as an essential reference point in such signature phrases as "the fierce urgency of now."

In fact, Obama's speech in the Tiergarten reads like a response to King's Nobel lecture on the "world house," delivered from the vantage point of the twenty-first century. Obama not only presented himself as "a fellow citizen of the world" but also employed the same transatlantic connection and global vision when he proclaimed:

> People of the world—look at Berlin, where a wall came down, a continent came together, and history proved that there is no challenge too great for a world that stands as one.... While the twentieth century taught us that we share a common destiny, the twenty-first has revealed a world more inter-twined than at any time in human history.[16]

The narrative of this book is thus one of entanglements and shared destinies on both sides of the Atlantic throughout the twentieth century. Although we focus on the period after 1945, we begin with W. E. B. Du Bois, whose experience as a graduate student in late nineteenth-century Berlin transformed his thinking about race and the color line, and World War I, which set the stage for the budding civil rights movement of the 1920s and 1930s. That movement was given tremendous momentum by the rise of Nazism and white America's revulsion for that racist regime.

By tracing the encounter between African Americans and Germany, we aim to broaden the understanding of how America's struggle against Nazi Germany and its leadership role in Europe after 1945, specifically in West Germany, were essential to advancing the cause of civil rights in the United States. At the same time, our goal is to move beyond the high-level politics and policymakers in Washington and Bonn to the activists on the ground. Their voices and the response to their demands from military and government representatives, as well as the media, make clear how the African American GI experience in Germany enunciated and spurred the struggle for civil rights. In telling that story, we hope to take a critical first step toward a more nuanced and sophisticated awareness of how America's struggle for racial justice reverberated across the globe.[17]

1

Closing Ranks: World War I and the Rise of Hitler

Only a transnational approach to American and German history reveals to what degree America's participation in World War I and its struggle against Nazi Germany influenced how African American civil rights activists framed their demands. President Woodrow Wilson's April 1917 call to action, in which he urged Congress to take up the struggle against Germany so that the world would "be made safe for democracy," empowered these activists to formulate a more forceful civil rights agenda. But it was the rise of Hitler and white America's condemnation of the Nazi racial state that allowed activists to highlight the discrepancy between America's ideals of democracy on the one hand and the reality of daily life for African Americans on the other. They used white America's denunciation of Nazi racism to expose the Jim Crow laws of the South and to indict the prevailing "separate but equal" doctrine as incompatible with the principles on which American democracy was founded.

When President Woodrow Wilson called on his fellow countrymen to send American soldiers abroad to save democracy in Europe, the great majority of African Americans and their leaders did not respond with enthusiasm. America's black population had been emancipated from slavery in the wake of the Civil War; however, liberation had come without any real financial support to help establish a new life. The situation was especially dire in the South, where 90 percent of America's black citizens lived before World War I. The great majority of them were forced to make their living as sharecroppers or tenant farmers, working in miserable conditions and for marginal incomes. Furthermore, state legislatures across the South had passed what became known as Jim Crow laws. These legal restrictions were designed to deprive African Americans of the political power that the Northern victory in the Civil War had conferred on them. By the end of the nineteenth century, these laws had made it all but impossible for most African Americans to vote in any Southern state.

In addition to political disenfranchisement, Jim Crow laws were also passed to assure the almost complete segregation of the races. These racial codes were affirmed in 1896 when the U.S. Supreme Court ruled in the landmark case *Plessy v. Ferguson* that segregated institutions were constitutional as long as "equal" facilities were provided. Schools, restaurants, water fountains, movie theaters, public transportation, hospitals, and cemeteries were segregated. Furthermore, strict miscegenation laws criminalized marriage between whites and blacks to prevent "the mixing of the races." These miscegenation laws provided the bedrock for the complex system of Southern white supremacy, in which all black men, often belittled as "boys" even if they possessed advanced degrees or were respectable members of their own community, were demonized as a sexual danger to white female respectability. The violence of the lynch mob hovered as an ever-present threat over black men to ensure that they did not cross the strictly drawn racial and sexual boundaries.[1]

An intricate web of informal and unwritten racial codes reinforced the system of white supremacy in everyday life. African Americans had to show deference to whites. They had to wait in line until all whites had been served, yield the right of way when walking or driving, and enter white homes and establishments only by the back door. Blacks who challenged the segregation laws and racial codes could expect the brute force of the local sheriff, or violence from vigilante lynch mobs.[2] So intertwined were the "legal" rules and "informal" traditions to maintain white supremacy that it was "somewhat difficult," as African American educator William Henry Holtzclaw wrote in 1915, "to draw...a sharp line marking off distinctly the point where the lynching spirit stop[ped] and the spirit of legal procedure commence[d]."[3]

"Separate but equal" was, of course, not equal at all, no matter how loudly proponents of this view declared that it was. The few schools built for black children were often in a deplorable state, and illiteracy rates among African Americans in the rural South remained unacceptably high at more than 30 percent. While a proud African American middle class of teachers, clergy, professionals, and business owners led lives more privileged than the poor sharecroppers and tenant farmers, they, too, were exposed to the daily humiliations of racial segregation, the racist legal system, and the unpredictable violence of white lynch mobs. As civil rights activist Charles Evers recalls,

> Being black was part of the air you breathed; it was part of the socializing any black youth had to undergo. Our mothers began telling us about being black from the day we were born. The white folks weren't any better than we were, Momma said, but they sure thought they were....We got it hammered into us to watch our step, to stay in our place, or to get off the street when a white woman passed.[4]

Matters were somewhat better for African Americans living outside the South, because the Jim Crow laws of disenfranchisement and racial segregation were not in force for them. But racism was deeply entrenched where they lived as well: African Americans were forced to work at menial and low-paying jobs, lived in substandard housing, and knew without being told which stores, hotels, and restaurants were open to them and which would refuse to serve them. An increasingly integrated market economy assured that racist stereotypes originating in the South rapidly spread throughout the nation by means of popular culture and advertising for consumer products. On the eve of Word War I, African Americans throughout the United States were at best second-class citizens.

Despite this low status and African Americans' lack of enthusiasm for defending American-style democracy, some black spokesmen did believe that participation in the Great War would finally earn full citizenship for blacks. W. E. B. Du Bois, for example, one of America's foremost advocates for the nation's black minority and a cofounder of the NAACP, called on his fellow African Americans to "close ranks" and join the war effort against Germany.

That call was not an easy one for Du Bois to make. More than twenty years earlier, while a graduate student at Harvard, Du Bois had won a prestigious fellowship to study in Berlin from the autumn of 1892 to the spring of 1894. Du Bois had relished his time in Germany, feeling that it constituted his first experience of a society without a color line, and he would recall Germany as a special place to the end of his life. Outside the United States, Du Bois recalled that he was judged not necessarily by the color of his skin but by his *class* status as an educated university student. It was an experience, he wrote, that allowed him to shed the collective African American experience of being "a problem" and instead "to look at the world as a man."[5] He later reflected on how radically his time in Germany had shaped the kind of an intellectual he became after his return to the United States. His friendships and encounters with white people outside the United States prompted him to "emphasize the cultural aspects of race" rather than biological ones because the "eternal walls between races did not seem so stern and exclusive" anymore.[6] Nonetheless, much as Du Bois had appreciated German *Kultur*, he had also come to loathe German militarism. Thus, even though he understood World War I as a struggle between European powers over control of people of color in Africa and Asia, he sided with France and Great Britain, and against his beloved Germany.

Yet African Americans remained unconvinced by Du Bois's call to "close ranks." Roi Ottley, one of America's foremost black journalists, spoke for many other blacks when he concluded: "The truth is, Negroes exhibited little enthusiasm for the war—actually their eyes were fixed on Washington, not London, Paris or Berlin."[7] Why, indeed, should African Americans risk their lives to defend democracy in Europe when they did not have it at home? On July 28, 1917, during a silent march in New York City organized by the NAACP after the bloody St. Louis race riots of May and July had taken the lives of more than 100 black Americans and driven some 6,000 from their homes, protesters carried signs that pleaded with President Wilson: "Bring Democracy to America before you carry it to Europe," and "Why not make AMERICA safe for Democracy?"[8]

Despite the discrimination and humiliation that defined their daily lives, many black Americans did eventually heed Du Bois's call to support their government. Some 400,000 African American GIs served in the U.S. military in World War I. Although the country needed their participation in the war effort, military leaders, with disproportionate numbers of Southern officers among them, were none too eager to bestow full "manhood" on black recruits by training them for combat duty. For the most part, military commanders considered blacks unsuited to the complex tasks of modern warfare. As a consequence, almost 90 percent of African American soldiers were assigned to manual labor battalions rather than to more prestigious combat units. Even college-educated African American men often ended up in menial positions that failed to make adequate use of their education and professional skills.

The great majority of black draftees served in the military equivalent of chain gangs commanded by Southern noncommissioned officers and officers chosen for their past experience as overseers in such work details. The military employed this placement strategy in the hope that it would protect "Southern sensibilities" (eight out of the nine military training camps were located in the South) from the sight of black soldiers in uniform. Once sent overseas, black draftees were relegated to performing the most unskilled labor. It would be up to the "laborers in uniform," as the military called them, to unload the ships once they got to France. They cleaned military camps, peeled potatoes, laid railroad tracks, repaired infrastructure, dug ditches and latrines, and took care of the livestock. For their efforts they received substandard food and housing, and were clad in fatigues and uniforms that had been deemed unsuitable for white troops. They also had to endure "abusive language, kicks, cuffs, and injurious blows" from their superiors.[9] Black activists, who traveled to France to check on the soldiers, bemoaned this discriminatory treatment, and were truly outraged when the military assigned to black labor battalions the difficult and unpleasant task of gathering the remains of fallen white soldiers strewn across battlefields or hastily buried by their comrades. Not considered good enough to fight side by side with white soldiers, black GIs, by their labor, assured that white soldiers would have dignified burials in cemeteries the black GIs had built for them.[10]

Despite this humiliation, the almost 200,000 African Americans who served in Europe distinguished themselves by their faithful service to their country. The black soldiers who were allowed to bear arms (92nd and 93rd Division) comported themselves with valor. Soldiers in the all-black 369th Infantry Regiment, also known as the "Harlem Hell Fighters," fought alongside French troops because their own country's officers refused to command them. Together with their French comrades, they were among the first troops to make it to the Rhine. For their bravery, they were awarded some of France's highest military honors. Their own country was less grateful to the heroic fighters. The military command withdrew black soldiers from German territory almost immediately so they could not be part of an occupation army and rule over a white population.[11]

World War I had profound repercussions for African Americans at home. For example, it accelerated the Great Migration of black sharecroppers and field hands from the agricultural South to industrial centers of the North, where factory jobs were open to them for the first time as cheap European labor had ceased to arrive during the war. Every day, hundreds of black men and women traveled to Detroit, Chicago, Pittsburgh, Cleveland, and New York to pursue opportunities created by wartime demand for manufactured goods and new sources of labor. By 1940, some two million African Americans had migrated northward, leaving behind Southern poverty, Jim Crow laws and humiliations, and the constant threat of vigilante violence. Asked why he had left the South behind, one man told an agent from the Department of Agriculture: "I just want to be somewhere where I won't be scared all the time." Said another: "I just want to feel safe."[12]

Fighting abroad and helping France and Great Britain defeat another "white" nation had a dramatic impact on individual soldiers. For many of them, and especially for soldiers from the South, their tour of duty abroad marked their first escape from lives defined by segregation, racial discrimination, and humiliation. One soldier recalled his time in France: "I have never before experienced what it meant to be really free, to taste real liberty—in a phrase, 'to be a man.'"[13] In the cities and hamlets of France and Belgium, African American soldiers had their first opportunity to enter establishments that were not racially segregated, and black musicians, both in and out of uniform, were fêted wherever they performed. Even more stunning for these soldiers was the fact that white women found them attractive and lovable human beings. Henry Berry, a World War I veteran, wrote how deeply his experiences abroad had touched him. In France, "he was not a savage, not a mere educated dog, but a human being…having the right to live and be happy."[14] Furthermore, fighting alongside units of colonial troops from the French and British armies in France, black soldiers came to understand their own racial oppression and America's color line in the larger international context of European colonialism in Africa and Asia. World War I and the Great Migration in its wake thus brought about not only a much more urban black population but also one with sophisticated and globally oriented views on the race question.

The participation of African American GIs in the war also exposed as never before the contradiction between the democratic ideals on which the United States was founded and the reality of daily life for the country's black population. Although the U.S. military was in Europe to defend democracy, commanders kept white and black troops strictly segregated. What's worse, the military even tried to introduce American-style segregation among the French, as Du Bois reported in outrage after his visit with the troops in 1918. U.S. officers instructed their French counterparts not to shake hands with African American officers, and they exhorted the civilian population, especially French women, not to interact with black soldiers.

Du Bois lamented after the war that a "nation with a great disease set out to rescue civilization [and in so doing]...took the disease...of race hatred and prejudice" to Europe.[15]

John Hope, Du Bois's friend and one of America's most distinguished black intellectuals, who later became president of Atlanta University, expressed the same sense of disillusionment in 1919 after observing how black soldiers were treated not only by their own officers but also by their white comrades: "If you should ask me whether the prejudice is southern or northern prejudice, I would be compelled to say that it was southern and northern, that it was American."[16] For Hope, too, the experience of witnessing American racism on European soil evoked a new perception of the American "race problem," as he wrote, "I know my country's faults in a clearer way than I had ever seen them before I was in France."[17]

This heightened awareness of black Americans' plight in the United States had tremendous implications for civil rights activists. Woodrow Wilson's appeal to make the world "safe for democracy" empowered them to address the failure of American democracy with respect to racial equality much more systematically, and also forcefully. Indeed, W. E. B. Du Bois also encouraged black GIs to take on the "battle against the forces of hell in our own country." He celebrated the veterans returning victoriously from Europe as "soldiers for democracy" and urged them to continue the struggle: "We return. We return from fighting. We return fighting. Make way

Figure 1 African American troops of the 505th Engineers illustrate how they "used cold steel on the Huns," May 5, 1919 (NARA).

for democracy! We saved it in France, and by the Great Jehovah, we will save it in the United States of America."[18]

Triumphant African American veterans returning from the battle-fields of Europe were ready to follow Du Bois's call, but white America, apparently, was not yet ready to grant blacks more freedom. On the contrary, during the war, the United States had seen a dramatic increase in violence and lynchings against black citizens in the South. To Southern reactionaries, African American educator Carter Woodson concluded in 1922, "the uniform on a Negro man was like a red flag thrown in the face of a bull."[19] The end of the war and the Red Scare after the Bolshevik Revolution in Russia made the situation for African Americans even more perilous. Complained one Natchez veteran: "You see they are afraid that if the Negro kept up his idea of his being a soldier and fighting, and wearing guns, etc. that these Negroes wouldn't stand for all the insults which they have to take from white people."[20] Thus, many Southern whites, including Mississippi Senator James Vardaman, believed that "French-women-ruined negro-soldiers" had to be reminded of the Southern race hierarchy. In 1919, seventy-seven African Americans, ten of them veterans, were lynched—one veteran had merely refused to step off a curb when told to do so by a white woman.[21] But violence against returning veterans and blacks in general was not limited to the South: race riots also erupted in the North where black workers now competed for jobs that white Americans claimed were theirs.

As a discouraged African American community soon realized, the hopes that had been raised during the war were not to be fulfilled. The "manhood" and full citizenship that had traditionally been the reward for serving one's country willingly were denied to African American men. The U.S. military, which had relied on black soldiers to defeat Germany, barred black volunteers from joining in peacetime throughout the 1920s and 1930s. Black officers were also being dismissed across the board and their requests to retain their commissions denied because, as one examining board ruled, "[n]egroes are deficient in moral fiber, rendering them unfit as officers and leaders of men."[22] By 1938, in a military some 230,000 enlisted men strong, fewer than 4,500 were African American and only 5 of the army's 1,359 officers were African American. Of those five, three were chaplains and the fourth was close to retirement.[23]

In the 1930s, the NAACP was increasingly active in bringing legal challenges to the Jim Crow system and socialists stepped up their efforts to advocate for greater civil rights in both the North and the South.[24] It would, however, take another world war, and America's entry into that war, to bring the civil rights agenda front and center. The rise of Nazism in the heart of Europe, and America's deep revulsion for the Nazi racial state, provided civil rights advocates with a whole new arsenal to indict the evil of white supremacy in the United States. African American civil rights activists watched developments in Germany closely, and they understood that Nazi racism also targeted black Germans and ethnic minorities like the Roma and Sinti. Yet they chose to discuss the emerging racial state in

Germany chiefly in terms of its anti-Semitism because that, rather than the persecution of other racial minorities, was what riled the Roosevelt administration and the American mainstream media, as well as churches, unions, and civic organizations.

Hitler's assumption of power in January 1933, the passing of the Nuremberg Race Laws in September 1935, and the increasing legal and social segregation of German Jews allowed activists to draw comparisons between the situation of Jews in Germany and that of blacks in the United States. Long before most of their countrymen, these activists recognized the full scope of Nazi racial hatred. Still, when they expressed empathy toward Germany's Jews, they also expressed deep dismay that white Americans were willing to stand up for the German Jews but not for Southern blacks. Civil rights activists were keenly aware of the difference between the state-sponsored racism of Nazi Germany and the U.S. federal government's refusal to interfere more forcefully in Southern states where the noxious Jim Crow laws prevailed. Nonetheless, they argued that "racial prejudice is racial prejudice wherever it exists. It is just as sordid and cruel when directed against the Negro in Mississippi as it is when directed against the Jew in Germany."[25]

In another development beneficial to the civil rights cause, the winning performance of black athletes against Germans and other white athletes during the Nazi years dramatically contradicted the regime's claims of Aryan supremacy (so similar to notions of white supremacy spouted in America's Deep South). In 1936, Jesse Owens bested some of Nazi Germany's greatest athletes at the Berlin Olympic Games, setting multiple Olympic and world records in the process, and in 1938, boxer Joe Louis won back the title of World Heavyweight Champion from the German fighter Max Schmeling in a rematch at New York City's Madison Square Garden. These victories over members of the alleged master race cheered African Americans and compelled white Americans, if ever so gingerly, to praise their black athletes.[26]

The comparison between German Jews and Southern blacks was underscored by parallel developments in Germany and the United States. Just as Nazi storm troopers escalated their violence against German Jews, U.S. senators Robert F. Wagner and Edward Costigan were drafting an antilynching bill. This bill was the culmination of a lengthy, nationwide campaign to make lynching a federal crime, and it was supported by millions of progressive Americans. German-Jewish refugee scholars, after escaping Nazi terror, were especially committed to support this bill. In addition to their experience with Nazism in Germany and Jim Crow laws in the United States, they came to understand the depth of America's race problem teaching at traditionally black colleges, where many of them found employment. A coalition of Southern senators, who feared that the antilynching bill would mark the first step toward full civil and political equality for African Americans, managed to defeat the Wagner-Costigan bill with a filibuster in 1938. The bill's failure, as well as President Roosevelt's unwillingness to

Twilight Of The Gods

Courtesy Baltimore (Md.) *Sun*

Figure 2   "Olympic Crisis," cartoon published in the September 1936 issue of the *Crisis* (reproduced by permission of the NAACP).

override it by issuing an executive order, provided black civil rights activists countless opportunities to compare Germany's treatment of the Jews with America's treatment of its black minority.[27]

To be sure, civil rights activists understood that a regime authorizing state violence against a minority was markedly different from one failing to intervene against vigilante violence. Yet they continued to draw the comparison between Nazis and Americans anyway because, as one observer asked in 1939, what is the difference to a "murdered man...between the government sanctioning his murder by decree, or permitting his murder" by sheer disregard for his humanity?[28] Once activists realized the full horror of Nazi racial hatred, these kinds of comparisons disappeared for the most part, although not completely. *The Chicago Defender*, for example, wrote in late 1942: "if Hitler wins, the poll-taxers of the South who now use lynching as a weapon of terror will use it as a weapon of extermination."[29]

Remembering the broken promises of World War I, African Americans, given the grim reality of their lives, were hardly motivated about fighting in another "war for democracy," in which they felt they had no stake. World War II veteran Charles Hanson recalled many decades later that he was not amused when black newspapers demanded that black soldiers be trained for combat units: "Why should somebody who's been beat on the head daily...say I demand to be sent to the frontlines?"[30] Another soldier wrote to the NAACP that the "Negro would rather give his life at home fighting for a cause he can understand than against an enemy whose principles are

Figure 3 "Your Hands Are Bloody," cartoon published in the February 1935 issue of the *Crisis* (reproduced by permission of the NAACP).

Figure 4 "Another Klansman," cartoon published in June 1939 (*Philadelphia Tribune,* Philadelphia, PA).

Figure 5 "It Does Happen Here," cartoon published in the November 1938 issue of the *Baltimore Afro-American* (Used with permission from the Afro-American Newspapers Archives and Research Center).

the same as our so-called democracy."[31] Indeed, some in the black press gave voice to this somber mood when an editorial asked, "Why die for democracy for some foreign country when we don't even have it here?"[32]

In the debates leading up to the war, African American activists were also keenly aware that they were being asked to come to the rescue of Great Britain and France, two colonial powers that ruled over millions of other people of color. The black intelligentsia had been following Gandhi's struggle in India with great interest, and they did not want their contribution to the war to prolong colonial rule. Freedom for African Americans, they argued, was intimately tied to achieving freedom for the millions of enslaved people in the non-Western world. In the *Crisis*, African American journalist George Schuyler called British colonial rule "Hitlerism without Hitler," while Du Bois eloquently posed the predicament that black Americans confronted: "If Hitler triumphs the world is lost; if England triumphs the world is not saved."[33]

At the same time, black activists also understood that the war offered unprecedented opportunities to advance the civil rights agenda. Thousands of factory jobs opened up in the industrial centers in the Northeast and the West Coast, and the desperate need for black labor gave activists new leverage to pressure the Roosevelt administration to integrate factories that had traditionally excluded black laborers. Furthermore, because of the Great Migration, 30 percent of African Americans were now living outside of the South, in places where they were not only able to vote, but where political candidates also courted their votes. The Democratic Party was eager to reach out to these new voters, who had in the past cast their lot with the party of Lincoln, their emancipator. To convince African Americans that progressive New Deal Democrats represented their interests better than pro-business Republicans, and to win over eligible black voters in the Northern and Western states, President Roosevelt appointed a number of prominent African Americans as advisors to members of his cabinet.

After France fell to the Nazis in the summer of 1940, civil rights activists shifted gears, and by December 1941, when Pearl Harbor was attacked, they were ready to fully endorse the government's decision to go to war. Thus, when they set out to encourage a largely reluctant African American community to support the war effort, the NAACP, the black press, and other civil rights organizations—such as the Urban League—insisted that a real choice had to be made. They reminded African Americans of Hitler's hateful language in *Mein Kampf*, where he had referred to blacks as half-apes: "If Hitler wins, every single right we now possess and for which we have struggled here in America for more than three centuries will be instantaneously wiped out by Hitler's triumphs. If the allies win, we shall at least have the right to continue fighting for a share of democracy for ourselves."[34]

In light of this larger threat, black leaders galvanized their constituents to step up to the plate. Yet they had learned from their unconditional patriotic support during World War I and entered this fight both with less idealistic hope and more firm resolve. The NAACP reminded African Americans that they had been "taken to the mountaintop" before, only to be bitterly disappointed after the war, when the Ku Klux Klan was revived and soldiers were murdered for "wearing the uniform they had worn in France fighting to preserve democracy."[35] This time, in a clear reference to their unconditional support during World War I, they insisted, "there can be no closed ranks on the race question, and no silence on injustice."[36]

One expression of this new resolve was the so-called Double-V Campaign, launched in January 1942 by the *Pittsburgh Courier*. Promising to "wage a two-pronged attack against our enslavers at home and those abroad who would enslave us,"[37] proponents of the Double-V Campaign insisted that African Americans who were willing to risk their lives in war and who labored on the home front to support their country's struggle against fascism and racism should finally receive full citizenship rights. The campaign was also envisioned as a strategy to prod white American liberals to discover "the paradox within their own democracy and join the struggle for civil rights."[38] Black newspapers, all civil rights organizations, and nearly all black churches lent their support to this campaign, which united and invigorated the black community.

A January 1942 editorial in the *Crisis* declared what was at stake in the bluntest terms. It is worth quoting at some length to show how centrally the struggle against Hitler's Germany figured in mobilizing black America:

> It must be that we declare the life blood of our fighters and the sweat of our workers to be a sacrifice for a new world which not only shall not contain a Hitler, but no *Hitlerism*. And to the thirteen millions of American Negroes that means a fight for a world in which lynching, brutality, terror, humiliation, and degradation through segregation and discrimination shall have no place *either here or there*. So we must speak even as we fight and die. We must say that the fight against Hitlerism begins in Washington, D.C., the capital of our nation, where black Americans have a status only slightly above that of the Jew in Berlin. We must say that if forced labor is wrong in Czechoslovakia, peonage farms are wrong in Georgia. If the ghettos in Poland are an evil, so are the ghettos in America.[39]

By using Nazi Germany as a mirror to reflect America's own racial shortcomings, African American activists gave new force and clarity to their argument that the prevailing Southern doctrine of "separate but equal" was anything but, and could, therefore, never assure the equality of black citizens. Consequently, white America's outcry against Nazi racism and America's entry into the war in 1941 made possible a civil rights agenda that insisted not just on ameliorating the consequences of segregation but on ending it altogether, both in its legalized form in the South and its unofficial practice in the North. Thus, when African Americans joined the war effort across the nation and on the battlefield overseas, they also called for an "unconditional surrender" of the "Hitlers" on the "home front."[40]

2

Fighting on Two Fronts:
World War II and Civil Rights

America's entry into World War II in December 1941 brought the civil rights agenda front and center. Since the Nazi regime presented not only a threat to democracy but was also ideologically grounded in racial inequality, America's entry into the war made possible never before imagined advances on the home front for African Americans. But there were also real limits to what could be accomplished. Those limits were most obvious in the debates and policies regarding the use of black troops. Despite all the debates on civil rights leading up to World War II, and throughout the war, the U.S. military that defeated Nazi Germany together with the Soviets, British, and French, was as segregated on Victory in Europe Day (VE-Day) in May 1945 as it was in 1940, when the United States began mobilizing for the looming conflict.

Still, being called upon to fight in a war whose express purpose was to defeat the Nazi racial state had tremendous implications for the advance of civil rights. Just like their brethren in World War I, black soldiers stationed in Great Britain, as well as fighting in France and Italy, encountered societies without a color line for the first time, interacting with white people who saw them not only as triumphant liberators but also as *Americans* (rather than "Negroes"), and furthermore considered them "men" rather than "boys." That experience outside the United States allowed many black soldiers to fully understand what one historian has called the "depth of their own degraded citizenship."[1] Many of the soldiers who had fought abroad would not be willing to return to the same conditions they had left behind, becoming instead the foot soldiers of the burgeoning civil rights movement.

Another Jim Crow Army

Between May and October 1940, the Roosevelt government began preparing for a possible intervention in the conflict raging in Europe and Asia. Military planners were, for the most part, veterans of World War I, and their views were heavily influenced by the military's past use of black draftees as "laborers in uniform" and by what they considered the disappointing performance of black combat troops in World War I. By and large, military analysts overlooked the units that had performed well under fire and focused instead on units that had performed below par. Ignored was the fact that poorly performing units were usually also those that had been inadequately equipped, had received very little or only mediocre training stateside, and were commanded by incompetent or racist white commanders.

While military policymakers grudgingly recognized the army's obligation to employ black soldiers, they insisted that strict segregation of the troops had to be maintained to uphold morale and ensure military efficiency. Army Chief of Staff General George Marshall supported efforts to eliminate *overt* discrimination in the army, but he also resisted all efforts by civil rights activists, many of whom were also veterans of World War I, to integrate the military. Doing so, argued Marshall,

> would be tantamount to solving a social problem which has perplexed the American people throughout the history of this nation. The Army cannot accomplish such a solution and should not be charged with the undertaking. The settlement of vexing racial problems cannot be permitted to complicate the tremendous task of the War Department and thereby jeopardize discipline and morale.

Secretary of War Henry Stimson did not believe in integration either, and he was ready to support his generals. Though he acknowledged "the individual tragedy" this sort of policy inflicted on "the colored man himself," he urged Roosevelt not to place "too much responsibility on a race which was not [known for] showing initiative in battle."[2]

Roosevelt sided with the military, and in October 1940, it was announced that the military would be segregated, just as in World War I. Still, concessions had to be made to civil rights activists, who used the national emergency as a moment to advance their cause. As part of the national mobilization that followed Japan's attack on Pearl Harbor, the U.S. Army reactivated the two black infantry divisions, the 92nd and 93rd, known popularly as the Buffalo Soldiers Division and the Blue Helmets. Initially barred from service in the Army Air Corps, African Americans were permitted to qualify as aviators in 1941 after a relentless national campaign in the black press compelled Congress to establish an all-black fighter squadron. Trained at Alabama's Tuskegee Institute, one of the nation's oldest and most prestigious black colleges, these fliers became known as the Tuskegee Airmen. Along with black ground crews and flight surgeons, they formed the four squadrons of the 332nd Fighter Group of the U.S. Army Air Corps, which flew more than 1,500 missions in Africa and Europe between April 1943 and April 1945.[3]

While the government's decision to mobilize and deploy a segregated military had already infuriated civil rights activists, Secretary Stimson's

Figure 6 Gen. John K. Cannon, commander of the 12th USAAF, congratulates Capt. C. B. Hall of the 99th all-black Fighter Squadron, who shot down two German planes over a bridgehead south of Rome, Italy, January 29, 1945 (NARA).

announcement just a few weeks after the attack on Pearl Harbor to maintain separate blood banks for white and black soldiers only increased their anger. In the *War's Greatest Scandal*, a pamphlet published by the March on Washington Movement (1941–1947), civil rights activists decried segregation in the military as "a fantastic situation in an Army supposedly dedicated to wiping out Nazi racialism. And yet, how can we expect anything else when we see those in command of this Army and Navy adopting as their official policy this doctrine of Hitler?" The activists taunted their government: " 'White supremacy,' which is simply Hitler's 'Nordic Supremacy' in Cracker Lingo, has become the official policy of the American armed forces. Racialism is monstrous in Nazi Germany but O.K. in the U.S. Army."[4]

By refusing to integrate the military, the federal government had once again officially sanctioned the Jim Crow system of segregation inscribed in state (rather than federal) law. Indeed, the U.S. military now authorized the legally ordained racism of the Deep South as standard practice on all its bases, even in states where no such institutionalized discrimination existed. The military's racial policies during World War II politicized a generation of African Americans, many of whom had never experienced firsthand the indignities and humiliations of Jim Crow that were the norm below the Mason-Dixon Line. Black soldiers traveling by train to army bases in the South, where 80 percent of all black GIs received their training, were usually crowded into the first car, right behind the coal-powered engine. As World War II veterans Walter Patrice and Spencer Moore recalled, as soon as the train arrived in Washington, DC, Jim Crow ruled. The air conditioner was turned off and open windows provided the only relief from the heat generated by the burning coal but left them covered with soot.[5] When changing trains, they rarely had access to refreshments of any kind, and they were allowed to board only after all the white soldiers had been seated. Encountering the full force of Jim Crow humiliation once in the South, recalled veteran A. William Perry, was "like a slap in the face."[6] As one disgusted editorialist wrote in the *Crisis* after a particularly jarring incident in North Carolina, "There they were, soldiers of democracy, not in Hitlerland, but in the greatest democracy in the world, in their own native land, branded, callously mistreated, humiliated. Looking about them in North Carolina, would it be any wonder if they had little enthusiasm for destroying the Master Race—in Berlin and Tokyo?"[7]

In this situation, many black recruits encountered other blacks hailing from significantly worse circumstances for the first time. Joe Stephenson of North Carolina, who graduated from college, for example, was shocked to see the very high illiteracy rates among his fellow soldiers from the Deep South and was furious about "what the country had done to them." Moreover, black soldiers discovered that they were treated worse than the enemy: they had to put up with segregated and substandard transportation and lodging whereas German POWs received the same accommodations and provisions as white American GIs. West Point graduate and World War II veteran Joseph Hairston had the "horrible realization" that "German war prisoners could eat in the establishments [on the military base] and we couldn't." Meanwhile, Southern sheriffs, who resented the officer training patches on black soldiers' uniforms, used the most derogatory language to instruct "uppity" Northern blacks of the Southern race hierarchy. Reuben Horner, who arrived in the South from Vermont as a young lieutenant, recalled that the military brass treated him and his fellow black officers "very much like dogs," addressing him as "boy" rather than by his military rank.[8]

This federalization of Jim Crow laws through the U.S. military had already occurred during the Spanish-American War of 1898 and World War I, but by 1941, the African American community had become more urban and political, as well as better educated and organized, and thus ready to defend the civil rights cause. African American representatives could now make a powerful and convincing case that the Southern "traditions" of Jim Crow were not merely an aberration in an otherwise admirable democratic system, as white Northern liberals sometimes claimed. Indeed, just as civil rights advocates such as John Hope had done after World War I, activists now argued that racial discrimination was not a *Southern* problem but an

American problem.[9] They were also empowered to raise again and again the troubling question of what distinguished the racial segregation in the military and American society from that of America's foe in the war. In one of his columns, poet Langston Hughes wrote, for example, that "the army put its official stamp upon Jim Crow, in imitation of the Southern states where laws separating Negroes and whites are as much part of government as are Hitler's laws segregating the Jews in Germany."[10] The *Crisis* was just as insistent that the prejudices undergirding segregation had to be "rooted out whether they reside in the *Mein Kampf* of a Hitler, or in a memorandum in the adjutant general's office of the American Army."[11]

As historians of the U.S. military have pointed out, the organization's racial policy during World War II merely continued practices that had been in effect since the War of Independence: blacks were permitted to bear arms in defense of their country only as a last resort, and when public pressure demanded it. Furthermore, African American soldiers were under no circumstances to be given authority over whites. If they achieved high rank, they could command troops of their own race but never white ones. A few commanders suggested that black soldiers, if provided the same training opportunities, would perform as well as white soldiers, especially with the firm leadership of a white officer. The majority, however, continued to "adhere to the belief that blacks had inherent biological and psychological traits that limited their suitability for military service" and especially for modern warfare. The 1936 Army War College manual for officers, for instance, asserted that the "Negro" is "careless, shiftless, irresponsible...unmoral, untruthful and his sense of right doing is relatively inferior." Moreover, blacks' "cranial cavity" was allegedly smaller than whites', leading military planners to conclude in 1940 that "the Negro is far below the white in capacity to absorb instruction."[12]

In contrast to these claims of 1936, a revised officer-training manual of 1944 insisted that the U.S. Army did not accept any "doctrine of racial superiority or inferiority." Rather, the policy of segregation was strictly a matter of "practical military expediency, and not an endorsement of belief in racial distinction." Although attempting to present the army's attitude toward race as progressive and even-handed, this publication reflected the conviction that black and white troops were incompatible, that contact between them would inevitably lead to "interracial friction," and that an integrated military could never be an effective fighting force.[13] With this view, the military gave expression to widely held assumptions among America's white population. Surveys conducted by the Office of War Information in July 1943 showed that 96 percent of Southerners and 85 percent of Northerners insisted on segregation in the military. The attitude among African Americans could not have been more different: 90 percent of Northern blacks and 67 percent of their Southern counterparts wanted to be trained and to serve in integrated units.[14]

In accordance with the majority opinion of whites and established practice from World War I, the U.S. military, after convincing America's thirteen million African Americans that they also had a stake in the fight against Nazism, deployed 80 percent of African American soldiers in manual labor and service units and excluded them from the more prestigious combat units. The one million black GIs who served in World War II understood how crucial their participation was to the war effort. But many also complained that they were being sent abroad to fight for a democracy that most of them did not yet enjoy at home. One soldier put this so eloquently in 1944 that it is worth quoting him at length:

> The truth is that there isn't a Negro here who feels that his greatest enemy is Germany or Japan. This is repeatedly brought out in statements made during the orientation periods when we are ostensibly learning what we are fighting for .... The crimes committed by the Nazis and Japanese seem unreal and far away to them while the crimes committed by Southerners in this country are known to all of us. Many of the boys...who come from the South can tell stories of being run out of town, of being threatened, and being intimidated. For every story of Nazi cruelty which is related, they can counter with an equally gruesome, true story of Southern inhumanity.[15]

The army and the War Department were aware of such attitudes. A July 1943 study expressed deep concern that only 39 percent of African Americans believed that the war against Germany and Japan was paramount, while 37 percent thought that the United States should first "make democracy work better here at home," and 24 percent held that both goals could be pursued at the same time.[16] Consequently, the War Department monitored both the black press and letters soldiers deployed in Europe wrote to black publications to get a pulse of what they called the "racial situation." They also gathered insights from censored letters soldiers sent home and from reports that commanders in the field sent along about the mood of the soldiers. These sources provide a jarring contrast to the celebratory histories of World War II that glowingly describe American GIs fighting in that war as the country's "greatest generation." They describe in great detail how being in Great Britain or France allowed black soldiers "their first experience of being treated as normal human beings."[17] Such positive encounters were often juxtaposed with humiliations and frequent violence from white officers and fellow soldiers furious that black soldiers were dating white British and French women.[18] Walter White, who visited the European Theater of Operations (ETO) in 1944 before the invasion of Germany, reported that he had "been greatly disturbed by the disheartened attitude" of many black soldiers. "Some of them have become so embittered that they call their white fellow-American soldiers 'the enemy.' Several of them have asked me, 'What are we fighting for? Were we sent to the ETO to fight the Nazis—or our white soldiers?' "[19]

Despite this disregard from their white comrades and from the military leadership, African American soldiers did what they were called to do. Vernon Baker, who finally received the Medal of Honor in 1997, the only African American among the 433 soldiers it was awarded to for

WWII service during his lifetime, recalled the segregated military at the ceremony: "I was an angry young man. We were all angry. But we had a job to do and we did it." Because these black GIs did their jobs, they enjoyed firm support from their own community, which was immensely proud of them. African American artist Charles Alston showed this pride in a drawing he made for the Office of War Information, which many black newspapers reproduced. It depicts a black soldier standing on African soil gazing fixedly at the south of Italy, ready to save the European continent, which is devouring itself. Referring to Africa as the "Springboard of Civilization," Alston reminded African Americans of that continent's central role in the birth of human civilization, rejecting the views of white supremacists in the United States and Europe, who saw nothing but barbarism there.[20]

Black soldiers played a crucial role in defeating the Nazi racial state. The Buffalo Soldiers of the 92nd Division fought valiantly in Italy despite the often mediocre leadership of their white officers and the substandard equipment they were forced to use. After D-Day in June 1944, the truck drivers of the Red Ball Express in France made sure that the 28 Allied divisions in the field received a daily supply of some 750 tons. Because all railroad

Figure 7 "Again the Springboard of Civilization," Charles Alston for the OWI, 1943 (NARA).

lines in France had been bombed by the Allies, the almost 6,000 trucks of
the Red Ball Express were the only means of bringing much needed materials to the front. African Americans made up 75 percent of the soldiers of
that vital supply and communications line. The famed all-black 761st Tank
Battalion was the first to break through the Siegfried Line, and fought decisive victories during the Battle of the Bulge. The horrific losses of that same
battle also made it possible for about 2,500 black GIs from service units to
serve in combat side-by-side with white GIs, when depleted lines needed to
be replenished. The War Department vetoed the commanders' suggestion
to integrate individual black soldiers into all white units and allowed the
"experiment" to proceed only at the platoon level. Still, the black volunteers who had to give up their military rank to be able to volunteer in the
combat units were thrilled to at last have their chance to "fight like men."
Wilson Evans was one of those volunteers, and he recalled that he never
"felt so free from the burden of color because this was the first time in
twenty-seven months of service that I was an American soldier."[21]

The War Department was most anxious to present to the American public images of the war effort that did not upset the social order at home.
Many images that the Signal Corps took of black soldiers participating in

Figure 8   Volunteers for Front-Line Duty Take a Break between Instruction Periods, March
28, 1945. All black volunteers had to surrender their military rank in order to fight in integrated units with white soldiers (NARA).

the struggle against Nazi Germany were propaganda photos, intended to broadcast a sense of racial harmony and to keep the black community committed to the war effort.

Most of these photos of black soldiers circulated in the United States portrayed their subjects as "helpers" rather than warriors. In other words, these photos also reveal the military's attitude that "there should be no Negro heroes." If extraordinary contributions of black soldiers had to be acknowledged, citations were to be given for "preserving supplies and other military properties, for saving the lives of Army personnel—especially of white officers—rather than for heroic performances, under fire, against the enemy."[22] Nonetheless, these photos conveyed to black Americans the crucial part that their sons, husbands, and brothers played in the war and especially in conquering the evil of Nazism.

In selecting propaganda photos, military officials also took pains to avoid circulating photos portraying black men poised to fire weapons or commanding tanks because such images presented a threat to the existing social order based on white supremacy.[23] Accordingly, few photographs in the army's official record depict black soldiers advancing into German cities or engaged in combat.

Figure 9   Tankmen of the all-black 761st Tank Battalion and infantry of the 3rd Battalion, 409th Regiment, 103rd Division (7th U.S. Army) fry pancakes together near Reisdorf, Germany, April 3, 1945 (NARA).

Figure 10   Corporal William E. Thomas and Private First Class Joseph Jackson on Easter Morning, March 10, 1945 (NARA).

Just as threatening to the established social order was the idea of black soldiers wielding power over white men, even if those white men were the defeated enemy. Black troops did play a role in the capture of Wehrmacht soldiers and in guarding them, but this seemed to elicit some unease among officials in the War Department. An official charged with monitoring the "Negro Press" reported with some concern that a military photo of a black soldier with a group of Wehrmacht soldiers in a forest had been reproduced on the front page of seven major black newspapers, including the *Atlanta Daily Word* (Figure 12). The photo was reproduced not with the caption assigned by the military but instead read "Superman Surrender."[24] The black soldier is proudly displaying a dagger he must have taken from a captured or killed Wehrmacht soldier.

Exit interviews conducted by military intelligence disclose the fears that were unleashed among whites because black soldiers had gained authority over white men. One white officer reported with some trepidation that the "authority exercised by the [black] troops as conquering and occupying forces has developed a staggering attitude of arrogance toward white people in their off-duty hours," and that he and other officers were "deeply concerned over the serious problems that will arise when the troops return to the U.S., where their activities will be limited by social-legal restrictions."[25]

Figure 11 African American GIs awaiting orders in Coburg, Germany, to crush any remaining Nazi military resistance, April 25, 1945 (NARA).

Figure 12 African American soldier of the 12th Armored Division guards a group of Nazi soldiers captured in the surrounding forest (NARA).

Figure 13   African American soldiers (12th Armored Division, 7th U.S. Army) guard a group of Germans they have ordered out of the farmhouse, April 1945 (NARA).

These officers were right to be concerned about how the participation of black GIs in a war far from home might impact the social order when they returned to the United States. Something had happened to black GIs "over there." They had become "men" and were no longer willing to be treated as "boys." African American veteran Dabney Hamner, who had been wounded fighting in Germany with the 125th Infantry Division, recalled that the "only time in my life I felt like a man was in Europe."[26] Another black soldier was convinced that "the Negro who returns to his farm or service position in the South will not be the docile laborer he was when he left. He will be a man who knows how to fight and who believes he should fight for those things which he fought for in World War II."[27] Yet another African American veteran explained candidly how his whole being had been transformed by his experience of fighting abroad: "I went into the army a nigger; I am coming out a man."[28]

Other returning soldiers shared similar convictions with military officials, albeit in somewhat less forceful language. Captain Richard Middleton, a chaplain, told his military intelligence debriefers about the treatment he would receive back in his home state of Mississippi from those who had served alongside him during the war: "I know when I walk down the street with my wife and family, those same people will say in a surprised and shocked tone, loud enough for us to hear, 'How can a Nigger become a captain in the Army?'" Middleton was also certain that returning "Negro soldiers will be more articulate and I know I certainly will be."[29] Weiman

Tyus, another African American chaplain, concluded that the "Negro soldier is returning to his native land with deep brooding in his heart and [a] dark smoldering resolve to start a new struggle, however hopeless, for the privileges that constitute his birthright."[30] Another veteran named Johnnie Stevens commented that, although "we came back to the same identical thing that we had left, in a way Word War II was good for the black soldier and the black people, for the simple reason that we learned a lot. We learned what it was like to live without prejudice. And believe it or not, we learned it from other countries."[31]

Fighting in World War II made these soldiers feel like "men" and expanded their worldview. But their role in helping defeat the evil of Nazi racism also had a terrific impact on many of them. Seeing with their own eyes the carnage that Nazi racism had wrought, African Americans GIs were stunned and, like Private William A. Scott III of the 183rd Engineer Combat Battalion, they often evaluated their experiences in Germany in light of their own complicated American heritage: "even though my ancestors had arrived as slaves in chains from Africa, and [were] subjected to torture and death during the long centuries of slavery, it all seemed to pale in comparison to the glaring impact of what I had witnessed in Buchenwald."[32]

But their encounters in the Nazi concentration camps such as Buchenwald also convinced them that the fight against segregation and racism in the United States was a righteous one, and one they wanted to be part of. As veteran Leon Bass remembers,

> The day that I walked through the concentration camp gates of Buchenwald ... I was totally unprepared for what I saw. And I? I just said to myself, "My God, what is this? This is some kind of insanity! Who are the people? What did they do that was so wrong?" And that's when I found out that they were Jews and gypsies, some were Jehovah Witnesses, they were trade unionists, they were Communists, they were homosexuals...There were so many different groups placed in that camp by the Nazis. And what did the Nazis use as a yardstick as to who would be chosen to go there? They said those people who were not good enough, those people...were inferior, they could be segregated. So, you see what I mean? Segregation, racism, can lead to the ultimate, to what I saw at Buchenwald.[33]

As it became clear how dramatically black GIs had been transformed by their experiences outside the United States, the War Department watched with concern. Commanders reported that "since these troops were free, while in Europe, from much of the racial discrimination existing in this country, and were at liberty to associate with white girls, many felt it would be a 'let down' to return home. For this reason 40 percent of those interviewed expressed a desire to remain overseas upon the cessation of all hostilities."[34] Even more troubling were assessments that grave conflict was bound to occur after the war "when the colored soldiers attempt to secure for their race that equality of treatment which they have received in foreign countries."[35] With dismay, officials read letters by young soldiers that

Figure 14 American troops, including African American soldiers from the 183rd Engineer Battalion, 8th Corps, U.S. 3rd Army, such as Leon Bass (third from left) view corpses stacked behind the crematorium at Buchenwald, Weimar, Germany, April 1945 (United States Holocaust Memorial Museum).

Figure 15 African American soldiers next to an oven in the crematorium at the Ebensee concentration camp, Ebensee, Austria, May 6–May 30, 1945 (United States Holocaust Memorial Museum).

asserted "that a new person (Negro) will come back home embedded [sic] with more hate than ever." They were just as anxious about black papers that predicted that trouble would ensue when black veterans returned home in large numbers and saw "that the home front...stood still on the race question while they fought and died for democracy abroad."[36]

The widely read African American magazine *Ebony* enthusiastically declared that these men were "not the same Negroes who put on uniforms after Pearl Harbor. The war has been an education...Travel, better health and living conditions, even higher income has made the Negro younger generation the most aware, most articulate, and the most militant in all U.S. history."[37] A 1947 publication on returning black veterans came to a similar conclusion. The authors asserted that matters for blacks in the United States were no worse than they had been before the war, but the veterans "were far more restless and dissatisfied when they returned to civilian life."[38]

Coming Home

Homecoming was often a bitter experience, especially for the 63 percent of African American veterans returning to the South. As veteran Chester White recalled, to the white soldiers, "we were just niggers. I'll never forget the one who yelled, 'just wait until the war's over, we know how to take care of you nigger bastards.'" One of White's friends "had all kinds of ribbons, but he was bitter as hell." Among Southerners, he remarked, "it didn't seem to make any difference if you fought or you didn't fight; [to them,] he was still only a black boy."[39] Veteran Dabney Hammer was equally dismayed. He had fought five battles "for American democracy" and proudly wore his medals on his uniform but was told by a white man in his hometown of Clarksdale, Mississippi, not to forget that he was "still a nigger."[40] Reverend Hosea Williams encountered the full force of that kind of attitude while traveling through Georgia after his discharge from the army. Despite all the medals on his uniform, including a Purple Heart, he was beaten nearly to death by a white mob in Americus, Georgia, because he tried to get a glass of water from a "white-only" fountain at a bus station. It took him months to recover from his injuries, and he later remarked on how he had "laid there crying eight weeks wishing Adolf Hitler had won the war."[41]

Significantly, violence aimed at veterans in uniform was perpetrated not just by individual vigilantes but also by local police officers, the alleged guardians of the law. Before Henry Murphy, a highly decorated veteran, returned home to Hattiesburg, Mississippi, his father warned him to take off his uniform and put on civilian clothing. "He told me not to wear my uniform home. Because the police was beating up [black] GIs and searching them. If they [sic] had a white woman's picture in his pocket, they'd kill him."[42] Matters were just as bad for veterans coming home to Alabama. Theophilus Eugene "Bull" Connor—the police commissioner of

Birmingham who in 1963 would become infamous for ordering the brutal use of fire hoses and attack dogs on civil rights protesters—unleashed a wave of police violence against black veterans in Birmingham, five of whom were beaten to death in a six-week period.[43] Just as after World War I, such figures apparently felt that the "manhood" black GIs had attained in Europe would have to be stripped from them. If they were to fit into Southern society again, they could not keep either their uniforms or any pictorial evidence that racial boundaries had been transgressed in Europe.

Even black veterans returning to states in the Northern United States were bitterly disappointed to see how little had changed during their absence. Oliver Harrington, the accomplished political cartoonist, wrote of his own homecoming after serving as a war correspondent for the *Pittsburgh Courier*: "You fought, if you [were] a Negro, to tear down the sign 'No Jews Allowed' in Germany," only to find that "the sign, 'No Negroes Allowed' " was still acceptable in the United States.[44] Another veteran, Henry Peoples, recalled that painful homecoming bitterly many years later: "I killed—I repeat I killed—other men in the name of democracy. Could the joke have been on me for being naive enough to believe in my government?"[45]

Many of these veterans resigned themselves to the old way of life, especially if they came from the South. The veteran Henry Murphy mentioned above, for example, followed his father's advice, and slipped on, as he put it, the only uniform that was acceptable to Southern whites: "overalls and a jumper, the uniform of a field hand."[46] But many others refused to resume an existence of submission and restricted opportunities, becoming instead the foot soldiers in a transformational movement. Oliver Harrington, for example, took on the struggle for civil rights by joining the NAACP; in search of a better life, he would later leave the United States for East Germany, where he became a renowned cartoonist and commentator. Reverend Hosea Williams, also mentioned above, joined the NAACP as well and subsequently became a prominent figure in the Southern Christian Leadership Conference, where he met and developed a deep friendship with Dr. Martin Luther King Jr. Many other veterans—less famous, but just as brave—were ready to take a stand, too: "I got through fighting in the ETO (European Theater of Operations)," said one, "and now I am fighting in the STO (Southern Theater of Operations)."[47] Another reflected on his decision to join the struggle by remarking that black veterans "had stood together and gained a new pride and unity," and when the "moment came...the men were going to be the cutting edge of a movement that would change America."[48]

Black veterans joined the NAACP by the thousands, both in the United States and from military bases abroad. Between 1940 and 1946, the number of local NAACP chapters nearly tripled, and membership increased from 50,556 to 450,000.[49] In defending the NAACP against charges of stirring up discontent among black soldiers, *Crisis* editor Roy Wilkins pointed out that veterans hardly needed the NAACP to tell them that it was "foolish to be *against* park benches marked '*Jude*' [Jew] in Berlin, but be for park benches marked '*Colored*' in Tallahassee, Florida."[50] Indeed, it was the veterans of World War II that the NAACP would rely on to provide some of the main plaintiffs in a series of court cases that tore down the segregation laws of the American South during the 1950s bit by bit. Veteran Oliver Brown most famously forced the desegregation of the school system when he agreed to let the NAACP take his child's case to the highest court of the country in the landmark 1954 case, *Brown v. Board of Education*.[51]

Veterans were key players in Mississippi's civil rights movement, and they took the lead in other Southern states as well. They were also involved in the so-called GI revolts across the South, where they sought to displace the entrenched and often corrupt local political machines. Veteran Jim Williams recalled that "little pockets of rebellion took place" in many parts of the United States after the war.[52] As a result of veteran activism, voter registration soared for the 1946 Democratic primary, the first national primary following the Supreme Court decision in 1944 that declared the white-only primaries of the South to be unconstitutional. The activism of veterans in Georgia raised the number of registered voters in Atlanta from 5,000 to 25,000, and more than 100,000 African Americans voted in that primary.[53] In Alabama, wrote a proud observer, "more than one hundred Birmingham Negro WWII veterans marched in double file to the Jefferson Country Courthouse to present their discharge papers as evidence of literacy."[54] Tragically, plenty of such attempts to assert civil rights failed, and whites' efforts to reassert their supremacy proved deadly for many black veterans. During the 1946 primary election, six veterans were lynched, while the corpses of others were found floating in the Mississippi or mutilated in the woods. Still others were forced to flee to the relative safety of the North.[55]

Clearly, the civil rights struggle begun in the early twentieth century was far from over. Changing people's hearts and minds in the country at large would be an arduous and long-lasting task. As discussed in the next chapter, the U.S. military that occupied the American zone in defeated Germany and was sent to de-Nazify and reeducate German society was just as segregated as it had been in 1941 when the United States had entered the war.

3

"We Will Never Go Back to the Old Way Again": African American GIs and the Occupation of Germany

America's occupation and reeducation of Germany (1945–1949) would prove to be a tremendous boost to the civil rights movement. During these years, activists were able to enunciate and clarify their message as never before. America's involvement in postwar Germany was, of course, not the only reason civil rights activists made significant advances after World War II, but events in Germany do comprise an integral piece of the puzzle of the larger narrative of the civil rights movement.

Two participants in the American occupation of Germany who later became noted commentators on American racism recognized postwar Germany as an unexpected location for confronting America's race problem, and for setting a stage for its future resolution. The African American journalist Roi Ottley traveled extensively during World War II and in postwar Germany as a war and foreign correspondent for several U.S. newspapers. His observations of race relations among U.S. troops led him to conclude that "American racialism would come into dramatic focus on German soil."[1] David Brion Davis, who served in Germany as an eighteen-year-old and was to become one of America's most distinguished historians of racism, also came to view the "early years of the American occupation...[as a] microcosm of the racial and civil rights struggle that would dominate America in the 1950s and 1960s and finally succeed in eradicating much of the evil of a Jim Crow South."[2]

Black soldiers, for their part, experienced their time in post-Nazi Germany as a "breath of freedom," and African American civil rights activists, as well as the black press, were eager to bring this news home. In much of its coverage, the black press depicted postfascist Germany as a sort of "Shangri-La" or "racial utopia" where African Americans could enjoy a better life than they could in their own country.[3] At the same time, much of the occupation coverage exposed the racism and violence that white enlisted men and officers inflicted on black soldiers in front of the very Germans they were sent to democratize. Significantly, the stories of post-Nazi Germany as a haven for black GIs also started to flow into the consciousness of a stunned white America.

America's Occupation Army

After the German surrender on May 8, 1945, the American military counted some 1.6 million American troops in Germany, with about 10 percent of those troops being African American. These troop levels, however, were quickly drawn down, as the anticipated resistance in Germany never materialized. Beginning with Victory in Europe Day (VE-Day), troops were sent to the Pacific to continue the struggle against Japan, or demobilized and sent back to the United States. By late 1945, only 614,000 GIs remained in Germany, and in 1946 another 400,000 GIs were returned to the United States. Given the mostly compliant and cooperative German population, a mere 90,000 soldiers were deemed necessary to ensure the goals of the occupation by 1948.[4] Some 10,000 of those troops were African American.

While these troops were in Germany to prevent any resurgence of Nazism, the U.S. forces also undertook the ambitious mission of democratization. At the Yalta Conference in February 1944 and the conference at Potsdam (July–August 1945), the Allies had decided that Germany would be divided into four zones of occupation, which were to be governed by America, the Soviet Union, Great Britain, and France. The Allies also agreed that their mission was to rid Germany of all vestiges of Nazism and to make it a democratic country. In their own zone of occupation, the Americans initially focused all efforts on demilitarizing Germany's war industry and prosecuting key Nazi war criminals. By 1946, however, it had become clear that eliminating Nazism was not sufficient. A much more concerted effort of reeducation was needed to build the institutional, social, and psychological framework necessary for a democratic Germany. With this shift in policy, the military government also made clear that the individual GI was to play an important role in converting Germans to the cause of democracy. In fact, the army saw its soldiers as democracy's best ambassadors.

The War Department and most military commanders saw no contradiction in employing a Jim Crow army to accomplish this noble mission. Not a single black officer served on the staff of the military governor of the American zone, General Joseph McNarney in Frankfurt, nor could any black soldier be found in his sprawling military government headquarters. In the early years of the occupation, blacks were not allowed to join the constabulary force whose job was to control the border with the East and to police the German civilian population. The army excluded them from the postal service, and they were not permitted to supervise or guard German workers.[5] The military commanders defended these restrictions by arguing that black GIs "ordinarily could not be utilized satisfactorily in a supervisory capacity over German personnel, since they required so much supervision themselves."[6] Furthermore, Deputy Chief of Staff General Paul suggested that Germans would find it offensive to be policed or guarded by African American soldiers, although he did not offer any evidence to back up this claim.[7] Citing the absence of black troops during the Rhineland occupation after World War I, commanders even tried to exclude black GIs completely from occupation duty; only manpower shortages and fears of an outcry from African American civil rights groups prevented this.[8] In fact, it was the Berlin Airlift of 1948–1949 that curbed all further efforts to keep blacks from participating in the occupation in Germany as it generated an urgent demand for troops in transportation and supply units.

It was ironic that this rigidly segregated and deeply racist army took on what commanders called "the most important job ever undertaken by the United States," namely, the reeducation and democratization of the defeated German foe. Moreover, it did it in a spirit of great optimism, as revealed in this written statement to the soldiers: "we ourselves prove that under the influence of an American environment, the German becomes a democratic, peaceful citizen."[9] Curing Germans of their race hatred was an important step in achieving democracy, and in this effort, the military command also envisioned a crucial role for the American GIs, whom it regarded as democracy's best ambassadors. An instruction manual informed soldiers and their families serving in the army of occupation that they were responsible for teaching Germans that "the whole concept of superiority...and intolerance of others is evil..." and that America was the "living denial of Hitler's absurd theories of a superior race."[10] One can only wonder what black soldiers must have thought when they read these instructions. Even the most insensitive observer could not miss the contrast between this soaring rhetoric of democratic ideals and racial harmony and the stark reality of the occupation army's Jim Crow policies.[11]

This disparity, however, did not stop key commanders in the military government from publicly expressing their resentment of African American GIs in the occupation force and trying to decrease their presence. Ernest Harmon, commander of the Constabulary, informed his cheering audience of all-white soldiers in 1947 that sending "colored soldiers" to Europe had been "America's stupidest mistake" and that he had warned the government not to send any "Niggers" because they had now become "a much bigger problem than the Germans."[12] General Geoffrey Keyes, commander of the Third Army, worked assiduously to reduce the number of African American troops. Military governor General Joseph McNarney declared in 1946 that it would take 100 years for Negroes to attain the developmental level of whites.[13] Even when this rabid segregationist returned to the United States in January 1947, the situation for African American GIs did not improve significantly, since his successor, Lieutenant General Lucius Clay, believed that if African American GIs had to be stationed in the prestigious Berlin command at all, they might best be used as ceremonial parade troops.[14]

These discriminatory and derogatory attitudes from military leaders notwithstanding, the participation of African Americans in the democratization and rebuilding of Germany offered the black community untold opportunities to celebrate its soldiers' contributions. The *Chicago Defender* was keen to highlight the "vital reconstruction role" that they played and, especially, to praise their contribution to democratizing German youth in the German Youth Activities (GYA) clubs. Some of the African American women who had been allowed to join all-black Women's Army Corps (WAC) units also went to Germany to serve as members of the occupation force. The black press invoked these young WACs, just as it did the many young black GIs serving in the occupation, again and again to underscore the value of their efforts, which it regarded as equal to those of whites.[15]

Because the war had politicized and mobilized America's black population as never before, representatives of various African American organizations and groups traveled to Germany both during the occupation and throughout the 1950s, keeping the black community in the United States informed about what its GIs were doing abroad: the African American press had its own correspondents in postwar Germany, and the *Pittsburgh Courier*, one of the most important black newspapers, ran a column titled "At Home and Overseas with Our GIs"; in addition, African American civil rights activists and members of African American churches and women's organizations traveled to occupied Germany, often reporting what

Figure 16 Members of the Women's Army Corps receive an orientation lecture from Jack Casey at European Command Headquarters (EUCOM HQ) in Nuremberg, Germany, October 17, 1949 (Courtesy of the Library of Congress).

they witnessed. Their reports from Germany, as well as the soldiers' reflections on their time there, provide a much needed corrective to the prevailing popular narrative that celebrates World War II veterans uncritically as "America's greatest generation"; they also add important new insights into how decisive the occupation of Germany was in exposing the limits of American democracy.

The Experience of Black Soldiers in Germany

Black soldiers experienced their occupation duty in Germany as a moment of liberation. Both in Great Britain before the invasion of Normandy and in France during the advance into Germany, black GIs had reported that sense of liberation because of the kindness the white civilian population in those countries had shown them. Yet they had never expected to be treated decently in the land where, as *Ebony* magazine observed, "Aryanism had ruled supreme."[16] In fact, soldiers were able to develop deeper relationships with the civilian population in Germany than they had during the war in Great Britain, France, or Italy, because, once hostilities were over, military units tended to remain in a particular locale for extended periods. They thus established day-to-day routines that fostered their connections to the local community; for example, attending local church services, dances in village pubs, as well as performances in the theaters and opera houses of Germany's bombed out cities.[17] These peacetime experiences proved especially electrifying for African American GIs from the South, but Northern blacks, too, were astounded to find themselves living in a society without a color line.

One of the most eloquent observers of the profound impact encounters in Germany had on black soldiers was the distinguished African American writer William Gardner Smith, who was born and raised in Philadelphia and was himself stationed in Germany in 1946/1947. During his time in Germany, Smith made a name for himself as a correspondent for the *Pittsburgh Courier*; he also wrote one of the most widely read novels of the postwar experience, *The Last of the Conquerors* (1948). In Berlin, Smith wrote a passage that echoed W. E. B. Du Bois's account of his time in that city, emphasizing that many black soldiers first experienced in Germany what it was like to be treated like "human beings" and "men": "Many black Americans came alive for the first time in the ruins of Berlin... Members of a victorious army, they found respect and consideration for the first time—but from the former enemies." Smith recalled, too, that "black soldiers often wept like babies when their time was up, when they had to return 'home.'"[18]

Living in a society without the dreaded "whites only" signs was a novel experience for many black soldiers. One of Smith's protagonists in *The Last of the Conquerors* gives voice to what this meant to him and countless other GIs: "Now I know what it is to walk into any place, *any* place, without worrying about whether they serve colored.... You know what the hell I learned? That a nigger ain't no different from nobody else. I had to

Figure 17 Corporal James Doughty hangs out his laundry in the city square of Coburg, Germany, May 16, 1945 (NARA).

come over here to learn that. I hadda come over here and let the Nazis teach me that. They don't teach that stuff back in the land of the free."[19] This sentiment reflected what real black soldiers felt as well: one said that the "Nazis in Germany treated me better than the white folks in Virginia, where I was born."[20]

For many black GIs, then, military service in Germany expanded their outlook and helped them to reimagine their own place in the world. Andrew Bowman, for instance, recalled that he "felt like a prisoner in the United States" before he went to Germany, but that Germany "opened [his] eyes to the variety of reactions a black could expect when dealing with whites."[21] Many years after the war, another soldier marveled that

> we were treated better by the civilian population than we were treated in America. See, in our country we could not buy a hotdog when we were in uniform, had to ride in the back of the bus when we were in uniform—but over there, you were treated like a king. We ate together, slept together. After the war was over and [the Germans] had dances again, you were invited. That is why a lot of blacks took their discharge in Europe. They said, look, ain't nothing in America for me.[22]

Of course, such glowing recollections of postwar Germany should not suggest that Germans had abandoned racism with the defeat of Hitler. On the contrary, racism toward people of color has a long history in Germany. Germany's nineteenth-century colonial ambitions in Africa only reinforced this racism, and after World War I, Germany's resentment at having lost the war fueled the hateful and racist "Black Horror on the Rhine" campaign against the occupiers, wherein nationalist politicians denigrated France's colonial troops from Senegal. The Nazi racial state, of course, directed its most virulent antipathy toward the Jews, but it also persecuted Afro-Germans as racially inferior. When the Nazis were defeated, these attitudes could not be eliminated overnight. Oral histories reflecting on the occupation years, even the positive ones, make it clear that racist stereotypes permeated German perceptions of black GIs. Recent studies of postwar Germany have confirmed such racism, showing, for example, how appalled many Germans were that white German women entered romantic and sexual relationships with black GIs.[23] African American soldiers' mostly positive recollections of their time in Germany, therefore, say much more about the dismal state of race relations in the United States and its military than they do about racial tolerance in postwar Germany.

Most notably, the interaction between black GIs and German civilians was marked by the absence of the legal and informal color line that still defined the lives of African Americans in the United States and in the occupation army. Despite the twelve-year rule of the Nazi racial state, German society did not have a long-standing tradition of institutionalized racial barriers. Furthermore, Germans, by and large, had had very little exposure to people of color, and were, therefore—much like the French—attracted to the "exotic otherness" that black soldiers presented. Some of these soldiers recall how Germans called them "chocolate soldiers" and openly admired their brown eyes, white teeth, and dark skin.[24] Like the British and French, Germans also viewed black soldiers first and foremost as Americans or Yankees—as conquerors who wore the uniform of the victor nation—and not as "Negroes." Indeed, one white German woman who married a black GI told her children that "Germans saw the blackness" of their father's skin "as visible proof that he was a U.S. soldier."[25] Moreover, as William

Figure 18   Private James Allen, the only motorcycle patrolman in the 90th Military Police in Kitzingen, Germany, undated (Courtesy of the Library of Congress).

Gardner Smith noted in 1959 when reflecting on his time in Germany, Germans understood power: "They were racists, but we were conquerors and the look in their eyes was respect."[26]

Though Germans may have feared and perhaps even resented the presence of black soldiers in the occupation army, they considered them the most generous of all the occupiers. Because these GIs were assigned to supply, labor, and service details, they had unfettered access to the food and goods that hungry Germans in their war-torn cities lacked. The military noted this development with some concern: "Germans were quick to sense that there were, on the whole, greater material advantages to be gained from fraternizing with Negroes than with white troops." The black soldiers, for their part, "embraced fraternization with enthusiasm."[27] Children were especially taken with the black GIs who kindheartedly handed out candy and indulged their every whim.

This image of the magnanimous, child-loving black soldier has taken on an almost iconic quality in Germans' memory of the end of the war and their first encounters with Americans. Many white soldiers shared their rations as well, but in the recollections of Germans, the generosity of the black GIs stands out to this day. The first encounter with other people of color for Hans Massaquoi—the longtime editor of *Ebony* magazine—who was born to a white German mother and a Liberian father in the 1920s and

Figure 19   African American GI distributing candy to German children, 1945 (bpk).

lived through Nazi Germany as an Afro-German child longing to fit in, was also with black GIs. Massaquoi was as startled as the GIs, who asked him "what in the world" he was doing "among the Krauts" before handing him a helmet overflowing with chocolates, army C-rations, and cigarettes in the rubble of his hometown of Hamburg.[28]

The severe food shortages during the early years of the occupation certainly contributed to black soldiers becoming such beloved occupiers. And, as World War II veteran Preston McNeil recalled, children were often the first to make contact with them, which often led to friendships with the children's families: "They were hungry, so we'd give them food. It's hard to see kids down in the garbage cans, getting food. So I used to take my mess kit, put food in there, and give it to them. And the next day, [the kid] will come out looking for you and then he'll invite you to his house. And you'd bring the food and everything. So they came to love us."[29]

Contemporary witnesses on the German side, for their part, reported that black GIs did not approach the defeated civilian population with the sort of arrogance displayed by many of the white soldiers. Indeed, a military survey found that 70 percent of Germans found the black soldiers friendlier than white troops.[30] Irmgard Achatz, a German woman who fell in love with a black GI in 1947 and later married him, explained the popularity of the soldiers by telling her children that they

> brought joy to the population. They were happy to be there. They smiled. They laughed. They were kind and polite and caring and humble. Everything about the black GIs was refreshing and a sharp contrast to the white GI troops who treated the German population as defeated and conquered. Not quite deserving the respect given to dogs. White GIs took things, demanded things...sometimes spat on people in the street. Black GIs came with gifts and flowers and stuff from the PX ... and that jazz music epitomized the sassy swing of the Swartze [sic]. It was refreshing not always to feel vanquished.[31]

According to these Germans and the GIs themselves, black soldiers could empathize with the conquered Germans because of their own experiences of poverty and second-class treatment back home.[32] Ollie Stewart brought that message home when he reported that "Tan Yanks taught Europe many things: democracy as it should be lived, not preached." He also observed that "the soldiers' generosity and consideration to the down-trodden... contrasted glaringly with the arrogance of some other men wearing the uniform."[33]

As the example of Irmgard Achatz shows, black GIs in Germany—as in other European countries where they had spent time—were able to establish romantic and sexual relationships with local women. Although these relationships might have provoked sullen service in local inns or rude stares on German streets, they did not subject the soldiers to arrest or the violence of the lynch mob, as would have been the case in the American South. Not surprisingly, the black press was riveted by this phenomenon as these relationships broke the ultimate taboo upon which the Southern system of white supremacy was erected. Reporting on this assault on the foundation

Figure 20   Corporal William A. Smith (playing guitar) and Sergeant Stanfort Osborne with the 654th Tank Destroyer Battalion, 35th Infantry Division (9th U.S. Army) at Herne, Germany, 1945 (NARA).

of the Jim Crow order, Roi Ottley called the "combination of Saxon blonde and Mississippi black" a "spectacular racial development."[34]

Clearly, black GIs' freedom to fall in love with white women and be loved by them in return fortified a sense of manhood, equality, and even democracy in them that they were denied in their own country. Again, one of William Gardner Smith's protagonists poignantly articulates what such experiences meant to black GIs:

I had lain on the beach many times, but never before with a white girl...No one stared as we lay on the beach together, our skins contrasting but our hearts beating identically and both with noses on the center of our faces. Odd, it seemed to me, that here, in the land of hate, I should find this all-important phase of democracy. And suddenly I felt bitter.[35]

The son of one such interracial couple recalls his parents' descriptions of their life together in Germany during the late 1940s: They told him of an "experience free of visible racial prejudice, especially in comparison to the vocal and visible prejudice confronted by them" when they returned to the United States in the early 1950s. He also remembered his father marveling at the ease with which he and his wife could be together in Germany: "Things that were unthinkable for an interracial couple to do in the U.S. or on the U.S. military base [in Germany] could be done naturally by them in almost any German town and in the countryside. They rented an apartment together; they sat on buses and trains together in the same section—front or back. They ate in restaurants together."[36]

Spreading the News

With black GIs enjoying such unprecedented freedoms and, for the most part, acceptance from the German civilian population, the African American press took on the crucial role of spreading the news in order to indict the limits of democracy in the United States. A 1946, six-page photo essay by *Ebony*, "Germany Meets the Negro Soldier," proved especially electrifying, and was recommended by the *Chicago Defender* as a must-read. Representative of the wider black press coverage of black GIs' experiences in Germany, this photo essay presented the full spectrum of interactions between black GIs and German civilians. It included not only photos of interracial romance but also of interracial families (e.g., a proud new dad going for a stroll with his white German partner and their baby), work environments (e.g., soldiers in their offices interacting with white German secretaries), and black GIs interacting with adoring German children.[37]

These black papers highlighted the irony of Germany's comparatively respectful treatment of black soldiers. The *Chicago Defender* emphasized a "Paradox in Race Relations" with a long, screaming headline—"In Berlin...One Time Citadel of Race Hatred ... Negro GIs Are Living in a New World of Social Equality.... Hitler Called Them 'Semi-apes,' but German Frauleins [*sic*] Find Negro GIs Likable and Human"—suggesting that the images of the interracial couples of the *Ebony* magazine spread were bound to "make Dixie gasp" while, at the same time, offering an opportunity for "frank talk to make America think."[38] The *Defender* was also stunned to relate that Germans presented "very little evidence of prejudice" toward black soldiers despite their anti-Semitism.[39] Similarly surprised, an *Ebony* correspondent reported in 1946 that in post-Nazi Germany, blacks were "finding more friendship, more respect and more equality than they would back home—either in Dixie or on Broadway," and concluded that many black GIs found that democracy had "more meaning on Wilhelmstrasse [in Berlin] than on Beale Street in Memphis."[40]

Male readers of the African American press responded approvingly to this sort of coverage—especially concerning interracial couples—but their observations also show that these stories from postwar Germany inspired hope for greater democracy and equal treatment at home. One *Ebony* reader praised the articles on "GIs in Germany" because

> they gave undeniable proof that the Negro is a human being, a creature who loves and is loved ... As a free people we Negroes want the right to live

wherever we choose and can pay the rent; to associate with, court or marry whomever we choose ... If a Negro boy and a white girl find things in common and desire to associate with each other, we as believers in democratic freedom should support their democratic right to do so.[41]

A writer for the *Chicago Defender*, while speculating that the "ability of the colored soldier to excel on the dance floor" had doubtlessly added to his "popularity among the frauleins [sic]," nevertheless expressed his wonderment that even the parents of the soldiers' girlfriends accepted the black GIs. "A great many boys get steady girlfriends whom they visit at their homes during furlough. The parents of the girls treat the soldiers with respect."[42] This respectful treatment was all the more surprising as it was so seldom encountered in the United States.

Beyond interracial relationships, another wellspring of friendly encounters between blacks and Germans that the black press seized upon was music, and especially jazz. Urban Germans had first fallen for jazz in the 1920s, but, as the Nazis were quick to ban the "despised" African American cultural import, postwar Germans reportedly had "no 'jump' in their music." Yet black GIs were more than willing to teach them to "swing all over again."[43] One report, characterizing most German music as "either too militaristic or sad enough to make you weep in your beer," pointed to the transformative role the "tan Yanks" were playing in the German music scene. They were not only "teaching German girls the delicate art of jitterbug" but were

Figure 21   Irmgard Achatz from Kollbach, Bavaria (second from left) and her future husband James W. Tanner (far right) from Philadelphia with friends, late 1940s (Debra Abell, Pittsburgh).

jamming with the "long-haired [German] musicians," who, as a result, were now "playing boogie-woogie and popular American music with skill and gusto." The writer added jokingly that if Hitler were alive, "nothing would kill him faster" than seeing how Germans embraced the culture that black GIs were bringing to Germany. The African American press clearly took a lot of pride in the fact that black GIs not only brought democracy to Germany but also taught Germans a different way of being in the world.[44]

Accordingly, black papers were keen to relate that interactions between American blacks and the German community had expanded significantly since the wives and children of the soldiers had arrived in Germany in greater numbers.[45] Such stories served a dual function: they celebrated the contributions of black Americans to their country's mission in Germany and offered readers examples of interracial friendships that were hardly possible in the United States during those years. In one such story, *Ebony* described black families as popular employers because they tended to be more generous with their food rations and hand-me-down clothing, which the German women working for them as maids or nannies greatly desired. *Ebony* also reported that African American families regularly met with their German friends, visited each others' homes, attended church, and went swimming at the beach. Naturally, their children also played together.[46]

Observers outside of the black press were just as astounded by Germans' acceptance of black soldiers. After one of his visits to Germany, Marcus Ray, the advisor to the U.S. secretary of war on matters pertaining to black soldiers, wrote that "Negroes were accepted by the native populations on the same basis as whites and that there was no problem whatsoever, as far as the people themselves were concerned."[47] Walter White, executive secretary of the NAACP, had similarly good news. A poll taken among black GIs in Germany revealed that the soldiers had been extended "more genuine friendship and democracy by the people who but lately were the guinea pigs of Hitler's racial theories than they get in the 'democracy' which had won the shooting war."[48] Roi Ottley also relayed African American GIs' enthusiasm for Germans' acceptance of them, emphasizing that soldiers who had already served in France uniformly declared Germans "freer of color prejudice than the French."[49]

Another phenomenon the black press was eager to convey was the high incidence of soldiers showing reluctance to return to the United States after having tasted equality—or love and sometimes even marriage—overseas. The percentage of black soldiers extending their tour of duty was three times that of white GIs.[50] The *Pittsburgh Courier* informed its readers that black GIs liked it so much in Germany that 37 percent of the men in the famed 761th Tank Battalion decided to extend their tour of duty.[51] To explain this trend, the black press emphasized the discrepancy between life in Germany and life in the United States for black GIs:

> Having experienced more democratic treatment abroad than they ever received at home, these men dread the thought of returning to their

homeland again to be subjected to injustice, indignities and the many irrita-
tions which are part and parcel of second-class citizenship. By re-enlisting
they are guaranteed...duty in countries where they feel that their acceptance is based upon ability and personality rather than upon their skin
pigmentation.[52]

The NAACP's Walter White, who was also a regular contributor to the
Chicago Defender, observed that even though the army was a deeply racist
institution, black GIs extended their tours of duty "for almost the sole reason that doing so would enable them as occupation troops to live anywhere
on earth except in their own United States."[53]

In fact, so many black GIs requested postings in Europe, and specifically
in Germany, that the military was compelled to end the postwar policy of
allowing enlistees to choose their post if they were sent abroad. This step
was necessary because the high proportion of troops signing up for service
in Europe (with most of those troops being sent to Germany) was threatening the military's policy that only 10 percent of its occupation army could
be African American. A whopping 85 percent of black enlistees in 1946
requested a posting in Europe.[54]

The American zone of occupation emerged as the favorite posting for troops
headed overseas, and some black GIs even chose to make the defeated country their permanent home, despite its widespread destruction and poverty.

Figure 22   African American soldiers who extended their service in the U.S. army (370th
Infantry Rifle Co, 7819th Transportation Trucking Co, 7765th Band Unit, Engineer Depot),
Nuremberg, Germany, November 2, 1948 (NARA).

A *Pittsburgh Courier* headline of February 1947 read: "Found Freedom in Germany: Few GIs Eager to Return to States."[55] Many of the black servicemen who decided to stay found work as civilian employees of the U.S. military government, or for the United Nations Relief and Rehabilitation Administration (UNRRA). Others, like Fez Roundtree of Lancaster, Pennsylvania, were able to make a living in the thriving jazz clubs of war-torn cities like Munich, Frankfurt, or Berlin.[56] Some soldiers took their military discharge in the United States and then came back to the American zone of occupation. One soldier spoke frankly about his decision to emigrate: "I am happy here in Germany…I got tired of being a second-class citizen. I feel like a man now, and people treat me like a man—which is more than I can say about the place where I was born."[57] Another soldier also stated that a "lot of black GIs took their discharge in Europe" because "they said, Look ain't nothing in America for me…I can't get a decent job…I can't even vote. So what the hell do I want to go back for?"[58] These stories from those who chose to remain abroad, whose numbers were small relative to those who went home, nonetheless served the important function of reiterating for African Americans that a world without racial boundaries was possible.[59]

Again, the novelist William Gardner Smith provides a figurative description for black GIs' response to Germany. African American GIs had literally become "drunk" on the experience of their "first absolute freedom," he said, and many vowed never to "get sober again." Smith explained why service in Germany was such a transformative experience for black GIs:

> Do you know what it's like for a Negro to be among the "conquerors" instead of the defeated? We learned about it for the first time when we "occupied" Germany and none of us ever got over it. We'll never go back to the old way again. It was the first time we had ever gotten out of the social nightmare in the States and were in a situation where we were equal, in fact more equal than the Germans.[60]

Jim Crow in Germany

Germany provides such an interesting locale to study American debates on race because the U.S. military had literally brought a slice of America into the heart of Europe. While white Americans were delighted that the U.S. military government was stamping out Nazism and instructing Germans in the American way of life, few were willing to consider that the darker aspects of that way of life had also been exported. Indeed, the U.S. military had taken Jim Crow racism to the very country the United States was committed to educating toward a democratic way of life. Thus, while the mainstream white media celebrated the achievements of America's democratization program, African American papers were full of headlines that decried the "Nazi Attitudes of White Soldiers," or declared "American Officers Abroad Propagating Race Hatred," all the while cautioning that the U.S. military might be "Losing the Peace" because "American Prejudice

[was] Rampant in Germany."[61] At the same time, as the black press noted, posters from the Soviets advertising their system's freedom from racial prejudice and their commitment to equality regardless of race dotted "every corner of Berlin and [the] Autobahns, like Barbersol ads back home."[62]

Civil rights activists and the black press insisted that the American racism on display in occupied Germany was not just a matter of a few bad apples, as the army liked to claim, but a larger problem grounded in the institutionalized racism of the segregated military. While segregated military units and installations were the norm in the United States as well, the situation in Germany exposed this fact to the very people the Americans wanted to convert to democracy. Germans were astonished to realize that the "GIs' service club in front of Lt. General Lucius Clay's Berlin headquarters [did] not permit black soldiers on its premises." They were just as puzzled that the swimming pool at the main barracks was "used on separate days by Negroes and whites," and that after the black soldiers used the pool, it was emptied and refilled with fresh water.[63] They also noted that the Palm Garden Red Cross Club at the U.S. military government headquarters in Frankfurt still did not admit black soldiers as late as January 1947.[64]

When the army set up a segregated training camp in Germany, an editorialist for the *Chicago Defender* expressed his outrage in no uncertain terms:

> Under peace-time Army regulations in former Nazi-dominated Germany, it appears that the States'-Rights, Jim Crow formula of Dixie America has been transplanted to famed Kitzingen training center.... This [segregated installation] is ironic because the slogan of the U.S. officials in occupied Germany is "Teach the Germans Democracy." It should be revised to read "Teach the Germans Democracy, American style." In other words, train the Germans to segregate Negroes, soldiers, and civilians, [and] keep them in a separate, restricted district.... It's Jim Crow any way you look at it or try to explain it.[65]

The editorialist closed his indictment with questions a World War II veteran had asked that highlighted the hypocrisy of America's democratic mission in Germany:

> Why is it that a Negro soldier can face death alongside a white soldier in the heat of battle but still can't sit alongside him and fraternize when the war is over?... Why have a White and Black rule for U.S. fighters, overseas or at home? If the Negro is good enough to die fighting overseas for America, why is not his brother good enough to enjoy civil rights at home?... America can't teach democracy abroad and practice bigotry at home. The two theories are diametrically opposed.[66]

Aside from the institutionalized racism of the military, American patterns of segregation were also carried into German neighborhoods in an imitation of Southern racial codes. Beginning with the occupation of Germany, all entertainment facilities in Germany bordering on military bases that catered solely to GIs were instructed not to allow the "mixing of races." Many Southern military commanders adhered to such segregation on principle whereas others did so out of fear that their military record would be damaged by too many racial incidents among their troops. White enlisted men and officers enforced these racial boundaries, using violence if necessary. Soldiers and military commanders also upheld the system by threatening to impose economic sanctions on German pub owners who failed to comply. Yet plenty of Germans were willing to accept this system of social segregation because of their own racial prejudices.[67]

Not satisfied with maintaining segregation between white and black troops, a number of military commanders tried to keep black soldiers as far away from the civilian population as possible. Time and again, black soldiers complained about commanders and military police discouraging them from associating with the locals.[68] Commanders tried to limit the interaction between black GIs and German civilians by not granting passes to soldiers who wanted to visit a German pub or attend a German church service. They also liked to place all-black units in isolated areas. In one especially egregious incident, a large number of troops were posted outside the city of Mannheim in a secluded area in the middle of the woods. Without any sanitary provisions, these black GIs were forced to live in tents and lean-tos under the most primitive circumstances.[69]

Another way commanders discouraged interracial interaction was to educate the German public about observing American racial codes. Roi Ottley reported that one officer in Teisendorf, a small village outside of Munich, went so far as to explicitly instruct the Germans that women were to stay away from the black troops: " 'I warn you,' he said without ceremony, 'the women are not to associate with the Negroes.' " When the Germans expressed bewilderment and pressed him for clarification, he told them with "obvious annoyance" that they "must understand... 'that the Negro has the same status in the U.S. as the Jew in Germany.' "[70]

Clearly, military authorities were appalled by the development of interracial relationships during the war and were most eager to put a stop to it. As postwar correspondent Grace Halsell concluded, when U.S. officers from the South "were sent out into the world to preserve Our Way of Life they took it to mean the Southern Way of Life, preserving the purity of the white blood."[71] Anxiety over the color line was also on the mind of Secretary of War Patterson, who, when reading a complaint by the Negro Newspaper Publishers Association about black soldiers and their white German partners being harassed by the military police, asked with a note of alarm, "are we going to mix races?"[72]

The rank and file were just as determined as commanders to rein in black soldiers after the fighting was over to restore the social order that the war had upset. The continuing breakdown of the color line only made them more vehement and violent in their reaction. They forced black GIs off the sidewalks, called them derogatory names in front of Germans, and beat them up for trying to enter establishments that white GIs considered "their

Figure 23 "When I told the colonel about it he just grinned. Said I shouldn't be spreading Russian propaganda!" The distinguished cartoonist Oliver Harrington lampoons the way in which the U.S. military exported the color line, and how eagerly some Germans adopted it, undated (Dr. Helma Harrington).

own." The *Crisis* reported with disgust that instead of "teaching Germans the tenets of democracy," white soldiers were poisoning them with "a good deal of jim crowism [*sic*]." Indeed, they instructed "innocent German teenagers" not to cross the "race line" and explained that "Negroes" should "'keep their place,' especially as regards white women."[73]

Indeed, the rise in interracial relationships proved especially provoking. Again and again, interracial couples were harassed or attacked. For example, one white soldier threatened a black GI strolling with his white German girlfriend, yelling: "A black s...of a b...with a white woman, I don't give a g...d.... If you are in Germany, or Japan, or any other place, you need to be killed. I'll cut your g...d...throat!" He then pulled razor from his boot and assaulted the soldier.[74] Given America's mission of de-Nazification, Germans could observe this sort of behavior only with disbelief. As David Brion Davis put it, "former Nazi youth gazed incredulously at the semifascist racism of white American officers and enlisted men infuriated when German girls happily dated African American troops, who experienced a racial freedom they had never known before."[75]

With the prevalence of such Jim Crow practices and attitudes, it is not surprising that representatives of the Negro Newspaper Publishers Association, when they traveled to Germany in 1946 to investigate complaints by black soldiers, found "widespread efforts" among commanders to discourage social interaction between Germans and black GIs and observed "strong arm methods" among hostile military police to separate interracial couples.[76] One soldier complained to the NAACP that the military police were raiding the homes of Germans who were "friendly with Negro soldiers." This made it impossible, he said, to maintain friendships as both the Germans and the soldiers feared the MPs and the humiliation the raids entailed.[77] News of such behavior also made its way back to the United States, where the black press alerted readers to this state of affairs. The *Chicago Defender*, for example, reported that "[w]hite officers, with few exceptions, did their darndest to break up interracial love affairs all the way from England in 1942 to Berlin in 1946," and the practice continued "in the army of occupation."[78]

As the color line continued to break down in occupied Germany, racial tensions rose. The military tried to hide the brewing racial strife, but individual servicemen, groups of soldiers, and veterans working as civilians for the military government could no longer be silenced. They alerted their superiors, as well as the black press and civil rights organizations, about the indignities they endured. One group of soldiers, for example, made a formal complaint to the General Staff Office about white officers encouraging enlisted men under their command to harass black soldiers. Describing the "mob violence" directed against them, they tried to shame the military leadership by contrasting this behavior with that of the Germans, their former foes: "the other allies [*sic*] have accepted us fully...even the Germans, the common enemy, have done likewise, the men we fought during the war...After we get attacked [by white soldiers], it is not the MPs who come and help us, but the Germans."[79] Another group alerted the NAACP about a "wave of intimidation" MPs were inflicting on black soldiers and implored the organization to do something about it.[80]

Some of those who filed complaints took their argument a step further by reminding their superiors that the treatment of blacks in the army in

Germany undermined the U.S. government's mission of democracy. One letter signed by eighteen veterans who had taken jobs in the military government, for example, stated: "One of the objectives of the U.S. forces in Europe is to teach the German people the democratic way of life. Beating of colored personnel, abusive language and remarks, discriminatory acts by military police etc., is most certainly a blinding step in reaching this end." And just as civil rights advocates in the 1930s had done (see chapter 1), these veterans embarrassed their government by comparing the racism of Americans to that of the Nazis:

[W]e as ex-combat soldiers did not fight the war for this sort of treatment and unfair practice...[T]he feelings of most of the Germans here are that what the American soldiers are doing to the Negro civilians is not the least bit worse than what the Nazis did to the Jews here on the same streets....If we are to educate these people in the line of democracy, we should practice it daily and not Nazism on a small basis.[81]

Figure 24 Cartoon with the figure of Jim Crow looking on as a U.S. soldier goose-steps past a reviewing stand in the American zone of occupied Berlin. Other onlookers include a German offering the Nazi salute, Truman's Secretary of Defense Louis Johnson covering his eyes, a laughing Russian soldier, and an applauding angel who resembles Hitler, 1949 (Committee against Jim Crow in Military and Training/Wisconsin State Historical Society).

These complaints notwithstanding, draconian punishment often awaited black soldiers who refused to observe "Southern traditions," even though they were asserting their democratic rights outside the United States. African American GIs were repeatedly charged with rape even when the German women involved assured the military police that their relationships were consensual.[82] Given the attitude of many Southern white officers toward "race mixing" or "miscegenation," it is hardly surprising that black soldiers were charged in 48 percent of the 620 rape cases brought to trial between VE-Day and the end of June 1946, even though they represented merely 10 percent of the manpower. Similarly but more disturbingly, 83 percent of soldiers executed for rape in the European Theater of Operations were African American. The racial imbalance in the application of this most severe punishment for such cases can be explained only as an effort by the military justice system to reestablish the American color line that had been increasingly undermined since the American troop deployment in Great Britain in 1943.[83]

The White Press and Black Soldiers

Significantly, news of the unexpected freedom and acceptance that black soldiers experienced in Germany also flowed into the mainstream American press. Although the coverage of the black soldiers' experience was not as extensive as in the black press, these reports reflect the mainstream press's greater interest in its African American counterpart since the beginning of the war. *Newsweek* magazine, for example, shared an overview of the extensive 1946 *Ebony* article and photo spread, "Germany Meets the Negro Soldier," which had energized black America. With astonishment, *Newsweek* concluded that many Americans were "more virulent than a large number of Germans" in "their attitude toward Negro troops." Because of the unexpected tolerance black GIs experienced in Germany, the article concluded, there had been an "overwhelming flood of requests by Negro enlistees for service in Europe, particularly in Germany."[84]

Progressive publications were also intent on broadcasting the startling news from Germany to a wider swath of white America. An exposé in the December 1945 issue of the *New Republic* detailed the humiliations black GIs had to endure once they returned to the United States. It then juxtaposed these observations with the reflections of a black soldier stationed in Germany explaining the desire prevalent among his peers to remain there: "You hear a lot about how homesick the overseas American soldier is for the 'good old USA,' he said. But you don't hear much about that from the Negro soldier...Hell, why should they be homesick? Homesick for Jim Crow, for poll taxes, and segregated slums? Homesick for lynchings and race riots?"[85]

Another source of information for white America on the overseas experience of black soldiers came from African American novelist William Gardner Smith. His novel, *The Last of the Conquerors*, was one of only a few to come out of the war. With more than 280,000 copies sold, it was widely read and reviewed. Both the novel and its reviews made a large audience aware of the profound impact the "sudden freedom" black GIs experienced in Germany, of all places, had on them. As one of Smith's protagonists, Hayes, said of Germany, "I like this goddamn country, you know that? That's right. I like the hell out of it. It's the first place I was ever treated like a goddamn man."[86]

The review in the *New York Times* was typical. Highlighting the "heady whiff of freedom" and the "measure of dignity and equality" black soldiers enjoyed in Germany, "the land of the pogroms," the reviewer praised Smith for sharing the black soldier's feelings, thoughts, and hopes, "and what he found—ironically in the wrong country."[87] The *Saturday Review of Literature* sharply contrasted the black soldiers' "overwhelming knowledge that there was a place on earth where there was no discrimination against them," with "their certain future back home where Jim Crow, in one form or another, must rule their lives."[88] Another reviewer pointed out that "life for Negro soldiers in Germany was no simple affair. They had to adjust to many different levels of living: life with the Germans, where they were men," and life in the army where all too often they were "just beasts of burden on which officers rode to higher ranks."[89] Still another reviewer exclaimed incredulously after having read that day's Associated Press (AP) report, which highlighted the story of a black soldier in Germany: "How true to life art is!:…An American Negro said today he believes Germany offers him a better future than the United States."[90]

At the same time, the disturbing stories of how American racism played out in the streets of Germany also made their way to white America by other means. In 1946, David Brion Davis wrote a letter to his parents expressing his shock over the actions of his fellow soldiers: "I am getting quite bitter on the race question. Perhaps I sound a bit shrill, but it is difficult not to become alarmed when not one or two but dozens of men openly proclaim their hatred of the black race and take every opportunity to shoot or arrest or beat up colored soldiers."[91] In their widely read account of the U.S. occupation of Germany, *Conqueror's Peace*, journalists Bud Hutton and Andy Rooney, in describing the violence that white military police inflicted on black soldiers in front of Germans, also brought their dismay about American racism to a broad American audience. Sarcastically referring to the aftermath of one such incident as the "bleeding remnants of an example of American democracy," the authors emphasized that America's prominent role in Germany brought its racial problem into the open. Given America's mission of reeducation in Germany, they asked what Germans were to make of the prevalence of racial violence against blacks: "For twelve years Hitler and the Nazis taught" the Germans a doctrine of hatred and they cautioned their readers that "the Germans were defeated by an army among whose ideals was that such [racial] distinctions and discriminations were wrong and should be destroyed."[92] Another commentator on the experience of black soldiers abroad suggested that such news from Germany should be "heard by arrogant nationalists who regard each white American soldier in Germany as a Galahad devoted to a holy mission."[93]

*   *   *

As these news reports make plain, America's occupation of Germany brought "American racialism" into sharp relief, just as Roi Ottley suggested it would. Individual soldiers were transformed by their encounters with a society that, though hardly free of racism, did not have an American-style color line and was greatly appreciative of the black soldiers' generosity. Soldiers returning home shared their experiences at their place of work, with their families, in barbershops and locker rooms—stories that have become a resilient memory of the black military experience. Significantly, news of post-Nazi Germany as a sort of racial utopia also made its way to a nationwide audience because of the efforts of the black press and civil rights activists. Their reports from Germany allowed African Americans in the United States to imagine a space where the freedom and equality denied them in their own country became possible. In many ways, these same articles also suggested that, if such a transformation was possible in the land "where Aryanism had ruled supreme," perhaps change could also be achieved in the United States of America. At the same time, white Americans increasingly realized that their country's mission in postwar Germany made them vulnerable to charges of hypocrisy. As the occupation, even more than the struggle against Nazi Germany during the war, revealed the contradictions between America's ideals and the reality of life for African Americans, postwar Germany emerged as an unexpected site for advancing the civil rights cause.

4

Setting the Stage for Brown: Integrating the Military in Germany

Fighting in World War II and being part of an occupation army in postwar Germany had a tremendous impact on black soldiers. Their experiences not only empowered them as individuals but also fostered a comprehensive debate within the African American community about these GIs' vital contributions at a time when they were at best granted second-class citizenship at home. Significantly, the war and the de-Nazification and reeducation of Germany after 1945 also exercised a profound influence on the racial attitudes of many white Americans, bringing them to understand the international implications of what the Swedish economist Gunnar Myrdal termed "the American dilemma"—that is, the coexistence of America's liberal ideals of equality and basic human rights with the deplorable status of the country's black minority.[1] In his 1944 study of race relations, Myrdal concluded that the race question had to be solved for American democracy to survive and also for the nation to take a leading role in the postwar world.[2] Prompted by the unrelenting attack on Jim Crow that civil rights activists and the black press waged between 1933 and 1945—particularly with their strategy of equating Nazism with Jim Crow—white liberals finally woke up to the grievances of African Americans and came to embrace Myrdal's conclusion. Under the continuing pressure from activists and the black press, and increasingly embarrassed by the hypocrisy of a Jim Crow army reeducating the defeated Germans, many white liberals decided that the time for change had come. Thus, the postwar occupation of Germany— even more than the struggle against Nazi Germany during World War II—*nationalized* America's race problem, making it an *American* rather than merely a *Southern* issue, at last impelling momentum for change.

A New Civil Rights Consensus

Just as the black community had hoped, the Double-V campaign during World War II alerted many white Americans to the discrepancy between

America's struggle against Nazism and the continued existence of Jim Crow at home. Again and again, African American activists and the black press warned white America that its own racial practices undermined its power in the struggle against Nazi racism: its voice would carry "far greater authority" if it could also "be heard against racial oppression at home."[3] This strategy paid off as white Americans began to see the point and make it themselves. Representative Samuel Dickstein of New York, for example, asked his colleagues in the House in 1941, "What good is it to defend democracy against attacks from without when we allow the basic principles of democracy to be violated right here in our own country?"[4]

Once the war started, progressive mainstream publications such as the *New Republic,* the *Nation, Common Sense, Atlantic Monthly, P.M.,* and *Survey Graphic* provided civil rights activists with a platform for making their case that the war against fascism had to be won both abroad and at home. One railed in the *Nation* against American hypocrisy in fighting Nazis but treating black soldiers so badly: "the Army puts them in uniform, transports them south and leaves them to be kicked, cuffed and even murdered with impunity by white civilians" while German POWs were afforded more respect and dignity than were African American GIs.[5] Others emphasized that this sort of violence was not merely a "Southern problem." In the North, too, when black workers and their families tried to move into formerly all-white neighborhoods, they were "mauled by the police and stoned by 'neighbors' " for trying to do so.[6]

The white press not only gave black activists a platform but also took up the pointed comparisons between the Nazi racial state and white supremacy in the United States, exposing the deep contradiction at the heart of American democracy. Just a few months after the Japanese attack on Pearl Harbor, *Common Sense,* for example, editorialized that Americans had done little "to wipe out the shame of our treatment of the Negro as a step toward the defeat of those who treat the Jews the same way."[7] In 1943, the *New Republic* reacted to the news that a white mob had confronted black families trying to move into a Detroit housing complex, somberly remarking that the white mob was "assuredly doing Hitler's work."[8] The *Nation,* too, emphasized the problem with fighting fascism abroad "while turning a blind eye to fascism at home," concluding that the United States could not fight under a banner that read "For democracy and a caste system."[9]

To put it in a nutshell, World War II and especially America's victory over the Nazi racial state had shaken the intellectual foundations of Jim Crow, making civil rights an issue that progressive Americans increasingly embraced. As Roy Wilkins, editor of the *Crisis,* commented in 1944, "Hitler jammed our white people into their logistically untenable position. Forced to oppose him for the sake of the life of the nation, they were jockeyed into declaring against his racial theories—publicly." Indeed, in order to justify the war, America had to declare: "Down with Hitlerism! Down with the Master Race theory! Away with racial bigotry!"[10] Philanthropist and civil rights activists Anson Phelps Stokes agreed: "[The] war, by raising the *Herrenvolk* issue in the case of Germany, has driven home to us in the United States that we are subject to attack on the ground of inconsistency and insincerity if we, as a democracy ... do not treat white men and colored men exactly on the same objective basis."[11] Moreover, it was clear to all reform-minded commentators and civil rights activists that things could not go back to the way they had been before the war; the impact of the war had been too great:

> The whole young male population of the race will never again fit into the serfdom of Southern feudalism or the second-class status of Northern industrial cities. It is too late ever again to keep Negroes "in their places." If we wanted that we should never have ... called them to the tremendous education of the armed forces.[12]

The war had had an impact on white soldiers and officers, too, spurring many of them to reflect critically on their own racial beliefs. One optimistic officer confidently declared that "thousands of Southern white officers developed a solid respect for their Negro troops" and were determined that they should be granted the same "rights, privileges and opportunities" they had helped to preserve.[13] Another officer, Lt. Colonel John Sherman, not only reiterated the sharp comparison between Nazi racial policies and American white supremacy but also highlighted just how bad the situation in America was: "It must be admitted that, thus far, the negro's life in America has given him very little to fight for. When one asked me, 'How come white folks fightin' Hitler for treating the Jews jes' lak they treat us?' I could not find an adequate answer in any Army regulation or textbook."[14] The shift in attitude of a white GI raised in Mississippi to hate "Negroes" is especially striking: "So if the Germans can have freedom ... why not let the Negro race have what they fought for? I feel that they should and a lot of Southern GIs feel the same way."[15]

World War II had indeed changed the hearts and minds of many white Americans, ushering in an opportunity for broader social change, as well. This manifested itself in the founding of new civil rights organizations, state and municipal laws, and legal advances on the federal level. In 1942, the Congress of Racial Equality (CORE), which started the first sit-ins to integrate lunch counters and movie theaters in the North, was established. Likewise, in the last years of the war, hundreds of interracial committees were set up across the country at the behest of the American Council of Race Relations, which succeeded in prompting several states and cities to pass civil rights laws by the late 1940s. Other progressive groups that focused on overcoming American racism were the American Civil Liberties Union (ACLU), the National Catholic Welfare Conference, and the American Jewish Congress. Knowledge of the horrors of the Holocaust especially encouraged progressive Americans to build interracial alliances with African Americans. The NAACP's long-term strategy of using the courts to effect social change was also beginning to pay off: it succeeded in winning a series of important court cases starting in 1944 that began the long process of desegregating juries, housing, interstate transportation, and higher education, as well as ending the all-white primaries in some states of the South.

To be sure, these signs of progress and declarations of solidarity with African Americans' demands for more equality were hardly representative, as the long, hard fight for civil rights makes abundantly clear.[16] Many white Americans, as the previous two chapters have shown, were determined to rebuild the boundaries of Jim Crow segregation that had been weakened during the war, and to reverse any advances African Americans might have made because of the war. Some enacted this determination in violence against their black neighbors and especially returning veterans.

While violence against veterans was not as extensive as after World War I, the brutal beating and blinding of Isaac Woodward, a highly decorated veteran, in February 1946 generated national outrage once the NAACP took on his case. After three years of military service, and still in his uniform, Sergeant Woodward was arrested on a bus trip for allegedly taking too long to use the men's restroom. The South Carolina sheriff who arrested him beat him so brutally with a blackjack that Woodward lost his eyesight. Woodward's case was not any more brutal than many other incidents of mob violence and lynchings that greeted returning veterans, but the fact that he was still wearing his uniform surely heightened people's indignation.

This case proved pivotal as it caught the attention of President Harry Truman, who proceeded to become a true leader in advancing civil rights, much to his contemporaries' surprise. When Walter White, the executive secretary of the NAACP, informed Truman about the Woodward case, the president exclaimed, "My God, I had no idea it was as terrible as that. We've got to do something."[17] Truman found it unacceptable that this could happen without state authorities doing anything against it. If that was possible, he told a friend who had served with him in World War I, then there was something "radically wrong with the system."[18]

Although Truman's championing of civil rights was clearly a political move to counter Republicans who had run on a civil rights platform in the 1946 election, he also acted out of principle, as his reaction to Woodward's case shows. After this outrage, Truman was ready to act. On December 5, 1946, he issued Executive Order 9808 to establish the President's Committee on Civil Rights, which was charged with exploring ways to ensure the equality of all Americans. It released its report, *To Secure These Rights*, with its wide-ranging list of recommendations, in December 1947. This comprehensive report covered all aspects of discrimination and inequalities that America's black minority faced. It also listed the economic, moral, and international reasons why these abuses had to be overcome, and laid out a detailed program of how to go about this.

The committee's language was frank, and its suggestions far-reaching. It called for a federal antilynching law, the establishment of a permanent Civil Rights Commission, a permanent Fair Employment Practices Commission (FEPC), legislation to overcome disenfranchisement, an end to a segregated military, and suggested that all civil rights work be located in the Department of Justice. The committee also forcefully attacked America's civil rights record and indicted the Jim Crow army, deploring, in particular, the "injustice" of asking men "to fight for freedom while subjecting them to humiliating discrimination in the fighting forces."[19]

In addition to establishing this committee, Truman underscored his commitment to civil rights by addressing the NAACP at its national convention in June 1947. He was the first president to do so since the organization's founding in 1909, and he was also the first to campaign in Harlem. Fully aware that he would not be able to convince the U.S. Congress to enact many of the recommendations made in his committee's report, Truman made use of the prerogative of the executive order. On July 26, 1948, he signed Executive Order 9980 to desegregate the federal work force. On that same day—and over the expressed opposition of the secretary of the army and many of the military's highest officers—Truman also issued Executive Order 9981 ending segregation in the armed forces with this statement: "It is to be the policy of the President that there shall be equality of treatment and opportunity for all persons in the armed services without regard to race, color, religion or national origin."[20] This order also established the President's Committee on Equality of Treatment and Opportunity in the Armed Services, which was tasked with recommending how the integration could best be achieved. This monumental act was a landmark development in the long history of the civil rights movement that set the stage for the desegregation of schools following the 1954 Supreme Court decision in the *Brown v. Board of Education* case, which paved the way for the legal transformations of the following decades.

Internationalizing Civil Rights History

Historians of the civil rights movement have told the story of Truman's rise as a champion of civil rights—and told it well. They have also given a comprehensive account of how domestic issues pushed Truman to pursue this path, particularly the integration of the military. 1948 was an election year. Truman feared that black voters in the Northeast would not support the Democratic Party, especially after Henry Wallace abandoned the Democratic Party over its tepid support of civil rights and ran as a presidential candidate for his newly founded Progressive Party. Made up of the left wing of democrats, the new party explicitly endorsed the integration of the military. Thomas Dewey, the Republican Party's presidential candidate, also made integration of the military a central element of his party's platform, and radical labor leader A. Philip Randolph put pressure on Truman as well. Together with the civil rights activist Grant Reynolds, who had served as a chaplain in World War II, Randolph had established the Committee against Jim Crow in Military Service and Training in 1947. During a meeting on March 22, 1948, Randolph and Reynolds told Truman in no uncertain terms that "Negroes were in no mood to shoulder guns again for democracy abroad while they were denied democracy at home." During a hearing nine days later, Randolph and Reynolds also told the Armed Services Committee of the U.S. Senate that they would urge "Negro and white youth not to submit to draft calls" if they would have to serve in a segregated military. When a NAACP survey found that 71 percent of black youths would refuse to register for the planned peacetime draft if the military continued to be segregated, it was clear that the time for desegregation had come.[21]

Histories of the civil rights movement since the end of the Cold War have added an interesting new angle to this narrative by revealing the centrality of U.S. foreign policy concerns after 1945 in advancing the cause of civil rights. In internationalizing the history of civil rights, such studies have focused foremost on the competition with the Soviet Union in the non-Western world. In particular, they have explored America's ambition after 1945 to win over the newly decolonizing nations of Africa and Asia into the Western bloc. It was in those young countries' best interest, America argued, to align themselves with the "Free West" under the leadership of the United States. Yet, as the U.S. government quickly found, this case was difficult to make when the Soviet Union, eager to attract these nations to its own bloc, was flooding them with a steady stream of news about lynchings, the continuing disenfranchisement of African Americans in the South, and the segregation of the races to indict American democracy as a fraud. The American government was also hardpressed to explain to newly appointed diplomats from Africa why some of Washington's finest hotels and restaurants, in accordance with existing Jim Crow segregation laws, refused to serve them.[22]

Despite this new internationalization of the history of the civil rights movement, however, America's involvement in Europe, and particularly in Germany, after 1945 has not been explored with the same sort of attention. The role that the establishment of the military base system and the sizable troop deployments in Germany played in advancing the civil rights agenda has also been largely ignored. Yet, as analyzed below, the U.S. record of race relations also presented a serious challenge to America's mission in Europe. Most notably, it undermined America's credibility in the eyes of Germans, especially concerning the nation's self-appointed aim to de-Nazify and democratize the defeated nation. Furthermore, beginning in 1946, the United States and the Soviet Union were engaged in an ideological battle to define Europe's destiny. In the immediate postwar years, this struggle was by no means decided in favor of the United States; postwar elections in both Italy and France had shown substantial support for communism. Not surprisingly, the battle over Europe's future raged most fiercely in Germany, divided in two by the Iron Curtain running through its heart. The city of Berlin, located inside Soviet-dominated East Germany, would become the Cold War metaphor par excellence. Equally important was Germany's role in America's evolving military strategy to contain communism. In order to fortify its strategic position vis-à-vis the Soviet Union, the United States halted its drawdown of troops and reactivated the 7th Army; by 1950/1951 some 250,000 American troops were deployed in West Germany, and their numbers would remain fairly steady until 1991. Fortified by tens of thousands of British, French, Canadian, and Dutch troops, these Americans (mostly combat troops) were poised to hold the line against a possible attack by the more than 350,000 Soviet troops stationed just across the border in East Germany.[23]

Struggling for Civil Rights Abroad

Taking up the idea of internationalizing civil rights history, it is fruitful to consider the December 1947 release of the report, *To Secure These Rights*, with its strong recommendations for change, within the momentous Cold War developments of that year in Europe. Just nine months earlier, in March of 1947, the president enunciated the Truman Doctrine, which promised U.S. support for "free people" struggling against communist repression. To keep Greek communists from overthrowing the repressive Greek monarchy that had been restored by Great Britain after 1945, Truman made substantial funds available so that Greece could become a "self-respecting democracy." Preventing a communist takeover in Greece was seen as essential to avoiding a possible communist takeover in Turkey, which in turn might threaten U.S. influence in the oil-rich Middle East. To convince the American people that this emerging Cold War foreign policy of containment was the correct approach, Truman framed it as an effort to ensure that Greece—and other threatened countries like it—could become democratic just like the United States: nations where "free institutions, [a] representative government, free elections, guarantees of individual liberty...and freedom from political oppression" were the rule.[24]

Yet, as civil rights activists were quick to interject, this description of American democracy was hardly one that black Americans could recognize. Why did the Truman administration believe that the United States was powerful enough to bring democracy to far-away Greece if it was impotent to assure "free elections [and] freedom from political oppression" for African Americans in the United States, they asked? Why didn't the principles of the Truman Doctrine apply to black Americans?[25] In a similar line of attack, the NAACP boldly submitted a resolution to the UN's Commission on Human Rights in October of that year. Entitled "An Appeal to the World," the 150-page document drafted principally by Du Bois depicted the lack of democracy for African Americans in great detail. "An Appeal to the World" denounced racism in the United States as barbaric and asked the government to redirect its efforts at democratization toward home: "It is not Russia that threatens the United States as much as Mississippi; not Stalin and Molotov, but Bilbo and Rankin."[26] However, the American members of the UN Commission on Human Rights refused to take up the appeal for fear of giving the Soviets ammunition.

The report of the President's Civil Rights Committee, *To Secure These Rights*, released just two months later, thus aimed to fix what "An Appeal to the World" had exposed without airing America's dirty laundry before the world. To be sure, the drafters of *To Secure These Rights* were confident of the righteousness of America's cause, and they reiterated with some pride that America's emerging Cold War foreign policy was designed to make the United States "an enormous, positive influence for peace and progress throughout the world." But they cautioned that America's poor civil rights record made it difficult for the nation to be such a force of good. Emphasizing the international effects of civil rights abuses at home, they declared that "a lynching in a rural American community" not only challenged that community's conscience but had repercussions that echoed across the nation and "from one end of the globe to the other."[27]

There could be no doubt that this statement was true. As concerned members of the State Department noted, the number one item requested at America's overseas libraries and information centers were publications related to the American race question.[28] Senator Henry Cabot Lodge called race relations "our Achilles' heel before the world," and the State Department agreed: "no American problem received more widespread attention" across the globe "than our treatment of racial minorities, particularly the Negro."[29] Interest in the American race problem was also extensive in Europe. In 1948, the *Crisis* counted more than 500 articles on race relations and discrimination in the United States in just 10 European newspapers.[30]

Civil rights activists in the United States were closely attuned to this global context of America's unresolved race question, as their debates in the 1930s and 1940s on the interconnectedness of the race problem in the United States and the exploitation of people of color in the colonies attest.[31] After World War II, when the process of decolonization was underway, they, therefore, kept a close watch on developments in the non-Western world and the escalating competition between the Soviet Union and the United States. Although the global context is vital to understanding the advance of civil rights, here we focus on how civil rights activists used developments in Germany, which was increasingly emerging as the main battlefront in the Cold War.

Given Germany's location in the heart of Europe, as well as its large size and economy, the question of securing freedom and democracy in West Germany was the most pressing issue for America. If Western Europe as a whole was to prosper under U.S. leadership, the parts of Germany controlled by the Western Allies (which increasingly meant the Americans) had to be revived. Furthermore, the Americans viewed the defeated country as a sort of social science laboratory for creating a new democratic Germany from the ashes of the Third Reich. To accomplish this goal, the United States invested unprecedented money, manpower, and talent. The escalating Cold War added significant urgency to that mission as the United States intended to prove the superiority of the American way of life to the Soviets and the world in Germany. Meanwhile, the Soviets were just as determined to prove the Americans wrong.

Ironically, America's profound disagreements with the Soviet Union over how best to democratize the Germans in their respective zones of occupation offered civil rights activists untold opportunities to comment on race issues in the United States. One high-profile instance was when Secretary of State George Marshall met with his Soviet counterpart Vyacheslav Molotov in Moscow in March 1947. Criticizing the Soviets for not having granted free elections in their zone of occupation, Marshall lectured Molotov on the meaning of the word "democracy," which, for the American government and its people, entailed human beings having "certain inalienable rights—that is rights, which may not be given or taken away." Further, Marshall continued, "a society is not free if law-abiding citizens live in fear of being denied the right to work, or [are] deprived of life, liberty and the pursuit of happiness." While Marshall emphasized the *ideals* of American democracy, the NAACP was quick to expose the gap between those ideals and the reality that black Americans faced in their daily lives. An editorial in the *Crisis* mocked Marshall, asserting that he "must have stuttered as he read these passages" since the Soviets knew perfectly well that blacks in the U.S. did not "enjoy the democracy as defined by Mr. Marshall." As the editorialist pointed out, most of them could not vote, were forced to live in constant fear of lynchings, and could not even get served a hamburger in the restaurant at the capital's airport.[32]

Civil rights activists also used America's ambitious goal of assuring freedom and equality abroad by contrasting it with the lack of urgency for change at home. Langston Hughes applied his acerbic tongue to exploring this issue in his regular column in the *Chicago Defender*. With biting sarcasm, Hughes told African Americans in 1948 to be patient with their demands since the government was currently busy "teach[ing] the rest of the world democracy." African Americans "shouldn't be so rude as to expect [the government] to bother much with democracy at home," and should realize that "the Germans and the Greeks come first." However, one big question remained, namely, whether Germans could "learn from folks with Dixie-like manners." Since a segregated army was in charge of the reeducation effort over there, could the Germans "learn to be democratic from gentlemen who practice only confederate democracy?"[33]

The black press was full of such criticism, as civil rights advocates were determined to expose the hypocrisy of America's mission in Germany to advance their cause. One such editorial was written by Lester Granger, a member of the National Urban League and advisor to the U.S. government on integrating the military. He concluded somberly that as long as "democratic living" was not possible in the United States, the country had "no chance...to exert leadership in making democracy real in Europe or anywhere else."[34] The *Crisis*, too, pointed out sarcastically that "America may preach about democracy and inalienable rights in her Senate" while killing an antilynching or an FEPC bill, "but preaching about democracy" abroad while "practicing lynching" was taking things too far.[35] And Nell Dodson Russell argued pointedly in the *Minneapolis Spokesman* that America was undermining its own foreign policy goals because of its unwillingness to effect change at home. As she wrote, "We have an Army of Occupation in Germany to teach Germans all about democracy, and yet biased and prejudiced members of that very Army [are] daily teaching the Germans to hate Negroes. Small wonder the Germans don't seem to be learning their lessons [about democracy] very quickly!"[36]

There can be no doubt that Germans noticed this gap between America's rhetoric and its deeds, for many of them commented on it. Roi Ottley reported that Germans were "sincerely bewildered by American racialism" and that they asked probing and insightful questions, such as "How wrong was the *Führer* in his hatred of Jews... when your white Americans encourage us to hate the blacks—their comrades in arms?!"[37] Walter White also informed the readers of his column that "Germans sneer at pious American enquiries about Nazi racism and how Germans ever fell for it." Their reply to such questions was irrefutable: "How can you talk about German racism as long as you maintain separate white and black armies?"[38]

Integrating the Army

President Truman's executive order to integrate the military on July 26, 1948, was, in a sense, a battle victory in the long war to end the Jim Crow army. That war, however, was still far from over. In the decades leading up to this success, no other civil rights organization was as vocal in speaking up for the rights of black soldiers and as relentless in demanding an end to the segregated army as the NAACP. Beginning in World War II, another group of activists significantly amplified the NAACP's efforts—the Negro Newspaper Publishers Association. In large measure, it was this group of publishers that brought news about developments in Germany back to the U.S. government and the American people.

The group organized as a political lobby during the war. In February 1944, thirteen representatives of the black press met with President Roosevelt to present him with a twenty-one-point program stating war and postwar aims, including their commitment to "fight for every right guaranteed by the Constitution."[39] Then, in 1946, representatives of the association traveled to Germany. Having observed the grievous consequences of a segregated army, they gave the secretary of war a warning that echoed the charges of hypocrisy, the need for education in democracy, and the damage to the U.S. mission abroad that had already been voiced by many civil rights activists and even the white press: they pointed out that those the army sought to democratize were aware of its segregation and questioned it for teaching what it failed to practice; that the United States needed to educate the armed forces in "the real meaning and spirit of democracy" and demonstrate that this ideal could and would be practiced; and that the segregated army was undermining America's mission in Germany.[40]

When the publishers traveled to Germany again in April 1948, the Cold War was escalating due to developments in the Soviet sphere of influence. In February of that year, Czech communists had taken control of the government in Czechoslovakia with the support of Moscow, and on March 31, the Soviets had stopped all train traffic bringing supplies from the Western zones to embattled Berlin. This divided city, with its western and eastern sectors controlled by the four Allies from World War II, now sat on the frontline of the Cold War, making it a very high-stakes locale for the Americans, who wished to keep control over their zone of occupation in Berlin as well as in West Germany. By June 1948, the situation had escalated when all traffic to Berlin had been cut off, and to save Berlin from starvation and inevitable Soviet domination, United States and British forces would organize an airlift to transport supplies into the city. This monumental effort ineluctably required the manpower of black soldiers, the great majority of whom were still amassed in service and transport units. This escalating crisis, along with America's desire to win the hearts and minds of the German people in the Cold War struggle, thus handed the publishers new and powerful ammunition for attacking segregation in the military.

During their April 1948 visit, the publishers found that, despite the recommendations in the report of Truman's Committee on Civil Rights, *To Secure These Rights*, not much had improved in the army of occupation since they had last visited. Consequently, they reiterated a number of the same criticisms they had voiced two years before. While they agreed that the military offered a better life than most black soldiers could expect in civilian life in the United States, they also despaired that the continuing segregation was crushing the men, exacerbated by the contrast between circumstances on and off base: all over Germany, black soldiers were free to go as they pleased and to interact freely and cordially with the white civilian population; it was only in their own military bases that segregation ruled. Even worse, the publishers reported, the Air Force had succeeded almost completely in "depopulating itself of Negroes." As in the past, they reminded the government that Germans, who were supposed to be learning "object lessons in practical democracy," could "not fail to question" a "democracy that makes distinctions based on color alone," and that abolishing segregation "immediately and completely" would provide a boost to the U.S. mission in Germany, taking "a tremendous step in the ideological capture of the German people."[41]

Upon their return home, the publishers decided to draw a hard line with Truman, precluding any offers for compromise and unequivocally demanding an end to segregation in the army. With this decision, they joined a number of distinguished African American leaders who had rejected any offers of serving as advisor for Secretary of the Army Kenneth Claiborne Royall, who continued to insist that all improvement for black soldiers had to be achieved "within the framework of segregation."[42] The representatives of the black press published these demands for an end to the Jim Crow army in all their papers. Expressing strong support for Truman's Cold War strategy of containment and informing the president that the Soviet threat had convinced them of the necessity of a strong troop presence in Germany, they nevertheless insisted that "it must not be Jim Crow"[43] for all the reasons they had already voiced—above all, the hypocrisy of preaching democracy without practicing it.[44]

Just as during the war, the arguments of the black press over developments in occupied Germany spilled over into ever-wider circles, making the segregated military more and more embarrassing to the U.S. government and progressive Americans. A number of commentators outside the black press voiced concerns very similar to those of the Negro Newspaper Publishers' Association. David Dempsey, a former World War II Marine Corps war correspondent, found a new metaphor for expressing the hypocrisy of America's mission in Germany, pointing out in the *New York Times* that the U.S. Army—an "instrument for guarding our democratic ideals and, at times, extending them to others"—was, in some sense, American "democracy's worst salesman." Not only were black GIs in Germany "rigidly segregated" by color; they were also the "victims of a 'cracker' mentality" that surprised America's allies and enemies alike.[45] Erika Mann, a German émigré and refugee from Nazi Germany, felt compelled to warn her new countrymen that the racial hatred of the American officers in the occupation army must be delighting the German Nazis who had not yet been converted to democracy.[46] Another critical observer of America's racial politics warned that the occupation of Germany put the treatment of black soldiers in a new, international spotlight: "one learns that the discrepancies between ideals and realities of the American way, such as those that allow us to assign the Negro soldier to the least desirable military jobs, as is customary in civilian life, can no longer be considered private national business when they are practiced in full view of Germans we hope to re-educate."[47] Moreover, according to the NAACP's Walter White, a "growing number of [white] American officers in Germany" were expressing similar concerns. While they comprised only a minority and would not go on record for fear of antagonizing their senior officers, they were deeply worried about the "image American democracy" presented to "an increasingly skeptical world."[48]

As such debates on developments in occupied Germany illustrate, Truman's Executive Order 9981 mandating the integration of the military, like the report *To Secure These Rights* that preceeded it, needs to be understood in an international context. Truman acted partly in response to the domestic pressures outlined above, but mainly to address international concerns, as American "domestic politics" had also been taken abroad once the United States stationed a substantial number of troops outside America's borders. Those who agitated for reform understood the interconnectedness of domestic and international politics and were prepared to take advantage of it.

Indeed, America's military's occupation in Germany provided those in favor of reform with a powerful argument for defusing the naysayers.

When Hanson W. Baldwin, the longtime and Pulitzer Prize–winning military editor of the *New York Times* criticized Truman's decision, he used an argument shared by most military leaders, namely, that the army would change only when the nation as a whole changed in regard to race relations. In this, he repeated the old mantra that the army was not and should not be an "instrument for 'social reform.'" But the NAACP adamantly refused to accept this reasoning. Walter White spoke for the organization in taking Hanson and the generals on in an open letter to the editor. He asked pointedly: "What is our Army doing in occupied Germany if it is not a mission of social reform—a reform against the very racism which the brass hats now justify as sound Army policy?"[49]

Achieving de facto Integration

As Hanson and other critics of Truman's order make plain, the road from the declared to the real integration of the armed services would be long. Although the newly established air force and the navy began the slow process of integration, the army remained firmly and even stubbornly opposed. In fact, it would take another war, this one in Korea (1950–1953), with its high casualties and unexpected manpower shortages, to make integration on the battlefield a military necessity. Off the battlefield, however, the integration of the soldiers' barracks, clubs, and movie theaters proceeded at a snail's pace, if at all. While army commanders were willing to accept integrated fighting units in Korea, they were still leery of "social integration" on its U.S. and especially West German bases because they worried about the implications such a policy would have. They might have been able to picture black and white soldiers swimming in the same pool on base, but what about the soldiers' wives and children? Were white military wives and their children to swim in the same pool as black GIs and their families? Just as tricky were the social events and dances that were regularly organized on military bases to entertain the troops. As most military bases were in the South, military commanders found it difficult to imagine Southerners accepting such mixed functions.

During the struggles to force integration on a reluctant army command after Truman's Executive Order had been issued, military commanders were so focused on the *social* implications of integration that they at times neglected the much larger issue of military efficiency. When opposing integration, commanders regularly "rang in a bedroom scene" to warn of the inevitable "mixing of the races" or "miscegenation" that would result from an integrated military.[50] Charles Fahy, chair of the President's Committee on Equality of Treatment and Opportunity in the Armed Services, was so exasperated with the recalcitrant attitude of the military leadership that he asked General Omar Bradley during one hearing: "General, are you running an Army, or a dance?"[51] Compellingly, anxiety over the "social aspects" of integration was especially pronounced among army commanders in Germany because the color line, which many of them still hoped to uphold, had broken down so completely there. Commanders argued that the situation "was complicated by social relations not only between white and Negro but between the Army as a whole and the civilian population." They also pointed to another issue which complicated matters in Germany, namely, the "competition between white and Negro troops for German girls," as a major reason for their opposition to integration.[52]

Despite their reservations, commanders would have to deal with the full integration of troops by 1951, when the Department of the Army finally forced them to desegregate their units. Several factors contributed to prompting this move, including the changing domestic political situation in West Germany and its strategic position in America's policy of containment, the ongoing escalation of Cold War tensions, the advent of the Korean War in 1950, as well as increasing criticism of America's hypocrisy from Germans themselves. Above all, West Germany's special position in the Cold War made the Jim Crow army there all the more visible to the whole world. Thus, as we will see, Germany again served as a major point of reference for supporters of equal rights.

In October 1949, the political situation in Germany changed dramatically. The U.S. military government had ended, and the Federal Republic of Germany (West Germany) had been created under American tutelage as a semisovereign state overseen to a considerable extent by the Office of the High Commissioner (HICOG), which was installed by the U.S. State Department. Just across the Iron Curtain, the Soviets had established the German Democratic Republic (East Germany), which stood under even firmer control of its "mentor." The division of Germany, and with it the division of Europe into East and West, had become a matter of fact. Consequently, Cold War anticommunist hysteria was already at a very high level and rose to an even higher pitch that same month when Chinese communists prevailed and created the People's Republic of China.

Into this new political landscape, the European Study Mission of the Foreign Affairs Committee of the U.S. Senate traveled to Germany in December 1949, almost eighteen months after Truman's executive order, to explore the situation with the still segregated army. To the senators' great dismay, they found that not much had changed since Truman's executive order. Almost none of the African American troops served in integrated units, and black officers were few and far between. Jacob Javits, the senator from New York who led the delegation, warned the secretary of defense that the segregated military was a major impediment to winning the existential struggle playing out in Germany—the "main front of the cold war." On his travels, he was rather taken aback by people's perceptions of America's racial policies, which, he noted, were all too often informed by inflated and inflammatory charges about the racial situation in the United States that were disseminated by the Soviet Union. Though he was able to reassure many Germans that Soviet claims were exaggerated, he had to acknowledge that there was "enough to it to damage our cause" significantly in the Cold War. Unequivocally, he declared that "non-segregation and non-discrimination" had now become "a question of foreign policy."[53]

Seven months later, in June 1950, the Cold War had escalated to the brink of real war, and on June 25, the Korean War broke out. The United States had been warning of communist aggression in Korea, and now this far-away conflict raised America's military stakes in Germany, prompting Truman to make his "Troops to Europe" decision. This shift in policy brought an activated 7th Army to Germany and replaced the remaining occupation troops with heavily armored combat troops.

Spurred by this atmosphere of increasing Cold War anxieties, as well as continuing complaints from black troops to the NAACP and the black press about the unwillingness of commanders in Germany to integrate, Raymond Pace Alexander, a distinguished lawyer and longtime civil rights advocate also traveled to Germany in October 1950.[54] After an extensive tour of bases, Alexander sent a long report to George Marshall, the former secretary of state who was by then secretary of defense, to plea for the full integration of the armed forces.[55] Alexander told Marshall that blacks were proud of their service, and that many of them were ready to make a lifelong commitment to the military. But the troops were demoralized by segregation and by the utter lack of "Negro-ranking officers." No such officers were to be found in the European Command (EUCOM), which was under the purview of the Defense Department. Moreover, Alexander's visit also revealed that overcoming discrimination was not just a matter for the military. High-ranking black officers could also not be found in the offices of HICOG, which was directed and staffed by the Department of State.[56] Alexander insisted that this situation was detrimental to troop morale. But even more importantly, it hurt America's cause of freedom. An integrated army, he argued, "is the strongest and most powerful answer to the oft repeated charge and propaganda of our communist enemies that we make false and dishonest claims of a liberal and free America."[57]

Alexander also charged that the prevailing situation in the military undermined America's strategic planning for Europe, particularly with its new policy of containment. He warned that the United States could not "contain communism abroad or fight its freedom-destroying germs at home, and at the same time compromise on such fundamental issues underlying our very existence as a nation." At that point, the United States was debating the possibility of creating an integrated European military with France and Great Britain. Such a European military would enable the rearmament of West Germany just five years after the defeat of Nazism, while assuring the French and the British that there would be no German military resurgence. This plan, therefore, gave Alexander another argument against continuing a segregated army: "maintaining two separate armies in Europe...one white, one Negro, especially in view of our plans to organize one great army of democracy in Europe among all the nations of the North Atlantic Pact, would be a shameful betrayal of the very bedrock and foundation of democracy." Furthermore, continuing segregation would be a "monstrous blunder" that would give the Soviets more leverage in the Cold War confrontation with the United States.[58]

Once again, Alexander stressed the threat to America's mission in Germany. If America was to win this struggle for the hearts and minds of the people, not just in Germany but in the world, a serious course correction was of utmost importance: "We can not [at] one and the same time preach the doctrine of the sanctity of the individual and condone persecution of fifteen million of our own loyal patriotic Negro Americans."[59] And Alexander made it clear that Germans had certainly noticed the discrepancy: he informed Secretary of Defense Marshall that people across Germany, including mayors and officials, had repeatedly raised the issue of the segregated military with him. Whether in the smallest villages or the largest cities, people had asked him again and again: "Why do they say that America is such a free, liberal and democratic country, so good to their people, that we should copy its way of life, when you maintain two separate armies of soldiers, when you segregate your soldiers?" He did not know how to answer them.[60]

As Alexander's account suggests, such queries from the German people were quite widespread, providing unexpected assistance to African American civil rights activists and black GIs in their efforts to advance desegregation. The U.S. military government, and after German sovereignty in 1949, the Office of the High Commissioner, organized lectures, exhibitions, and town hall meetings as part of its ambitious effort to reeducate Germans in the principles of American democracy. The reeducation program aimed to help Germans overcome their racist Nazi past while also strengthening their resolve against the new totalitarian dictatorship, Soviet Communism.

Not surprisingly, at such events, debates about race could lead to most embarrassing moments. This was especially true once the military occupation was over and Germans felt they could speak more freely. At Heidelberg University, for example, the Americans had organized an event at which the new university president, Karl Heinrich Bauer, was to explain to his audience of students that there would be no more teaching "based in discrimination" in the new Germany. African American journalist Roi Ottley, who had been in the audience that day, reported with a certain amount of glee that a "cocky youngster" asked the red-faced American organizers: "don't you in the U.S.A. believe in the superiority of the white race?"[61]

Another indication of just how widespread such cynical attitudes toward American assertions of democracy were can be found in a study of the Civil Affairs Division (CAD) in HICOG. The division had asked German youths to write letters explaining what they considered the most urgent impediment to world peace. Some of the answers were rather startling.[62] In analyzing these letters, CAD's military intelligence officer, William Harlan Hale, ascertained that racial discrimination was doing serious damage to how German youths viewed America. This was no small matter, since youths were the ones who needed to be educated as future democratic leaders of the country. Hale reported, "many of the youth asked how Americans can square [American discrimination] with their condemnation of Nazi racist teachings." One young person, for example, had asked: "Shouldn't you clean up your own house before you presume to tell us what's right?" This was a question Hale felt that no American could afford to ignore.[63]

Significantly, in these letters, some of the German youths focused particularly on the American racism on display in Germany as a threat to world peace. They mentioned especially the mistreatment that black soldiers endured at the hands of their white countrymen; one wrote, for example: "It is often said that American MP's [sic] beat up their Negro comrades." Given this behavior in the army of occupation, writers such as this one joined others in wondering how Americans could "possibly reproach the Nazi regime and the SS."[64] Similarly, another German youth, without any prompting by the CAD, wrote a letter to the editor of an American-sponsored paper in Germany, condemning the gap between Americans' democratic preaching and the behavior in the army: "How do you expect the impression on my people to be when soldiers beat up or even shoot their colored fellow soldiers? How do you expect to talk Germans out of this silly racial hatred nonsense?"[65]

German youths were not the only who felt this way. Older Germans, too, were concerned, but they tended to be less cynical and were much more circumspect in voicing their opinions for a number of reasons. Some felt that Germans had no right to criticize Americans after the crimes their country had committed during the Third Reich. But even more, they believed that it was not prudent to attack America with the communist parties of the Soviet Union, as well as East and West Germany, relentlessly attacking the American race problem to undermine U.S. leadership in Europe. Thus, older Germans generally expressed their thoughts on the unresolved race problem in private conversations with the Americans. Consequently, one must look to reports on such conversations by the Americans with whom they conferred.

We have already seen above that both Jacob Javits of the European Study Mission in December 1949 and Raymond Pace Alexander on his visit to Germany in October 1950 related Germans' questions and concerns about American democracy, particularly in light of the segregated military. For pro-American and anticommunist Germans, the segregated military was a serious impediment to America's success in Europe, and hence a threat to West German security against the Soviets in the Cold War. In his report, Javits further relayed that in all of his meetings, "segregation and discrimination" were "constantly raised as points invalidating [his] protestations of democracy," and that all his meeting partners referred to the Jim Crow army as a serious impediment to America's ability to succeed against the Soviet Union.[66]

Dr. Dorothy Ferebee, president of the National Council of Negro Women, who traveled to Germany in May 1951, also encountered a great deal of criticism of American democracy. Despite her eagerness to assure her government of its just cause in the Cold War struggle, she had to acknowledge that the critics she had talked to had a point. Germans had asked her how black troops could "fight for freedom in Korea and serve as defenders of western freedom in Germany" yet have "their liberty restricted at home."[67]

Edith Sampson likewise heard numerous complaints from Germans. A prominent black attorney, she was an officer of the National Council of Negro Women and an alternate member of the United States delegation to the United Nations. In 1949, she was asked to join the Round-the-World Town Meetings that were sent abroad by the State Department to counter Soviet propaganda about racism in the United States by highlighting the advances that African Americans had made. Sampson was beloved in Germany for her efforts at the United Nations on behalf of the hundreds of thousands of German POWs in the Soviet Union. Yet, when she conducted a series of town hall meetings as part of a three months tour in Europe in 1951, she, too, had to listen to harsh criticisms of the United States. "German civilians," she reported to the Office of the High Commissioner, "frequently commented on the contrast between our democratic pretensions and our practice of segregation in the occupation forces. They often asked me to explain this contradiction. It was obvious to me that our chief objective, which is to cultivate a democratic spirit in Germany, is definitely handicapped by the continuation of segregation and discrimination."[68]

With this mounting censure of American hypocrisy, officials in Washington finally listened. Because of America's role in Germany, and because of Germany's strategic location in the Pentagon's defense strategy to contain Soviet expansionism in Europe, the State Department beseeched the Department of the Army to put pressure on its commanders in Germany, and by 1951, the Department of the Army came around. Anna Rosenberg, assistant secretary of defense, who had been instrumental in pushing the Department of the Army, called the step absolutely necessary because an integrated military was a "living example of democracy in action—the only answer to Communist propaganda."[69] William Gardner Smith was more sober in his assessment of the change. He surmised that, without foreign pressure, fewer African Americans would have been appointed to prominent posts in the government or sent abroad to represent the country, and the integration of the military also would not have been accomplished. In an essay, he quipped triumphantly, nonetheless, that "the embarrassment of the government [was] the gain of the American Negro!"[70]

It is perhaps ironic that in its effort to defeat Nazism and reeducate the Germans, the United States was forced to take a long hard look at itself. African Americans had made their case about the deficiencies of American democracy for many decades, and by the early 1950s, a good number of white Americans had come to understand that as well. James Goodnight, one of the Resident Officers in HICOG, provides a thoughtful commentary on this journey that white Americans were forced to make. At one of the regularly scheduled town hall meetings, in which Germans were exposed to the principles of American grassroots democracy, he talked of the advances that black Americans had made over the past centuries. Goodnight framed his story in the by then established Cold War narrative that emphasized an honest engagement with the shortcomings of American democracy, while also portraying that very democracy as a story of redemption and national reconciliation.[71] He stressed that African Americans' slow and steady journey toward equality had been sped up considerably in recent years and praised Germans for the role they had played in this. Their knowledge of the situation of the "American Negro," and their willingness to take on white Americans who tried to lecture them about racism, had allegedly "helped to trigger a wave of 'contemplation' that was transforming the state of race relations in the South."[72]

Unfinished Business

Despite the acceleration of African Americans' "journey" Goodnight referred to and the speed with which de facto integration of the military was accomplished, the real situation in this new army—and especially in the civilian communities surrounding military bases—was not changing fast enough. For one thing, in the American South, segregation still ruled daily life outside of military bases. While the color line in Germany was not so clearly drawn, it was apparent that there, too, many commanders, white soldiers, and German locals still had some "unfinished business" concerning racial integration.

Nonetheless, it was far easier to desegregate the army in West Germany than in the United States, as the media coverage of this revolutionary change stressed. De facto integration of the military was accomplished in just two short years—from 1951 to 1953—on all military installations, including those in Germany and the United States. The whole process was undertaken without much fanfare, being presented to the American people as a fait accompli. The military was able to be so effective because of its top-down hierarchical structure. Yet in West Germany, the social situation off base made it possible for the U.S. military to do in military communities such as Kaiserslautern, Ramstein, and Landstuhl what it could only dream of in places like Fort Hood, Texas, or Fort Rucker, Alabama. The ongoing integration of the military went so smoothly, reported the *Saturday Evening Post*, because in Germany there were "no external social pressures to complicate the integration picture."[73] One officer, involved in ensuring the success of the program, explained why this was so: "[It] is difficult to make such a program stick, in, say, Mississippi, if, after you've practiced equality all day, you leave the post and run smack into the strictest of Jim Crow restrictions downtown. In Europe, people are more apt to ignore the color line." In other words, when soldiers left base in Germany, they did not have to deal with Jim Crow buses, segregated diners, or movie theaters in the surrounding civilian communities.[74] The Department of Defense noticed this effect, too, apparently realizing what so many black soldiers had been pointing out since the start of the war, namely, the paradox "that the Negro citizen in uniform has frequently been made to feel more at home overseas than in his home town."[75]

In a hopeful spirit, some in the media wondered whether this ease of integration in Germany might have an impact on race relations at home. The *Saturday Evening Post*, for example, asked speculatively: "Given the special situation [over there], will the effects of integration carry over into the lives of those exposed to it in the European Command? Will it have a lasting impact on their thinking and the way they act when they get back to the United States?" A colonel from Chicago stationed in Germany believed that it would: although he had harbored doubts about the whole program at first, he had quickly changed his mind when he found that it was working and had "of course" been easier in Germany, adding "I'd be very much

Figure 25 Interracial German-American couples dancing at a New Year's Eve party in the Noncommissioned Officers' Club (NCO), Ramstein Air Base, late 1950s (Ramstein Air Base Documentary & Exhibition Center, Ramstein).

surprised if that fact didn't percolate back to the United States and have an effect on us there too."[76]

The effect on America that this officer alluded to was twofold, as both blacks and whites living in West Germany as soldiers or accompanying families had an opportunity to experience the less restrictive racial environment. Although blacks comprised only about 10 percent of the troops in Germany, the troop deployment was so extensive that some 30,000 black GIs (and their families) were stationed there on a regular basis, with soldiers usually staying for two- or three-year tours of duty. Thus, every couple of years, a new cohort of African American GIs, and often also their wives and children, found themselves living in Germany, which made it possible for hundreds of thousands of African Americans to be exposed to a life outside the United States. Just as it had been for soldiers during the war, this experience marked the first chance to escape the Jim Crow South or the de facto segregation of the North for many of these black soldiers and their families. While Northern blacks occasionally complained that Germans stared at them, especially in communities without American military bases, most black GIs, and especially those from the South, continued to embrace their time in Germany.[77]

Many African Americans in Germany echoed the sentiments soldiers had been expressing since they first began deploying to Europe. One black officer interviewed by *Ebony* magazine in 1952, for example, said that a man could have "more personal freedom [in Germany] than in most places in the United States."[78] One soldier recalled his time in Germany as a "three-year breathing period" and was shocked at having to "deal with Jim Crow" again once he returned home.[79] Felix Goodwin, returning to the United States in 1953 after an extensive tour of duty in Germany, was equally dismayed when his young daughter, born and raised in Germany, was reprimanded for using the "whites only" water fountain at the local Sears in New Orleans and was directed to the blacks only fountain in the basement. This obliged him to explain the facts of life in her home country to her.[80] And Colin Powell, America's most famous African American soldier who served as a young lieutenant in Germany from 1958 to 1959, shared similar positive recollections in his memoir: "For black GIs, especially those out of the South, Germany was a breath of freedom." For the first time, they "could go where they wanted, eat where they wanted, and date whom they wanted, just like other people. The dollar was strong, the beer good, and the German people friendly, since we were all that stood between them and the Red hordes."[81]

Much like the soldiers who fought during World War II and served in the occupation, many of these soldiers who served in Germany in the 1950s and 1960s returned to the United States with a new hope and determination for change. Joe McPhee, for example, returned to his hometown of Poughkeepsie after serving in Germany during the early 1960s and joined the NAACP because of the "worse than disconcerting" contrast between the situation in Europe and that in the United States. As he explained, after serving in the U.S. military to assure "rights and privileges for people in Europe," he returned home to find that he still did not possess those same rights.[82] Many such disillusioned veterans became foot soldiers in the civil rights movement that an older generation of World War II veterans

Figure 26   Marchers, including a veteran who had served in Germany, pause for a prayer during the Selma to Montgomery March for Voting Rights, March 21, 1965 (Take Stock/ Matt Herron).

was leading throughout much of the South. Names such as Medgar Evers, Aaron Henry, and Amzie Moore immediately arise in this context, but there were many other lesser known but equally determined activists who joined and led the cause.[83]

Serving in the U.S. military outside the United States also had an emancipating effect on some white soldiers who were able to develop friendships with African Americans, which would not have been possible with the existing race barriers back home. While such interracial friendships like the one depicted in Figure 27 could flower in the clubs on U.S. military bases, such pairs were more likely to meet over beer and Wiener schnitzel at one of the many German restaurants that, unlike typical GI bars, welcomed both white and black Americans equally.

Despite the relative ease of integrating the military in Germany, there was still a great deal of racism and segregation both *on* base and *off*. Throughout the decade and even into the 1960s, the overwhelming majority of troops

Figure 27   Interracial German-American couple (right) in the NCO Club, Ramstein Air Base, late 1950s (Ramstein Air Base Documentary & Exhibition Center, Ramstein).

continued to spend their leisure hours with others of their own race. While the military argued that this happened because Southern blacks preferred it this way, the record makes clear that this was not the case. White GIs imposed segregation by threatening the German owners of bars and clubs with an economic boycott if they allowed black soldiers on their premises. For all too many bar owners, that was an easy calculation to make given that black GIs only constituted 10 percent of the troop strength. Often enough, the choice of hillbilly or Country Western music was enough to keep black soldiers away.

Commanders rarely took action against this sort of segregation off base. On the contrary, investigations by civil rights advocates found that a good number of commanders "used their authority to reinforce racial segregation and other forms of off-base racial discrimination."[84] Just as during the occupation years, many commanders continued to instruct local proprietors to observe the American model of racial segregation, defending it as, allegedly, what the men wanted and as a way to preserve the peace.

Alarmingly, commanders even supported German forms of racism at times. Whereas a good number of German landlords refused to rent to black soldiers because white American tenants threatened to move out, plenty of Germans had their own "unfinished business" when it came to race relations and plainly did not want black tenants in their homes. Yet, when soldiers complained about such discrimination, the military refused to act. In 1955, the Department of Defense (DOD) went so far as to declare that it could not intervene on behalf of black GIs on the grounds that such matters were beyond its purview because "community mores with respect to race" varied.[85] The department repeated that line in 1959 when a German landlord denied housing to a black soldier, and in the early 1960s investigators found that "local military commanders seemed unwilling to take the matter [of discrimination] seriously."[86] Suggestions from civil rights leaders to address these abuses brought only negative responses from the military commanders.[87]

There can be no doubt that the unwillingness of American military commanders to intervene in German communities on behalf of black soldiers had nothing to do with them trying to be polite guests. In fact, the military ran roughshod over German communities all the time, for example, when conducting military maneuvers. Rather, commanders from the South, especially, ignored these issues because they found social segregation to be an appropriate norm. But even more importantly, until the early to mid-1960s, the American military and the Department of Defense resisted such intervention on behalf of black soldiers in Germany for fear that such actions would force the military to intercede in the still segregated communities surrounding military bases in the United States, and especially the American South, as well.

This disinclination on the part of the U.S. military to adjudicate on behalf of black soldiers stood in stark contrast to the military's usual concern for its troops. For example, the military occasionally declared German swimming pools off-limits to GIs and their families because the water quality failed to meet "American standards." At times, the military also declared German pubs or bars off-limits for GIs if they did not fulfill the military's standard of hygiene.[88] No such economic sanctions were ever imposed on local bar owners who denied service to black GIs, or German landlords who refused to rent apartments to black families.

It is easy to see how German and American forms of racism mutually influenced and reinforced one another in these garrison communities, generating widespread patterns of discrimination against black soldiers and often also their families. The Germans insisted that they had nothing against black soldiers, but that white Americans forced their hand. If there was racism in Germany, they averred, it was a thoroughly American import. The American military, for its part, pleaded helplessness as well, arguing that the Americans were merely guests in the country, and, therefore, it was impossible for military commanders to instruct German nationals about how to behave toward blacks.

Not surprisingly, the civil rights struggle unfolding in the United States during the 1950s and 1960s also played out in West Germany, particularly on and around military bases. Now that the military was formally integrated, white soldiers who resented this development had to express their hostility in the German communities surrounding the military bases to avoid demotion. Black soldiers also carried many of their frustrations over the slow pace of integration and the emerging civil rights struggle in the United States into these same communities.[89] Thus, whenever a civil rights confrontation occurred in the United States, German authorities and the American military police were put on alert to deal with the expected clashes between the soldiers. In 1956, when the University of Alabama refused to admit black student Autherine Lucy, violence erupted in garrison towns across West Germany as black soldiers reacted in anger.[90] Similarly, the crisis over school integration in Little Rock, Arkansas, in the fall of 1957 triggered even more serious street battles between black and white soldiers.[91] Accordingly, Germans in garrison communities braced themselves for trouble when they heard about developments on the civil rights front in the United States.[92]

As the civil rights movement coalesced under the leadership of Dr. Martin Luther King Jr. and gained strength over the course of the 1950s, black GIs also started to challenge the Jim Crow rules that had been introduced to garrison towns. This happened, for instance, in 1958, when black soldiers stationed in Baumholder staged a sit-in at a bar whose owner, as instructed by the base commander, had put up a sign stating that he did not serve "colored soldiers." The soldiers knew that such U.S. style segregation was illegal in Germany and protested the policy by shouting: "Where do you think you are, in Little Rock?" When they refused to leave, the owner called the American military police, who, instead of defending the soldiers' right to equal treatment (which was guaranteed by the German constitution), arrested them for disturbing the peace. When the German media discovered that the captain of the military police had brutalized the soldiers in the military jail, they loudly denounced such racial hatred as not acceptable in a democratic society.[93]

With ongoing civil rights protests both in the United States and on bases abroad, attitudes within the military did finally begin to change in the mid- to late 1960s, but even then, it was not enough. In 1961, Robert McNamara issued a number of civil rights directives from the Department of Defense that were to do away with the remnants of discrimination in the military. In July 1963, on the 15th anniversary of Truman's executive order, these efforts were extended to assure integration in the civilian communities bordering on military bases in the American South as well.[94] Beginning in 1964, the Department of Defense threatened to use economic sanctions to enforce this policy, and issued a series of directives to alleviate racism in housing and at off-base stores, diners, and clubs. But then the Pentagon turned its attention elsewhere, namely the war in Vietnam, as former Secretary of Defense Robert McNamara acknowledged in hindsight.[95] Consequently, discrimination endured and racial tensions continued to rise, culminating in a crisis on U.S. military bases around the globe in the late 1960s that nearly destroyed the armed services and prompted real change. Until that racial crisis, however, which is discussed at length in chapter 8, the military's laissez-faire attitude concerning racial questions and the dramatic events of the civil rights movement unfolding in America were not lost on the Germans. With this social revolution effectively on their doorstep, West Germans could not fail to be influenced by it, and East Germans, too, had strong reactions, though without black GIs in their midst and under the sway of communist propaganda. The next three chapters explore these themes in detail.

5

Bringing Civil Rights to East and West: Dr. Martin Luther King Jr. in Cold War Berlin

> The church is absolutely packed...And the entire time Dr. King is speaking, you can hear a pin drop. Nobody coughs, nobody sneezes...These people are in a kind of a prison not of their own choosing. They don't have any freedom to claim. And he's talking to them about passive resistance. In other words, admitting to them, "you are in a situation that needs to be resisted." And that was radical in and of itself.

With these words, Alcyone Scott, one of the local interpreters for Dr. Martin Luther King Jr., remembers King's sermon in East Berlin's St. Mary's Church, the largest and oldest Protestant church in the divided city, on the night of September 13, 1964.[1] King's visit to Berlin in the fall of 1964, only a month before winning the Nobel Peace Prize, stands out as an important point in the reception of the African American civil rights movement in Germany. Coming to one of the major battlegrounds of the Cold War to spread his message of nonviolence and brotherhood, King underlined the global dimension of the struggle for racial justice and also had a profound impact on the people of Berlin, East and West.

The transnational dimension of the civil rights movement with regard to Germany was thus twofold: in the same way that the experience of black GIs in Germany transformed debates about civil rights in the United States, the movement, in turn, influenced German politics from the late 1950s onward. The presence of American GIs, media coverage, transatlantic exchange programs, and visits by prominent African American leaders all contributed to Germans' perceptions of the racial situation on the other side of the Atlantic and their image of the United States. Looking at the movement from the German side highlights its global reach and once again underscores the entanglement of the two countries' histories.

From its very beginning, the African American civil rights struggle captured the attention of Germans. While in East Germany it prompted an official call for revolutionary solidarity with oppressed segments of the U.S. population, in the Federal Republic it fed criticism and doubts about

America's democratic mission and leadership in the "Free World." The West German media tuned in closely to the major events of the struggle: the landmark Supreme Court ruling in *Brown v. Board of Education of Topeka* banning segregation in public schools in 1954, Rosa Parks's courageous refusal to give up her seat on a Montgomery, Alabama, bus that triggered the Montgomery bus boycott in 1955, and the turbulent integration of an all-white high school in Little Rock, Arkansas, in 1957 all provoked widespread reporting and commentary on the progress of race relations across the Atlantic.[2] This coverage increased at the beginning of the 1960s, when eyewitness reports, historical analyses, and contributions by African American civil rights leaders frequently found their way into West German periodicals.[3]

Sabine Lietzmann, U.S. correspondent for the *Frankfurter Allgemeine Zeitung*, was a particularly perceptive observer of the civil rights struggle who constantly emphasized the magnitude of social and political transformations unfolding in the United States. She maintained, for example, that the "twenty million American Negroes with the law on their side" were "no longer satisfied with nuggets begrudgingly tossed at them in accordance with the law" and that "the Second World War, the court decisions of the postwar period, and the rise of the black world from Africa" had roused black consciousness. In her view, the American South was a "powder keg" ready to explode, and no American could claim not to have known about it.[4] Lietzmann even declared 1963 the "Year of the Negro" in light of the events that had recently occurred: in the spring, authorities had unleashed police dogs on demonstrators in Birmingham, Alabama; on August 28, hundreds of thousands of people had come together for a March on Washington and to hear Dr. King's "I Have a Dream" speech as they demonstrated for equality and social harmony between the races; and on September 15, four young African American girls had been killed in a church bombing by the Ku Klux Klan (KKK), also in Birmingham. Although realistic about the severe obstacles that lay ahead, Lietzmann was convinced that white Americans could "no longer close their eyes and hearts" to the plight of the African American population.[5] Most of her fellow commentators shared this belief and agreed that the movement, which had formerly been dominated by religious leaders, was now on its way to becoming a political mass movement that would fundamentally change the country.[6]

Not just reporters but also segments of the German population now began to voice their support for the U.S. civil rights movement. On September 25, 1963, when President John F. Kennedy visited Frankfurt, a bipartisan coalition of conservative, Social Democratic, and left-leaning German students joined forces with American and African students to demonstrate for civil rights in the United States. This crowd of more than 100 demonstrators marched through the city's streets in a silent procession, bearing banners with slogans such as "Equal Rights for All Americans," "Give Me Liberty or Give Me Death," and "1963: Time to Practice Civil Rights Granted in 1865." Arriving at their destination—the U.S. Consulate—they delivered a petition addressed to the president and signed by 450 people. Although this petition recognized Kennedy's past efforts on behalf of the rights of African Americans, it called for further measures to combat domestic racism and discrimination.[7] Expressing similar solidarity, a banner reading "For Colored People We Stand Behind President Kennedy" was visible in the crowds that gathered when Kennedy spoke at the Römerberg Plaza in Frankfurt that same day.

King's visit to Cold War Berlin took place within the context of these larger German debates about the U.S. civil rights struggle. Yet his trip was specifically initiated by Willy Brandt, then mayor of West Berlin and later minister for foreign affairs and West German chancellor. During his visit to Washington to meet Kennedy in May 1964, Brandt encountered King in person for the very first time. He listened to him elaborate on "his dream of an America that had overcome racial segregation" at the banquet of the Americans for Democratic Action convention, where they were both scheduled speakers.[8] Brandt was "deeply moved by this joint appearance" and impressed by King's eloquence, his reflections on the American Dream, and the seriousness of his efforts to gain equality for his fellow countrymen. He, therefore, extended an invitation to King to come to Germany the following September, which the civil rights leader immediately accepted.[9]

Figure 28 Silent March for African American Civil Rights, Frankfurt/Main, Germany, September 25, 1963 (Institut für Stadtgeschichte Frankfurt am Main/Renate Dabrowski).

Another important facilitator of King's visit was Provost Heinrich Grüber, the former pastor of East Berlin's St. Mary's Church. Grüber had been an active opponent of the Nazi regime and had garnered international attention in 1961 when he testified during the trial of Adolf Eichmann, one of the leading architects of the Holocaust, in Jerusalem. Invited by U.S. churches, Grüber began to travel across the United States delivering sermons and visiting a variety of Jewish and African American religious leaders in the following years, as well as Attorney General Robert Kennedy in September 1962. On these visits, Grüber encountered the civil rights struggle firsthand.[10]

In the course of 1963, Grüber took up correspondence with Dr. King and invited him to Berlin. As he explained in his first letter, Grüber perceived King's quest for racial equality as similar to his own resistance to fascism:

> I remembered the time during the Hitler regime when my precious wife and family fought with and for me and I decided to write you. I write in the bond of the same faith and hope, knowing your experiences are the same as ours were. When Hitler published the so-called Nur[em]berg "Race Codes," I allied myself with many pastors of the confessed church [the Confessing Church] in opposition of this act and founded an office to help the suppressed and discriminated; this office bore my name. Because of this, Eichmann sent me to a concentration camp in 1940: first to Sachsenhausen, then to Dachau.[11]

Recounting his time in the Nazi camps and his participation in the Eichmann trial, Grüber further elaborated on the motives of his support and solidarity: "During the time of Hitler, I was often ashamed of being a German, as today, I am ashamed of being white. I am grateful to you, dear brother, and to all who stand with you in this fight for justice, which you are conducting in the spirit of Jesus Christ."[12] Thanking Grüber for his support and for the invitation, King replied that he would "be happy to come to Berlin" when he had an opportunity to do so and his schedule would allow it.[13]

It did not take long for this opportunity to arise. Just months later, King traveled to Berlin to take part in the fourteenth annual cultural festival of the city (*Berliner Festwochen*) from September 12 to 14, 1964, whose theme was European interactions with Africa.[14] From the moment of his arrival in Berlin, King was subjected to a schedule that whisked him from one official function to the next. Shortly after landing at Tempelhof Airport in West Berlin on the afternoon of September 12, King and the Rev. Dr. Ralph Abernathy, his close associate and the vice president of the Southern Christian Leadership Conference (SCLC) that King was heading, were greeted by Provost Grüber, as well as government representatives and church dignitaries (such as West Berlin Senator for Science and the Arts, Walter Stein, and General Superintendent of the Protestant Church in West Berlin, Hans-Martin Helbich). The American civil rights leader was also immediately surrounded by a whole host of eagerly awaiting journalists, both local and international.[15] Right after this welcome, King was escorted to his first press conference and then to his accommodation at the West Berlin Senate guest house by the Wannsee in Berlin-Grunewald.

The next morning started with King's signing of the Golden Book of Berlin in West Berlin's city hall (Rathaus Schöneberg) and a reception with Mayor Willy Brandt. Honoring his guest, Brandt presented King with a small replica of the Berlin Liberty Bell, a ten-ton bell given to the city in 1950 by the United States as part of an initiative chaired by General Lucius D. Clay. Inspired by the Philadelphia Liberty Bell, this gift, which was inscribed with the motto "That this world under God shall have a new birth of freedom," was intended to be a symbol of the struggle against communism. At the same time, the motto was a direct reference to Abraham Lincoln's Gettysburg Address during the American Civil War, which marked an important turning point in the history of African American emancipation in the United States, a connection that, however, did not seem to have played a large role in the postwar situation. Together with a "Declaration of Freedom" signed by sixteen million Americans, the bell was put up in West Berlin's city hall from where its knell emanated daily across the divided city. The city produced small replicas of this bell now to present them to distinguished American guests as a token of gratitude for the U.S. defense of the city's freedom by means of the airlift during the Soviet blockade of 1948/1949 and during the Berlin crisis of 1961 that led to the building of the Wall.[16]

This reception was followed by the official opening ceremony of the city's annual cultural festival at the Berlin Philharmonic Hall. This year, to honor the late president Kennedy, the organizers had turned it into a memorial service featuring four international choirs.[17] One year earlier, Kennedy had paid his spectacular visit to the city. Amidst the cheers of thousands and thousands of Berliners, he had famously declared that he was a citizen of Berlin ("Ich bin ein Berliner"), reinforcing America's commitment to West Berlin in the face of the communist threat.[18] This speech has remained unforgettable to Berliners, Germans, and to historical memory to this day.

Drawing on Kennedy's determination from the year before, Mayor Brandt, in his speech during the opening ceremony, situated the struggle of the city within the global struggle for freedom and liberty:

> Here in Berlin, a miracle occurred—people asserted themselves, surrounded by threatening force, but borne up by the awareness that freedom is stronger. This was and continues to be more than a national task. We know that it is about freedom for all. All people, regardless of their skin color, of their faith, of their social background, of their nationality. In this spirit, we begin this Festival 1964.

This inclusion of racial equality and justice was an integral part of Brandt's notion of freedom. It was also a source of his admiration for his American guest, who had "devoted his life to this great task with courage and determination: to further the cause of freedom and help his country."

In Brandt's view, the cultural festival of 1964 was to serve as a signal of freedom coming from a place that, against all odds, understood "how to assert the demand for humanity and cosmopolitanism." Thereby claiming freedom as a fundamental human right for people across the globe, and especially for those who had been and continued to be victims of discrimination and oppression, Brandt subsumed the fight against communism, the decolonization process and national liberation movements, as well as the American civil rights movement, under a larger quest for liberty around the world:

> I would be pleased if a message of self-confidence and hope were to emanate from this place and from our festival to many peoples. Especially to the peoples of Africa as well. And over the ocean. But also into the quiet streets beyond the wall that Kennedy spoke of. To all people who strive to get past the sometimes rather narrow issues of politics and live their lives in peace and freedom and dignity.[19]

King bolstered this global dimension of the struggle for equality and justice, which was to become one of the rhetorical hallmarks of his time in Berlin, in his own remarks on John F. Kennedy at the opening ceremony. In King's eyes, the president had understood that the era was one in which

Figure 29   Dr. Martin Luther King Jr. and West Berlin Mayor Willy Brandt during the opening ceremony of the Berliner Festwochen, September 13, 1964 (SZ Photo).

human rights had become "the central world issue" and that "the struggle of Negroes" in the United States "was a component of this world movement." Although he saw "storm clouds forming on the American political horizon" indicating the depth of "the roots of violence and extremism" in his country, King remained optimistic that "the forces of good" would ultimately prevail.[20]

In the fall of 1964, one of the clouds looming on the horizon was the candidacy of Barry Goldwater, the staunchly conservative Senator from Arizona, for the presidency. Commenting on him during the press conference the day before, King had already provoked substantial consternation in Washington. Asked about the upcoming U.S. elections, the civil rights leader had declared that there were "signs of Hitlerism" in the candidacy of the Republican senator. Should Goldwater win, he predicted, the country would witness "a dark night of social disruption," as well as violence "on a scale...never seen before."[21] According to King, Goldwater himself was not necessarily a "racial fanatic" but rather represented a philosophy that opened the door for fascism, helping and providing a home for "race fanatics—like in Mississippi." One potential consequence, King averred, was "the danger of a Third World War," since "[n]ationalistic feelings and chauvinism—fed by Goldwater—could lead to total destruction."[22]

It is striking that both Brandt and King employed references to the history of the other's country to boost their own definitions of freedom. During a keynote speech on the occasion of the "Day of the Church," King was quite specific in this regard. Before 20,000 Berliners assembled at the Waldbühne, an open air theater in West Berlin, he compared the divisions in his home country to the separation of his host city, which, he argued, had become "a symbol of the divisions of men on the face of the earth."[23] As one of the hot spots of the Cold War, King explained, the city had not only become a center of world attention but also acquired a deeper historical meaning:

> Here in Berlin, one cannot help being aware that you are the hub around which turns the wheel of history. For just as we [in the United States] are proving to be the testing ground of races living together in spite of their differences, you are testing the possibility of co-existence for the two ideologies which now compete for world dominance. If ever there were a people who should be constantly sensitive to their destiny, the people of Berlin, East and West, should be they.[24]

King was, of course, fully aware of the stark differences between the respective situations in Berlin and the Unites States. He underscored his reluctance to "attempt to bring you God's word for your situation" because of his lack of familiarity with local politics and the very short period of time he had been there. As he put it, his stay was "not...long enough to discern God's plan for you and his calling to you."[25] Nonetheless, King

Figure 30   Dr. Martin Luther King Jr. preaching before more than 20,000 Berliners at the Waldbühne, West Berlin, September 13, 1964 (ullstein bild—dpa).

used his time in the divided country to expand on a spiritual message of brotherhood that transcended national differences:

> Regardless of the barriers of race, creed, ideology, or nationality, there is an inescapable destiny which binds us together. There is a common humanity which makes us sensitive to the sufferings of one another. And for many of us, there is one lord, one faith and one baptism which binds us in a common history, a common calling, and a common hope for the salvation of the world.

With respect to the Cold War division that manifested itself so vividly in Berlin, the conclusion King drew from this was clear: "on either side of the Wall are God's children, and no man-made barrier can obliterate that fact. Whether it be East or West, men and women search for meaning, hope for fulfillment, yearn for faith in something beyond themselves, and cry desperately for love and community to support them in this pilgrim journey."

King dedicated the major part of his sermon at the Waldbühne to introducing his German audience to the civil rights struggle in the United States—from the Montgomery bus boycott and the lunch counter sit-ins in Greensboro, North Carolina, to the SCLC's campaign in Birmingham in 1963 and the passage of the Civil Rights Act by Congress in 1964. Extrapolating from this overview of the major events of the movement, King outlined his vision of how "to transform the jangling discords of the nations into a beautiful symphony of brotherhood."[26]

King's appearance as a principal speaker during the "Day of the Church" was greeted with enthusiasm by both his audience and church leaders. Even before his sermon, when Hans-Martin Helbich, General Superintendent of the Protestant Church in West Berlin, announced that the American guest was also scheduled to speak in East Berlin that night, the crowd broke into applause. Another Protestant leader Otto Dibelius, Bishop of the Protestant Church in Berlin-Brandenburg, explicated the political implications of King's message: "for the sake of the blessedness of our souls, the Wall has to go." Addressing King directly, Dibelius promised the support of Christians in Berlin and Germany if King maintained his nonviolent course: "If you begin your struggle for freedom with the firm resolve to lead a struggle without violence and to fight the good fight of believing in the spirit of rec-onciliation, then all the Christians of Berlin and Germany will stand beside you and declare: we want to lead the same nonviolent struggle."[27]

Another expression of local church officials' admiration for King's work was the conferral of an honorary doctoral degree from the Theological School of the West Berlin Protestant Church. Bestowed on King after the open air church rally during an award ceremony in Dibelius's home, the degree honored him for being "a shining example of Christian responsibil-ity" and a "courageous and selfless leader in the struggle for the rights and freedom of oppressed peoples." The text on the diploma specified that he was being recognized as someone "who had thought through, seriously and in a scholarly manner, the question of the meaning of Christian love for political life and the understanding of love and violence, thus opening new paths for Christian participation in political life."[28]

Despite King's very short time in Berlin and his lack of familiarity with the tense nature of local politics, he had encountered the city's political reali-ties during a tour earlier that day. That morning, the young East German jockey Michael Meyer had attempted to escape to the West, resulting in a gun battle between East German border guards and the U.S. soldier on duty on the Western side of the Wall. East German border guards had opened fire, hitting Meyer when he crawled beneath the barbed wire at Stallschreiber Straße in Berlin-Mitte. Yet West Berliners and U.S. Private First Class Hans Puhl managed to rescue him. While terrified residents and firefighters cut the barbed wire, Puhl threw a grenade and returned fire until he was able to pull Meyer over the Wall with a rope. Meyer survived the incident, though hospitalized, and an East German border guard was wounded.[29]

As soon as King heard about this incident later that afternoon, he vis-ited the scene, both inspecting the site of the escape and talking to West Berlin residents whose building had been struck by East German gunfire. Witnessing the full extent of the fortifications separating the two parts of the city, he regarded the "incredible" episode as further evidence of the neces-sity of détente between the superpowers.[30] When asked at a press confer-ence what, specifically, he would do to bring freedom and liberty to people behind the Wall, King admitted that he had no concrete answer but favored nonviolence as the only method with any prospect of success.[31]

Figure 31 Dr. Martin Luther King Jr. talking to the Grossmans of Stallschreiber Straße, whose building was struck by gunfire during a skirmish between East German border guards, West Berlin police, and American soldiers at the Berlin Wall, September 13, 1964 (akg—images).

Figure 32 Dr. Martin Luther King Jr. and Dr. Ralph David Abernathy at the Berlin Wall, Bernauer Straße and Schwedter Straße, September 13, 1964 (Landesarchiv Berlin/Karl-Heinz Schubert).

Then, only a few hours later, King had the opportunity to engage directly with East Germans. That afternoon, he crossed the Iron Curtain at Checkpoint Charlie to hold the sermon in communist East Berlin that Helbich had announced at the Waldbühne. It was primarily Provost Grüber who was responsible for this speaking engagement at St. Mary's Church. Ever since his visit to the United States, Grüber had become a passionate supporter of King's cause, for example, assisting in the translation of King's key texts into German, such as his "Letter from Birmingham Jail" of 1963, and calling for congregations across the country to discuss them. In an afterword to a German collection of King's writings whose publication coincided with his visit, Grüber stressed that segregation was "one of the major sins of our time." Due to their past, German Christians, in his view, bore a special responsibility to speak out against this form of discrimination:

> In the Third Reich, we found it hard to bear when theologians calling themselves Christians wanted to separate brothers and sisters classified as Jews according to the Nuremberg Laws [German Jews who had converted to Christianity] even in worship services and demanded a separate service—even their own churches—for them. We do not know how this can be reconciled with people confessing one common, holy church and singing the song "One Herd and One Shepherd." This schizophrenia is much more widespread in America now than it was then for us.[32]

Given his strong feelings about racial injustice in the United States, Grüber had not only extended a written invitation to King but also lobbied among local church officials to facilitate a speech in his former church, the historic St. Mary's Church at Alexander Square in the center of East Berlin that had been built around 1250.[33]

In the end, King actually gave two sermons because so many people came to hear him. Indications that King was to speak in East Berlin had already been reported in the Western media before his arrival.[34] Although no official announcement had been made by the East German government, the news had spread quickly by word of mouth in the communist half of the city. Two hours before the event, the doors of St. Mary's already had to be closed since the church could not accommodate the more than 2,000 East Berliners who had gathered to see King. When the stream of people did not dwindle even an hour before the event, church officials were forced to schedule a second sermon in the nearby Sophia Church.[35]

However, the arrival of the American guest was delayed by problems at Checkpoint Charlie. Escorted by American pastor Ralph Zorn and his parish worker Alcyone Scott, King had arrived at the border crossing without a passport. Scott, a twenty-five-year-old graduate of the University of Chicago, had come to Berlin at the beginning of 1963 to work for the Lutheran World Foundation in Zorn's parish in Berlin-Wedding, a workers' district bordering directly on the Wall. Asked to accompany Zorn and help interpret for Dr. King during his time in East Berlin, she had to negotiate the party's entry into East Germany with the border guard whom she knew from previous crossings. Since King was not carrying his passport, the guard brusquely refused to allow them to enter. The guard did eventually recognize King, though, and, after consulting his superiors, requested an alternative form of identification. The report prepared for the East German Ministry of State Security described the scene as follows:

> Asked whether Dr. King had any other sort of passport with him, he presented a check card of the USA (similar to an identity card)....Furthermore, Z[orn] remarked that K[ing] himself would be holding the sermon in St. Mary's Church. Thereupon, the three citizens [individuals] were permitted to enter after consultation with on-duty officers....Dr. King and the others repeatedly expressed their appreciation and drove into the democratic Berlin at about 19:52.[36]

Ebony magazine later noted that "it was the first time on record that anyone other than a defector had been allowed to enter East Berlin without presenting an official document."[37]

As the crowd outside the church had now been waiting for King for quite some time, it was difficult to control when he finally arrived. People immediately swarmed around the van, as Scott recalled: "I could not get out of the van because people were pressing against it to get to King. And you thought you were with the Beatles because the people mobbed him, just mobbed him. They all wanted either to touch him or to get an autograph; they handed him matchbooks or anything, saying 'Please sign this.' It was just phenomenal!"[38]

The somewhat chaotic situation was exacerbated by the fact that St. Mary's Church, at that particular time, did not have a pastor in charge of managing parish affairs who could have planned a more orderly reception for King. After the Berlin Wall was built, Provost Grüber, who had once held this position, was denied reentry to East Berlin because of his criticism of the East German state. Since then, two replacements had come and gone: Pastor Martin Helmer had fled the country, and Pastor Werner Arnold had been arrested and imprisoned after facilitating the escape of thirty East Germans to the West and smuggling Western goods and medicine into East Berlin.[39] Consequently, King was welcomed by Gerhard Schmitt, the recently appointed General Superintendent of the Protestant Church in East Berlin, who managed only with great effort to haul his American guest through the crowds into the church.[40]

Echoing the remarks of his West German peers Grüber and Helbich, Schmitt, in his introduction of King to the audience in St. Mary's Church, underscored Germany's unique responsibility in the global struggle against discrimination, while at the same time voicing implicit criticism against the East German regime: "We know about our guilt as German people. But we also developed a special sensitivity that is attuned, in international relations, to people anywhere in the world having to fight for their rights and human dignity on account of the color of their skin or their beliefs."[41]

When King took the pulpit, he extended his greetings not only from "Christian brothers and sisters of the United States" but also from those of West Berlin, where he had just spent what he described as "one of the most rewarding days of my life."[42] After brief introductory remarks, King essentially gave the same speech as in the Western half of the city, presenting an overview of the civil rights struggle in the United States and extolling the virtues of using nonviolence to effect social change.

While King's plea for passive resistance had been received warmly in West Berlin, it elicited a far greater emotional response on the other side of the Wall. A reporter from the *Frankfurter Allgemeine Zeitung* characterized the scene: "Spellbound—it can hardly be described any other way—the thousands sitting at his feet listened. What's more, they looked up to him...More than anything he could have said, it was the fact that he had come to them, to East Berlin."[43] In East Germany, where freedom of speech

Figure 33 Dr. Martin Luther King Jr. speaking to the congregation at East Berlin's St. Mary's Church with Pastor Ralph Zorn interpreting, September 13, 1964 (Landesarchiv Berlin).

and freedom to travel were severely restricted, no one in the audience failed to notice the political implications of King's message. It became particularly obvious when, right after King's first words, "My dear Christian friends of East Berlin," the choir intoned the spiritual "Go Down Moses," whose chorus includes the repeated phrase "Let my people go" in both the German and English versions. Scott reflected on the reaction to Dr. King in the church:

> [I]t was the power of his message, and it was also couched in very clear Christian terminology. This was clearly a man of a faith with a profound belief in humanity and in reconciliation. He believed it, and you felt it. And for people in this audience, who really saw no future for themselves because the Cold War was hot (no one ever imagined at this point in time that it would ever end), for him to talk about hope was electrifying.[44]

King evoked the same response at his second sermon in East Berlin that night. As he was finishing at St. Mary's Church around 9 p.m., about 2,000 people, many of them adolescents, had already poured into nearby Sophia Church. When every last seat had been filled, they continued to come, cramming into the aisles and around the altar and the baptismal font. They had come with shopping bags, briefcases, and some had even unwrapped their dinner. The local West Berlin paper later described this occasion as "no longer a church service but a political event, an assembly around a man from the West."[45] The audience besieged King after his speech, embracing him, shaking hands with him, and asking him to come back. According to *Ebony*, King's attempt "to leave East Berlin proved almost more difficult than entering as hundreds of East Berliners blocked his path."[46] But King patiently answered their questions and signed autographs for them before he was hustled away to meet with local church representatives at the Albrecht Street Hospice for a small reception. Close to midnight, King finally returned to the elegant guest house of the Senate at Wannsee in West Berlin before leaving for Munich the next morning.

King's visit to the East is particularly striking in two respects. First, apart from his adventurous border crossing, he did not encounter East German government representatives, and second, his visit generated relatively little coverage in the East German media.[47] In order to situate this omission, it is important to recall that the German Democratic Republic (GDR) and the United States had no formal relations at that time. Since the GDR's founding in 1949, the United States had not recognized it as a sovereign state, viewing it as a Soviet-occupied zone and satellite instead. The two countries did not initiate official diplomatic relations until 1974. America's relationship to East Berlin was shaped by its firm alliance with Bonn and depended on Washington's relationship to Moscow.[48] In the eyes of U.S. officials, East Germany was no match for its Western counterpart in strategic, economic, or political significance. Its rigid communist ideology deeply anchored it in the Soviet camp, so that even official cultural contacts between the two countries did not exist before 1966.[49]

Figure 34   Dr. Martin Luther King Jr. speaking to East German and African students from the Humboldt University in East Berlin after his sermons, September 13, 1964 (Siegfried Krüger).

East German party officials, for their part, considered American imperialism the greatest threat to global revolutionary progress since fascism. In step with Soviet ideology, East German propaganda portrayed the United States as the leader of reactionary forces and the declared enemy of the state. However, alongside these official pronouncements, transnational networks connected the two states in a variety of areas, for example, with regard to international church organizations or informal contacts between religious communities.[50] In addition, a rich reservoir of images and perceptions of the United States existed in the GDR that was marked by material desires, intellectual curiosity, and historical legacies of interaction. Such private and intellectual fascination with the transatlantic enemy often stood in contrast to the official party line, although the regime shifted its attitude toward these notions over time.[51] Nonetheless, the "other America," consisting of the downtrodden and the persecuted, had always enjoyed widespread sympathy among GDR decision makers.

In fact, official propaganda often turned representatives of these oppressed minorities, such as African American singer and actor Paul Robeson, into popular heroes. The correspondence between King and Gerald Götting, the chairman of the conservative Christian satellite party in East Germany, the Christian Democratic Union (CDU), shows this process in action. Like Provost Grüber, Götting began writing King in 1963, emphasizing early on that the people of East Germany felt a special connection to him and stood behind him in his struggle against "racist terror."[52] Nonetheless, East German officials failed, for whatever reason, to seize upon the opportunity of King's visit to underscore the image of the "other America." Although certainly well aware of King's imminent arrival, functionaries in East Berlin were either too surprised by the actual course of events or too concerned about the possible political impact of King's words and charisma on their own citizens to exploit his visit ideologically. Above all, they may have feared that King would inspire East Germans to articulate their own dissent using the passive resistance King espoused for the civil rights movement.[53]

It appears, however, that such fears were unfounded because it would be more than twenty years before GDR citizens would employ such tactics in larger numbers. In the shorter term, the repercussions of King's visit were felt primarily in the religious sphere. East German publishing houses thus considered it politically safe to extensively publish texts by and about him in the following years. In this way, these publishers helped incorporate King into official doctrine by insisting that "Christianity and the humanistic goals of socialism" were not opposed to one another.[54] This ideological usurpation notwithstanding, King's writings and actions, as well as his theology, did undoubtedly serve as an inspiration for the East German opposition movement in the long run.[55] Yet the exact ways in which his reception and the civil rights movement of the early 1960s, among a multitude of other factors, contributed to the emergence of a civil society based in East German churches that would eventually bring down the communist regime in 1989 remains to be explored.

Despite the significance King's visit had for contemporaries, only few historians and commentators have reflected on his time in Berlin.[56] His trip to the divided city is largely overshadowed by the private audience he had with Pope Paul VI at the Vatican before his return to the United States, as well as the Nobel Peace Prize he accepted in Oslo in December 1964.[57] King himself, however, went back to the United States certain of the support for his cause among the German people of both the East and West. As he had declared upon accepting his honorary doctor of theology degree, "I shall cherish this moment as long as memory lives. When I go back I will know that we do not struggle alone; that millions are with us."[58] After an East German publishing house adopted his texts, he even stated that he felt "both humbled and honored" to have contributed "in greater Germany" to "the stepping up of the pace, at least in terms of attitudes, in our striding toward that dawning day of [a] world at peace."[59]

In contrast to the East German press and American historians, the contemporary African American press at the time *did* take notice of Dr. King's Berlin visit as a major success and an indicator of the crucial progress Germany had made in race relations since the end of World War II. According to *Ebony*'s description, Germans had literally

> spread the red carpet [and] lavished on [King] one of the most enthusiastic welcomes ever extended to an American since the late President Kennedy

visited the divided city...Twenty years ago, even the wildest imagination could not have envisioned what thousands of Berliners witnessed: a Negro being honored by high German officials, including dignitaries of state and church. But times have changed, and so have the Germans.[60]

Putting it even more bluntly, New York's *Amsterdam News* wrote that King "was treated quite differently than was track star Jesse Owens, who was openly snubbed by Adolph [*sic*] Hitler and his henchmen back in 1936 at the U.S. Olympics in Berlin."[61]

At the same time, the coverage of King's visit failed to raise the issue of racial discrimination of African American soldiers by West German land-lords and in West German restaurants, although the civil rights leader had promised to examine this situation and perhaps even alert the U.S. govern-ment to potential problems in an interview beforehand.[62] In part, this omis-sion was no doubt due to the enthusiastic acceptance King had received while abroad. As the *Baltimore Afro-American* cynically noted, "The thought surely must have crossed Dr. King's mind that while welcomed in Germany, the high wall of American prejudice denies him the privilege of appearing in any of the major pulpits in the South."[63]

King's visit to the front line of Cold War Europe gave him new perspec-tives to draw upon when he continued his civil rights struggle back at home. Just as he had compared America's racial strife with Germany's ideological division when speaking at the Waldbühne, he compared Berlin's Wall with the walls of segregation in the United States. In August 1965, King pro-tested the segregation policies at Philadelphia's Girard College, an all-white boarding school for boys located in an African American neighborhood and surrounded by a stone wall: "At this stage of the 20th century in the city that has been known as the cradle of liberty, the Girard College wall is like the Berlin wall. This wall, this school, is symbolic of a cancer in the body politic that must be removed before there will be freedom and democ-racy in this country."[64]

Although King's prime focus had always been on improving the situa-tion in the United States, he was mindful of the global dimension of the civil rights struggle in his country early on. His visit to Berlin and the com-ments he made there were another demonstration of this.[65] He later invoked this notion not only in his Nobel Peace Prize lecture in Oslo at the end of 1964, when he talked about a "great 'world house' in which we have to live together—black and white, Easterners and Westerners, Gentiles and Jews, Catholics and Protestants, Moslem and Hindu."[66] Shortly before his death on April 4, 1968, he also told one of his aides that "[i]n our next campaign, we have to institutionalize nonviolence and take it international."[67] In fact, at least in the case of Germany, he had already done so.

6

Revolutionary Alliances: The Rise of Black Power

On February 17, 1968, the auditorium of the Technical University in West Berlin was packed. More than 5,000 international guests had come to the divided city to attend the Vietnam Congress, a gathering of intellectuals, activists, and students determined to voice their opposition to the war in Southeast Asia in one of the hot spots of the Cold War. In a variety of plenary sessions, workshops, and demonstrations, international antiwar activists deliberated ways to stop the war effort and establish a global opposition network. One of them was Dale Smith, a delegate of the Student Nonviolent Coordinating Committee (SNCC). In his speech to the congress, Smith reflected on the transformation that the civil rights struggle had undergone since the mid-1960s and offered a passionate plea for a move from protest to resistance: "We have allowed the forms of our protest to be determined by others.... We believe that the war in Vietnam is being waged exclusively against the Vietnamese, but we, too, are its victims.... This is not only a war against the Vietnamese people. It is a war against us and against the bit of humanity that remains to us." As a consequence, Smith called for a greater militancy and resolve, emphasizing the solidarity that citizens of the West should feel with the Vietnamese: "As long as parents in Vietnam cry about their children, the parents in the US should also cry about their children."[1]

Congress participants greeted Smith's words with enthusiastic applause. His hosts, members of the German Socialist Student League (Sozialistischer Deutscher Studentenbund [SDS]), seconded Smith's views with equal conviction. One of its representatives, Rudi Dutschke, a sociology student from the Free University, expressed the same kind of urgency. Exclaiming that "[i]n Vietnam, we are also battered every single day, and that is no image and no phrase," Dutschke argued that this kind of solidarity went beyond mere rhetoric. Just like Smith, Dutschke contended that the war had immediate consequences for the political struggles at home and could possibly launch "a long period of authoritarian world domination from Washington to Vladivostok." Therefore, people should come together to create a "second front" to fight against "global imperialism" as represented by the United States.[2]

The Vietnam Congress displayed a revolutionary alliance between civil rights and Black Power activists and their West German supporters with an explicit global agenda. From the very beginning, African American activists had seen their struggle for racial equality in the United States in international perspective and as part of a larger struggle against colonialism in Africa, Asia, and South America. Organizations such as the NAACP, the Council of African Affairs (CAA), and the National Negro Congress (NNC), in campaigns for human rights and colonial independence, helped to intensify the quest to put an end to oppression around the globe, particularly during World War II and the early postwar years. Yet the Cold War and the emergence of McCarthyism thwarted this aim. Political pressure to present a united, anticommunist front led the NAACP to abandon its international agenda and focus on domestic progress. Public critics of U.S. race relations such as W. E. B. Du Bois and Paul Robeson were dismissed and marginalized, and their ability to travel overseas was hampered by the State Department.[3] Although many African American activists and civil rights leaders only grudgingly acquiesced and continued to look beyond national borders in private, they publicly conformed to the Cold War domestic focus. Finally, in the second half of the 1960s, the Black Power movement was able to break this ideological consensus by popularizing the connection between discrimination at home and oppression and imperialism in the Third World, returning to the debates in the African American community of the interwar years. Dale Smith's articulation of his solidarity and identification with the Vietnamese at the West Berlin congress exemplified this strategy.[4]

The Vietnam Congress marked the climax of another development that had been building throughout the 1960s, as well, beginning with growing German awareness of the American civil rights movement. West Germans had not only learned about the civil rights struggle through high profile events such as the 1964 visit of Martin Luther King Jr. and the general media coverage. German emigrants from the 1930s, tourists, and Germans working in the United States, as well as exchange students, also transported information about developments on the other side of the Atlantic back home.

One such student was Günter Amendt of Frankfurt, who had spent an extended period in Berkeley in 1964 and visited people across the United States. Only a few months after King's visit to Germany, Amendt recounted his experiences in the leftist periodical *neue kritik*. Highlighting the enthusiasm white Northern students had exhibited for the civil rights movement during "Freedom Summer," a voter registration drive and educational campaign for the African American community in Mississippi coorganized by SNCC in the summer of 1964, Amendt noted a shift. In his view, it had become "more than just a race movement struggling for integration." As civil rights activists had come to acknowledge that there was "a close correlation between black skin color and [one's] economic circumstance," they had adjusted their goals so that the movement was now "rooted in a desire for change in American society."[5]

Figure 35 SNCC delegate Dale Smith and West German student leader Rudi Dutschke during the Vietnam Congress in West Berlin, February 17, 1968 (ullstein bild/The Granger Collection, New York).

The mainstream German press recognized this shift as well. The West German weekly *Die Zeit* wrote that, although, formally, "the chains of legal segregation and degradation have been broken... racial separation has de facto remained," manifesting itself in the urban ghettos of the North and the Southern resistance against federal integration laws.[6] Nonetheless, the press hailed the Civil Rights Act of 1964 and the Voting Rights Act of 1965 as major political achievements that would make institutionalized racism difficult to maintain, since this legislation established African Americans as an important constituency in U.S. politics.[7]

Despite these legal advancements, many journalists in the Federal Republic voiced great concern about the rise of violence and the racial tension in American cities, for example, characterizing "[w]hat began as a struggle for the basic rights of blacks" as "becoming a latent war of civil rights."[8] Especially after the riots in Watts, a neighborhood of Los Angeles, in August 1965, and similar racial confrontations in Newark and Detroit in July 1967, German observers feared that the conflict had spun out of control. As one journalist asked anxiously, "Is this another one of those 'hot summers' that have been disturbing the population of the United States sporadically for five years now? Or is it already the open rebellion, the civil war between black and white?"[9]

The rise of Black Power was registered with similar worries in the West German press. As Dr. King was faced with the militant ideology of Malcolm X and the more radical positions of SNCC representatives such as Stokely Carmichael, who became chairman of the organization in 1966, he was perceived as having lost control over the direction of the civil rights movement.[10] Consequently, many journalists expected that the campaign would splinter and drift onto "a collision course" with the political establishment, which would endanger the very idea of racial integration.[11] In sum, the mainstream West German media propagated an image of the United States as a country haunted by its racial problems. Domestic opposition to the war in Vietnam, the emergence of a counterculture, and the availability of the birth-control pill all exacerbated the sense of crisis in the United States, where the racial conflict seemed to be tearing the social fabric apart.[12]

However, from the mid-1960s onward, West Germany had to face some problems of its own. After the establishment of the Federal Republic in 1949, the country had experienced an unprecedented economic boom. Because of the Cold War, the young West German democracy soon found its way back into the international community as a crucial partner in the Western alliance. Domestically, the country was shaped by the fourteen-year reign of Chancellor Konrad Adenauer (1949–1963), who steered the country toward a path of political and social stability. At the same time, however, Adenauer's policies of Western alignment and the specter of the Federal Republic's rearmament propelled by the United States drove substantial numbers of dissenting West Germans onto the streets during the 1950s. In addition, the nation only very slowly came to terms with the legacies of Nazism, and several political and administrative decision makers remained tainted by their questionable past.[13] Furthermore, the country's political culture continued to be influenced by authoritarian notions; for example, its rigid anticommunism led to the ban of the Communist Party in 1956. Similarly, in 1962, the press and the executive branch were provoked only too easily into a showdown concerning what came to be known as the "Spiegel Affair": Defense Minister Franz-Josef Strauss had initiated the unlawful arrest of journalists for alleged treason, thereby overstepping his powers and violating due process. Despite the relative political and social stability of the Adenauer years, these other persistent issues prompted many domestic and foreign observers to wonder, as German philosopher Karl Jaspers phrased it in a widely read book in the mid-1960s, where the Federal Republic was drifting.[14]

In the second half of the decade, West Germans' concerns about the strength of their democracy mounted with the debate about the so-called emergency laws. These threatened to vastly expand executive powers if a vaguely defined state of internal or external emergency should arise. In response, the trade unions, pacifists, and parts of the Social Democratic Party came together in a broad-based coalition to safeguard constitutional rights and to oppose this potential weakening of democracy, which they perceived as similar to the Nazi seizure of power in 1933. They were joined by a small but vocal minority of university students who criticized the lack of democracy in the country's university system. They also lamented a Cold War mentality that stifled domestic political culture and constrained foreign policy. The main organization representing these views was the SDS. Originally the youth organization of the Social Democratic Party, the SDS was expelled by party elders in 1962 and moved closer to the international New Left.

Since the beginning of the 1960s, the SDS and its key representatives had entertained strong connections to their peers in the United States. As a result, the political strategies and techniques of the American New Left and the civil rights movement profoundly influenced them.[15] Karl Dietrich (also known as KD) Wolff, German SDS president from 1967–1968, is a case in point. Having grown up in rural Hesse, Wolff first came into contact with the United States when American troops arrived in Germany in early 1945. It was his encounter with the generosity of a black GI that left the most striking impression on him, as on so many of his generation:

> [A] tank drives into the Schlosshof, the turret with cannon twists around once, and a big black GI with sweat-glistening face jumps down. The mothers, the nannies, the children watch him, keeping their distance. Suddenly, the GI has gum and little bars of Cadbury's chocolate in his hand. Yet we are not supposed to "fraternize"; the mothers hold us children back. I am able to slip under their arms. The GI rolls me an orange, the first one in my entire life.[16]

But Wolff had other direct experiences with American culture and the civil rights movement, as well. As an adolescent, he frequented U.S.-sponsored "America Houses," which provided West Germans of his generation ample access to American literature, and in 1959, he traveled to Michigan as a high school exchange student with the support of the U.S. government's "Youth for Understanding" program. At a local Quaker youth club in Michigan, Wolff learned about the civil rights movement for the first time, as well as about the lunch counter sit-in conducted by four African American students in Greensboro, North Carolina, in February 1960 and the "Freedom Rides" to integrate interstate travel into the South the following year. After his return to Germany, he continued to watch the development of the civil rights struggle, and when he later enrolled at the universities of Marburg, Freiburg, and Frankfurt, he came across the SDS.

At that point, the SDS, in addition to advocating democratic university reform and more freedom in West Germany's political culture, was also becoming a part of the international opposition to the war in Vietnam. Responding to the escalation of the American war effort, it organized anti-war rallies, teach-ins, and conferences with speakers such as German émi-gré and Frankfurt School philosopher Herbert Marcuse in 1965/1966. By the end of 1966, the SDS had established itself as the leading representative of opposition to the Vietnam War in the Federal Republic.

In the meantime, the Berlin chapter of the SDS spearheaded by Rudi Dutschke was gaining more and more ground in the overall organization. Dutschke and others pushed their interpretation of the war as an imperi-alist effort to suppress revolutionary forces and liberation movements in impoverished countries around the world. Faced with this situation, the task of opposition groups in the industrialized countries of the West was to show solidarity with the "Third World" by weakening imperialism from within. In addition to demonstrations, political education, and direct action campaigns, this strategy included reaching out to the domestic opposition in the United States.

Since the mid-1960s, the German SDS had paid close attention to the radicalization of the civil rights movements and its key players. It had not only adopted the protest methods of its African American peers, but also frequently borrowed political ideas and phrases from the civil rights strug-gle.[17] During its national convention in September 1967, the organiza-tion officially declared its solidarity with the rising black power faction in the movement. From the students' perspective, the nonviolent strategy of Dr. Martin Luther King Jr. had been unable to effect meaningful social change for most African Americans since it had failed to overcome fun-damental economic inequities in U.S. society. As SDS member Gerhardt Amendt observed after two months of study in Harlem in 1967, "The suc-cesses of the civil rights movement celebrated in the press have demonstra-bly reached only the small black middle class; they have changed nothing in the living conditions of ghetto residents."[18]

Proponents of "black nationalism" such as Malcolm X, for their part, saw the civil rights struggle in the United States as part of an international class struggle to be waged in solidarity with liberation movements world-wide. With this view, they found immediate support among members of the German SDS. As the organization declared in one of its resolutions at the 1967 national convention,

> The violent struggle of the blacks who conceive of themselves as 'Afro-Americans' in the USA makes the solidarity with the national liberation movements of the Third World concrete. As they create a second Vietnam in the USA itself, their struggle against American capitalism is tied, in practice, to the international class struggle against imperialism.[19]

In the eyes of West German activists, the transformation of SNCC and the call for Black Power illustrated the emergence of yet another front in the battle against U.S. imperialism—this time from within.

Members of the SDS had met key representatives of the Black Power movement not only in the United States during visits or exchange years but also during international conferences. In July 1967, for example, an SDS delegation traveled to London to participate in the congress "Dialectics of Liberation," where they heard Stokely Carmichael speak.[20] Bernward Vesper, a member of the delegation, described this experience, which had a profound impact on him:

> A couple of hours later Carmichael. The auditorium is now black and brown. Dock workers, students. And Carmichael hammers it into them to strike back. "If we have to die, then we will strike back!" And for the first time, I hear: "We are the majority, we, the colored people of the world! We will confront imperialism in its heartland, and if we do not gain the freedom to be humans, we will burn America down from one coast to the other!"[21]

After the congress, Vesper began to publish German translations of Black Power and Black Nationalism literature through his publishing house, thereby supplying a growing demand among his peers.[22] His fiancée Gudrun Ensslin, who would later become one of the leaders of the West German terrorist group the Red Army Faction (Rote Armee Fraktion [RAF]), supported him in these efforts. Ensslin had studied in the United States, was active in the GI desertion campaign in West Germany, and helped with the translation of these texts. Both Vesper and Ensslin understood Black Power as a prime example for the global dimension of revolutionary struggle at the end of the 1960s. In its militancy and determination, they also viewed it as a reference point and role model for their own efforts in the industrialized countries of the West. As Vesper wrote, "the freedom struggle of the colored people of the whole world is also the hope for the whites cut off from their future."[23]

The murder of Dr. King on April 4, 1968, only six weeks after the Vietnam Congress in West Berlin, seemed to confirm the failure of nonviolence and the legitimacy of Black Power. Whereas official obituaries, silent demonstrations, and other expressions of mourning across the Federal Republic emphasized King's achievements for nonviolent social and political change in the United States, West German activists interpreted his murder differently. Despite their previous criticism of King, his killing now became a clarion call for revolutionary action on behalf of his legacy. As Berlin activist Ekkehart Krippendorff proclaimed, "We are the ones who must satisfy his demand for a truly revolutionary change of our society in our own way as well. We have learned from his methods and also from his own insights on the nature of the society in which we ourselves live. The legacy of Martin Luther King is, for us, the continuation of his social-revolutionary struggle with his—but also with our—methods, here in our own country."[24]

The assassination attempt on West German student leader Rudi Dutschke only seven days later lent an even greater urgency to this task. Dutschke's assailant, a struggling loner named Josef Bachmann, claimed that he had been inspired by the murder of King. Among activists, this reinforced the notion that both the civil rights movement in the United States and the student movement in the Federal Republic were exposed to similar threats. This comparison was heavily contested in public. As a local newspaper in Hamburg wrote, "Berlin is not Memphis, and the Federal Republic is not America. Here we do not have a race problem rupturing a whole people with its profound social aspects. Here we do not have the Ku-Klux-Klan or fanatical race opponents on both sides."[25]

Despite these objections, West German activists continued to pursue the coalition with the militant parts of black America. KD Wolff, especially, can be credited for elevating this affiliation to the next level at the end of the 1960s. After his tenure as German SDS president, Wolff went on a lecture tour through Canada and the United States at the invitation of the American SDS in February 1969. In California, he visited the headquarters of the Black Panther Party for Self-Defense in Oakland, as well as its chairman Bobby Seale. There he established a long-lasting relationship with the group that would deepen in the following years through correspondence, mutual visits, and publications in each other's journals.

During his stay in the United States, Wolff had the chance to elaborate on this connection when subpoenaed to a hearing of the Senate internal security subcommittee. Confronted by the infamous segregationist senator Strom Thurmond from South Carolina, Wolff declared the SDS's solidarity with the Black Panthers: "The victories of the movement in the United States are considered our victories...the repression against the radical movement in the United States, which is being stepped up, is repression against us."[26] When he expanded on the persecution of the Black Panther Party in the United States, the officials questioning him asked, in a deliberately provoking and potentially racist manner, whether he was talking about "animal species" or "people." Wolff's answer elicited an enthusiastic response among his many supporters in the audience: "Well, I would like to say one thing to that. I prefer panthers to pigs."[27]

After his return to Germany, Wolff launched the Black Panther Solidarity Committee in Frankfurt in November 1969. The committee became part of the international support network that emerged after one of the party's imprisoned leaders, Eldridge Cleaver, escaped from U.S. custody in November 1968. The Black Panther Party's minister for information, who had risen to national prominence when his prison memoir, *Soul on Ice*, had been published in 1968, had gone on to set up his base in Algiers in 1969, where he headed the party's international section.[28] Within this international solidarity network, Wolff's committee had three major goals:

1. Education about the party's struggles and about the fascist terror of the ruling class in the USA.
2. Agitation and propaganda among GIs stationed in Germany.
3. Material support of the Black Panthers.[29]

In practice, this meant that the committee would produce and sell German translations of key texts of the party both to inform people and collect funds for its cause. It did so through Wolff's publication house "Roter Stern," which disseminated the words of Eldridge Cleaver, the party's cofounder Huey Newton, and others to a West German audience.[30] In addition, the committee organized solidarity demonstrations, film screenings, and went to local high schools educating people about the African American civil rights struggle and the Black Power movement. Wolff also launched a reading group called "Red Panthers," which introduced young blue-collar apprentices and trainees from the region to the texts of the Black Panthers and other literature from the socialist canon.

But it was not only the shared struggle against the war in Vietnam or a general anti-imperialist ideology that connected West German students to the Black Panthers at the end of the 1960s. Another essential feature reflected in these activists' solidarity efforts was the deep disillusionment they felt with the United States. Growing up in postwar Germany, the young generation had welcomed the material benefits of the Marshall Plan in the reconstruction of the country and eagerly embraced American popular culture as part of the U.S. occupation. Whether it was fashion, music, or movies, the American way of life exercised a profound influence, strongly attracting German youth, especially because their parents often viewed it critically. Jazz, GIs, and Hollywood conveyed a new cultural openness and individualism, testing social conventions and traditional hierarchies.[31]

Figure 36 African American exchange students from Lincoln University (Pennsylvania) at a Black Panther solidarity rally at the University of Frankfurt, 1971 (Barbara Klemm, Frankfurt/Main).

Politically, German youth perceived the United States as a force of democracy and freedom, an example for the Federal Republic to emulate. In this positive climate, the rising awareness of Jim Crow racism, bolstered by media representations of U.S. authorities' brutal reactions to integration efforts and civil rights demonstrations in Little Rock or Birmingham, dealt a massive blow to the image of the United States among young people. As one of them recalls, "When one saw that blacks have fewer rights and white Americans come here and tell us that all people are equal before the law, one suddenly had to admit that a considerable contradiction between claims and reality existed."[32]

Their disappointment grew in proportion to the escalation of the Vietnam War, which provoked them to anger, cynicism, and frustration with the seeming hypocrisy of the nation they had admired: America's official portrayal as the leader of the "Free West" in the face of its political actions at home and abroad seemed false. As racial tensions in the United States grew and the conflict in Southeast Asia intensified, the positive image of the American government began to crumble. More importantly, West German activists began to characterize American policy as "fascist," comparing it to Nazi Germany, as one of them recently recalled:

> We voiced criticism that started with the insight that, for example, racism had led to the murder of the Jews in the concentration camps, and one saw that blacks in America were treated brutally like scum, that people had recognized that one had to take sides, and with the blacks, with the civil rights movement and not with the Ku-Klux-Klan or other similar crazies or the American government.[33]

These rhetorical references were applied not just to Vietnam; the legacies of Nazi ideology and the German atrocities during World War II were also apparent in how this young generation perceived the discrimination against African Americans in the United States. During his high school year in Michigan, for example, German SDS president Wolff shocked his American hosts, the local Rotary Club, when, after reciting the pledge of allegiance at a local Boy Scout meeting, he interjected "in a voice shrill with apprehension: 'Except for Jews, Negroes, and all the other nasty foreigners!'"[34]

Dagmar Schultz, another German activist who had spent time living in the United States, where she was active in the civil rights movement in the South in the 1960s, also noted similarities between attitudes in the South and the Nazi past.[35] In a 1965 account, she explained how public reactions to her interactions with African Americans prompted her to compare the situation in the United States to Nazi Germany and made her sensitive toward the notion of "collective guilt." When local police harassed them for their activities, for example, Schultz linked this behavior to the hatred and sadism of personnel in German concentration camps.[36] Reflecting on her experience, Schultz concluded: "The similarities and differences between Hitler's Germany and Mississippi have often been disputed, but one common conclusion is certain: The practice of a system founded on racial dominance has a devastating effect on individuals as well as on humanity in general."[37] In the mid-1980s, Schultz would contribute to raising awareness about the history and situation of blacks and black women in Germany, coediting the first volume on Afro-German identity from a female perspective.[38]

Strikingly, such comparisons to Nazi Germany were also applied in reverse, that is, by the mainstream West German press in more critical evaluations of the Black Power movement. For example, one paper depicted Malcolm X as a "black Goebbels." Another compared a speech by H. Rap Brown, who became SNCC chairman in 1967 and the Black Panther Party's minister of justice the year after, to the rhetoric of the Nazi propaganda minister's total war speech in the Berlin Sportpalast in February 1943.[39] These depictions sometimes converged with racist prejudices and superficial stereotypes rooted in German colonialism, such as characterizations of urban race riots in the United States as a "breakout of the jungle" or portrayals of black people as naturally more emotional and prone to ecstatic and erratic behavior than other people.[40] However, more enlightened observers of African American culture also voiced their opposition to what they perceived as radical excesses in the civil rights struggle under the banner of black nationalism. In 1970, Joachim-Ernst Behrendt, who as a music journalist and producer became one of the most acclaimed authorities on jazz in the Federal Republic, openly accused Eldridge Cleaver and Leroi Jones of propagating an ideology that bore fascist tendencies.[41]

This did not, however, detract members of the Black Panther Solidarity Committee and the radical parts of the West German Left from their position in any way. Their comparison of the German past with current racial discrimination in the United States strengthened their solidarity with Black Power and served as a boost for greater militancy. That way, they not only situated their individual campaigns in a worldwide revolutionary uprising of the suppressed classes but also construed them as a belated resistance to contemporary injustices they deemed similar to the atrocities of Nazism—an attempt to avoid both their own victimization and atone for the sins of their parents. In imitation of the Black Panthers, as well as of revolutionary inspirations such as Che Guevara or Frantz Fanon, some of them came to regard violence as a legitimate tool for individual liberation and empowerment. In their view, the African American minority was an "internal colony" in the United States. The Federal Republic and the transatlantic alliance, on the other hand, were in an "external colonial relationship" that implicated West Germans in the crimes committed by "U.S. imperialism" worldwide. As a consequence, attacking this association and representatives of the West German and U.S. government became political and moral imperatives.[42]

This notion is particularly evident in West German terrorist groups of the 1970s. In June 1970, the RAF—the most well-known of these—published its founding manifesto in the underground newspaper *agit 883,* which featured a black panther alongside a Russian Kalashnikov (later the visual trademark of the group).[43] In its writings, the group also frequently referred to the Black Panthers and even adopted their language, for example, when labeling the police "pigs" (using the English word).[44] Most importantly, however, the RAF admired the outbreak of violence in the urban race riots in the United States and considered it an example for its own actions: "The Afro-Americans and their allies did not weigh the distribution of power of the classes, nor did they count the divisions of the counterrevolution. They did not calculate their chances. They just let themselves go for a moment and turned their violence against their oppressors. In the streets of Watts, they ignited the fire of the revolution, which will not go out before their final victory."[45] In the eyes of the RAF, the Black Panthers became both a role model and partner in what they conceived of as an international revolutionary struggle stretching from Vietnam, Africa, and South America all the way to the industrialized countries of the West.

In addition to these political alliances, German activists' affinity with the African American cause also stemmed from a deep fascination with the "authentic," which white Germans, more generally, saw represented in their concepts of blackness and black culture. Afros, blues, and soul music, as well as a variety of consumer products associated with blackness and frequently advertised with African American models, are just a few of the many examples of cultural items young people in West Germany eagerly identified with in the 1960/1970s.[46] They came to see whiteness as the epitome of reason and conformity, whereas blackness seemed to represent emotionality, fulfillment, freedom, and empowerment. By admiring and emulating black role models, they strove to transcend the constraints of their own society and create a new identity in solidarity with black people worldwide, often projecting their own desires onto African American militants as a result.

This sort of projection is particularly apparent in the case of Angela Davis, who emerged as the undisputed icon of the black power struggle at the beginning of the 1970s, both in the capitalist Federal Republic and in the communist German Democratic Republic. Born in 1944 in Birmingham, Alabama, to African American middle-class parents, Davis established an especially meaningful personal and intellectual association with Germany early on. This began when she became interested in German philosophy through her studies with Herbert Marcuse at Brandeis University. Then, from 1965 to 1967, she studied at the University of Frankfurt with another key thinker of the Frankfurt School, Theodor W. Adorno, as well as his students Jürgen Habermas and Oskar Negt. During that time and through Adorno's seminars, Davis became acquainted with members of the German SDS and also participated in demonstrations against the war in Vietnam. She even traveled to the congress on "Dialectics of Liberation" in July 1967 together with the delegation of the German SDS, after which she decided to return to the United States to support the Black Power movement.[47] In

California, where she continued her studies with Herbert Marcuse, who had moved from Brandeis to the University of California at San Diego, she joined SNCC and eventually the American Communist Party (CPUSA), soon advancing as a leading intellectual representative of black power after being appointed to an assistant professorship at UCLA.

In the course of 1970, her association with the Soledad Brothers, a group of black prisoners at the Californian Soledad Prison in Salinas, brought her international notoriety. Davis had become involved in the defense campaign of the three inmates, who were accused of murdering a prison guard and were facing capital punishment. Davis gave speeches about the California penitentiary system, helped with the legal aid, and met the family of George Jackson, who was one of the inmates. In August 1970, his younger brother Jonathan Jackson entered a Marin County courtroom armed and took the presiding judge, the assistant district attorney, and a member of the jury hostage in an attempt to free three other inmates who stood trial that day. In a subsequent shootout with the police, both hostages and kidnappers died. Soon thereafter, the police ascertained that the guns used in the kidnapping attempt were registered in Angela Davis's name. The authorities immediately indicted her for being an accomplice to criminal conspiracy, kidnapping, and homicide, and issued a warrant for her arrest. Though she was charged in August, she evaded capture for two months—until October 1970—during which she was on the FBI's list of Ten Most Wanted Criminals.

As Davis's former peers in the Federal Republic reacted with shock, anger, and disbelief, Herbert Marcuse fueled these feelings through agitation on her behalf.[48] Only a month after her arrest, Marcuse published a call for solidarity in an Austrian leftist journal, arguing that her story was "the story of a threefold political repression: against a woman, against a militant black woman, against a leftist rebel." Whether or not Davis was guilty, Marcuse stressed, the trial itself would be unjust as "the trial of a society of violence and injustice, of a society responsible for the situation Angela finds herself in today." In his view, she was "fighting for her life," so strong action was needed: "only a powerful protest, a protest that is present everywhere and cannot be stifled, can save her life."[49]

This was exactly the kind of protest Davis's West German supporters had in mind. The Black Panther Solidarity Committee in Frankfurt had started to disseminate informational material on the Soledad Brothers illuminating the background of Davis's indictment as early as September 1970.[50] The committee's strategy was to launch a public information campaign to build up international pressure for her to be acquitted.[51] On November 24, 1970, about a thousand students gathered for a Frankfurt teach-in, where they listened to speeches by KD Wolff and Daniel Cohn-Bendit, among others.

Davis's plight garnered support from more established sectors as well. On December 22, 1970, faculty members of the University of Frankfurt—with the support of the rector of the university—issued a call for solidarity with

Angela Davis, condemning "U.S. imperialism" with surprisingly harsh language. They expressed their concern that she was being

> charged and convicted for her participation in organizing resistance to a system that ha[d], for centuries, subjected the colored population of America to the most ruthless economic and cultural exploitation. Within this system, a hundred thousand murdered Vietnamese serve[d] the same purpose as the feared judicial murder of Angela Davis: the maintenance of rotted, historically obsolete power and privileges.[52]

As this statement shows, the notion that Angela Davis's case represented a concerted attempt by U.S. authorities to criminalize and silence the Black Power movement in a "prefascist" manner underlay most of these efforts.[53]

The Angela Davis Solidarity Committee, founded in May 1971, held this view as well. As a politically independent body, the committee's goal was to coordinate all support campaigns for Angela Davis in the Federal Republic.[54] It provided basic information about Davis's life, her studies with Marcuse and her time in Frankfurt, her work in the African American freedom movement, as well as the upcoming trial. Given Germany's racist history, the committee felt that it had special obligation to shine a light on racial discrimination in other parts of the world: "The German people, especially, have a right to be educated about the ongoing racism in the

Figure 37   On March 13, 1971, women's groups in Frankfurt organized a women and children's demonstration in support of Angela Davis, in which about 200 participants marched to the U.S. General Consulate to deliver a petition (Manfred Tripp/Archiv: Hamburger Institut für Sozialforschung).[55]

world. And precisely those who have made their inner peace with the Jews should consider that their credibility depends on their willingness to fight without compromise against the social causes of racial discrimination, wherever it appears." Solidarity with Angela Davis, according to the committee, not only expressed opposition to a system whose "inhumanity" had been "unveiled by its genocide in Vietnam," but also served as an indicator of whether Germans had come to terms with the Nazi past by testing their readiness to speak out against a supposed return of fascism at home or abroad.[56]

Within this framework, the German past functioned as an interpretative lens through which the struggle of African Americans was displayed for a West German audience. As a consequence, support for Davis was considered just as important for Germany as it was for the United States. A group of activists at the Free University's John F. Kennedy Institute summed up this perceived link between Angela Davis's situation and their own: "In the USA, as in the Federal Republic, we must prevent political organizations from being criminalized and, therefore, liquidated without the need for the state to legitimize its actions, by propaganda campaigns of the state apparatus and the bourgeois press.... The struggle to free Angela Davis is thus directly linked to the struggle for our own democratic rights."[57]

* * *

On June 3–4, 1972, the Angela Davis Solidarity Committee organized a congress "Am Beispiel Angela Davis" (The Example of Angela Davis), which drew more than 10,000 people for the opening rally at the Frankfurt Opernplatz. Once again, the congress participants highlighted the exemplary character of the case, emphasizing that fighting for a fair trial for Angela Davis was tantamount to fighting for democracy at home. In addition to drawing these analogies, the congress also prompted discussion about the legitimacy of violence for social change. Only a few days before the congress opened, key members of the RAF (Andreas Baader, Holger Meins, and Jan-Carl Raspe) had been arrested after a series of terrorist attacks in May. These included bombings at a U.S. military installation in Frankfurt, law enforcement agencies in Augsburg and Munich, the Axel Springer publishing house in Hamburg, the European headquarters of the U.S. Army in Heidelberg, as well an assassination attempt on a federal judge in Karlsruhe, which all together caused the death of four U.S. soldiers and injured seventy-four other people. Therefore, the congress took place in an unsettled atmosphere marked by nationwide searches and media hysteria. This situation transformed a solidarity event for an African American activist into a central forum for discussing pressing domestic concerns, including terrorism, the legitimacy of militant actions, and the state's monopoly on violence in the Federal Republic.

Consequently, the congress "Am Beispiel Angela Davis" was as much a soul-searching of the West German Left at the beginning of the 1970s as it was about the African American struggle in the United States. Despite honest compassion and concerns for her fate, West Germans, in a sense, used Angela Davis as yet another Black Power icon upon which to project the hope of an international revolutionary alliance. As Herbert Marcuse observed in 1969, Davis was the "ideal victim" for this sort of projection: "She is black, she is militant, she is a communist, she is highly intelligent, and she is pretty—and this combination is more than the system can take!"[58] Together with the personal connection she had to the Federal Republic, these features spurred the solidarity movement for Angela Davis in West Germany, which to many observers seemed even more active than that in the United States. However, even these widespread solidarity efforts were no match for the government-orchestrated campaign for the civil rights struggle and the "heroine of the other America" on the other side of the Wall, in communist East Germany.

7

Heroes of the Other America: East German Solidarity with the African American Freedom Struggle

Rising out of the ruins of the Soviet-occupied zone of defeated Nazi Germany, the German Democratic Republic (GDR) was founded in October 1949, a product of the Cold War division of Germany after World War II. By the early 1950s, the Socialist Unity Party of Germany (Sozialistische Einheitspartei Deutschlands [SED]), resulting from a forced merger between the Communist and Social Democratic Parties in April 1946, dominated the political, cultural, economic, and administrative branches of society as well as the media. This one-party rule and the legal framework that was established to support it allowed the regime to control political opposition and the electoral and government system. Although its institutions formally resembled those of a parliamentary democracy, the state apparatus was firmly in the hands of the SED and its various party organizations, led by First Secretary Walter Ulbricht from 1950 to 1971.

As a satellite state of the Soviet Union, East Germany was solidly tied in to the Warsaw Pact system and followed Marxist-Leninist ideology. The state had nationalized major parts of industry, collectivized the agricultural sector, and regulated the economy by means of central planning. It also penetrated and exercised ideological oversight over the cultural sphere and set up a powerful secret police with the Ministry of State Security, which infiltrated nearly all aspects of life in the GDR, monitored the political behavior of its citizens, and relied on a vast network of unofficial informants. A worker's uprising in June 1953 that was quelled with the help of Soviet tanks proved to be the only serious challenge to the SED regime before 1989. Nonetheless, economic standards lagged behind those in the Federal Republic, prompting hundreds of thousands of East German citizens—many of whom were also politically motivated—to emigrate to West Germany by crossing from the East sector to West Berlin before the Wall was built in August 1961.

What followed was a short period of limited political relaxation that found its end with the Eleventh Party Congress of the Central Committee of the SED in 1965, which suspended all forms of liberalization in the cultural and political sphere, subjecting these areas once again to the supreme ideological authority of the party. Subsequent years saw a crackdown on the "damaging influence of Western culture," official East German support for the Soviet invasion of Czechoslovakia in 1968, and Erich Honecker's succession to power in 1971, replacing Walter Ulbricht as head of state.[1]

In East Germany, the African American struggle for civil rights elicited an interest at least as strong as in the Federal Republic. The major difference to West Germany, however, was that the East German solidarity movement was engineered and enforced by the government. Ever since the regime's beginning, the fight against racism was deeply ingrained in East German ideology, with "Rassen-" and "Völkerhaß" (racial and ethnic hatred) explicitly prohibited in the country's constitution and punishable by law. Official sources also claimed that racism simply did not exist in the GDR.[2] Since it perpetuated social hierarchies in addition to those of economic class and prevented the "oppressed" from uniting and rising up against their "oppressors," racism was seen as directly opposed to communism. In the government's ideology, racism, imperialism, and anticommunism were thus intertwined and regarded as enemies of peace and progress. Furthermore, the horrible consequences of racist ideology in German history yielded special obligations for the young communist regime, as one East German scholar noted: "We Germans, especially, whose country under the imperial regime was the starting point of atrocious racial persecution, have a duty to the international workers' movement and all peace-loving forces in the world to take a stand against racism and fight it without compromise." From the East German perspective, this was particularly vital, since West Germany's "imperialism" relied equally on racism for its "aggressive, chauvinistic policies."[3]

Not surprisingly, given this perspective, the situation of African Americans came to the attention of the East German party leaders early on. Already in 1951, a translated petition of the Civil Rights Congress—an American civil rights organization with ties to the Communist Party USA (CPUSA)—to the United Nations on behalf of the black minority in the United States was published in East Berlin.[4] Using this publication to alert East Germans to this issue, the state, following communist dogma, blamed the continued existence of Jim Crow laws on "U.S. monopolies," which, it claimed, maintained racial discrimination "as a means of dividing and weakening the working class," including the use of African Americans as "wage depressers and strikebreakers." In the eyes of East German officials, the unfair and prejudiced treatment blacks received from U.S. trade union organizations was equally responsible for this situation.[5]

Within this framework, the institutionalized racism in the Southern United States gained particular significance due to America's elevated role in the Cold War and the global reach of its political and military power: "The Negro question is not an issue that concerns *only* Americans. It concerns us all because discrimination, oppression, and terror in the domestic policies of a country can lead to the transfer of such methods to other countries and have already done so."[6] For the East German dictatorship, the importance of racial discrimination in the United States, therefore, derived from its interpretation of the German past as much as it did from the imperatives of the present. East German leaders saw the oppression of African Americans in the United States as part of an international class struggle, in which former colonies across the globe were striving for liberation and independence. They thus actively championed what they considered the "other America" of black civil rights activists, focusing especially on those who openly shared their Marxist and socialist convictions or were engaged in international peace activities like the World Peace Congress in Paris in 1949. These voices largely fell silent with the rise of McCarthyism and the submission of civil rights organizations such as the NAACP to an anti-communist Cold War consensus that focused on the domestic rather than the international scene. This offered the regime a welcome opportunity to exploit racial inequality in the United States for propaganda purposes and to gain international stature. Frequently referring to the African American civil rights movement in domestic and foreign policy matters to discredit the Western system of democracy and capitalism, the East German government argued that the racial question in the United States was "a test case for the stronghold of imperialism" that revealed "the whole lie and hollowness" of American democracy.[7] This ideological mindset explains the contrast between the regime's lack of an official reception for Dr. King, who at that point still mostly adhered to the NAACP's consensus, during his 1964 visit in East Berlin and its enthusiastic embrace of other black civil rights leaders, who did not. Moreover, it showcases the stark differences between East and West Germany's ways of taking up the U.S. civil rights issue.

Yet East German solidarity with African Americans also transcended mere rhetoric. In October 1958, the communist German state welcomed W. E. B. Du Bois, who had not only been dismissed by the NAACP in 1948 but was also monitored by the CIA and the State Department for his international criticism of the racial situation in the United States and his political move to the left.[8] After his days as a student at the then Kaiser Friedrich Wilhelm University of Berlin from 1892 to 1894, Du Bois had returned to Germany several times, most notably visiting the country in the summer of 1936, when Berlin was the capital of Hitler-dominated Germany.[9] By the mid-1950s, Du Bois had become increasingly alienated from the NAACP, which he had cofounded, and had developed a profound interest in African liberation movements and sympathies for socialism as a solution to global and domestic divisions of race.

In 1958, at age ninety, Du Bois was honored for his lifelong achievements by his alma mater in Berlin, which had been renamed Humboldt University after the acclaimed German scholars Wilhelm and Alexander von Humboldt. It awarded him with an honorary degree of Doctor of Economics for his "meaningful scholarly accomplishments" and "his outstanding service in the struggle to free African peoples and to maintain world peace."[10] Stressing that "this new, socialist university" in 1958 was very different from the one that Du Bois had attended more than sixty years earlier, Heinz Mohrmann, the dean of the Faculty of Economics who explained Du Bois's merits at the ceremony, noted that "the progressive tradition" had "found a home" there, and that the university was proud to "renew its connection with such an eminent American scholar."[11] East German officials sought to maintain this connection even after this event: they visited Du Bois in his new home in Ghana in April 1963 shortly after his 95th birthday and offered condolences to his widow when he died four months later, laying a wreath at his graveside.[12]

Only a few years later, another African American civil rights activist with ties to the NAACP visited East Germany. Unlike Du Bois, however, he would eventually settle there permanently. Oliver Harrington had gained national recognition in the late 1930s working as a political cartoonist for several newspapers of the black press, including the *New York Amsterdam News*, the *Baltimore Afro-American*, and the *Pittsburgh Courier*. His character Bootsie, in particular, an ordinary African American who encountered everyday racism in American society, became very popular.[13] In 1943, the *Pittsburgh Courier* sent him to Europe as a war correspondent. Accompanying NAACP Executive Secretary Walter White in Italy, Harrington documented the situation of black GIs firsthand and became director of the NAACP Public Relations Department after World War II (See chapter 3, Figure 23). Disillusioned, he left the United States in 1951 and settled in France, where he was part of the African American expatriate community, befriending writers such as James Baldwin, Richard Wright, and William Gardner Smith.

In 1961, Harrington traveled to East Berlin to accept an offer from the Aufbau Publishing House to illustrate a series of German translations of American literary classics. Although critical of the regime's cultural policies, he decided to remain in East Germany for the following three decades of his life, only returning to visit the United States in 1972 and 1991.[14] In East Germany, Harrington worked for Berlin Radio International organizing broadcasts directed at U.S. troops stationed in West Germany. He also came to enjoy particularly high esteem for his skills as a political cartoonist. He specialized in addressing the political situation in America and frequently drew attention to racism, poverty, and imperialism in the world at large. Harrington supplied numerous U.S. and international periodicals with his cartoons, including the *Daily Worker*, the New York-based paper of the CPUSA, the humor magazine *Eulenspiegel*, and the general interest monthly *Das Magazin*, one of the most popular papers in East Germany.

Yet East German connections to African Americans were not limited to intellectual representatives of the civil rights movement. From 1953 to 1963, the GDR accommodated a small group of five black deserters in Bautzen, a medieval city in Eastern Saxony located between Dresden and the Czechoslovakian and Polish border, which became infamous for its penitentiaries where political opponents of the regime were imprisoned. Similar to about forty other American deserters, these five African Americans had left their units by crossing over to the GDR from West to East Berlin in the course of the 1950s before the Wall had been built.[15] Their reasons for deserting varied from having fallen in love to not wanting to be shipped to the front line of the Korean War. The East German government put them up in a "House of International Solidarity," which the *Washington Post* labeled an "espionage, propaganda and sabotage school," where they received German language lessons, political education in Marxism and communism, as well as the opportunity to learn a trade or be trained for industrial labor.[16]

These deserters fared relatively well in East Germany. The first to arrive in Bautzen, Charles Lucas, born in 1916 in Xenia, Ohio, for example, took up a job in a state-owned bakery and became a local boxing star.[17] Arthur Boyd from Long Island got married to a woman from East Berlin and became a metal worker; Raymond H. Hutto from Georgia went on to get his state qualification to work at a coal and gas combine near Dresden; former sergeant Willie Avent even gained the "Silver Pin of the National Front" and became a distinguished member of the "Society for German-Soviet Friendship."[18]

Of the five, the deserter with perhaps the most visible achievements was James W. Pulley, a black GI born in 1936 in Philadelphia, who managed to launch a very successful career as a popular singer. After deserting from his unit in Augsburg to escape to Halberstadt with his East German girlfriend in 1955, Pulley received training as a metalworker in Bautzen and had taken a job as a boilermaker in Görlitz when his singing talent was discovered at a dance event in 1957. In the following years, he went on tour with the Dresden dance orchestra "Black and White" and with East German show stars such as Dagmar Frederic. His repertoire included American songs like "Blueberry Hill" and a variety of pieces from gospel, rock 'n' roll, and Harry Belafonte tunes, as well as German hits.[19]

Although the majority of black deserters integrated themselves into East German society, the authorities and the East German secret police and Soviet intelligence kept a watchful eye on them and their treatment by the local population. In April 1954, a Soviet report drew a first balance sheet of the desertion by American military personnel and their residence in Bautzen in general. It described the situation of the deserters as somewhat isolated from the community and acknowledged difficulties with the political education and professional training program. Furthermore, it stated that local authorities displayed an inattentiveness to their needs and concerns, and that they frequently had to endure racial discrimination.[20] After the fall of the Wall in 1989, the Pentagon—with the help of German authorities—ascertained the names and whereabouts of these Americans but did not press any charges for their evasion of military service.

The East German fascination with the civil rights struggle, however, was not only visible in the warm personal receptions or official propaganda, but was also reflected in the descriptions of African Americans in East German literature of the time. Max Zimmering's poem "Schwarz-weiße Liebesballade" (1949), for example, describes the obstacles a black GI and his white English wife faced after his return to Virginia, a state that still prohibited interracial marriage, following World War II.[21] Anna Seghers's *Der erste Schritt* (1953) chronicles the path to socialism of two African Americans from different social backgrounds. In the story, Pat from Mississippi, the son of a wealthy lawyer, returns home after his military service in World War II only to find Jim Crow segregation still in place in his native town. After being beaten by a white mob ("so that you all don't believe you have become something better because you were in the war"), Pat becomes a socialist.[22] The second protagonist, Richard from Detroit, on the other hand, is a worker in a factory and witnesses how the black employees are pitted against their white colleagues in being used as strike-breakers during a labor conflict. When two white workers who happen to be communist later come to Richard's defense in discussions with the management, he adopts their political persuasion, realizing that they, too, suffer discrimination (for their political views).

Seghers's story, and many other accounts—both nonfictional and fictional—tried to illustrate the link between racism and class-based exploitation and how both were used to maintain an unjust economic and political system. East German works relating to the civil rights movements of the 1960s, such as Wolf Biermann's popular song "Ballade vom Briefträger William L. Moore" (1963), echoed these sentiments. In addition to exposing racial divisions in the United States, however, they also frequently signaled their potential transcendence. All in all, about 250 works—a surprisingly large number—dealing with the situation of African Americans, including translations and academic publications, were available in East Germany by the beginning of the 1970s.[23]

Other cultural products related to the black experience in the United States made their way into East Germany in the 1950/1960s as well, where they were loaded with ideological implications. The most interesting one was jazz. Just as in West Germany, debates about jazz in the GDR always included discussions about race, culture, sexual digressions, and commercialization.[24] Although authorities at the beginning of the 1950s branded all jazz as a Western import, and, thus, discouraged its enjoyment among East Germans, supporters of this musical genre made a fine distinction between "authentic" (such as blues and Dixieland) and "commercial" jazz (like swing, sweet, and bebop). Whereas the former remained true to "black traditions" and outside the mass market, the latter were considered a product of a capitalist music industry and American imperialism; consequently, they were perceived as "decadent" or "degenerate."[25] East German officials, however, were only partially persuaded by this argument, and eventually came to permit musical trends such as blues, Dixieland, and swing.

On the other hand, the regime held African American folk music and spirituals in particularly high esteem. They were considered the truest and most "authentic" expressions of the oppressed. Accordingly, the East German government treated representatives of this music almost like folk heroes. Paul Robeson, one of the first major concert stars who popularized this music internationally, is a prime example of this. Robeson was an actor, intellectual, and activist who spoke out against racism and fascism after World War II and made no secret of his sympathies for the Soviet Union and Russian culture, as well as the African liberation movement. Thus, as a friend of communism, Robeson was invited to participate in the World Youth Festival in East Berlin in 1951. Under the spell of McCarthy-era communist paranoia, the U.S. government had revoked Robeson's passport from 1950 to 1958, which prevented him from attending the event. Nevertheless, he became a widely popular figure in East Germany, even being honored with a concert in absentia for his sixtieth birthday on April 9, 1958, at the Friedrichstadt-Palast in East Berlin.[26]

After the State Department had restored Robeson's passport, he traveled through Europe and the Soviet Union from July 1958 to December 1963, during which time both he and his wife made their way to the GDR. Eslanda Robeson traveled to East Germany in September 1959 while her husband was playing Othello at the Shakespeare Festival in Stratford-on-Avon. She spoke at a rally honoring the victims of fascism in East Berlin, visited the Nazi concentration camp at Ravensbrück, and met with Rosa Thälmann, the widow of German communist leader Ernst Thälmann.[27]

Robeson himself then came to East Berlin in October 1960, where he was regaled with admiration, awards, and honors. He gave several concerts, cheered on by thousands of people. For example, as part of the festivities for his award of an honorary degree of Doctor of Philosophy by Humboldt University, Robeson, overlooking a crowd of thousands of East Germans at Unter den Linden (a boulevard in the center of Berlin) sang "John Brown's Body" and "Ol' Man River" flanked by East German professors. He was also awarded the German Peace Medal by the German Peace Council, the "Großer Stern der Völkerfreundschaft [Great Star of Friendship among the Peoples]" by East German communist party leader Walter Ulbricht, and became a corresponding member of the German Academy of Arts. Helene Weigl, the widow of German writer Bertolt Brecht, presented Robeson with a silk cloth displaying the peace dove from the logo of their theater company Berliner Ensemble. The Free German Youth (Freie Deutsche Jugend, FDJ), the youth organization of the SED, also invited Robeson to a performance of folk songs and dances in his honor before 5,000 people, during which he joined a group of African students from Leipzig on stage, announcing that this was "one of the most moving days of [his] sixty-two-year-old life."[28]

Robeson's visit offered East German officials the opportunity to underline their solidarity with the African American struggle for civil rights and the African liberation movement; they also used the event to discredit the Federal Republic and compare its policies toward black people from the United States

Figure 38 Paul Robeson speaking in front of the Humboldt University to a crowd of East Berliners at Unter den Linden, October 6, 1960 (Zentralbild/Sturm/Bundesarchiv).

Figure 39   Paul Robeson is honored with the "Great Star of Friendship among the Peoples" in silver by Walter Ulbricht, Chairman of the Council of State of the German Democratic Republic, in East Berlin on October 6, 1960 (dpa—Bildarchiv).

and Africa with their own. In a speech honoring Robeson's efforts for global peace, Albert Norden, a member of the Politbüro of the Central Committee of the SED, for example, accused West Germany of condoning apartheid in South Africa and commemorating military generals involved in the Herero and Namaqua Genocide in German South-West Africa from 1904 to 1907 by naming military installations after them. Distinguishing East Germany's solidarity with the "oppressed" around the globe from that of the West, Norden waxed poetic in explaining the reason for the award: "We in the G.D.R.... feel a deep sympathy with all people, no matter what colour skin they have, who struggle for their national liberation and independence and we honour therefore the man who keeps hammering at the chains that still bind 20 million Negroes in the United States and millions of others in Africa."[29]

Robeson himself was overwhelmed by the enthusiastic response he received in East Germany. His visit once again confirmed his belief in the power of socialism to bring about international peace and national independence. At the same time, he did not fail to mention the "many brave fighters in West Germany" who were working "against racial discrimination despite greatest difficulties." Expressing his great admiration for the socialist experiment, he nonetheless maintained that "especially from the vantage point of East Berlin," he considered himself fundamentally American: "I am, as an American, devoted to my land, to the decent traditions of America, and...I am a friend, was a friend, and will always be a friend of the Soviet people and the peoples of the democracies of socialism."[30]

With deteriorating health, Robeson returned to the GDR in September 1963 to be treated at a clinic in East Berlin before returning to the United States at the end of the year. During this visit and thereafter, his friendship with East Germany remained unbroken and continued to be reciprocated by the state.[31] Among his other numerous honors, East Berlin named a street and local high school after him, a Paul Robeson Archive was opened at the Academy of Arts in 1965, and various symposia were held in his honor during the 1970s.[32] Even more than W. E. B. Du Bois, who had also received an honorary degree from Humboldt University in 1958, Robeson thus emerged, in the words of Albert Norden, as one of the most celebrated "black pioneers of humanity" in the GDR.[33] After he died, the honors kept coming. In 1983, he appeared on an East German stamp with the inscription "For Peace Against Racism, Paul Robeson 1898–1976."

Given Robeson's celebrated status, it was a symposium held in his honor that prompted discussions among East German party leaders to strengthen the issue of racism in their overall ideological work.[34] The first opportunity to do so presented itself when Reverend Dr. Ralph Abernathy, by then Dr. King's successor as president of the Southern Christian Leadership Conference (SCLC), visited East Berlin from September 27 to 29, 1971. Abernathy's visit was part of a larger trip of SCLC leaders to communist nations. Before his stay in East Berlin, he had visited Moscow for a weeklong tour of the Soviet Union and, before his return to the United States, would also stop in Prague, Czechoslovakia, for the Christian Peace Conference. Abernathy made the trip, he explained, because he wished to "see Communism in practice" since "the hope of the world rests in coexistence" and "[t]here must be closer ties between people of all nationalities, ideologies and beliefs."[35]

During his 1964 visit to Germany, Abernathy had accompanied Dr. King to West Berlin, where he had spoken at the First Baptist Church in Tempelhof. On his 1971 trip, in contrast, Abernathy visited East Berlin,[36] and East German officials were ready to utilize the visit to full ideological advantage. Together with Reverend Dr. Joseph Lowery of Atlanta and Reverend Dr. Wyatt Walker of Harlem, Abernathy received an extensive welcome by representatives of the East German state.[37] During his two-day stay in the country, he signed the Golden Book of the city, delivered a lecture at the Humboldt University, and gave a sermon at St. Mary's Church.[38] Standing in the very same spot where Dr. King had spoken to the congregation seven years earlier, Abernathy placed his visit to East Germany within a tradition that included the previous visits by Du Bois, Robeson, and King. Abernathy, however, used even stronger language than his predecessors to assail the continuing economic divide and racial discrimination in the United States. Interrupted by roaring applause, he called for the withdrawal of troops from Vietnam, the acquittal of Angela Davis, as well as an end to apartheid in South Africa, freedom for political prisoners, and civil rights for blacks in America:

> It would be good news for the world, if it could go out from Marin County in California that Angela Davis is free. [*Applause*] It would be good news for the world if we could read in the headlines that the United States of America was not spending 30 billion dollars to send somebody to the moon, but was giving 30 billion dollars to South Africa to get rid of racism and inequality. [*Applause*] It would be good news, the best news, to the world if the United States of America would free all political prisoners and let the black people enjoy the blessings of our democracy. [*Applause*][39]

With such severe criticisms of the United States, Abernathy easily endeared himself to the state apparatchiks, who eagerly incorporated him into their propaganda campaigns.[40]

Figure 40   Reverend Dr. Ralph Abernathy on his way to the Humboldt University in East Berlin together with Reverend Dr. Joseph Lowery and University Rector Professor Dr. Karl-Heinz Wirzberger on September 28, 1971 (Zentralbild/Mittelstädt/Bundesarchiv).

Following his sermon, Abernathy was awarded East Germany's "Medal of Freedom" during a dinner with dignitaries of the state.[41] Albert Norden's congratulatory speech at this event gave the regime the opportunity to drive its ideological message home: Norden honored Abernathy as a "close friend and comrade-in-arms," explaining East Germany's continuing support for the African American civil rights struggle as motivated, in part, by the German past: "We are against racism because it is an exponent of the war of aggression, which claimed the lives of 20 million Soviet citizens, 6 million Polish people, and many other people by 1945." He expanded on this comparison by professing that the people of the GDR considered the U.S. government and the Pentagon the "heirs of Hitler" due to the war in Vietnam and the exploitation and suppression of its black citizens. In his view, the struggle of the "other, better America" thus deserved the prominent place that it occupied in the kindergartens, universities, and mass media in East Germany, which, in contrast to the United States, had succeeded in eradicating racist ideology within its borders.[42]

With such strong ideological statements, it was impossible for Abernathy not to become embroiled in political controversy about this visit in the United States. Although he avoided commenting on these references to fascism, he did tell his hosts that he was "filled with joy" and "moved to tears" by his medal, which he vowed to wear "in prison and fighting in the streets" in order to prove to "be worthy of this honor."[43] He also promised to advocate for the international recognition of East Germany after his visit and explained that he would leave the country "knowing that in the German Democratic Republic we have countless numbers of friends who will help us to free Angela Davis and to solve the problems of racism, poverty, and war in the world."[44] Predictably, conservative commentators in the United States dismissed Abernathy's statements in East Berlin, turning around the references to Nazism to direct them at East German officials themselves. As William Buckley Jr. put it, "[i]t is as if the American director of the Anti-Defamation League had taken a decoration from Hitler, and pledged himself on his return to America not to let Hitler down in the fight for race relations."[45]

Despite the success of Abernathy's September 1971 visit, however, a much broader, state-funded campaign for Angela Davis already overshadowed it in terms of importance for the regime's ideological purposes. Only a few days before Abernathy's arrival, about 700 students and young people had assembled at the Humboldt University to express their solidarity with Davis as part of the international "Day of Action for Angela Davis" the next day. As a telegram from this meeting to the New York Committee to Free Angela Davis stated, "The youth of the German Democratic Republic raise their voice of protest against the terror justice of the USA, which has held the upstanding communist and patriot Angela Davis behind bars for twelve months."[46]

Events like these were embedded in the regime's nationwide push to mobilize solidarity for Angela Davis, whom it portrayed as the heroine of the "other America" alongside W. E. B. Du Bois, Paul Robeson, and Martin Luther King, among all segments of East German society. On Davis's twenty-seventh birthday on January 26, 1971, for example, about 2,000 Berliners assembled in a congress hall at Alexander Square, carrying banners and chanting slogans such as "Freedom for Angela Davis," "Pluck Angela from Death by Gas," or "Imperialism = Death of Peoples."[47] In preparation for this event, the FDJ, endorsed by the communist party, called for a comprehensive public solidarity campaign with the theme "A million roses for Angela Davis, which became one of the signature features of East German support for Davis.[48] In February, a group of prominent East German officials, academics, athletes, writers, and actresses published a call to solidarity entitled "Save Angela Davis!" The signatories declared that Davis represented "the best traditions of America" and, referring to political persecution under National Socialism, charged that her trial constituted an attempt to frame her that was indicative of the "growing fascist tendencies in American life."[49] Members of "Free Angela Davis" committees in the United States, such as visiting professor Wallace Morgan or Fania Davis, Angela's sister, also spoke at official solidarity events in East Berlin and across the country.[50]

All of these events were planned and discussed by the Central Committee of the SED, which also coordinated how they were to be represented in the East German media.[51] Still without diplomatic relations with the United States, the East German regime hosted various representatives of U.S. peace organizations and the CPUSA during Davis's trial, seeking to underline its principled support of her cause and trying to commit these groups to advocate for official international recognition of the GDR.[52] It also went to great lengths to negotiate an arrangement with the American government whereby the editor of the East German party newspaper could cover Davis's trial firsthand in California. Alongside his articles, a whole host of other publications, songs, and radio plays about Davis was made available to the population as the solidarity campaign was augmented toward the beginning of her trial in January 1972.[53] Perplexed by the intensity of this campaign, *Time* magazine concluded that the country was "deeply in the grip of Angelamania."[54] East German citizens signed petitions on Davis's behalf, collected "solidarity donations" for "Free Angela Davis" committees in the United States, and children painted "sunflowers for Angela Davis." Youth clubs and workers' teams were named after Davis, and schools sent solidarity postcards to her in prison, as well as protest letters to President Richard Nixon and Governor Ronald Reagan of California.[55] One child later remembered the impression of the crucial importance this campaign had for him and the country at the time:

> With burning hearts, we painted bright postcards in school, always signed with the demand for President Nixon: Freedom for Angela. The cards were then collected with the assurance of our teachers that all of them would be

sent to the White House. We were convinced of the justness of the cause she was fighting for, without really knowing the circumstances that had led to her arrest. ... About a year later, it became clear that my postcard must have had an effect. Angela Davis was freed on account of my protest and others around the world.[56]

Shortly after news of her acquittal on June 4, 1972, in a San José court room reached East Germany, Erich Honecker himself, as the newly appointed first secretary of the Central Committee of the SED, congratulated Davis via telegram, stressing the unconditional solidarity East Germans continued to feel for her: "Your name, dear Angela, has become a symbol of the struggle against imperialist caprice and oppression. Your courage and steadfastness as a communist and as a representative of your country's African American population have made you a shining role model for the youth."[57]

Only a few months later, Davis went on a tour through Eastern Europe and the Soviet Union to express her gratitude for the international solidarity campaign this part of the world had waged on her behalf. While studying in West Germany, Davis had already visited East Berlin once in May 1967. Her 1972 reception in East Germany, however, was marked by mass rallies with thousands of people, by meetings with government officials, as well as tours through the country's universities and industrial centers. Günther Jahn, first secretary of the Central Council of the FDJ, characterized the warm atmosphere for this fellow communist and

Figure 41   Angela Davis with first secretary of the Central Committee of the East German communist party Erich Honecker, East Berlin, September 11, 1972 (Bundesarchiv/Peter Koard).

representative of the other America as follows: "In the country of Kant and Hegel, whose philosophy Angela Davis has studied, in the country of Schiller and Goethe, whose works Angela Davis has read in the original language, in the liberated homeland of Marx and Engels, millions of hearts are beating for her and her American comrades."[58] During her stay in the GDR from September 10 to 17, 1972, Davis received an honorary degree from the Karl-Marx University of Leipzig, was granted honorary citizenship in the city of Magdeburg, and spoke with border guards at the Berlin Wall. Just like Paul Robeson in 1960, she was awarded the "Great Star of Friendship among the Peoples" by Walter Ulbricht, then chairman of the Council of State of the GDR.

In response to all these honors, Davis explained that she admired East Germany and stressed the power of solidarity among the socialist nations. She emphasized that she felt like she was in a "completely new dimension of space and time" that foreshadowed a progressive and just order: "We find ourselves, indeed, in a new historical era, when we compare life in the socialist countries with that in the United States. We see here what it means for the working class to wield the power."[59] When meeting with Erich Honecker, Walter Ulbricht's successor as East German communist party leader, she extended greetings from the CPUSA leadership and praised the defeat of racist and fascist ideology in her host country, which she regarded as "one of the greatest achievements of the working class and the SED of Germany." She praised the party for having "overcome the racial prejudice resulting from Hitler's brutal master race ideology by which the German people were corrupted" and for planting "the seeds of international friendship in the hearts of the people."[60] Accordingly, in her thanks to the East German people for their support and letter campaign, Davis also highlighted that the international solidarity among the socialist countries had played a major role in her acquittal, which to her was "a victory of proletarian internationalism and the class solidarity of the workers of the world, which, in the court room of San José was achieved by the efforts of many people."[61]

Davis's perfectly orchestrated visit in 1972 turned her into a communist superstar in the GDR. It also pleased East German officials who kept a watchful eye on the overall reception and evaluation of her visit among the population across the country.[62] In addition, they used her sojourn to strengthen their relationship with their communist peers in the United States. The movie "Angela Davis besucht die DDR" (Angela Davis Visits the GDR) produced by East German television was even supposed to be used by the CPUSA as campaign material in the 1972 U.S. elections. To generate funds for the CPUSA, the regime also produced a photo postcard with Davis's autograph that was sold through the branches of its youth organization.[63]

Davis returned to East Germany only one year later at the invitation of Erich Honecker and as the head of the American delegation for the Tenth World Festival of Youth and Students in East Berlin. The

Figure 42   Angela Davis arrives in East Berlin, where she is enthusiastically welcomed by Erika Havemann (née Berthold), daughter-in-law of renowned East German dissident Robert Havemann, September 11, 1972 (Archiv/Berliner Verlag).

festival, which was labeled "Red Woodstock" or "Summer of Love" retrospectively, brought more than 25,000 foreign guests, youth and student groups to East Berlin from all around the globe. Under the slogan "For Anti-Imperialist Solidarity, Peace and Friendship," the organizers held about 1,500 events (seminars, mass demonstrations, concerts, etc.) between July 28 and August 5, 1973. During these nine days, the GDR presented itself to the world as an open, progressive, and tolerant society. The secret police had given orders to show "a maximum of generosity" with regard to political actions by foreign delegations that departed from official East German doctrine. This sudden liberalization and permissiveness concerning appearances and musical choices surprised the domestic youth.[64]

For Honecker, the festival served as a test case for his policy of "controlled opening," whereby he sought to gradually expose the East German population to foreign influences again and lobby for international recognition of the sovereignty of the GDR.[65] Behind the scenes, state authorities had carefully planned to ensure security during the festival. Among other things, they had preemptively been arresting and prosecuting potentially subversive, previously convicted, and mentally ill people since the beginning of the year.[66] This mixture of superficial thaw and continued domestic control turned out to be a viable strategy for the East German leadership in the following years.

Given these circumstances, Angela Davis's appearance at the festival was used even more extensively for propaganda purposes than her previous visit and boosted what the U.S. Department of State described as "a colorful propaganda feather in [the] hat of [the] East German regime in general and Erich Honecker in particular."[67] Greeted by chants of "Angela, Angela," she gave a passionate speech for international solidarity at a major outdoor rally on Alexander Square and was the star at many other events. East German officials lauded her presence and performance at the festival, in particular her strong support for the policies of the Warsaw Pact and her criticism of the U.S. role in Vietnam. Davis herself credited the event as being one of the "three unforgettable experiences in her life" next to her entry into the Communist Party and her release from prison.[68]

Despite all the criticism directed at Davis for her association with the reviled East German regime, the connection between Davis and the communist country remained strong. In 1975, she helped cofound the U.S. Committee for Friendship with the German Democratic Republic.[69] In the following years, East Berlin continued to strive for an alliance with African American civil rights and black power activists. These efforts also deepened its relationship with the CPUSA and helped denounce the U.S. "imperialist" policies on a domestic and international level. Subsequent efforts on behalf of African American solidarity, as in the case of Benjamin Chavis and the "Wilmington Ten," however, did not come close to reaching the intensity and breadth of the campaigns orchestrated for Davis at the beginning of the 1970s.[70]

Nonetheless, the impact of the East German drives for solidarity with the civil rights struggle since 1945 *were* felt in the United States and abroad. When the regime invited sixteen African American editors and publishers, most of whom were neither self-described socialists nor communists, for a ten-day stay in East Germany in May 1975, it was able to make a lasting impression on them. Having met with leading party officials and Oliver Harrington, who was a friend to several members of the delegation, the visitors were particularly surprised by the public status leading representatives of the African American community enjoyed in their host country. One of them even listed several such figures and the high regard East Germans had for them after his return: "Paul Robeson won their hearts as a singer and worker for peace. Angela Davis has been adopted as a folk heroine by the students because of her fight for the downtrodden, and Dr. Ralph Abernathy... is prominently recalled. All are household names in the GDR. Their pictures are frequently seen, especially Robeson's and Angela's."[71]

*   *   *

The East German solidarity with African American civil rights has to be understood within the larger context of the state's intentions: stemming

from official doctrine, it was part of the antiracist and anticolonial component of the state's socialist ideology. Furthermore, as an expression of international solidarity with "the oppressed," it provided a connecting point to
the efforts of the CPUSA and its representatives; it could draw on black civil
rights activists' potential interest, sympathy, and commitment to communism, most prominently in the case of W. E. B. Du Bois, Paul Robeson, and
Angela Davis. At the same time, East German officials used this solidarity to distance themselves from West Germany and to discredit the United
States by pointing to the failures and hypocrisies of these Western capitalist, liberal democracies and the whole system of international alliances of
which they were a part. Consequently, the displays of solidarity with the
cause of African American civil rights became a fundamental ideological
tool for East Germany in the propaganda battles of the Cold War.[72]

In the course of the 1960s, the image of the United States as the imperialist, transatlantic enemy thus found its equal complement in an alternative
America of protest and resistance. Next to the antiwar movement, it was
the civil rights and Black Power movements that dominated this picture and
came to infuse popular East German culture. This ambivalence between
admiration of and solidarity with the "other" America, on the one hand,
and profound criticism and Marxist-Leninist rejection of the fundamentals
of U.S. economic and political structures, on the other, not only spurred
American studies in the GDR but also became one of the country's most
palpable features—and remains one of its most lasting legacies in popular
consciousness to this day.[73]

East Germany's solidarity with the African American civil rights struggle, however, cannot overshadow the fact that the GDR was hardly a society
free of racism and xenophobia. These were not exclusively West German
phenomena or "imports," as East German officials maintained, or as urban
legend after the collapse of the regime in 1989 would have it. Rather, xenophobia in the GDR had a unique quality that stemmed, among other things,
from the dominance of antifascism as an all-encompassing ideological
umbrella for the communist system and its silence about the Holocaust as
part of its politics of memory with regard to National Socialism. Antifascism
and a Marxist-Leninist view of history became the integrative framework
that allowed East Germans to project individual guilt and responsibility
onto leading figures of the Nazi dictatorship or externalize them to West
Germany. The failure to acknowledge and address personal involvement
and the country's historical continuities with a criminal regime prevented
East Germans from engaging in a thorough debate and coming to terms
with the anti-Semitic and racist crimes of the German past.[74]

Ideologically, racism and xenophobia were discouraged and suppressed
in the GDR. Given the SED's supreme control over the public sphere, these
social problems were thus not always clearly visible phenomena. Yet for the
people who suffered from their effects, such as Afro-Germans, foreign students, workers, visitors, or refugees from Africa and Asia, they were noticeable and well-known facts that would eventually rise to the surface and

reach a new quality with the emergence of right-wing extremism in the late 1980s and after German unification, when both the Eastern and Western parts of the country experienced a series of xenophobic attacks.[75]

Consequently, African Americans visiting or residing in East Germany after 1945 were well aware of these prejudices. The internationally renowned concert singer Aubrey Pankey, for example, who lived in East Germany from 1954 until his death in 1971, complained about an "unfortunate instance of Jim Crow" he experienced in the GDR. In 1959, he was invited to perform in a program of American music directed by the U.S. conductor Earl Robinson at East Berlin's State Opera. Among the many other parts that were available, Pankey had been asked to play the minor role of a black preacher, a request he believed was based on his race. In his eyes, this was the sort of proposal for which "in any other country," even in the United States, "an immediate protest would be forthcoming from all progressive people."[76]

Alfred Kurella, director of the Cultural Commission of the Politbüro of the Central Committee of the SED, was equally upset about this suggestion and promised Pankey an immediate investigation. He apologized for this form of racial discrimination, which, in his view, was based on East German "pseudosympathies" with blacks.[77] In a letter to his colleague Albert Norden, Kurella went even further, alleging that "behind the very loudly proclaimed propaganda for the 'poor Negro'" and his "culture" that certain people propagated, there actually lay "a racial hatred with inverse indicators."[78]

Along the same lines, Oliver Harrington characterized this disjunct between official doctrine and everyday reality as a "special condition" for the "hidden" and "undercover" racism in the GDR. In 1991, he argued, for example, that living in East Germany, he was "insulted on the streets on an average of about 5 times a day."[79] Testimonies like these do not lessen the impact of solidarity efforts launched by the GDR on behalf of the "other" America. Yet, they help to contextualize them in a larger perspective on the nature of the regime's striving for international recognition, its internal dynamic, as well as its policies and traditions, much of which remains the topic of future research.

The revolutionary alliances that emerged between civil rights and black power activists with East and West Germans in the 1960/1970s were in many ways different: one was a government-sponsored solidarity campaign firmly rooted in an unfree state's ideology and propaganda, whereas the other one was driven by students and intellectuals identifying with Black Power in opposition to their own government and its transatlantic partnership. What the campaigns on both sides of the Iron Curtain shared, however, was an extensive use of the Nazi past as a driving force for their efforts, as well as elevation of the civil rights struggle to the realm of international politics in the Cold War. Although the campaigns had unique agendas of their own, both of them, along with their domestic repercussions, are thus an integral part of the global dimension of the African American journey for equality and freedom.

8

A Call for Justice: The Racial Crisis in the Military and the GI Movement

Although the racial crisis of the late 1960s and early 1970s brought upheaval to U.S. military bases across the globe, the most extensive interaction between African Americans and local civilians took place in Germany. This fact once again underscores the close interconnectedness of German and African American history. Politicized black GIs—and African American veterans who had decided to make Germany their home after they were discharged from the military—like German students were appalled by America's war in Vietnam and the failure of the civil rights agenda and increased their protest activities tremendously. Radical German student activists hoped that an alliance with these African American GIs and veterans would make possible a transnational revolutionary movement. Such a movement would be powerful enough, they believed, to unseat the centers of the "American military empire" in both Germany and the United States and, thus, push forward the freedom struggle in the United States and the liberation movements in the Third World.

In fact, only a small number of the 30,000 African American GIs stationed in Germany and a minority of student activists would form this revolutionary alliance, which lasted a little over two years (late 1969–1972). Though small, and transient, given that the soldiers were usually stationed in Germany for a limited time, this transnational and cross-cultural collaboration had repercussions at the highest level of government, in both Germany and the United States. The agitations of these soldiers and students substantially contributed to what the Black Caucus in the U.S. Congress called the "New American Revolution" in the U.S. military—the American government's response to the unfolding events.[1]

The 1970/1971 Racial Crisis in the Seventh Army

The unusual alliance of black GIs and German students was made possible because of the poor state of the U.S. Army Europe (USAREUR), also known as the 7th Army. Although considered the backbone of the North Atlantic Treaty Organization's (NATO) defense strategy in the Cold War struggle with the Soviet Union, the 7th Army had been used by the Pentagon as a reserve for materials and personnel for the Vietnam War. By 1970, the 7th Army in West Germany was close to collapse, lacking 50 percent of majors and 37 percent of captains and lieutenants. Just one lieutenant colonel, one major or captain, and eighteen to twenty lieutenants led whole battalions.[2] Exacerbating this leadership crisis was the high turnover rate of officers caused by the personnel demands of the Vietnam conflict; some officers were reassigned after just four months.[3] This practice undermined any sort of continuity in leadership and unit cohesion. General Michael Davison of USAREUR admitted after the worst of the crisis had passed that "we had to wreck the 7th Army to keep Vietnam going."[4]

Deteriorating living conditions in crumbling military barracks, many of them built during the late nineteenth century or under the Third Reich, aggravated an already tense situation. The *Los Angeles Times* painted a grim picture of it: "Bats in the billets, flooded basements, clogged plumbing and flaking walls," were not unusual, and soldiers contrasted their own miserable surroundings "with the clean and pleasant barracks German troops enjoy" on their bases.[5]

Between the bad living conditions and the gaps in the command structure, unprecedented discipline and morale problems arose.[6] At military roll calls, soldiers at times greeted commanders with the cry "FTA" (F--k the Army); in some instances, they lobbed grenades into commanders' offices; and unit-wide incidents of insubordination were regularly reported.[7] On all military bases, underground newspapers—such as the *Baumholder Gig Sheet* (Baumholder), *Graffiti* (Heidelberg), *Speak Out* (Hanau), *Venceremos* (Frankfurt) and *Forward* (Berlin)—emerged to provide outlets for the widespread anger of soldiers. One frustrated soldier gave voice to the sentiments of many at the time when he summed up the situation: "We, the unwilling, led by the incompetent, perform superfluous duties for the ungrateful military."[8] That West Germany served as a deployment base to Vietnam and also as a way station for returning GIs to cool off before heading stateside did not help morale.

Brutalized by the Vietnam War, and alienated by the mind-numbing military drills and the boredom of army life in West Germany, white and black soldiers increasingly turned to alcohol or drugs. Military studies showed that drug use among GIs stationed in West Germany was even higher than that of soldiers in the United States; only GIs in Vietnam had higher consumption levels. Drinking alcohol to excess was an even bigger problem than drugs, and by 1972, the military operated some eighty-four detoxification centers in West Germany.[9] Not surprisingly, crime rates among American GIs also exploded. In 1971, American GIs committed 2,319 violent crimes against German civilians, an increase of 75 percent over 1969.[10] American observers and German commentators agreed that German communities surrounding military bases were increasingly subject to a "reign of terror."[11]

Certainly, a major factor in escalating this crisis within the military was the racial tension aggravated by developments in the United States. After the widely perceived failure of the liberal civil rights movement, and especially after the murder of Dr. Martin Luther King Jr., the mood among black enlisted men had reached a boiling point. But the mood was also tense among white GIs. Many of them resented the emergence of the Black Power movement and expressions of black pride—the elaborate handshakes or "dabbing" that black GIs had developed, the Afro hairstyles, the demonstrative Black Power Salute (or "power checks" as the GIs called it), the carrying of soul sticks, and the insistence that soul music be played at clubs for servicemen. In some spectacular instances, white GIs organized Ku Klux Klan gatherings and burned crosses in front of barracks where black GIs lived.[12] Black soldiers, inspired by the Black Panther Party for Self-Defense, responded by organizing militant self-defense groups. By 1970/1971, dozens of these had been founded on U.S. military bases across West Germany.[13] Among the most important were the Black Action Group (Stuttgart), Black United Soldier (Karlsruhe), Black Defense Group (Karlsruhe), United Black Soldier (Heidelberg), Unsatisfied Black Soldier (Heidelberg), and Blacks in Action (Mannheim).

Though plagued by the crumbling infrastructure of its bases, the rise in crime, as well as drug and alcohol abuse, USAREUR admitted that the racial crisis and tensions between whites and blacks presented the greatest challenge. Said one white noncommissioned officer (NCO) in Germany: "Race is my problem, not the Russians, not Vietnam, Jordan, nor maneuvers. I just worry about keeping my troops—black and white—from getting at one another."[14] Unfortunately, effective military leadership for dealing with this racial crisis was sorely lacking. Not only had the Vietnam War decimated its command structure; the military had also failed to train its commanders in handling the more assertive and militant African American soldiers then being drafted.[15]

As racial strife between white and black GIs increasingly spilled out from military bases into the surrounding communities, Germans looked on with dismay.[16] Interior spaces of German bars and discotheques were routinely demolished when black soldiers tried to enter places that white soldiers had traditionally claimed as their own. It is true that such confrontations had happened in the past as well, but not to the degree that had become the norm. Romantic relationships between African American GIs and white German women further stoked existing tensions. The combination of too much alcohol and the competition over access to local women and off-base entertainment facilities often proved explosive.[17]

A Most Unusual Alliance

Yet this was not all there was to it. A glance at German or American newspapers of 1970/1971 would easily lead one to conclude that alcohol, drugs, and women were the root of most of the racial strife on and near bases between white and black GIs.[18] However, since some German students reached out to collaborate with African American GIs, their grievances could be heard outside of the often sensationalist media coverage of the garrison towns, providing us with a much more differentiated picture of the racial crisis.

Chapter 6 detailed how German student activists adopted the ideas and tactics of the civil rights movement during the 1960s and how many of the more radical activists became enamored with the Black Panther Party for Self-Defense after 1967. This theoretical engagement with the ideas of the Black Panther Party became praxis when the students, as part of their protest against the Vietnam War, organized a campaign in late 1967 to convince both white and black GIs to desert their posts in Germany.

At its national convention, the German Socialist Student League (SDS) had officially established that American military installations in the Federal Republic were legitimate targets for protest activities.[19] Adopting GI-organizing techniques used in the United States, the German student activists began to approach American soldiers in local bars or reach out to them with flyers in English, which they distributed in front of military barracks, in bars frequented by GIs, or by placing them on cars with military license plates. In October 1967, a small rocket was even used to disperse flyers advocating desertion over an American military installation in West Berlin. Providing detailed contact information, the flyer asked: "Are you sure you'll survive Vietnam? Play safe! [sic] Don't let them send you there! Your government cannot defeat a people fighting for national independence. We offer you a safe place in Canada, Sweden or Denmark."[20]

African American soldiers occupied a particular place in this desertion campaign and in the GI-organizing efforts. U.S. officials noticed as early as October 1967 that "[f]or the first time strong racial appeals were made to negro soldiers" by antiwar activists.[21] The Republican Club at the University of Mannheim, an association of left-leaning intellectuals and students, for example, specifically tried to reach out to African American soldiers by highlighting the similarity of discrimination against them. Claiming that "the governing system in our society is going to act against us similar to the way they act against Afro-Americans in the states," the club solicited the cooperation of black GIs, invited them for discussion, and reprinted Black Power texts to be distributed among them.[22]

Some German activists later recalled that the desertion campaign first made them aware of the revolutionary potential black GIs presented. While the Vietnam War had politicized and radicalized both white and black soldiers, African Americans, the students surmised, had felt the contradictions of fighting this war more poignantly given their own subjugation in the United States. Student activists were convinced that black GIs, in their role as soldiers for the U.S. military, had learned that "the only freedom they were defending in Vietnam was the freedom to be exploited" and the freedom to "serve as the bull's eye for every racist police pig" once they returned home.[23]

Black GIs who spoke out against the war confirmed much of the students' assessment of the situation. As one said,

> Why should I go to Vietnam? You know they are turning over buses on kids, blowing up churches, little kids getting runned [sic] over. Why should I be willing to give up my life for somebody 14,000 miles away, and when I come back, I am treated worse than those people 14,000 miles away. For what? What would really come out of it?...Once I get back [to the United States], I am just a nigger on the street, and that is that.[24]

Another black soldier, recently returned from Vietnam, told a German newspaper: "We see the army on a whole different basis. All I can see is that the black man is used as a symbol for free America. Whenever we got a parade or something, you got the black man out front to show equal rights of man or something. It's bullshit." He also exhorted other black men to stop fighting in the U.S. military because they were doing "to other people around the world" the "same thing that [was] happening to our people at home."[25] Other GIs bitterly insisted that they had no reason to be fighting in a white man's army and in "a white man's war" and that their "place was back in the States: New York, Chicago, Atlanta, Detroit, Jacksonville, where they could fight to liberate and free their black sisters and brothers from the dirty stinking, teeming ghettos and from all forms of racial bigotry and oppression."[26] One young black sergeant expressed the same idea more succinctly: "I've bled for my country way off in the Nam. Now, if need be, I'll bleed for myself—for my people."[27]

Disaffected GIs like these were the ones German students reached out to. At the center of much of this effort was the Black Panther Solidarity Campaign organized by KD Wolff and described in chapter 6. Aside from trying to forge an alliance between white German students and the Black Panthers in the United States, KD Wolff was also intent on organizing a revolutionary alliance with black GIs stationed in Germany. Wolff and his compatriots in Frankfurt regularly joined black GIs on the bases to participate in Black History study sessions or reading groups focused on the Black Panthers. German women students who were dating black GIs also helped to make connections. Female student activists, called "brides of the revolution," were also instrumental; they would forge contacts with black GIs at discotheques, asking them to dance and then involving them in political discussions on the war in Vietnam and the Black Power struggle. Students also invited the GIs to rallies and demonstrations at which representatives of the Black Panther Party that they brought to Germany would speak.

The collaboration that would emerge—based as it was on an alliance between white, middle-class German students and radicalized African American GIs, often from disadvantaged economic backgrounds, was indeed most unusual. Despite heady excitement, and constant reiterations of revolutionary class and race solidarity among its participants, the alliance

Figure 43 Elbert "Big Man" Howard gives a speech at a Black Panther solidarity rally in Frankfurt (on the right: former German SDS President KD Wolff), 1970 (Barbara Klemm, Frankfurt/Main).

was fraught with problems from the beginning. Not all black GI activists, for example, believed in aligning with white activists,[28] and German students, no matter how idealistic their goal, "instrumentalized" the black GIs. To them, Black Panther GIs presented novel forms of masculinity and a revolutionary authenticity that their own privileged middle-class upbringing could not provide them. Thus, the student activists relied on this alliance because they believed that their intimate, face-to-face encounters with African American GIs would make abstract ideas such as international class and race solidarity immediate and real. These students hoped that enacting solidarity with the Black Panther GIs would help them to achieve the transformation of consciousness requisite for revolutionary action.[29]

No matter how passionately they envisioned their solidarity campaign as an emancipating tool, the students themselves often failed to rise above their own racial and cultural prejudices. An "instructional sheet" on how to interact with black GIs reveals that they were aware of this dilemma but were not always able to overcome it. The flyer advised students to approach black GIs as "individuals" and not as "victims," and to conduct conversations with "genuine humility" informed "not by guilt but an understanding of injustice." Yet, that same document betrayed a certain haughtiness and lack of understanding for black sensibilities when it admonished activists not to be arrogant in their conversations even though their English was "probably better than that of the Negro [*Neger*]."[30] The flyer's authors clearly did not realize that this American minority now wanted to be identified as black or Afro-American and passionately denounced the use of the term "Negro" or the German equivalent *Neger* as racist.

In collaboration with black GIs and black veterans who had taken their military discharge in Germany, the German student activists in the greater Frankfurt area produced the *Voice of the Lumpen*, a newspaper printed by Roter Stern, a small press owned by KD Wolff. The veterans, black GIs, and an American art student studying in Germany were responsible for most of the content of the paper, but at the same time also made up the core of the activists who worked most closely with the students. The *Voice of the Lumpen* acquainted GIs with the Black Panther Party and its program, reported on developments in the United States and the non-Western world, and also kept them abreast of the struggle at military bases across the globe. In all their efforts, the editors wrote, they aimed to further "the GIs' capacity to deal with their situation in the military and to understand how it relates to the struggle [of the Black Panthers] being waged today inside Babylon (Amerikkka)."[31] The usual press run was about 20,000 issues, with German subscribers subsidizing it so that black GIs could have copies for free.[32]

While the revolutionary alliance between African Americans from the Voice of the Lumpen as well as assorted militant GI self-defense groups and German student radicals lasted, its members organized rallies and teach-ins at German universities, attracting substantial audiences.[33] One of the most spectacular events, and one that drew the particular attention of both American and German authorities, was a demonstration on July 4, 1970, with about 700 African American GIs and their German allies filling the halls of the largest auditorium of the venerable University of Heidelberg. Students from the English Department had initiated this "Call for Justice Day," which they envisioned as a countercelebration to America's Independence Day in an indictment of the United States for its failure to grant freedom and equality to its black citizens. The protesters met at the university auditorium because the military had forbidden GIs to hold the rally at the local military base.

This highly visible and well-attended event proved to be a resounding success, fostering solidarity and cooperation among black GIs and student activists. A number of groups from both camps joined in, including the Unsatisfied Black Soldier, the Black Defense Group, the Black Action Group, the Frankfurt-based Solidarity Committee, and the Voice of the

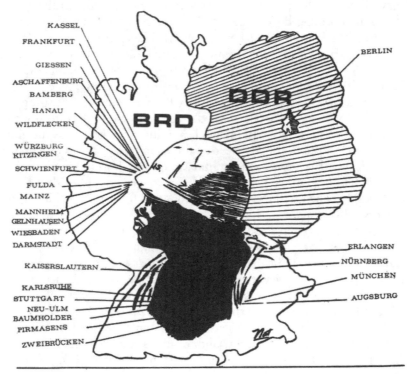

Figure 44 This image was part of the back cover of *Voice of the Lumpen* and emphasized the soldiers' role in the U.S. base system in West Germany and West Berlin/Cover: *Voice of the Lumpen*, Winter 1970 (Archiv für Soldatenrecht).

Lumpen. By the early afternoon, a jubilant crowd filled the hall with shouts of "freedom now," "Power to the People," and "right on, right on." When a band finally played Stevie Wonder's protest song "A Black Man," the hall erupted, with participants singing along and passionately embracing as "brothers." In between music, poetry recitations, and fiery speeches, the soldiers were given opportunity to voice their grievances and demands. They called for the creation of a civil committee to hear soldiers' complaints; for better accommodations, more career opportunities, and education in Black Studies; for the withdrawal of all troops from Indochina, the abolition of U.S. bases in Africa, and a commission on the treatment of black inmates in military prisons.[34] Significantly, the soldiers also accused their German hosts of racism by pointing to the discrimination black GIs encountered on the German housing market.[35]

The event was reported on in the German press, broadcasting the soldiers' determination to fight for their rights to a wide German audience. A black GI who helped organize the meeting made clear what was at stake for them. He insisted that it was "time for the black GIs to stand up and to come to grips politically with what is going on in the world." Praising the event as the start of a peaceful fight for equality and justice, he pledged that the struggle would be conducted with "courage and determination even if the military stockades in Heidelberg and Mannheim [would] burst from the seams."[36]

Figure 45 At this 1971 Black Panther solidarity rally at the University of Frankfurt, African American GIs, veterans, and students cheer for Kathleen Cleaver (Barbara Klemm, Frankfurt/Main).

Aside from this spectacular event, the Black Panther Solidarity Campaign also took its rallies and demonstrations outside the universities, bringing the concerns of African Americans, in general, and black soldiers, in particular, into the center of German cities. This gave black soldiers a political voice outside the narrow circle of leftist student activists. During numerous demonstrations in the spring of 1970, for example, Black Panther GIs marched with German students through downtown Frankfurt, protesting the war in Vietnam and calling for "Freedom for Bobby Seale," the imprisoned Black Panther leader.[37]

To maintain the momentum created by the "Call for Justice" protest, the Kaiserslautern "branch" of the Solidarity Committee organized a huge rally in October 1970 at the Fruchthalle, the local convention hall. A sleepy town of just 80,000 inhabitants, Kaiserslautern was just a few miles from neighboring Ramstein and Landstuhl, which housed a U.S. air base and military hospital, respectively; at that time, some 40,000 American GIs called these three communities home. The evening was advertised as a German-American friendship "happening" intended to alleviate the rising tensions between African American GIs and Germans of the previous year. From the start, city officials and police were suspicious but authorized the event anyway. Nonetheless, they were stunned when more than 1,000 Black Panther GIs and hundreds of their German supporters marched into the Fruchthalle to shouts of "Right on, Brother" and "Black Power." The popular TV news report *Panorama* devoted a whole segment of its show to the meeting, thus broadcasting the activities and grievances of black GIs across the country.[38]

When the German police arrested two editors of the *Voice of the Lumpen* in November 1970 after a shootout with a German guard at Ramstein Air Base, the collaboration between GIs and students entered its most organized and engaged phase. The defendants, Edgar Jackson and William Burrell, had tried to gain access to the base to hang posters advertising a talk by Kathleen Cleaver, the communication secretary of the Black Panthers. Cleaver was to speak as part of a solidarity rally in Frankfurt for Angela Davis, who had just been arrested in the United States. The arrest of Jackson and Burrell, two black veterans who had settled in Germany after their discharge from the U.S. military, gave the Black Panther Solidarity Campaign its own political "martyrs" to the cause, the Ramstein 2.[39] For the activists, the trial of the Ramstein 2 was a godsend because it allowed them to connect their struggle in Germany to the larger struggle that the Black Panthers in the United States were enduring. Thus, when protesters marched through German cities demanding freedom for Bobby Seale or Angela Davis, they also brought along banners demanding "Freedom for the Ramstein 2."

The trial itself offered the students and GI activists numerous opportunities to enlighten Germans about the persecution of the Black Panthers in the United States, to expose both American and German racism, and to further strengthen their transnational solidarity campaign.[40] Students rallied around the two defendants, providing them with excellent legal counsel and trial observers, and raising awareness for the issues of the case. According to the students' understanding, Jackson and Burrell had shot in self-defense only *after* the German guard had gone for his holster.[41] Comparing the guard's action to those of American police forces against Black Panther activists in the United States, the two men, so the students argued, were fully justified in their actions. To rally support for the defendants, the Voice of the Lumpen and the Black Panther Solidarity Committee held demonstrations and teach-ins on university campuses and organized such events in Zweibrücken, the town where the trial was to be held in June 1971.

To generate solidarity for the two defendants among GIs, rallies and political education classes were also held on U.S. military bases.[42] May and June 1971 saw four large fundraisers on military bases for the Ramstein 2 organized by the Black Panther Solidarity Committee, Voice of the Lumpen, and Unsatisfied Black Soldiers of Heidelberg. At one of these events, the hall was decorated with Black Panther flags, guns, and a pig-shaped U.S. flag.[43] The Solidarity Committee and the Voice of the Lumpen also convinced hundreds of black GIs to sign letters petitioning the German court to free the Ramstein 2.[44]

News of these sorts of protest and awareness-raising activities, especially those organized by the Black Panther Solidarity Campaign, reverberated throughout the United States. The *New York Times* compared the "soldier-activists" in West Germany to "organized black students groups"

Figure 46   Kathleen Cleaver, prominent representative of the Black Panther Party, speaks at the University of Frankfurt, 1971 (Barbara Klemm, Frankfurt/Main).

Figure 47 The Ramstein 2: Demonstration of German students and GI activists at the Zweibrücken Courthouse (Stadtarchiv Zweibrücken/Photographer: Imhoff).

on college campuses in the United States, and pointed out that the most active among them were Vietnam veterans. In another article, the *Times* properly noted that such protest activities by black soldiers *outside* their own country were unprecedented though their tactics mirrored those of "community activists" at home. At the same time, the paper differentiated developments in Germany from those in America by registering the "global dimension" since the soldiers protested against "racial discrimination both at home and overseas." Moreover, the *Times* stressed the unparalleled development of black soldiers "questioning whether they should fight for the United States" if discrimination continued—a perspective that threatened U.S. security in Cold War Europe.[45]

Of course, the collaboration between black GIs and German student activists caught the attention of the German media as well. While they had been covering the civil rights and the Black Power movements in the United States extensively, the black GI-student alliance brought that struggle and its increasing radicalization much closer to home. Some German observers did not understand why black GIs would conduct their struggle "on German soil," wondering, "What do we have to do with it?"[46] Others, however, pointed out that the black soldiers' protests forced the country's citizens to acknowledge a problem that they had largely dismissed as someone else's: "Perhaps people realized," one commentator remarked, "that problems such as oppression, discrimination, and injustice cannot be pushed away to a distant America."[47]

The American Response

The alliance between white German students, African American GIs, and black veterans who had stayed in Germany, fraught with problems from the beginning, did not last. To the great dismay and disappointment of German student radicals, the Black Panther Solidarity Campaign and the collaboration with African American GIs did not overthrow the "American war machine." The students and GIs had not only overestimated their own strength but also did not expect the powerful response of the U.S. government to address the grievances of African American soldiers. When government officials in the United States and West Germany began to take black GIs' concerns seriously, it alleviated the racial crisis, and the movement lost its urgency. The alliance also fell apart because the ideological divisions that cleaved the Black Panther Party in the United States also split the activists in the Voice of the Lumpen.[48] The emergence of black separatist activists who rejected collaboration with white revolutionaries effectively ended the collaboration with the students by early 1972.

In a way, the alliance's moderate successes also led to its collapse because it prompted both U.S. and German officials to act in order to deflate the crisis. The "Call for Justice" protest at Heidelberg University was especially important in this regard because of its high visibility and apparent legitimacy.[49] Not only had that meeting been held in one of West Germany's most distinguished universities—with the explicit support of the president of the university—but Heidelberg was also home to the headquarters of USAREUR. In response to the 4th of July protest, government agencies at the highest levels in both the United States and West Germany came to believe that the radicalization of black GIs and their deteriorating morale undermined not only military discipline but also threatened the security of West Germany's position—and thus America's in the Cold War struggle.[50]

Looking back from the less anxious perch of the post–Cold War world, these concerns may seem exaggerated, but for German and American officials at the time, these fears were very real indeed. While events in West Germany were in many ways similar to the racial crisis that plagued U.S. military bases everywhere, they were unfolding in front of Cold War foes East Germany and the Soviet Union. Consequently, West Germany presented a special case for the military, just as it had in the postwar decade during the crisis over integrating the military. It was in West Germany that the United States had drawn a line in the sand vis-à-vis the Soviet Union and asserted its leadership of the "Free World." With unease, *Time* magazine observed how communist propaganda, just as it had in the 1940s and 1950s, thrived on the racial crisis playing out in West Germany as a means of diminishing American leadership claims. The East German government's official newspaper, *Neues Deutschland*, for example, had seized on the racial discontent of the black soldiers and the recent spate of cross burnings to "portray the U.S. Army in Europe as a sort of K.K.K. expeditionary force."[51]

Given West Germany's special place in the U.S. defense strategy, and as America's poster child of the superiority of capitalism in the Cold War struggle, the situation called for intervention at the highest level. To begin with, a number of investigations were undertaken. In September 1970, as a direct response to the "Call for Justice" protest, the White House and the Pentagon sponsored a commission led by Frank Render II, the deputy assistant secretary of defense for equal opportunity, to take a hard look at the increasingly unmanageable situation in military bases across West Germany. In spring 1971, the NAACP then sent its own delegation led by Nathaniel Jones, general counsel of the NAACP, Julius E. Williams, head of the NAACP Department of Armed Services and Veterans Affairs, and Melvin Bolden from the Legal Department. They visited military bases in Heidelberg, Mannheim, Frankfurt, Karlsruhe, Stuttgart, Augsburg, Munich, Nuremberg, Berlin, Wiesbaden, Mainz, Bamberg, and Würzburg, where they met thousands of black and white military personnel and talked in depth with more than 500 African American GIs, both officers and enlisted men.[52] The Congressional Black Caucus (CBC) also sent an investigative team led by Thaddeus Garrett Jr., assistant to Representative Shirley Chisholm (D-NY), for a six-week tour of military bases in Europe, with a special focus on Germany.

The Render Report, despite its brevity, presented a stunning indictment of the discrimination and racism that African American soldiers faced both in the military and in German communities, and the more comprehensive NAACP and CBC investigations, by and large, confirmed these findings. "Generally," the NAACP reported, "our three week visit to military installations in Germany reinforced the Render Committee's conclusion that the problems that have surfaced in the European theater are, in many ways, an outgrowth and manifestation of racial tensions and unrest in the States." The main problems they found were "rooted in discriminatory policies in off-base housing, bars and recreational facilities; institutionalized racism in promotional procedures and advancement opportunities; and the misapplication of the UCMJ [Uniform Code of Military Justice]." However, they also stressed another point that had bedeviled black-white relations on U.S. military bases in Germany since World War II: relationships between black GIs and white German women; German women's apparent "distinct preference for the young, aggressive blacks" seemed to rile many white soldiers.[53]

After these reports came out in early 1971, the CBC was outraged that the Armed Services Committee of the U.S. Congress failed to call hearings to consider these findings. In light of that, the CBC called ad hoc hearings, cochaired by representatives Shirley Chisholm and Ron Dellums, for November 14–18, 1971. Both Dellums and Chisholm expressed their frustration that ad hoc meetings had to be held because their colleagues were "on the floor calling irrelevant quorum calls" rather than addressing "the very serious problems" that needed to be dealt with. Not to be deterred, Chisholm expressed the CBC's determination to bring about change at

Figure 48 Members of the NAACP team visiting Germany in spring 1971. On the far right is Julius E. Williams, head of the NAACP Department of Armed Services and Veterans Affairs; second from right is Nathaniel Jones, General Counsel of the NAACP, and on the far left is Melvin Bolden from the Legal Department (NAACP, Baltimore, MD).

last: "We have at least now served notice to everyone here in Washington, D.C., and all over this country, that the Blacks in the military now are tired of tokenism, that together we are going to bring all of the pressures that we know how to bring to bear on the Department of Defense."[54]

During those 1971 ad hoc hearings, representatives of the NAACP were heard. Frank Render and a number of expert witnesses and black soldiers were also invited to present testimony. Given the explosive situation in West Germany, they did not mince words, but used stern language to warn their government about just how dire the situation was: "the increasing polarization of Blacks and whites in our armed forces is rapidly approaching the point where the overall effectiveness of the military as a fighting force will be seriously hampered if not completely stalemated."[55] They further expressed concern about the "fearsome" potential "for large-scale violence, not to mention intensified morale problems," and warned that the army would "lose the support of many young black men who have real potential to rise to leadership positions in the military."[56] To prevent this, it was of the utmost importance that commanders convince these soldiers "that somebody cares about them."[57] The NAACP was hardly exaggerating with its conclusions. General Michael Davison, who took over command of USAREUR in spring 1971, assessed the situation in similarly grim terms, describing it as "on the verge of being completely riotous and out of control."[58]

Although the NAACP thus supported black GIs in seeking redress for their grievances, the organization rejected the demands of the more radical soldiers who had aligned with German students and called for revolution. Though acknowledging that "some of the younger servicemen seemed intent on pressing for change outside of the system," the NAACP held that "[s]uch a course would of course be catastrophic." Remaining true to its core principle of seeking change *within* the system, the NAACP assured white Americans that most black soldiers, despite the widespread increase in political radicalism, were still committed to doing so as well.[59]

Soldiers far from home have always had plenty of gripes even under the best of circumstances, but as the hearings and the report of the NAACP made abundantly clear, black enlisted men and officers had real grounds for their complaints. The military had distinguished itself after World War II by giving African Americans unprecedented opportunities for advancement. By the late 1960s, however, the military had lost that edge: with a leadership that, by its own admission, had become complacent, it was losing black talent to the private sector, which had begun a determined affirmative action drive in the 1960s. Accordingly, there were very few blacks in leadership positions in the 7th Army in West Germany. Although about 15 percent of U.S. soldiers there were African American in 1970/1971, only 2.2 percent of officers were, and at the junior officer level, less than 1.9 percent of lieutenants were, black—this marked a decline from the already paltry figure of 3.5 percent in 1965. Blacks were also vastly overrepresented in low-skilled combat and service and supply jobs that provided little chance of promotion. Heavily clustered in the lowest rank (E-1 and E-2), blacks comprised only 4.2 percent of the highest level (E-9). Not surprisingly, 72 percent of black enlisted men believed that whites were treated better, and 48 percent of black officers agreed. The situation in Europe was, of course, not that different from that of the United States, but this was hardly comforting to those who suffered the brunt of these institutionalized discriminatory practices.[60]

From their discussions with army personnel in Germany, the NAACP delegation concluded that "nearly all blacks and a considerable number of whites" believed that promotions were "rigged" to keep blacks from advancing. One black officer told the team that black enlisted men had to be "twice as good as whites to get promoted—and some white NCOs agreed." One black NCO's experience seemed to confirm this. He bitterly told the NAACP team that "You don't see any black commanders here. To tell you the truth, with my 18 years of service, I only heard of a few, but I've never seen or served under any." Only five African Americans held the rank of general (three Army, one Air Force, and one Navy), a fact that was not lost on the soldiers. Indeed, the NAACP reported that both black enlisted men and officers they had talked to in the air force did not regard the "presence of *one* black general as a sign of equal treatment, but as the most unabashed tokenism."[61] Another black NCO quipped: "One black general every 25 years!! All the black cats will have to wait until *he* retires or dies before another is made."[62]

Even more disturbing than this lack of black advancement were the NAACP's findings on the arbitrary application of the military justice system. The team deemed "the maladministration of justice" to be "the cancer that erodes America's ability to maintain an effective fighting force." Black GIs were disciplined not only more often but also for infractions that white GIs could get away with. For example, the NAACP found that commanders imposed Article 15, a nonjudicial punishment for minor offenses, inordinately on blacks. The discretionary power of that punishment left plenty of room for abuse. When a white soldier was late for duty four times in one week, nothing happened to him, but a black GI would be punished with Article 15 for the same offense. The NAACP also determined that black soldiers were getting Article 15 for simply expressing racial pride: for wearing Afros, black arm bracelets, black rings, for holding up the mess line with overly long "daps," or for giving the Black Power salute.

Black soldiers complained that officers and NCOs interpreted any questioning of authority, token of nonconformity, or expression of black pride as a sign of militancy.[63] "These whites," complained one soldier, "think that every time colored guys get together, well he is a Panther. He is a militant."[64]

Soldiers took exception to constantly being monitored and punished for expressing racial pride, while all too many commanders turned a blind eye to the display of the Confederate flag. Many were assured that the Article 15 punishments could be cleared from their records later on, but this was not necessarily the case. Furthermore, a string of such administrative punishments could lead to a dishonorable discharge, which was tantamount to a "life sentence": it was almost impossible for individuals so discharged to find suitable employment back in the United States.

Figure 49   These soldiers at Rhine-Main Air Base are provoking their superior officer with a Black Power greeting instead of a traditional salute. Soldiers were often punished for using this gesture ("power-check") among themselves or with their superiors (*Stern*, October 11, 1972/picture press/Perry Kretz).

Although the NAACP agreed with the military that its justice system, in principle, was based on equality of treatment regardless of race, it emphasized that, in practice, race played a significant role. As Captain Culver, an air force judge advocate from the Judge Advocate General Corps (JAG) who had defended a number of black GIs in Germany, put it in the hearings, "Military justice is White justice. There are White judges. White court members, and White lawyers." Indeed, of 136 judge advocates, only 3 were black, and of the 46 military judges in Europe, only 2 were.[65] Furthermore, racial prejudice figured into which infractions or incidents of insubordination were reported and thus came to the attention of this overwhelmingly white justice system. Since one could not escape the fact that "a substantial number of NCOs"—who were often the ones to make such reports—were racially prejudiced, it was in this "discretionary use of military justice" that "the greatest racism" came out.[66] Moreover, as Culver stressed, there was "a disproportionate number of southern whites in the officer corps" as well as among "senior NCOs," which influenced interpretations of black soldiers' behavior toward authority figures throughout the armed services.[67]

In consequence of this uneven application of military justice, the NAACP also ascertained that the population of military stockades in West Germany resembled that of U.S. prisons, with blacks making up more than 50 percent of inmates. Just as with Article 15, black soldiers endured incarceration as punishment, often for perceived insubordination, more often and more severely than whites. Although the 7th Army's crisis in discipline and morale affected both white and black GIs, it was black GIs who were most often subjected to disciplinary action: in 1970, even though only 15 percent of soldiers were African American, two-thirds of prison sentences for willful insubordination were handed out to black GIs. Stockades were also filled with soldiers who had not been tried for any crimes. A pretrial confinement prerogative allowed commanders to imprison alleged offenders for up to thirty days without filing charges; in 1970, three out of five black prisoners in military stockades were held under this rule, routinely well beyond the thirty-day limit, and sometimes for up to sixty or ninety days.[68] These periods of confinement could be very hard on soldiers, not only because they lost all pay for the duration, but also because commanders often ignored rules stipulating that they visit the prisoners, supply clean clothing, and provide counsel.

In its investigation, the NAACP discovered that 28 percent of African American prisoners (912 individuals) freed in 1970 had been released without any charges ever having been pressed against them. Commanders had imprisoned these GIs to intimidate them, and to silence and remove "troublemakers" and so-called black militants from their units.[69] But this practice was grossly unfair, as the NAACP noted, because it entailed a sweeping application of the label "militant" that covered "all aspects of black consciousness, black civil liberties, even expectations of equal treatment."[70] Frank Render was able to confirm this prevailing attitude among much of the brass, and how easily officers associated any sort of activism or demands for equal rights with militancy. During his inspection tour, one commander had told another that Render himself was "a top grade militant" who "[i]f he were not in the Army...would be a leader in the Black Panthers."[71]

Overtly racist behavior by commanders was also an issue. The NAACP reported on one commander who had the word "rebel" painted on his jeep, and they had also heard "lots of complaints [from soldiers] about verbal abuse and racial epithets from NCOs." Another example came from Augsburg, where white soldiers had painted the phrase "Hitler should have killed one million Negroes instead of the Jews" on one of the barracks. The fact that the offensive message stayed for months before military authorities had it removed speaks volumes for the sorry state of affairs within the 7th Army.[72]

One black GI gave this assessment of what it felt like to be a black soldier in USAREUR in 1970, when General Polk led the command: "We're here in the U.S. Army's black ghetto in Europe; on Polk's Plantations supervised by all the racist misfit pigs, who failed to make it somewhere else, but have that special qualification of how to control the brothers."[73] Another insisted that the time for talking was over and called for immediate action:

> We don't need all the cats running around from the Pentagon and Congress checking on the brothers....The facts are there loud and clear. If they really wanted to change things and eliminate the problem all they have to do is look at the statistics. It's the brother who gets the most court-martials. It's

the brother who gets the most Article 15's. It's the brother who is lowest in rank, last to be considered for promotion—why? Hell, any fool could look at this and see that all these things start with the "man," some racist pig commander—and that's the problem, that's where the brother's trouble lies.[74]

Noting the uneven application of the military justice system and nonjudicial punishment, the lack of black advancement, and the pervasive racism in the command structure, this black GI's pithy statement essentially sums up the findings of the NAACP investigation reviewed thus far.

In addition to calling for these imbalances to be addressed, black soldiers articulated one other demand to the NAACP team: they wanted the military to show more cultural sensitivity, among other things, by allowing and providing support for their cultural preferences, just as it did for white soldiers. Black soldiers were proud to sport their Afros, but military regulations and insensitive commanders often failed to appreciate how central this hairstyle was to their sense of identity and expressing Black Pride. The barbers and beauticians working on U.S. military bases were all German nationals with no training in cutting or styling black hair, so black soldiers and often their wives had to rely on their own know-how. They wanted the military to fix this and to start stocking black hair and beauty products in post exchanges. In the same way, they wanted military libraries and the Stars and Stripes bookstores to carry more black authors and for clubs on base to play more black music. Although NCO and Enlisted Men's Clubs (EM clubs) had started playing soul music during the week to appease the black GIs, on the weekends, Country and Western still ruled, making black GIs feel unwelcome. Complained Captain Edmond Robinson, "hill-billy music [sic] seems to be the official music of the Air Force."[75] They also felt unwelcome, and were often harassed, as they had been in the past, when they brought their white German girlfriends to the clubs on base.

The military's insensitivity to black culture also extended to education and military publications. The complaints about the Department of Defense (DOD) school system make especially clear that not only young hotheads but also older soldiers who were married and had children in school voiced frustration. Soldiers complained that the DOD school system employed almost no black teachers and that the curriculum lacked any sort of Black History or Black Studies. They also denounced the military newspaper Stars and Stripes for the unequal use of race in its coverage. The paper would regularly mention race, especially when reporting charges of rape, but not if the alleged offender was white.[76] In other publications, however, blacks were often absent, so black GIs wanted to "see more black faces in military publications" and for their white comrades to know what had been "accomplished by members of their race."[77]

In the NAACP's conclusions at the November 1971 hearings, the organization reiterated its indictment of pervasive discrimination in the military but finished on a note of hope. "Blacks and other minority servicemen are

Figure 50   The soldier at a music festival in Frankfurt, Germany, is decked out in "ethnic" clothing that he crafted from a military blanket. Lack of ethnic clothing in the post exchange was a main point of complaint among the GIs, June 1970 (Institut für Stadtgeschichte Frankfurt am Main/Philipp Kerner).

victims of discrimination from the time that they enter the services until the time that they are discharged," the report entered into the Congress in October 1972 insisted. But the military, with its unique command structure and almost absolute control over individual action, presented a terrific opportunity for America to "begin the work of eliminating racism." Echoing suggestions made by civil rights activists during the integration of the military between 1948 and 1954, the CBC prodded the U.S. military to take the lead once again in overcoming the country's racist legacy: "This is the paradox uncovered by the Caucus hearings; the military, which is such a blatant example of the worst in American racism, can become a source of reform for the whole society."[78]

Another conclusion the NAACP drew from the intense focus on development in West Germany was that the unrest there was not so much a result of the military doing worse than in previous years but of the different kind of soldier it was dealing with. Officers had told the NAACP investigators that racial brawls had been going on for years. The big difference now, however, was in the nature of the soldiers being sent abroad. The root of the developments in West Germany, suggested one observer, lay in "the more aggressive attitude of the young blacks coming into the Army, their unconcealed racial pride, and their much greater expectations as to how they should be treated both in the Army and elsewhere in society."[79] Terry Wallace, who served as *Time* deputy bureau chief in Vietnam for six years and authored the book *Blood: The Black Soldier from Vietnam*, probably understood the mood of the black soldier at the time better than most, and the CBC had called on him as an expert witness. "The military has not changed. I don't believe it," Wallace argued; "I think the reason we are having unrest today is because the Black population has changed." Along with enormous societal changes over the previous decade, blacks had grown more assertive: "the Blacks that we have here now," Wallace continued, "are determined to take no more licks. No more name calling, no more slurs, no more cross burnings, and no more confederate flags." Wallace also agreed with the NAACP that the military, because of its hierarchical structure, was *the* place to bring about change. Though it could not wipe out racism overnight, it could assure that a commander who had a cross burning or a "race riot" on his base should forget about ever being made "an admiral or general."[80]

Meanwhile, the military at last began to respond to the crisis with concrete measures. General James Polk was forced into early retirement and replaced by General Michael Davison as the commander of USAREUR in spring 1971. A number of other commanders, who had been unresponsive about the racial crisis, were also removed from the European Command. Davison acknowledged the depth of the problems much more forthrightly than his predecessor, as well as the 7th Army's central role in assuring the future integrity of the U.S. Army in general, and suggested concerted action to address the crisis.[81] Agreeing with Harold Sims, the acting executive director of the National Urban League, he also maintained that the military in Germany could "build an example of American society" in Germany that did not exist back home.[82]

To accomplish the goal of truly integrating the military, Davison called for a number of changes in the command and culture of the 7th Army. He insisted that his command be much more racially diversified and that the 7th Army needed "more black teachers, more black lawyers, more black counselors, more black chaplains, and more black officers and non-commissioned officers" so that African Americans and their families would feel that it was also *their* military. Further, Davison demanded more "black content" in overseas school operations, "not only in faculty but also in curricula, [the] civilian work force, and in our management echelon."[83] The race situation would not improve, Davison held, unless officers became more sensitive to the needs of black GIs and stopped interpreting every expression of racial pride as a challenge to their authority. "Black symbols, such as the 'dap' handshake, Afro haircut, black bracelets and the black power salute," said Davison, "shouldn't be considered anti-establishment" but represented, rather, "an establishment defect."[84] He set up a USAREUR Race Relations School in Munich to train qualified military personnel how to teach and resolve racial and ethnic problems. This school was modeled on the Defense Race Relations Institute in Florida that had been (and remains today) at the forefront of dealing with racial issues in the military since its creation in 1971.[85]

Addressing these demands, the military launched an affirmative action program to attract minority officers. Furthermore, Secretary of Defense Melvin Laird established the Task Force on the Administration of Military Justice in the Armed Forces to study not *whether* there was discrimination in the military but to assess the extent of it and to provide remedies.[86] Moreover, a much more deliberate effort to attend to the needs of black soldiers was undertaken. Military stores began stocking ethnic clothing, books by African American authors, and black beauty products, and African American barbers and beauticians were even flown in to train Germans to cut and style the hair of their African American clientele.[87]

Three years after the Render, NAACP, and CBC investigations, significant improvements had been made, as reported by *Ebony* magazine editor Hans Massaquoi when he traveled to Germany. For one thing, the army had developed a much more hands-on approach to dealing with racial issues. As Sergeant William Turner of Detroit put it, "before the Army got scared about this race thing, race relations was something the chaplains would talk about once in a while... now, at least in USAREUR, they have put teeth into equal-opportunity. It's no longer the chaplains' business; they made it everybody's business." These teeth consisted, among other things, in officers now being judged on their equal opportunity-race relations record when they were up for promotion.[88]

At the same time, Massaquoi cautioned that a long hard road lay ahead when he related two revealing slips of tongue made by Major General Hayward, USAREUR's top equal opportunity enforcer. Hayward had commented, "(as if reading from an Archie Bunker TV script)," on the special challenges that black soldiers faced in Germany: "He (the black soldier) can't just blend into downtown Heidelberg as *our* (meaning white) soldiers can because of his skin color. He has more difficulty making the acquaintance of reputable German girls than *American*, (brief pause) than the white soldier does."[89]

German Reactions to the Investigations

The investigations by the Render Commission, the NAACP, and the CBC had disclosed the extent of racism and discrimination not only in the military but also in German communities, prompting the German government to take active measures to combat it. This was a most unusual wake-up call for the Germans given that they had always taken pride, as chapters 3 and 4 demonstrated, in the fact that black GIs enjoyed their time in Germany. In the eyes of black GIs, Germany's image had declined markedly since the postwar decade, and even since just a few years earlier. A 1965 survey, for example, had shown that 64 percent of black GIs still believed that they experienced more racial equality in West Germany than in the United States, whereas 6 percent thought that they were treated better in the United States, and 30 percent saw little difference between the two countries.[90] Yet by the time of the investigations, black soldiers had numerous complaints about the way Germans treated them. Service in German restaurants and discotheques was often unfriendly; some establishments told black GIs that they were private clubs that admitted only members, yet white GIs who were not "members" had no problems. "Why are we here protecting the Germans when they won't even serve us?" asked one soldier.[91] Soldiers also lamented the practice of German landlords refusing to rent apartments to them and their families.[92] One African American captain expressed his outrage on national German television, asking indignantly why black GIs should risk their lives to defend German homes when they were not even welcomed to live in those very homes.[93]

How can we explain this radical shift? Germans were hardly more racist in 1970 than they had been in 1945. In fact, in the early 1960s, German media had become much more sensitive to incidents of racism in German society, reporting on them as part of a larger trend of interrogating the German Nazi past.[94] Thus, what had changed by the later 1960s was not so much Germans' attitudes and behavior but black GIs' expectations. The advance of the civil rights movement in the United States had radically diminished the contrast between an overtly racist America and a more hospitable Germany that had so impressed black soldiers from the 1940s to the early 1960s.[95] Furthermore, the more politicized and radicalized Black Power GIs now serving tours of duty in Germany, often after a stint in Vietnam, were no longer satisfied with mere "tolerance" and a less hostile environment than in the Southern United States. Much as younger Germans admired the martial posture of the new generation of black soldiers being sent to Germany, older Germans were—like the officers in the military—at a loss over how to deal with them. As one puzzled older German saw it, "We used to like black soldiers...But today they are so different. Most act angry and rough all the time. We don't hate them, but we just don't know what is bothering them."[96]

Hans Massaquoi explained in a way worth quoting at length why Germany was no longer the racial utopia of years past. Having grown up as an Afro-German in Nazi Germany, Massaquoi encountered other people of color first in 1945 when he befriended black GIs in his hometown of Hamburg, giving him a compelling perspective on which to draw.

The mixed feelings many black soldiers express toward Germans and Germany are in sharp contrast to the pro-German euphoria that prevailed among black occupation troops during the decade following WWII....The Jim Crowed black GI, a veritable underdog in his own right...generously shared his cigarettes and food rations with the starving and totally demoralized former foe. Germans, in turn, opened their hearts—and what was left of their bombed-out homes—to their black Samaritans in olive drab.

Decades later, Massaquoi concluded, Germans no longer needed "black friends and American cigarettes."[97]

Both Massaquoi and members of the NAACP delegation insisted that discrimination toward the black soldiers was not just a matter of indigenous German racism. Rather, it was a well-known fact that, in the past, white soldiers and commanders had pressured German business owners and landlords not to do business with black GIs if they were interested in keeping their white customers. Massaquoi maintained, for example, "much of the bias experienced by black soldiers at the hand of Germans—especially landlords and bar owners—is a direct import from the good old U.S.A. and reflects in many ways the racial polarization at home."[98] These observers also stressed that Americans had brought the Germans not only democracy but also the patterns of America's color line. While the NAACP's Nathaniel Jones was "inclined to give the Germans a lot of credit of being prejudiced without any help," he also reminded Americans that it was the U.S. military that had brought Jim Crow to Germany. "Desegregation did not come to Europe until the early 1950s, and by that time differing treatment for black and white soldiers no doubt had entered the living patterns in Germany, and made some impression upon the Germans."[99]

Be that as it may, German authorities were anxious to address the problem of German racism head-on. While army investigations found that the problem of discrimination among landlords and pub owners was not as widespread as anticipated—33 incidents of discrimination were reported in 1970 from some 19,000 troops renting on the German market—German officials wished to convey that even these numbers were unacceptable.[100] Just as importantly, they no longer insisted that discrimination was an American problem but acknowledged German responsibility. To combat the problem, they spread the news of discrimination in West Germany throughout the country: The Render Report was printed in full in a number of German newspapers, and the lengthier NAACP investigation was excerpted as well; the editors of the *General Anzeiger* in the city of Bonn, which was then the capital of West Germany, were especially disturbed, stating that they found the NAACP Report "alarming and deeply embarrassing";[101] and the *Stuttgarter Zeitung* cited Captain Curtis Smothers, the only black military judge in West Germany, to emphasize how determined black GIs were to effect change: "We are fighting for rights that are ours. No more, no less. And we want all those to be held responsible who do not respect our rights. Here in Germany as well as at home."[102]

*   *   *

Both the German and American responses to the racial crisis have to be viewed within the larger Cold War context. In America, the crisis erupted at the very moment when some congressmen, led by Senate Majority Leader Mike Mansfield (D-Montana), were questioning the rationale of continuing the extensive U.S. military presence in Germany. In light of Germany's ongoing détente with Eastern Europe (*Ostpolitik*) under Willy Brandt and the resulting reduction in tensions with the Soviet Union, Mansfield and his supporters concluded that a 50 percent reduction in troops in West Germany was called for. Consequently, it was easy for civil rights advocates to put pressure on the American and German governments. The NAACP and the CBC were quick to seize the moment in order to push forward their own civil rights agenda, both in the U.S. military as well as in West Germany. Resolutely declaring that there was "no reason why, repeat no reason why we must tolerate racism by the Germans," the NAACP was determined to change the laissez-faire way racist incidents had been handled in the past, when local military commanders and mayors of garrison towns had dealt with them. As black GIs, given their legal status under the Status of Forces Agreement, could not turn to the Germans, and the army had "already shown it w[ould] tolerate racism in the military," the NAACP called on the U.S. government to conduct conversations with the highest levels of the German government to address the issue. The CBC was just as adamant in its demands: "When racism rears its ugly head in Germany or Korea, the Americans assigned to 'protect freedom' have every right to expect, and indeed demand, the vigorous intervention" of their government. To ensure that neither the United States nor West Germany ignore the issue at hand, the CBC threatened to reconsider its support of appropriations for stationing "troops in countries where the human dignity of the black soldiers ha[d] been violated."[103]

Mansfield's call for a drawdown of 50 percent of U.S. troops in West Germany posed a serious threat to the Pentagon's European defense strategy, which was based on maintaining military forces in Germany at their current level. USAREUR representatives assured the West German government that the Nixon government was doing all it could to preserve the level of U.S. forces stationed in Germany as part of the NATO shield but also warned that every report about German discrimination undermined that goal.[104] Given Germany's precarious location in the Cold War struggle, the West German government was as eager as the Pentagon to preserve U.S. troop strength in Germany.[105] Defense Minister Helmut Schmidt made clear what was at stake when he encouraged the governors of states with U.S. troops to be vigilant about incidents of racism because there was "no substitute [for U.S. troops], not militarily, but especially not politically or psychologically."[106]

Important as the maintenance of U.S. troops in Germany was, politicians at the highest levels of the German government reacted to the allegations of racism in the three reports. To assure their American alliance partner as well as the African American community in the United States that West Germany was not hostile toward black soldiers, Chancellor Willy Brandt, President Gustav Heinemann, Foreign Minister Walter Scheel, and Defense

Minister Helmut Schmidt all made personal statements condemning the racism that black soldiers experienced in German society. Willy Brandt was especially eloquent. In his statement, he told Germans to stop criticizing other countries, such as the United States or South Africa, for their racism, and to take a hard look at the situation "at home" instead: "I am against self-righteousness, which is often noticeable when foreign and far-away countries are being criticized. Charity begins at home, but also the rights of man start at home." Brandt further exhorted Germans to practice a new kind of patriotism based not on feelings of superiority but on open-mindedness toward individuals who come to Germany from other continents, whether as soldiers or as students—an open-mindedness that could bring honor to Germans across the globe. Brandt then concluded with the clever epigram: "Tolerance made in Germany: that would be something we could be proud of."[107]

Aware that words had to be followed by deeds if black soldiers were to feel more welcome in their country, the West German government authorized an extensive $600-million construction program to modernize deteriorated military barracks for single or unaccompanied soldiers. To alleviate the situation in West Germany's notoriously tight housing market, the German government also built new family housing for U.S. military personnel.[108] While these new apartments benefited both white and black soldiers and their families, the impetus of the program was to address the complaints of black GIs over housing shortages and discrimination. Meetings about how to ensure nondiscriminatory policies were held at the federal, state, and local levels and in collaboration with civic and business associations to educate landlords and owners of bars, discotheques, and restaurants. Strict new rules imposed economic sanctions on individuals who continued to discriminate against blacks. German government officials also instructed media outlets to stop identifying alleged offenders by race when covering crimes committed by U.S. soldiers. Newspaper editors were also urged to exert greater effort in educating Germans about the accomplishments and contributions of African Americans to American history.[109] These steps were necessary, the German defense minister made clear in his instructions to governors of states with U.S. troops, because the problems and "concerns of [black] American soldiers in the Federal Republic must also be our concerns."[110]

This elevation of the race question to the highest levels of the U.S. and West German governments marked a dramatic shift from its treatment earlier in the postwar period. In the 1950s, charges of racism by black GIs were largely denied, and even in the early 1960s, such charges at most brought about ad hoc and often reluctant responses on the part of local military commanders and German mayors.[111] The German government's open acknowledgment of German racism, too, signaled a profound turn away from the practice of previous decades, when German officials had generally assured themselves that the discrimination black GIs encountered in West Germany was an "American import." In this view, affirmed by both the American military command and civil rights advocates in the 1950s and 1960s, such discrimination emerged when white soldiers pressured German pub owners to keep black GIs out or convinced German landlords not to rent to black families, making it an *American* rather than a *German* problem (the military never publicly admitted its commanders' complicity in this practice). The racial crisis in the late 1960s and early 1970s exposed the inadequacy of this view and brought German forms of racism and discrimination front and center.

In summary, many of the moderate demands of the civil rights movement going back to World War II finally became reality because the protests of more radical groups forced the German and American governments to act. Significantly, the voices of the minority soldiers were only heard so clearly and so loudly, both in the U.S. and in West Germany, because of the moral and logistical support they received from the radical German students activists. The students' eagerness to reach out to black GIs resulted in a much more complex historical record of how the radicalization of the African American civil rights movement of the late 1960s took on a global dimension. After the crisis in the military in 1970/1971, the situation of African American GIs in the military became a priority of foreign policy, both for the German and American governments. Just as importantly, concepts such as "discrimination," "equal opportunity," and "affirmative action" were introduced to German bureaucrats and the country's citizenry. How intertwined German, American, and African American concerns had become was brought home to all involved when the NAACP opened its first branch in West Germany in 1971.

Conclusion

A day before attending the 2009 commemoration of the 65th anniversary of the landing of American troops in Normandy, U.S. President Barack Obama visited the Nazi concentration camp at Buchenwald. Reflecting on the "human capacity for evil," Obama stressed that these sights had "not lost their horror with the passage of time."[1] He recalled his great uncle Charlie Payne: among the American forces that liberated a satellite camp of Buchenwald in 1945, Payne had suffered a great shock from the inhumanity he was confronted with when he arrived at the camp. The president concluded by underscoring the constant effort that is needed not only to preserve the history of the Holocaust but also to combat all forms of intolerance. In a subsequent interview, Obama highlighted the role of the veterans of this war: "as we see so many of our World War II veterans coming to the twilight of their years, it is especially important, I think, for us to remember, to record, to remind ourselves of how much that generation did on all of our behalves."[2]

This book has been about documenting the experience of African American soldiers, whose contributions during and after World War II have not yet been adequately acknowledged and made part of America's history and collective national memory. *A Breath of Freedom* coincides with other initiatives—political and scholarly—that have started to pay closer attention to the crucial role that black servicemen and women played not only in America's wars but also in the country's journey toward a greater and more inclusive democracy.[3] In July 2009, a month after Obama's visit to Buchenwald and Normandy, the NAACP, in a resolution during its centennial convention, honored black veterans for their crucial contributions to U.S. history and the civil rights movement. In February 2010, the U.S. House of Representatives passed a similar resolution, which acknowledged that "there has been no war fought by or within the United States in which Blacks did not participate." Enumerating their accomplishments, the House resolution affirmed that "Black veterans who were in the forefront of the Civil Rights Movement, with their strong resolve to address the paradox of military service abroad and the denial of basic rights at home, brought a deeper meaning to the word 'democracy,' and through their example, transformed the face of the United States."[4]

Our book captures a glimpse of this transformation by focusing on Germany, and the way in which that country emerged as a locale where the demands of the civil rights movement could be clarified and brought into sharp focus. Our choice of Germany in this study is due to the major role the country played in American politics in the twentieth century, both domestic and foreign. Even more importantly, Germany is a logical choice because of the hundreds of thousands of black GIs who helped liberate its people from Nazism. As we have seen, black soldiers were profoundly affected by this experience and by their encounters with a society that, while hardly free of racism, did not have an American-style color line. Many of these soldiers and those who served in Germany during the 1950s and 1960s returned to the United States with a new determination to become foot soldiers in another struggle—the one that still needed to be fought for full democracy and freedom at home.

David Brion Davis, the distinguished historian of U.S. slavery, who was often cited in this book regarding his experiences as an eighteen-year-old soldier in occupied Germany, came to see this confluence of the U.S. involvement in Germany and the struggle for civil rights as well. In reflecting on that time, he realized that as a teenager in Mannheim he had "glimpsed the contours of the United States" he would mature into:

> a relatively benign, good-natured, and well-intentioned desire to democratize the world, combined with signs of the coming cold war and with conflicts initiated by African Americans' expressions of freedom that would begin to heal the cancerous racial division and persecution that has corrupted the core of American society since the founding of the Republic.[5]

Yet this interconnected history of Germans and African Americans not only transformed the African American civil rights movement and U.S. politics: it also fundamentally altered the image of the United States among Germans, who followed the civil rights struggle on the other side of the Atlantic with great attention, both in East and West Germany. The freedom struggle of African Americans was particularly inspiring to a young generation of student activists in West Germany. Born in the last years of the Nazi regime, many of them first encountered black GIs when these soldiers gave them chocolate or gum at the end of World War II. As they grew up, many of them learned about the depth of racial discrimination and the burgeoning civil rights movement while spending time in the United States as exchange students in the late 1950s and early 1960s. During the 1960s, the student activists eagerly adopted techniques of this movement, such as sit-ins, for their own campaigns to expand German democracy. The rise of Black Power also fit in neatly with their emerging global revolutionary vision, which was based on anti-imperialism and the vanguard role of the liberation movements of Africa, Asia, and South America.

On the other side of the Wall, in East Germany, the infatuation with the African American freedom struggle was not an expression of grassroots democracy. Rather, the regime launched a comprehensive solidarity campaign for what it called the "other" America. Focusing on the political oppression, economic exploitation, and racial discrimination of African Americans in the United States, East German officials courted leading civil rights activists such as W. E. B. Du Bois, Paul Robeson, Ralph Abernathy, and, above all, Angela Davis with a variety of honors and splendid state receptions. In supporting civil rights in the United States, the East German regime sought to distance itself from West Germany, as well as to situate the African American struggle within a global class struggle, the national liberation movements in the former colonies, and the communist peace efforts during the Cold War. At the same time, as Dr. Martin Luther King's encounter with worshipers in East Berlin illustrates, the African American civil rights movement could also reverberate very differently in the communist state when framed in a religious context outside the regime's immediate control and carefully laid out propaganda plans.

African Americans, despite their seemingly positive reception and the freedoms they enjoyed in the two Germanys, encountered pervasive racism and xenophobia. Although both Germanys had made the equality of all races a basis of their constitutions, racism was deeply rooted in German history and culture and lingered in popular consciousness in both societies. Accordingly, though many Germans viewed black soldiers as especially kind and gentle to children and older people, others perceived them as aggressive and less able to restrain their passions than whites. All too often, Germans assumed that the social problems associated with the large American military presence in general (e.g., crime, alcohol abuse, sexual attacks on local women) stemmed from black GIs. In West Germany, not all landlords were willing to rent to black soldiers and their families, and pub and restaurant owners occasionally gave them the cold shoulder, or claimed that the premises were open to members only. In this way, the Federal Republic showed itself to be a society hardly free of racism, despite the advantages—both economic and security-related—that the African American soldiers provided. Likewise, racism was also a daily reality for people of color that lived in the other Germany, the proclamations of international class and race solidarity by the East German regime notwithstanding.

In the course of the 1980s, a group of black individuals in West Germany began to more publicly assert their identity as both German *and* black. Inspired by the African American feminist poet Audre Lorde, who led a workshop in Berlin in 1984, they adopted the term "Afro-Germans" or "Black Germans."[6] The two main engines for this movement were ADEFRA, an organization of black women in Germany founded in 1986, and the Initiative for Black People in Germany (ISD).[7] The goal of both groups was to foster the recognition of black culture and history in Germany, make visible the needs and demands of black people, and combat racial discrimination in all areas of German society. A variety of cultural and professional organizations across the country representing the black community have since complemented their efforts.[8] Their activities to establish an intercultural dialogue and a more inclusive German identity include seminars, workshops, exhibitions, as well as the annual Black History Month.

Increasingly, individuals sharing their biographies and experiences of living in Germany as black Germans have boosted these endeavors for greater public awareness.[9] The most famous of these is undoubtedly Hans Massaquoi, the son of a Liberian diplomat and a German mother. His life story of growing up in Hamburg during the Nazi regime and advancing to a successful career in the United States as an editor at *Jet* and *Ebony* magazines has mesmerized Germans and was only recently adapted for television.[10] In many ways, Massaquoi's biography exemplifies the many links between Africans, African Americans, and Germany in the twentieth century and the need for a more comprehensive, transnational perspective when narrating these lives. An organization that specifically targets such transatlantic histories of black people living in Germany, as well as the United States, is the Black German Cultural Society. It was established by black German children born after World War II—often the children of fathers who were U.S. soldiers—so many of its members share a dual heritage (German and American). The group tries to bring together black Germans on both sides of the Atlantic, answer questions about cultural identity, and help build relationships between extended families, for example, assisting children of African American GIs and German mothers who lost touch with one of their parents during the Cold War to reconnect with them.[11]

Today, there are between 300,000 and half a million black people living in Germany, many of whom are African immigrants or students married to German partners, as well as their children. A substantial part of the Afro-German population is comprised of descendants of children born to African American and French colonial soldiers after World War II (and to a much lesser degree also after World War I), as well as black people from the former German colonies. The existence and work of the aforementioned organizations illustrate that there is a fundamental need to address questions of black identity and racial discrimination in today's Germany, which is still struggling to forge a common identity after the more than forty-year separation of the two German states. This was most recently underscored by the controversy surrounding the documentary of a well-known German investigative journalist who darkened his skin and passed himself off as a black person to expose the daily racism in his country.[12] These and other political and cultural initiatives showcase the continuing shortcomings in German society and raise awareness about the mutual benefits to be gained from working toward a diverse society.[13]

Likewise, academics have begun in recent decades to dedicate their attention to the black presence in German history.[14] They have focused on racist ideology and the treatment of blacks during Nazi Germany and in the postwar period, as well as on the larger transatlantic connections between African Americans and Europe.[15] The civil rights struggle itself has also proven to be an exceptional point of attraction in the German academy.

Many German scholars who dedicated themselves to the study of U.S. politics and society were personally or professionally shaped by the experience of the civil rights movement.[16] As a result, the field of American Studies in both Germanys was marked by special attention to the history and culture of African Americans (as well as Native Americans), although this attention stemmed from vastly different political motivations and ideological backgrounds. As Sabine Sielke has noted about the development of the discipline, "If one reads this shared and continuous interest as a mediated interrogation of Germany's own history of racial discrimination and genocide, yet another culturally specific function of American Studies in post-war German academia comes to the fore, highlighting the 'darker' dimensions of the interdependencies of German and American history, many of which remain to be explored and theorized."[17]

Although the story of the interconnectedness of African American GIs, the civil rights struggle, and Germany touched a great number and variety of people, we feel that one person's biography uniquely embodies it: Colin Powell's. As we have used his words for the title of our book, we find it appropriate to close by relaying one of his experiences. In November 1986, Powell, then lieutenant general and commander of V Corps in Frankfurt, was invited to address the Eighteenth Equal Opportunity Conference of the U.S. Army in Europe (USAEUR) held at the Armed Forces Recreation Center in Garmisch, Germany. In his talk, Powell reflected on the history of the African American quest for freedom since the nation's founding, paying particular attention to the effect of the civil rights movement of the 1950/1960s on his own life as he was growing up in Harlem and when he entered the army in 1957.

Illustrating the harsh realities of racial discrimination at the time in the United States, he told the audience of young soldiers about an incident in Fort Benning, Georgia, in 1963, where he had just relocated with his young family after serving tours of duty in West Germany and Vietnam. On his way back to the Base Officers' Quarters, Powell stopped for a burger at a local drive-in restaurant. Unable to enter the establishment because of still-existing Jim Crow segregation, he decided simply "to park in the parking lot, not bothering anybody" and wait for the waitress to come and take his order:

> And when the car hop came out, asking for a hamburger, to be told as Captain of the United States Army, just back from a year in Vietnam, a year totally away, having been wounded, fighting for my nation...to be told that I could not have that hamburger. She could not bring it out to me, but if I wished to, I was welcome to come out of the car and go around the back of the restaurant and they would hand it out the back of the kitchen.

Angered by this blunt rejection, Powell replied defiantly: "Thank you madam, I am not that hungry and don't think I ever will be."[18]

Powell returned to the drive-in in the summer of 1964 after the passage of the Civil Rights Act. This time, he proudly walked into the restaurant to order his hamburger inside and was served, no questions asked. He told the young soldiers that not only "would [he] have torn the place up" had he not been served, but also that he had "never enjoyed a hamburger more in [his] life."[19] For Powell, the story that he shared on this occasion in 1986 encapsulated both the "trauma even after the achievements of the mid-sixties" and the progress of race relations in the United States.

In his view, this story also exemplified the continuing need to come closer to the fulfillment of the American promise of liberty and justice for all, inside as well as outside the military. According to Powell, striving to achieve that goal, which he traced from the democratic aspirations of Thomas Jefferson to Dr. Martin Luther King, was a guiding vision for "enlightened leaders" in the military and for any commander-in-chief. At the same time, he found it personally of prime significance "that the kind of Equal Opportunity that [he] fought for, and the progress [he] lived through" in the twenty-eight years he had been in the military continued "to be built upon" and extended "to every person in our society of whatever racial origin, [or] whatever sex." He ended by stressing that this ideal could be achieved but still required a great deal of work: "[F]ull Equal Opportunity is a reality that catches up to a dream, and hopefully in my lifetime, and hopefully while I am still in the army. There is a lot left to do."[20]

The unwavering pursuit of this dream for a more tolerant and democratic society is certainly not bound to any particular institution, ethnic group, or country like Germany or the United States; rather, it is a fundamental vision for people across the globe. Consequently, historians will undoubtedly continue to document its repercussions in the past and the present for some time to come.

Notes

Introduction

1. William Gardner Smith, interview, *New York Post*, September 29, 1959, Clipping File William Gardner Smith, Schomburg Center for Research in Black Culture, New York.
2. Colin Powell, *My American Journey* (New York: Random House, 1995), 53.
3. Brenda Gayle Plummer, *Rising Wind: Black Americans and U.S. Foreign Affairs, 1935–1960* (Chapel Hill: University of North Carolina Press, 1996); Mary Dudziak, *Cold War Civil Rights: Race and the Image of American Democracy* (Princeton: Princeton University Press, 2000); Azza Salama Layton, *International Politics and Civil Rights Policies in the United States, 1941–1960* (Cambridge, UK: Cambridge University Press, 2000); Thomas Borstelmann, *The Cold War and the Color Line: American Race Relations in the Global Arena* (Cambridge, MA: Harvard University Press, 2001). For a discussion of recent literature, see Kevin K. Gaines, "The Civil Rights Movement in World Perspective," in *America on the World Stage: A Global Approach to U.S. History/The Organization of American Historians*, ed. Gary W. Reichard and Ted Dickson (Urbana and Chicago: University of Illinois Press, 2008), 189–207. For the limitations imposed on the civil rights agenda by Cold War politics in the area of anticolonialism or Pan-African solidarity, see Penny von Eschen, *Race Against Empire: Black Americans and Anticolonialism, 1937–1957* (Ithaca: Cornell University Press, 1997); and Carol Anderson, *Eyes Off the Prize: The United Nations and the African American Struggle for Human Rights, 1944–1955* (Cambridge: Cambridge University Press, 2003); Manfred Berg, "Black Civil Rights and Liberal Anticommunism: The NAACP in the Early Cold War," *Journal of American History* 94.1 (2007): 75–96. See also Maria Höhn, " 'Ein Atemzug der Freiheit.' Afro-amerikanische GIs, deutsche Frauen, und die Grenzen der Demokratie (1945–1968)," in *Demokratiewunder. Transatlantische Mittler und die kulturelle Öffnung Westdeutschlands, 1945–1970*, ed. Arnd Bauerkämpfer, Konrad H. Jarausch, and Marcus Payk (Göttingen: Vandenhoeck & Ruprecht, 2005); and idem, " 'When Negro Soldiers Bring Home White Brides': Deutsche und amerikanische Debatten über die 'Mischehe' (1945–1967)," in *Amerikaner in Rheinland-Pfalz. Alltagskulturelle Begegnungen*, ed. Werner Kremp and Martina Tumalis (Trier: WVT Wissenschaftlicher Verlag, 2008).
4. See Maria Höhn, *GIs and Fräuleins: The German-American Encounter in 1950s West Germany* (Chapel Hill: University of North Carolina Press, 2002); Heide Fehrenbach, *Race after Hitler: Black Occupation Children in Postwar Germany and America* (Princeton: Princeton University Press, 2005); Tim Schroer, *Recasting Race after World War II: Germans and African Americans in American-Occupied Germany* (Boulder: University of Colorado Press, 2007).

5. Recent exceptions include Adriane Lentz-Smith, *Freedom Struggles: African Americans and World War I* (Cambridge, MA: Harvard University Press, 2009), which stresses the impact the encounter with French civilians and African troops had on black soldiers during World War I and on the civil rights struggle at home, as well as Manfred Berg, "American Wars and the Black Struggle for Freedom and Equality," in *The American Experience of War*, ed. Georg Schild (Paderborn: Ferdinand Schöningh, 2010), 133–54. For an extensive bibliography on the participation of African Americans in the U.S. armed forces, please see www.aacvr-germany.org/blackGIs.

6. We do not argue that the civil rights discourse that emerged in the United States was determined solely by America's growing entanglement with Germany. As Glenda Elizabeth Gilmore has shown in *Defying Dixie: The Radical Roots of Civil Rights, 1919–1950* (New York: W. W. Norton, 2008), radical leftist interracial alliances in the South during the 1920s and 1930s and their indictment of fascism already helped to sharpen the discourse on civil rights. In *How Far the Promised Land? World Affairs and the American Civil Rights Movement from the First World War to Vietnam* (Princeton: Princeton University Press, 2006), Jonathan Rosenberg demonstrates how the anti-colonial struggles influenced the internationalist outlook of African American intellectuals and framed debates on civil rights. See also his "'Sounds Suspiciously Like Miami': Nazism and the U.S. Civil Rights Movement, 1933–1941," in *The Cultural Turn: Essays in the History of U.S. Foreign Relations*, ed. Frank A. Ninkovich and Liping Bu (Chicago: Imprint, 2001). For the emerging collaboration between American Jews and African Americans over civil rights, see Harvard Sitkoff, "African Americans, American Jews, and the Holocaust," in *The Achievement of American Liberalism: The New Deal and Its Legacies*, ed. William H. Chafe (New York: Columbia University Press, 2003), 181–204.

7. David Brion Davis, "The Americanized Mannheim of 1945–1946," in *American Places: Encounters with History. A Celebration of Sheldon Meyer*, ed. William E. Leuchtenburg (Oxford: Oxford University Press, 2000), 79–91, esp. 79, 91.

8. For the full text of President Harry S. Truman's Executive Order 9981, see http://www.trumanlibrary.org/9981a.htm.

9. On the black press, see Lee Finkle, *Forum for Protest: The Black Press during World War II* (Rutherford, NJ: Fairleigh Dickinson University Press, 1975); and Patrick Washburn, *A Question of Sedition: The Federal Government's Investigation of the Black Press* (New York and Oxford: Oxford University Press, 1986). On the centrality of the press in creating and maintaining the black community, see Gunnar Myrdal, *An American Dilemma: The Negro Problem and Modern Democracy* (New York: Harper, 1944), Chapter 42; and Roi Ottley, *New World A-Coming* (New York: Houghton, Mifflin, 1943), Chapter 19.

10. At U.S. military bases in the Pacific, where Navy and Marine personnel were usually stationed for relatively short periods of time before rotating to another location, such alliances between black servicemen and civilians rarely had enough time to develop; and in South Korea, U.S. troops were much more isolated from the civilian population and served only year-long tours of duty.

11. See Frank W. Render, Department of Defense, U.S. Assistant Secretary of Defense, Manpower and Reserve Affairs, Memorandum for the Secretary of Defense, "U.S. Military Race Relations in Europe—September 1970"; and NAACP, *The Search for Military Justice: Report of an NAACP Inquiry Into the Problems of Negro Servicemen in West Germany* (New York: NAACP, 1971).

12. For more global outlooks on U.S. history, see representatively Thomas Bender, *A Nation among Nations: America's Place in World History* (New York: Hill and Wang, 2006); Ian Tyrrell, *Transnational Nation: United States History in Global Perspective since 1789* (Basingstoke: Palgrave Macmillan, 2007). The

emergence of African American diaspora studies, as well as the turn to transnational history, have also greatly expanded the boundaries of American history and African American studies. Particularly influential in reassessing the significance of European and African connections have been the works of Paul Gilroy, e.g., Paul Gilroy, *The Black Atlantic: Modernity and Double Consciousness* (Cambridge, MA: Harvard University Press, 1993), which spurred a plethora of new studies, topics, and approaches. For glimpses into this booming field, see, e.g., Brent Hayes Edwards, *The Practice of Diaspora: Literature, Translation, and the Rise of Black Internationalism* (Cambridge, MA: Harvard University Press, 2003); Michelle Wright, *Becoming Black: Creating Identity in the African Diaspora* (Durham: Duke University Press, 2004); Gerald Horne, *Black and Brown: African Americans and the Mexican Revolution* (New York: NYU Press, 2005); Nikihil Pal Singh, *Black Is a Country: Race and the Unfinished Struggle for Democracy* (Cambridge, MA: Harvard University Press, 2005); Kevin K. Gaines, *American Africans in Ghana: Black Expatriates and the Civil Rights Era* (Chapel Hill: University of North Carolina Press, 2006); Manning Marable and Vanessa Agard-Jones, eds., *Transnational Blackness: Navigating the Global Color Line* (New York: Palgrave Macmillan, 2008); Mary Dudziak, *Exporting American Dreams: Thurgood Marshall's African Journey* (Oxford: Oxford University Press, 2008); Marilyn Lake, *Drawing the Global Colour Line: White Men's Countries and the International Challenge of Racial Equality* (New York: Cambridge University Press, 2008); Gerald Horne, *Red Seas: Ferdinand Smith and Radical Black Sailors in the United States and Jamaica* (New York: NYU Press, 2009); Idem, *The End of Empires: African Americans and India* (Philadelphia: Temple University Press, 2009); Michael West, William Martin, and Fanon Che Wilkins, eds., *From Toussaint to Tupac: The Black International since the Age of Revolution* (Chapel Hill: University of North Carolina Press, 2009); Susan D. Pennybacker, *From Scottsboro to Munich: Race and Political Culture in 1930s Britain* (Princeton: Princeton University Press, 2009); Oliver Schmidt, "African American Troops in World War II: Transnational Perspectives on the 'Race War,'" *European Journal of Transnational Studies* 1.2 (Autumn 2009): 5–24; Simon Wendt, "Transnational Perspectives on the History of Racism in America," *Amerikastudien/American Studies* 54.3 (2009): 473–98; Jason C. Parker, "'Made-in-America Revolutions'? The 'Black University' and the American Role in the Decolonization of the Black Atlantic," *Journal of American History* 96.3 (December 2009): 727–50; Andrew Zimmermann, *Alabama in Africa: Booker T. Washington, the German Empire, and the Globalization of the New South* (Princeton: Princeton University Press, 2010). Scholarly networks, such as the Collegium for African American Research (CAAR), the Association of the Study of the Worldwide African Diaspora (ASWAD), the Black European Studies Program at the University of Mainz (BEST), as well as the Society for Multi-Ethnic Studies: Europe and the Americas (MESEA), have also facilitated this geographical expansion and broadened the scope of such studies beyond U.S. slavery and its aftermath. Almost all of these publications and networks, however, have paid no attention to the black GIs stationed in Germany.

13. See Gaines, *The Civil Rights Movement in World Perspective*.
14. For the full text of Dr. King's Nobel lecture, see http://nobelprize.org/nobel_prizes/peace/laureates/1964/king-lecture.html.
15. Martin Luther King Jr., "East or West—God's Children," Sermon, September 13, 1964, 1, 4f., Papers of Dr. Martin Luther King, Jr., The King Center, Atlanta, GA (hereafter KCA).
16. For the full text of Barack Obama's speech in Berlin on July 24, 2008, see http://my.barackobama.com/page/content/berlinvideo/.

17. Gerald Horne, "Toward a Transnational Research Agenda for African American History in the 21st Century," *Journal of African American History* 91.3 (2006): 288–303. Despite Horne's plea, few graduate programs have inspired their students to explore African American history outside the United States.

1 Closing Ranks: World War I and the Rise of Hitler

1. For gender and race relations in the South, see Tara McPherson, *Reconstructing Dixie: Race, Gender, and Nostalgia in the Imagined South* (Durham: Duke University Press, 2003); Hannah Rosen, *Terror in the Heart of Freedom: Citizenship, Sexual Violence, and the Meaning of Race in the Postemancipation South* (Chapel Hill: University of North Carolina Press, 2009); Crystal N. Feimster, *Southern Horrors: Women and the Politics of Rape and Lynching* (Cambridge, MA: Harvard University Press, 2009). For a history of miscegenation laws, see Paul Spickard, *Mixed Blood: Intermarriage and Ethnic Identity in Twentieth-Century America* (Madison: University of Wisconsin, 1989); Martha Hodes, ed., *Sex, Love, Race: Crossing Boundaries in North American History* (New York, NYU Press, 1999); Werner Sollors, *Interracialism: Black-White Intermarriage in American History, Literature, and Law* (Oxford: Oxford University Press, 2000); Elise Lemire, *'Miscegenation': Making Race in America* (Philadelphia: University of Pennsylvania Press, 2002); Kevin Johnson, *Mixed Race America and the Law* (New York: New York University, 2003); Renee Romano, *Race Mixing: Black-White Marriage in Postwar America* (Cambridge, MA: Harvard University Press, 2003); Peggy Pascoe, *What Comes Naturally: Miscegenation Law and the Making of Race in America* (Oxford: Oxford University Press, 2009).
2. For a good overview of the Jim Crow South before 1940, see, e.g., Neil McMillen, *Dark Journey: Black Mississippians in the Age of Jim Crow* (Urbana: University of Illinois Press, 1990).
3. Ibid., 197.
4. Ibid., 26.
5. W. E. B. Du Bois, quoted here from Sieglinde Lemke, "Berlin and Boundaries: *sollen* versus *geschehen*," *boundary 2*, 27.3 (2000): 45–78, esp. 50.
6. W. E. B. Du Bois, *Dusk of Dawn: An Essay toward an Autobiography of a Race Concept* (1940; New York: Oxford University Press, 2007), 51. For Du Bois's experiences in Germany and their impact on his thought, see Kenneth Barkin, "'Berlin Days,' 1892–1894: W. E. B. Du Bois and German Political Economy," *boundary 2*, 27.3 (2000): 79–101; Hamilton Beck, "W. E. B. Du Bois as a Study Abroad Student in Germany, 1892–1894," www.frontiersjournal.com/issues/vol2/vol2-03_beck.htm; W. E. B. Du Bois, *The Autobiography of W. E. B. Du Bois* (New York: International, 1968).
7. Theodore Kornweibel, *"Investigate Everything": Federal Efforts to Compel Black Loyalty during World War I* (Bloomington: Indiana University Press, 2002), 81.
8. Ibid.
9. Arthur Barbeau and Florette Henri, *The Unknown Soldiers: African American Troops in World War I* (Philadelphia: Temple University, 1974), 106.
10. Ibid., 165–66.
11. On the experience of African American soldiers in World War I, see also Stephen Harris, *Harlem's Hell Fighters—The African American 369th Infantry in World War I* (Dulles: Potomac Books, 2002); Adriane Lentz-Smith, *Freedom Struggles: African Americans and World War I* (Cambridge, MA: Harvard University Press,

2009). For good historical overviews of racism in the military, see Ulysses Lee, *The Employment of Negro Troops* (Washington, DC: Office of the Chief of Military History, U.S. Army, 1966); and Bernard C. Nalty, *Strength for the Fight: A History of Black Americans in the Military* (New York: Free Press, 1989). See also the special issue of *Journal of Negro Education* 12 (Summer 1943).
12. McMillen, *Dark Journey*, 264.
13. Herman Graham, *The Brothers' Vietnam War. Black Power, Manhood, and the Military Experience* (Gainesville: University Press of Florida, 2003), 8–9.
14. Cited in Lentz-Smith, *Freedom Struggles*, 129.
15. W. E. B. Du Bois, "An Essay toward a History of the Black Man in the Great War," *Crisis* 18.2 (June 1919): 63–87, 87. See also W. E. B. Du Bois, "The Negro Soldiers in Service Abroad during the First World War," *Journal of Negro Education* 12 (Summer 1943): 324–34.
16. Ridgely Torrence, *The Story of John Hope* (New York: Macmillan, 1948), 207–40.
17. Ibid.
18. W. E. B. Du Bois, "Returning Soldiers," *Crisis* 18 (May 1919): 13–14, 14. See also Jennifer Keene, "W. E. B. Du Bois and the Wounded World: Seeking Meaning in the First World War for African-Americans," *Peace & Change* 26.2 (April 2001): 135–52.
19. Cited in Barbeau and Henri, *The Unknown Soldiers*, 175.
20. McMillen, *Dark Journey*, 306.
21. Barbeau and Henri, *The Unknown Soldiers*, 177. Significantly, when white mobs attacked black neighborhoods, black veterans took up guns to defend their homes. See Simon Wendt, *The Spirit and the Shotgun: Armed Resistance and the Struggle for Civil Rights: New Perspectives on the History of the South* (Gainesville: University Press of Florida, 2007), 13f.
22. Ibid., 173.
23. Sherie Mershon and Steven Schlossman, *Foxholes and Color Lines: Desegregating the U.S. Armed Forces* (Baltimore: Johns Hopkins University Press, 1998), 8.
24. See, e.g., Glenda Gilmore, *Defying Dixie: The Radical Roots of Civil Rights, 1919–1950* (New York: W. W. Norton, 2008).
25. Elmer Anderson Carter, "On Racial Prejudice at Home and Abroad," *Opportunity: Journal for Negro Life* 17 (1939): 2. For a detailed discussion of interwar comparisons between Nazism and Jim Crow, see Gilmore, *Defying Dixie*; Jonathan Seth Rosenberg, *How Far the Promised Land? World Affairs and the American Civil Rights Movement from the First World War to Vietnam* (Princeton: Princeton University Press, 2005); and idem, " 'Sounds Suspiciously Like Miami': Nazism and the U.S. Civil Rights Movement, 1933–1941," in *The Cultural Turn: Essays in the History of Foreign Relations*, ed. Frank Ninkovich and Liping Bu (Chicago: Imprint, 2001), 105–30; Johnpeter Horst Grill, "The American South and Nazi Racism," in *The Impact of Nazism: New Perspectives on the Third Reich and Its Legacy*, ed. Alan E. Steinweis and Daniel E. Rogers (Lincoln: University of Nebraska Press, 2003), 19–38. See also the classic study by Harvard Sitkoff, *A New Deal For Blacks: The Emergence of Civil Rights as an Issue* (New York: Oxford University Press, 1978); Patricia Sullivan, *Days of Hope: Race and Democracy in the New Deal Era* (Chapel Hill: University of North Carolina Press, 1996); and Maria Höhn, " 'We Will Never Go Back to the Old Way Again': Germany in the African American Debate on Civil Rights," *Central European History* 41.4 (2008): 605–37. For the general perception of Nazi Germany in the United States, see Michaela Hoenicke Moore, *Know Your Enemy: The American Debate on Nazism, 1933–1945* (New York: Cambridge University Press, 2010).
26. On Joe Louis, see David Margolick, *Beyond Glory: Joe Louis vs. Max Schmeling and a World on the Brink* (New York: Knopf, 2005); Lewis A. Erenberg, *The*

Greatest Fight of Our Generation: Louis vs. Schmeling (New York: Oxford University Press, 2006); Randy Roberts, *Joe Louis: Hard Times Man* (New Haven: Yale University Press, forthcoming). On Jesse Owens, see William J. Baker, *Jesse Owens: An American Life* (Urbana: University of Illinois Press, 2006); Jeremy Schaap, *Triumph: The Untold Story of Jesse Owens and Hitler's Olympics* (Boston: Houghton Mifflin, 2007). See also Donald McRae, *Heroes without a Country: America's Betrayal of Joe Louis and Jesse Owens* (New York: Ecco, 2002).

27. For a detailed discussion of the failure of the antilynching bill, see Sitkoff, *A New Deal For Blacks*, 274–95. On the refugee scholars, see Gabrielle Simone Edgcomb, *From Swastika to Jim Crow: Refugee Scholars at Black Colleges* (Malabar, FL: Krieger, 1993). For the case of Georg Iggers, who escaped from Nazi Germany in 1938 and started teaching at Philander Smith College in Little Rock, Arkansas, together with his wife Wilma in 1950, becoming active in the local NAACP chapter, see Wilma and Georg Iggers, *Two Lives in Uncertain Times: Facing the Challenges of the 20th Century as Scholars & Citizens* (New York: Berghahn Books, 2006), 35–43, 61–87, 103–20. For an opposite case, namely, the racist portrayal of Howard University by German ethnologist Julius Lips, who worked there from 1937 to 1939, see Berndt Ostendorf, "Forschungsreise in die Dämmerung: The Strange Transatlantic Career of Julius Lips between Howard University and Leipzig University," in *Transatlantic Cultural Contexts: Essays in Honor of Eberhard Brüning*, ed. Hartmut Keil (Tübingen: Stauffenburg, 2005), 115–27.

28. Kate Stack, "Lily White Democracy," *Crisis* 46 (December 1939): 49.

29. "Nazi Butchers," *Chicago Defender*, December 26, 1942, 14.

30. Charles Hanson, "Plenty of Space to Exist In," interview by Maggi Morehouse, 1998, www.aacvr-germany.org/oralhistory.

31. Lucille Milner, "Jim Crow in the Army," *New Republic*, March 13, 1944, 339–42.

32. Editorial in the *Chicago Defender* from 1940, quoted here from Mershon and Schlossman, *Foxholes and Color Lines*, 38. On blacks' reluctance to support the war, see Sterling A. Brown, "Count Us In," in *What the Negro Wants*, ed. Rayford W. Logan (Chapel Hill: University of North Carolina Press, 1944), 308–44.

33. W. E. B. Du Bois, "As the Crow Flies," *Amsterdam News*, April 19, 1941, cited in Lee Finkle, *Forum for Protest: The Black Press during WWII* (Cranbury: Associated University Presses, 1975), 199; George Schuyler, "Hitlerism Without Hitler," *Crisis*, December 1941, 384, 389.

34. "Fight for Liberties Here while Fighting Dictators Abroad, NAACP Urges," *Crisis*, January 1942, 36.

35. Ibid.

36. "Says Now Is Time to Rap Hypocrisies," *Chicago Defender*, January 17, 1942, 6.

37. *Pittsburgh Courier*, February 14, 1942. The paper announced the Double-V Campaign on its front page and would sport the logo of the campaign and related stories throughout the war.

38. Finkle, *Forum for Protest*, 189.

39. "Now Is the Time Not to Be Silent," *Crisis*, January 1942, 7. See also the War Department's 1944 propaganda film, *The Negro Soldier*, directed by Stuart Heisler.

40. "Revolution in Dixie," *Chicago Defender*, August 5, 1944, 12.

2 Fighting on Two Fronts: World War II and Civil Rights

1. Neil McMillen, "Fighting for What We Did Not Have: How Mississippi Veterans Remember World War II," in *Remaking Dixie: The Impact of World War II on*

the American South, ed. Neil McMillen (Jackson: University of Mississippi Press, 1997), 93–110, 102.

2. Morris MacGregor, *Integration of the Armed Forces, 1940–1965* (Washington, DC: Center for Military History, 1981), 20–21. See also Sherie Mershon and Steven Schlossman, *Foxholes and Color Lines: Desegregating the U.S. Armed Forces* (Baltimore: Johns Hopkins University Press, 1998); L. D. Reddick, "The Negro Policy of the American Army since World War II," *Journal of Negro History* 38.2 (1953): 194–215; Ulysses Grant Lee, *The Employment of Negro Troops* (Washington, DC: Office of the Chief of Military History, U.S. Army, 1966); Maggi M. Morehouse, *Fighting in a Jim Crow Army: Black Men and Women Remember World War II* (Lanham, MD: Rowman and Littlefield, 2000).

3. See, e.g., Lawrence P. Scott and William M. Womack, *Double V: The Civil Rights Struggle of the Tuskegee Airmen* (East Lansing: Michigan State University Press, 1994); Todd J. Moye, *Freedom Flyers: The Tuskegee Airmen of World War II* (New York: Oxford University Press, 2010).

4. Dwight MacDonald and Nancy MacDonald, *The War's Greatest Scandal! The Story of Jim Crow in Uniform* (New York: March on Washington Movement, 1943), 3–4. On the issue of separate blood banks, see Thomas A. Guglielmo, "'Red Cross, Double Cross': Race and America's World War II–Era Blood Donor Service," *Journal of American History* 97.1 (June 2010): 63–90.

5. Spencer Moore, "No Time to Think about Civil Rights," interview by Maggi Morehouse, Magnolia, NJ, 1998; Walter Patrice, interview by Maria Höhn, Poughkeepsie, NY, 2010, both available at www.aacvr-germany.org/oralhistory.

6. A. William Perry, "Like a Slap in the Face," interview by Maggi Morehouse, Cleveland, OH, 1998, available at www.aacvr-germany.org/oralhistory.

7. "Meanest Trick," *Crisis*, April 1943, 105.

8. Joe Stephenson, "I Put Blinders On and Shut Out Bad Things," interview by Maggi Morehouse, Washington, DC, 1998; Joseph Hairston, "We Structured the March on Washington Like an Army Formation," interview by Maggi Morehouse, Washington, DC, 1998; Reuben Horner, "Fighting against My White Superiors," interview by Maggi Morehouse, Tucson, AZ, 1998, all available at www.aacvr-germany.org/oralhistory.

9. For racial discrimination and the civil rights movement in the Northern United States, see, e.g., Thomas J. Sugrue, *Sweet Land of Liberty: The Forgotten Struggle for Civil Rights in the North* (New York: Random House, 2008).

10. Langston Hughes, "My America," in *What the Negro Wants*, ed. Rayford W. Logan (Chapel Hill: University of North Carolina Press, 1944), 299–307, esp. 301 and 303.

11. Editorial: "The Negro in the United States Army," *Crisis*, February 1942, 47–49, 49. For the significance of World War II for the political mobilization of African Americans, see also Nikihil Pal Singh, *Black Is a Country: Race and the Unfinished Struggle for Democracy* (Cambridge, MA: Harvard University Press, 2005), 101–33.

12. Mershon and Schlossman, *Foxholes and Color Lines*, 15.

13. U.S. War Department, *Command of Negro Troops: War Department, 29 February 1944*, Pamphlet No. 20–6 (Washington, DC: US Government Printing Office, 1944), 13. See also Mershon and Schlossman, *Foxholes and Color Lines*, 1–22.

14. "The Negroes' Role in the War," July 8, 1943, 45, Office of War Information, Folder Negroes and Negro Race, RG 165/390, Box 472, National Archives and Records Administration, Washington, DC/College Park, MD (hereafter NARA).

15. Letter from Pvt. James N. Williams, Aide, Headquarters First Service Command Field Office, Security and Intelligence Division, December 20, 1944, 2, Office of Army Sec. Of War/Civilian Aide, RG 107, Box 261, NARA.

16. "The Negroes' Role in the War," July 8, 1943, 17.

17. Walter Francis White, *A Rising Wind* (Garden City: Doubleday, Doran, 1945), 21. White's book on his visit to troops gives a moving account of the soldiers' experiences in Europe and Africa. See also his records from that visit in the NAACP Folder, RG 107, Box 221, NARA. Graham Smith, *When Jim Crow Met John Bull* (New York: I. B. Tauris, 1987), describes the positive encounters African American GIs had in Great Britain, and how badly they were treated by their own officers and comrades. For reports from Great Britain, see, e.g., Army Service Forces Technical Intelligence Report: "Relations of Negro Troops with U.S. and British Soldiers," December 21, 1944, RG 107, CA, Box 265; and RG 498, Box 43, HQ ETO, NARA.

18. The breakdown of the miscegenation taboo was one of the most widely discussed concerns for the military. See, e.g., "Racial Situation in the United States," January 20 to February 3, 1945; War Dept. General Staff Decimale RG 185, Box 44 File 46–46; and excerpts from censored letters, RG 498, Box 43, HQ ETO, NARA.

19. Observations and Recommendations of Walter White on Racial Relations in the ETO February 11, 1944, 3–4, NAACP Folder I, RG 107, Box 221, NARA.

20. On Vernon Baker, see Richard Goldstein, "Vernon Baker, Medal of Honor Recipient, Dies at 90," *New York Times*, July 15, 2010, B17. On Alston's artwork and its distribution, see Harry Amana, "The Art of Propaganda: Charles Alston's World War II Editorial Cartoons for the Office of War Information and the Black Press," *American Journalism* 21.2 (2004): 79–111.

21. Cited in McMillen, "Fighting for What We Didn't Have," 100.

22. Reddick, "The Negro Policy," 196.

23. For military anxiety over upsetting the social order at home because of a war far away, see George H. Roeder Jr., "Censoring Disorder: American Visual Imagery of World War II," in *The War in American Culture: Society and Consciousness During World War II*, ed. Lewis A. Erenberg and Susan E. Hirsch (Chicago: University of Chicago Press, 1996), 46–70. The military, for example, also forbade the circulation of pictures portraying black soldiers and white women.

24. "Report of Trends in the Negro Press" (Weeks of May 26–June 2, 1945), June 11, 1945, 4, War Dept. General Staff Decimal File, RG 165, Box 260, NARA.

25. Secretary of War, Civil Aide to the Secretary, Attitudes of Negro Soldiers, Interview with Captain George Gitskin, June 28, 1945, Box 265, RG 107, NARA.

26. Cited in McMillen, "Fighting for What We Didn't Have," 103.

27. Letter from Pvt. James N. Williams, Aide, Headquarters First Service Command Field Office, Security and Intelligence Division, December 20, 1944, 2, Office of the Army Sec. of War/Civilian Aid, RG 107, Box 261, NARA.

28. Cited in Steve Estes, *I Am a Man! Race, Manhood, and the Civil Rights Movement* (Chapel Hill: University of North Carolina Press, 2005), 11.

29. Secretary of War, Civil Aide to the Secretary, Attitudes of Negro Soldiers, Interview with Captain Richard Middleton, July 26, 1945, RG 107, Box 265, NARA.

30. Secretary of War, Civil Aide to the Secretary, Attitudes of Negro Soldiers, Interview with Chaplain Weiman Tyus, July 26, 1945, RG 107, Box 265, NARA.

31. Lou Potter, *Liberators: Fighting on Two Fronts in World War II* (New York: Harcourt, Brace, Jovanovich, 1992), 270. For a discussion of the controversy surrounding the book and movie project *Liberators* (1992, dir. William Miles and Nina Rosenblum), as well as the official U.S. military definitions of "liberators", see Phyllis R. Klotman, "Military Rights and Wrongs: African Americans in the U.S. Armed Forces," in *The Black Studies Reader*, ed. by Jacqueline Bobo, Cynthia Hudley, and Claudine Michel (New York: Routledge, 2004), 113–37.

32. William A. Scott III, "World War II Veteran Remembers the Horror of the Holocaust," illustrated pamphlet published c. 1991 and accessible online as a pdf file at http://www.aacvr-germany.org/scott.

33. Leon Bass and Pam Sporn, " 'I Saw the Walking Dead': A Black Sergeant Remembers Buchenwald," interview segment of the documentary "Blacks and Jews: Are They Really Sworn Enemies?" produced by the Educational Video Center, text and audio accessible online at http://historymatters.gmu.edu/d/142. For more information on Leon Bass's experience, see www.aacvr-germany.org/oralhistory.

34. Army Service Forces Technical Intelligence Report: Operations of a Negro Engineer Dump Truck Company; Report No. 855, July 4, 1945, RG 107, CA, Box 265, NARA.

35. Military Attaché Report: Relations Between White and Negro—United States Troops in England; Report No. 84, September 7, 1944, Military Intelligence Division, RG 107, Box 265, NARA.

36. "Negroes," Overviews of the racial situation in the United States from the War Department, April 1944, RG 319, Box 380, NARA.

37. Editorial, "The Negro Veteran Tests America," *Ebony*, May 1946, 40.

38. Charles G. Bolté and Louis Harris, *Our Negro Veterans*, Public Affairs Pamphlet No. 128 (New York: Public Affairs Committee, 1947), 5–8.

39. Ralph G. Martin, "Where Is Home?" *New Republic*, December 31, 1945, 898–900.

40. McMillen "Fighting for What We Didn't Have," 103.

41. Rev. Hosea Williams, quoted in Richard Wormser, *The Rise and Fall of Jim Crow* (New York: St. Martin's Press, 2003), 166. For additional incidents of violence against veterans and the explosion of KKK activity, see James Cobb, "World War II and the Mind of the Modern South," in *Remaking Dixie*, ed. McMillen, 3–20, 6–7; Adam Fairclough, *Race and Democracy: The Civil Rights Struggle in Louisiana, 1915–1972*, 2nd ed. (Athens, GA: University of Georgia Press, 2008), 106–34.

42. McMillen, "Fighting for What We Didn't Have," 99.

43. Wormser, *The Rise and Fall of Jim Crow*, 166.

44. Oliver Harrington, "Frontiers Still Left in America: The Negro's Part," in *The Struggle for Justice as a World Force: Report of the* New York Herald Tribune *Annual Forum* (New York: Herald Tribune, 1945), 50–55, 52.

45. Cited in Moore, *Fighting in a Jim Crow Army*, 197.

46. McMillen, "Fighting for What We Didn't Have," 99.

47. Ibid.

48. Cited in Estes, *I Am a Man*, 38.

49. Ibid., 36. On the postwar jump in NAACP membership, see Mary White Ovington, *The Walls Came Tumbling Down* (New York: Harcourt, Brace, 1947), 280; Manfred Berg, *'The Ticket to Freedom': The NAACP and the Struggle for Black Political Integration* (Gainesville: University Press of Florida, 2005), 109–15; Patricia Sullivan, *Lift Every Voice: The NAACP and the Making of the Civil Rights Movement* (New York: New Press, 2009), 267–87.

50. Original emphasis. Roy Wilkins, "The Negro Wants Full Equality," in *What the Negro Wants*, ed. Logan, 130.

51. Despite continued employment discrimination for African Americans, the expanded opportunities for training and education for returning black veterans provided by the 1944 GI Bill and the subsequent Veterans' Adjustment Act of 1952 also fostered greater political mobilization. See David H. Onkst, " 'First a Negro...Incidentally a Veteran': Black World War Two Veterans and the G.I. Bill in the Deep South, 1944–1948," *Journal of Social History* 31 (Spring 1998): 517–44; Suzanne Mettler, *Soldiers to Citizens: The G.I. Bill and the Making of the Greatest Generation* (Oxford: Oxford University Press, 2005), 136–43.

52. Jim Williams, "They Treated the German POWs Better than Us," interview by Maggi Morehouse in Philadelphia, 1998, available at www.aacvr-germany.org/oralhistory.
53. Estes, *I Am a Man*, 263; and Ovington, *The Walls Came Tumbling Down*, 280. On the role of veterans in the civil rights movement, see also McMillen, "Fighting for What We Didn't Have"; James Cobb, "World War II and the Mind of the Modern South," in McMillen, *Remaking Dixie*, 6–7; Borstelman, *The Cold War*, 54; David Brion Davis, "The Americanized Mannheim of 1945–46," in *American Places: Encounters With History. A Celebration of Sheldon Meyer*, ed. William Leuchtenburg (Oxford: Oxford University Press, 2000), 88.
54. Jack Pollack, "Literacy Tests" (1947), reprinted in *Reporting Civil Rights, Part One: American Journalism, 1941–1963*, ed. Clayborne Carson, David J. Garrow, Bill Kovach, and Carol Polsgrove (New York: The Library of America, 2003), 85–91, 87.
55. Charles G. Bolté and Louis Harris, *Our Negro Veterans*, Public Affairs Pamphlet No. 128 (New York: Public Affairs Committee, 1947), 5, 6, 8. For the strengthening of political determination among African Americans in Louisiana, see Fairclough, *Race and Democracy*, 106–34.

3   "We Will Never Go Back to the Old Way Again": African American GIs and the Occupation of Germany

1. Roi Ottley, "*No Green Pastures* (Installment VIII)," *Chicago Defender*, December 15, 1951, 13, excerpted from Ottley's book *No Green Pastures* (New York: Charles Scribner's Sons, 1951). Some of the issues raised in this chapter have previously been discussed in Maria Höhn, " 'We Will Never Go Back to the Old Way Again': Germany in the African American Debate on Civil Rights," *Central European History* 41.4 (December 2008): 605–37. See also Maria Höhn, *GIs and Fräuleins: The German-American Encounters in 1950s West Germany* (Chapel Hill: University of North Carolina Press, 2002), Chapter 3, where Höhn first showed how the civil rights struggle came to Germany through the U.S. base system. See also Heide Fehrenbach, *Race after Hitler* (Princeton: Princeton University Press, 2007), Chapter 1; and Timothy L. Schroer, *Recasting Race after World War II: Germans and African Americans in American-Occupied Germany* (Boulder: University Press of Colorado, 2007), especially Chapter 2.
2. David Brion Davis, "The Americanized Mannheim of 1945–46," in *American Places: Encounters with History: A Celebration of Sheldon Meyer*, ed. William Leuchtenburg (Oxford: Oxford University Press, 2000), 79–91, 79.
3. William Gardner Smith used the term "Shangri-La" in his *Return to Black America* (Englewood Cliffs: Prentice Hall, 1970), 63. See also Georg Schmundt-Thomas, "America's Germany: National Self and Cultural Other after World War II," PhD diss. (Northwestern University, 1992). Schmundt-Thomas coined the term "racial utopia" in discussing Smith's novel.
4. Johannes Kleinschmidt, *"Do Not Fraternize." Die schwierigen Anfänge der deutsch-amerikanischen Freundschaft 1944–1949* (Trier: WVT, 1997), 133.
5. For the military's efforts to keep black soldiers out of positions that entailed police power over white Germans or supervision of white workers, see Margaret Geis, "Negro Personnel in the European Command, 1 January 1946–30 June 1950" (Office of the Chief Historian of Military History, European Command, Historical Division, 1952), 54–56; and Schroer, *Recasting Race*, 47–81, especially.
6. Geis, "Negro Personnel," 56.

7. Morris J. MacGregor, *Integration of the Armed Forces, 1940–1965* (Washington, DC: Center for Military History, 1981), 214.

8. On efforts to get African American GIs out of Germany, see Joseph Starr, *Fraternization with the Germans in World War II*, Occupation Forces in Europe Series 67 (Frankfurt: Office of the Chief Historian, Headquarters European Command, 1947), 153; John Willoughby, *Remaking the Conquering Heroes* (New York: Palgrave, 2001), 53–55; and Schroer's thoughtful discussion in Chapter 2 of his *Recasting Race*.

9. Cited in Kleinschmidt, "*Do Not Fraternize*," 204. A similar sense was conveyed in another manual, where soldiers were told that it was up to them to be "selling democracy to the Nazis and controlling them until they really believe it." Cited in Willoughby, *Remaking the Conquering Heroes*, 107.

10. "Orientation Program for Dependents," Occupation of Germany 1944–48, Misc. Files, 7 and 17, U.S. Army Military Institute, Carlisle, PA.

11. On the segregated army, see Ronal Sher, "Integration of Negro and White Troops in the U.S. Army, Europe, 1952–1954" (Heidelberg: Office of the Chief Historian, Headquarters USAREUR, 1956). See also Roy Wilkins, "Still a Jim Crow Army," *Crisis*, April 1946, 106–25. For an overview of the institutionalized racism experienced by black soldiers serving in Germany, see the Negro Newspaper Editors' Report to the Secretary of War, July 1946, RG 407, Box 719, NARA.

12. Davis, "The Americanized Mannheim," 91. On commanders who addressed their troops as "Niggers" in front of the Germans, see also Negro Newspaper Editors' Report to the Secretary of War, July 8, 1946, RG 407, Box 719, NARA.

13. For McNarney's views, see Schroer, *Recasting Race*, 67–70. See also "The *Meader Report*: Another Black Eye," *Chicago Defender*, December 14, 1946; and "Racial: Mädchen and Negro," *Newsweek*, September 16, 1946, 30.

14. Schroer, *Recasting Race*, 67.

15. See, e.g., "Negroes Play Vital Reconstruction Role," *Chicago Defender*, April 10, 1948; "Negro Troops Win Praise on 'Operation Vittles'. Truck Goods Flown in by Air Lift," *Chicago Defender*, October 16, 1948, 4; Lou Swarz, "'Harlem Tigers,' Veteran QM. Co., Become German Occupation Troops," *Chicago Defender*, October 13, 1945, 14. See also Hon. Helen Gahagan Douglas, *The Negro Soldier: A Practical Record of Negro Devotion and Heroism in the Cause of Freedom Gathered from the Files of the War and Navy Department*. Remarks of Douglas were entered into the congressional record on February 1, 1946. On the WACs and black women's wartime activism, see Martha S. Putney, *When the Nation Was in Need: Blacks in the Women's Army Corps During World War II* (Metuchen, NJ: Scarecrow, 1992); Brenda L. Moore, *To Serve My Country, To Serve My Race: The Story of the Only African American WACs Stationed Overseas during World War II* (New York: NYU Press, 1996); Charity Adams Earley, *One Woman's Army: A Black Officer Remembers the WAC* (College Station: Texas A & M University Press, 1996); Kathryn S. Dobie and Eleanor Lang, eds., *Her War: American Women in WWII* (New York: Universe, 2003), 115–26; Nikki Brown, *Private Politics and Public Voices: Black Women's Activism from World War I to the New Deal* (Bloomington: Indiana University Press, 2006); Doris Weatherford, *American Women during World War II: An Encyclopedia* (New York: Routledge, 2010) 8–12. See also www.aacvr-germany.org/wacs for image galleries and further information.

16. "Germany Meets the Negro Soldier: GIs Find More Friendship and Equality in Berlin than in Birmingham or on Broadway," *Ebony*, October 1946, 5–11.

17. Bill Smith, "Found Freedom in Germany: Few GIs Eager to Return to States," *Pittsburgh Courier*, February 22, 1947, 1. William Gardner Smith used the name Bill Smith when writing for the *Pittsburgh Courier*.

18. Smith, *Return to Black America*, 62.
19. Smith, *Last of the Conquerors* (New York: Farrar, Straus, 1948), 67–68.
20. "Fighters for Christian Brotherhood," *Chicago Defender*, July 4, 1953, 2.
21. Andrew Bowman, quoted in Monroe H. Little Jr., "The Black Military Experience in Germany: From the First World War to the Present," in *Crosscurrents: African-Americans, Africa, and Germany in the Modern World*, ed. David McBride, Leroy Hopkins, and C. Aisha Blackshire-Belay (Columbia, SC: Camden House, 1998), 192.
22. Lou Potter, William Miles, and Nina Rosenblum, *Liberators: Fighting on Two Fronts in World War II* (New York: Harcourt, Brace, Jovanovich, 1992), 258–59.
23. See, e.g., Höhn, *GIs and Fräuleins*; Fehrenbach, *Race after Hitler*; and Schroer, *Recasting Race*. See also Yara Collette Lemke Munzia de Faria, *Zwischen Fürsorge und Ausgrenzung. Afro-deutsche Besatzungskinder im Nachkriegsdeutschland* (Berlin: Metropol, 2002); and David Posner, "Afro-America in West German Perspective, 1945–1966," PhD diss. (New Haven: Yale University Press, 1997).
24. Smith, "Found Freedom in Germany."
25. Ronald Noble, e-mail to Maria Höhn, April 14, 2001. For Europeans regarding black soldiers as "Yankees," see also Lawrence Johnson, "A Lot of Pleasure in Berlin," interview by Maggi Morehouse, Cleveland, OH, 1998. Walter Patrice, a veteran who was also interviewed for this project, only spent a few weeks in Germany and was not impressed with the Germans; he found the Belgians friendlier; Walter Patrice, interview by Maria Höhn, Poughkeepsie, NY, 2010. Both interviews are available at www.aacvr-germany.org/oralhistory.
26. Joseph Barry, "An American in Paris–III," *New York Post*, September 29, 1959. See also Smith's *Return to Black America*.
27. Starr, "Fraternization with the Germans," 89.
28. Hans Massaquoi, *Destined to Witness: Growing Up Black in Nazi Germany* (New York: William Morrow, 1999), 271.
29. Preston McNeil, cited in Kleinschmidt, "*Do Not Fraternize*," 176–77. For other depictions of how easily these friendships developed, see also Roi Ottley, "No Color Lines for Frauleins," *Negro Digest* (February 1946): 11–12 (condensed and reprinted from *Pittsburgh Courier*, December 8, 1945). See also the photos of black soldiers and German children in "Germany Meets the Negro Soldier," 6.
30. Survey result cited in Schroer, *Recasting Race*, 46.
31. Debra Abell, e-mail exchange with Maria Höhn, June 2009.
32. Rosemarie Lester makes the point that in many of the serialized novels of the post-war years, Germans compare their own suffering with that of blacks in the United States; see Chapter 2 of her *Trivialneger: Das Bild des Schwarzen im westdeutschen Illustriertenroman* (Stuttgart: Akademischer Verlag H.-D. Heinz, 1982). See also Kleinschmidt, "*Do Not Fraternize,*"184; and Interdisziplinärer Arbeitskreis für Nordamerikastudien (hereafter IANAS) video collection, Video No. 60. These oral histories, conducted in 1993/1994, are a wonderful source for exploring German reactions to the American military presence in general. They can be viewed at Johannes Gutenberg Universität, Mainz.
33. Ollie Stewart, "What Negro GIs Learned from Women in Europe," *Negro Digest*, September 1947, 24–27, 25.
34. Ottley, excerpt from his book *No Green Pastures*, *Chicago Defender*, December 15, 1951, 13.
35. Smith, *The Last of the Conquerors*, 35.
36. Ronald Noble, interview by Maria Höhn, April 4, 2001 (e-mail in Maria Höhn's possession).

37. "Germany Meets the Negro Soldier," 5–11; "Racial: Mädchen and Negro," 29–30. For contemporary U.S. studies on this phenomenon, see Negro Newspaper Editors' Report to the Secretary of War, July 1946, RG 407, Box 719, NARA.
38. *Chicago Defender*, September 14, 1946, 7, advertisement (emphasis in original).
39. Louis Martin, "Tan Yanks in Germany Destroy Last of Nazi 'Culture': Swing Music Big Favorite," *Chicago Defender*, May 8, 1948, 5.
40. "Germany Meets the Negro Soldier," 5–11.
41. Letter to the Editor, *Ebony*, March 1947, 3–5. As Renee Romano has shown, in the 1950s and 1960s only very few people in the African American community argued that these relationships "betrayed the race." Most objections were based on the reasoning that approval of such relationships would make life even harder for African Americans. Renee Romano, *Race Mixing: Black-White Marriage in Postwar America* (Cambridge, MA: Harvard University Press, 2003), 89. African American women were far more guarded, if not critical, in their response to such stories. One woman expressed the feelings of many who did not object to these relationships per se but saw themselves as "victims of progress" because each new "war bride" meant "one less brown man" in the marriage market for them. Nor did all African American women agree that interracial love was an integral expression of democracy. One black woman conveyed her disappointment that *Ebony* associated the achievement of equality for black men with their ability to associate with white women. She raised a valid point, since this vision of democracy ignored black women's aspirations for full citizenship. See "Are White Women Stealing Our Husbands?" *Negro Digest*, April 1951, 55; and *Ebony*, November 1947, Letters to the Editor section.
42. Martin, "Tan Yanks in Germany Destroy Last of Nazi 'Culture,'" 5.
43. "Song of Girls and GI's," *Ebony*, October 1946, 10–11.
44. Martin, "Tan Yanks in Germany Destroy Last of Nazi 'Culture,'" 5 and "Negro GIs Play Vital Reconstruction Role," *Chicago Defender*, April 10, 1948. See also Willie Lee Wong, "Nazis Gone, Germans Rave Over 'Sweethearts of Rhythm' Band," *Chicago Defender*, September 8, 1945, 14, for a black women's band that came to Germany. On jam sessions between German jazz fans and African American GIs, see Schroer, *Recasting Race*, 175. See also the 1957 German TV production, "Wie Toxi Wirklich Lebt," which shows a great depiction of a black-only bar frequented by German women and male German teenagers who obviously enjoyed the music and enthusiastically watched the dance steps of the black GIs.
45. Very few black families were in Germany during the occupation since only wives of officers and high-ranking NCOs were allowed to come initially. The numbers increased significantly after the build-up of troops in the 1950s, when about 30,000 black GIs were stationed in Germany on a regular basis.
46. "The New Germany and Negro Soldiers," *Ebony*, January 1952. See also "Germany's Tragic War Babies," *Ebony*, December 1952, 78, and "Wives of Negro GIs Still Draw Stares in Germany," *Chicago Defender*, July 16, 1955. For an article on the occupation years, see "Christmas Finds These Americans in Germany," *Baltimore Afro-American*, December 1947. This article also stressed that many African American families had German friends and that contact with white Americans was much more limited.
47. Joseph Shepard, "Ray Defends GIs Serving Overseas," *Chicago Defender*, December 28, 1946, 1–2, esp. 1.
48. Walter White, "People, Politics, Places," *Chicago Defender*, May 18, 1946, 15.
49. Ottley, excerpts from his book *No Green Pastures*, *Chicago Defender*, December 15, 1951. For another essay that claims that the Germans were more liberal toward

the black soldiers than the French, see Ethel L. Payne, "Wives of Negro GIs Still Draw Stares in Germany," *Chicago Defender*, July 16, 1955, 12.

50. Frank E. G. Weil, "The Negro in the Armed Forces," *Social Forces* 26.1 (1947): 95–98, esp. 98. See also interview with Lieutenant General Clarence Huebener, cited in MacGregor, *Integration of the Armed Forces*, 214; and "Racial: Mädchen and Negro," 29–30.

51. Trezzant W. Anderson, "Germans Gradually Accepting Colored Occupational Troops," *Pittsburgh Courier*, February 2, 1946, 13.

52. Trends of the Negro Press, 2, War Dept. General Staff Decimale File, April 22, 1946, RG 165, Box 262, NARA. For coverage of this phenomenon in the press, see "Racial: Mädchen and Negro," 29–30.

53. White, "People, Politics, and Places."

54. "More Negroes Expected to Enlist in Army," *Chicago Defender*, June 15, 1946, 12; and "Choice of Station Ends as GIs Select Europe," *Chicago Defender*, July 6, 1946, 1. See also "Racial: Mädchen and Negro," *Newsweek*, September 16, 1946, 29–30, for a report on how many GIs wanted to sign up for Germany.

55. Smith, "Found Freedom in Germany." See also "Nothing to Go Back For," *Crisis*, February 1949, 52.

56. "Many Ex-GIs Taking Jobs in Germany," *Chicago Defender*, March 30, 1946, 2.

57. "Why Negroes Leave America: Many GIs Find More Freedom Overseas Than in Their Native Land," *Negro Digest*, March 1949, 10–11. On how many soldiers wanted to stay abroad, see also Peter Pollock, "GIs Come Home Older and Wiser," *Chicago Defender*, September 8, 1945, 10; and Walter White's regular column in the *Chicago Defender*, "People, Politics, and Places."

58. Lou Potter, *Liberators: Fighting on Two Fronts in WWII* (New York: Houghton Mifflin Harcourt, 1992), 259.

59. For the black expatriate communities after World War II in cities across Europe, see Smith, *Return to Black America*, 62. Smith himself had gone to Paris by the early 1950s, where he became part of the black expatriate community of writers and artists. The black expatriate communities in Germany have received little attention because they were comprised mostly of "regular people" rather than the prestigious writers and musicians who started the expatriate community in France in the 1920s.

60. Barry, "An American in Paris–III" (Schomburg Clipping file William Gardner Smith). See also Smith, *Return to Black America*.

61. Bill Smith, "American Prejudice Rampant in Germany," *Pittsburgh Courier*, March 1, 1947, 13; "American Officers Abroad Propagating Race Hatred," *Pittsburgh Courier*, June 8, 1946; and Roi Ottley, "Nazi Attitudes of White Soldiers," *Pittsburgh Courier*, September 29, 1945, 1, 4. See also Allan Gould, "Germany's Tragic War Babies," *Ebony*, December 1952, 74–78, which also talks about the racism that white soldiers were spreading among the Germans.

62. Edward Toles, "Where Is Hitler? German-Born Negroes Free in Berlin," *Chicago Defender*, July 14, 1945, 1.

63. "Bishop Walls Blasts Army German Jim Crow Policy," *Chicago Defender*, November 1, 1947, 7.

64. "Memorandum, Sec. of War Robert Patterson for deputy chief of staff, 7 January 1947," written by Marcus Ray reprinted in *Blacks in the Military. Essential Documents*, ed. Bernard Nalty and Morris McGregor (Wilmington: Scholarly Resource, 1981), 217.

65. Albert Barnett, " 'U.S. Democracy,' in Germany and at Home," *Chicago Defender*, January 21, 1950, 7.

66. Ibid.

67. Höhn, *GIs and Fräuleins*, Chapter 3, provides a detailed overview of German attitudes toward the black occupiers. Interviewed by Maria Höhn in May 2010, Max Neiman related that his father ran a number of white-only and black-only bars in Munich after 1945 and in Baumholder during the 1950s. The local commanders instructed him to create segregated spaces and threatened to make his establishments off-limits to all troops if he were to relax this policy in any way. See also the discussion of this policy in chapter 4 of the present book.

68. "Report of the Negro Newspaper Publishers Association to the Honorable Secretary of War, Judge Robert P. Patterson, on Troops Conditions in Europe, 18 July 1946," Adjutant General, RG 407, Box 719, 6, NARA.

69. Bill Smith, "McNarney Ignores Report, Isolates GIs," *Pittsburgh Courier*, October 26, 1946, 1, 4; and Smith, *The Last of the Conquerors*; "Report of the Negro Newspaper Publishers Association to the Honorable Secretary of War, Judge Robert P. Patterson, on Troops Conditions in Europe, 18 July 1946," 8, Adjutant General, RG 407, Box 719, NARA.

70. Ottley, *No Green Pastures*, 159.

71. Grace Halsell, *Black/White Sex* (New York: William Morrow, 1972), 144. Halsell was a correspondent for the *Fort Worth Star Telegram* in Texas who reported from Europe in the late 1940s and early 1950s.

72. Negro Newspaper Editors' Report to the Secretary of War, July 1946, 6, RG 407, Box 719, NARA. The biggest smear on black soldiers fraternizing with German women came from the so-called Meader Report, which expressed revulsion about that development. See Editorials: "Smearing our Soldiers," *Crisis*, January 1947, 9.

73. Alfred Werner, "Germany's New Pariahs," *Crisis*, May 1952, 296. For how the wives of military officers were educating the Germans in Jim Crow, see Dorothy Otis Wyre, "Mr. Jim Crow and I," *Crisis*, January 1956, 11–14, 11.

74. Complaint by War Department civilians to Military Personnel Branch, Headquarters, U.S. Forces, European Theater, APO 747, August 27, 1946, RG 498, Box 85/1, Folder 291.2, NARA.

75. Davis, "The Americanized Mannheim," 79.

76. Negro Newspaper Editors' Report to the Secretary of War, July 1946, 6, RG 407, Box 719, NARA.

77. Letter of August 1946, Discrimination in the U.S. Armed Forces, 1918–1955, Part 9: Series C, Reel 10, NAACP Records at Schomburg Archive (name and signature not legible). On commanders' refusal to grant passes, see Negro Newspaper Editors' Report to the Secretary of War, July 8, 1946, RG 407, Box 719, NARA. Such raids continued in the 1950s. For a complaint by a soldier in Kaiserslautern, see the November 12, 1954, letter from Sgt. Hely R. Harrell to Congressman Adam Clayton Powell, Jr., forwarded to the Army Liaison Officer on December 7, 1954, RG 407, Box 129, NARA. See also Höhn, *GIs and Fräuleins*, Chapters 7 and 8, for a detailed description.

78. Ollie Stewart, "How War Brides Fare in America," *Negro Digest*, April 1948, 26. See also "Bishop Walls Hits Army Bias," *Washington Afro-American*, October 25, 1947, 8.

79. ETO Secretary General Staff, RG 498, Box 20, NARA.

80. Letter of August 19, 1946, Part 9: Discrimination in the U.S. Armed Forces, 1918–1955, Series C, Reel 10, NAACP (name and signature not legible).

81. Complaint by civilian employees of the U.S. war department stationed in Germany, Classified Decimal File, August 27, 1946, ETO Secretary General Staff, RG 498, Box 20, NARA.

82. "Negro GIs Fraternize—But Wisely!" *Chicago Defender*, July 21, 1945; "A Double Standard of Morals," *Chicago Defender*, April 28, 1945.

83. Margaret Geis, *Morale and Discipline in the European Command 1945–49*, Occupation Forces in Europe Series (Karlsruhe, Germany: Historical Division, European Command, 1952), 27; idem, "Negro Personnel," 138. The bias in U.S. military justice is shown in J. Robert Lilly, "Dirty Details: Executing U.S. Soldiers during WWII," *Crime & Delinquency* 42.4 (1996): 491–516; and J. Robert Lilly and J. Michael Thomson, "Executing U.S. Soldiers in England during WWII: The Power of Command Influence and Sexual Racism," *British Journal of Criminology* 37.2 (Spring 1997): 262–88.

84. "Racial: Mädchen and Negro," 29–30.

85. Ralph G. Martin, "Where Is Home?" *New Republic*, December 31, 1945, 898–900, 898. Also Lt. Colonel John Sherman, "A Communication: Our Negro Soldiers," *New Republic*, November 19, 1945, 678, and Thomas Sancton, "Big Brass and Jim Crow," *Nation*, October 2, 1948, 365–66. See also Max Lerner, "The Negroes and the Draft," *PM*, April 11, 1948 (reprinted in the *Crisis*, May 1948), 140, 150–55; and Vernon Stone, "Baby Crop," *Survey*, 1949, 579–80.

86. Smith, *The Last of the Conquerors*, 57.

87. David Dempsey, "American Dilemma," *New York Times*, September 5, 1948, book review section, 6.

88. "Land of Freedom?" *Saturday Review of Literature* 15 (Schomburg Clipping File William Gardner Smith).

89. Abner Berry, "Last of the Conquerors, Important First Novel against Army Jim Crow," *Daily Worker*, August 31, 1948 (Schomburg Clipping File William Gardner Smith).

90. James Fenwick, "Novel Explores Theme of Negro GIs in Germany," August 15, 1949 (Schomburg Clipping File William Gardner Smith).

91. Davis, "The Americanized Mannheim," 88.

92. Bud Hutton and Andy Rooney, *Conqueror's Peace: A Report to the American Stockholder* (New York: Double Day, 1947), 54.

93. Jack Conroy, "Negro Soldier and a Fraulein [sic]," *Chicago Sun-Times*, August 17, 1948, 17.

4   Setting the Stage for Brown: Integrating the Military in Germany

1. Gunnar Myrdal, *An American Dilemma: The Negro Problem and Modern Democracy* (New York: Harper and Brothers, 1944). See also Junfu Zhang, "Black-White Relations: The American Dilemma," *Perspectives* 1.4 (February 29, 2000) at http://www.oycf.org/oycfold/httpdocs/Perspectives2/4_022900/black_white.htm.

2. Peter Kellogg, "Civil Rights Consciousness in the 1940s," *Historian* 42 (November 1979): 18–41.

3. Elmer Anderson Carter, "On Racial Prejudice at Home and Abroad," *Opportunity* 17 (1939). On African Americans' reluctance to support the war, see Sterling A. Brown, "Count Us In," in *What the Negro Wants*, ed. Rayford W. Logan (Chapel Hill: University of North Carolina Press, 1944), 308–44.

4. Kellogg, "Civil Rights Consciousness," 31.

5. Charles Houston, "The Negro Soldier," *Nation*, October 21, 1944, 496–97, 496. Houston was a black member of the Fair Employment Practices Committee founded by President Franklin Delano Roosevelt in 1941.

6. Edwin Embree, "Balance Sheet in Race Relations," *Atlantic Monthly*, May 1945, 87–91, 87.

7. "Propaganda and the War," *Common Sense*, February 1942, cited in Kellogg, "Civil Rights Consciousness," 32.

8. Kellogg, "Civil Rights Consciousness," 32.

9. Cited in ibid., 33.

10. Roy Wilkins, "The Negro Wants Full Equality," in *What the Negro Wants*, ed. Logan, 115.

11. Anson Phelps Stokes, "American Race Relations in War Time," *Journal of Negro Education* 14.4 (1945): 535–51, esp. 537, 538.

12. Embree, "Balance Sheet in Race Relations," 87, 91. See also Houston, "The Negro Soldier," 496–97.

13. Lt. Colonel John Sherman, "A Communication: Our Negro Soldiers," *New Republic*, November 19, 1945, 678. See also James Cobb, "World War II and the Mind of the Modern South," in *Remaking Dixie: The Impact of World War II on the American South*, ed. Neil McMillen (Jackson: University of Mississippi Press, 1997), 3–20, for the impact of the war on white soldiers.

14. Sherman, "A Communication: Our Negro Soldiers," 678.

15. "Takes War to Make Dixie GIs Lose Hate for Negroes," *Chicago Defender*, September 22, 1945.

16. Cobb, "World War II and the Mind of the Modern South," 6.

17. Truman cited in Bernard Nalty, *Strength for the Fight: A History of Black Americans in the Military* (New York: Free Press, 1986), 205.

18. Truman cited in Nalty, *Strength for the Fight*, 237.

19. President's Committee, *To Secure These Rights*, 162 (available at Truman Library, http://www.trumanlibrary.org/civilrights/srights1).

20. Nalty, *Strength for the Fight*, esp. 204–54; and Morris J. MacGregor, *Integration of the Armed Forces, 1940–1965* (Washington, DC: Center for Military History United States Army, 1981), esp. 291–314. For the full text of the order, see MacGregor, *Integration of the Armed Forces,* 312.

21. L. D. Reddick, "The Negro Policy of the American Army Since World War II," *Journal of Negro History* 38.2 (April 1953): 194–215, 200. A civil rights activist and curator of the Schomburg Archive, Reddick was involved in these debates. For Truman's relationship to the civil rights movement, see Harvard Sitkoff, "Harry Truman and the Election of 1948: The Coming of Age of Civil Rights in American Politics," *Journal of Southern History* 37 (November 1971): 597–616; Steven F. Lawson, ed., *To Secure These Rights: The Report of Harry S. Truman's Committee on Civil Rights* (Boston: Bedford/St. Martin's, 2004); Patricia Sullivan, *Lift Every Voice: The NAACP and the Making of the Civil Rights Movement* (New York: New Press, 2009), 352–67; Raymond H. Geselbracht, ed., *The Civil Rights Legacy of Harry S. Truman* (Kirksville, MO: Truman State University Press, 2007); Steven F. Lawson, *Running for Freedom: Civil Rights and Black Politics in America since 1941*, 3rd ed. (Malden, MA: Wiley-Blackwell, 2009), 36–71.

22. Mary Dudziak, *Cold War Civil Rights: Race and the Image of American Democracy* (Princeton: Princeton University Press, 2000); Thomas Borstelmann, *The Cold War and the Color Line: American Race Relations in the Global Arena* (Cambridge, MA: Harvard University Press, 2001); Brenda Gayle Plummer, *Rising Wind: Black Americans and U.S. Foreign Affairs, 1935–1960* (Chapel Hill: University of North Carolina Press, 1996). See also Penny von Eschen, *Race Against Empire: Black Americans and Anticolonialism, 1937–1957* (Ithaca: Cornell University Press, 1997); and Carol Anderson, *Eyes Off the Prize: The United Nations and the African American Struggle for Human Rights, 1944–1955* (Cambridge: Cambridge University Press, 2003).

23. Although America also had a mission to democratize Japan, the segregated military was less damaging to its cause there. The great majority of U.S. troops were stationed on Okinawa, an island a thousand miles from mainland Japan and a former Japanese colony. Okinawa remained under U.S. military occupation

until 1972, and large sections of the island were essentially an extended military compound. The segregation of the military was thus less visible to the local population. In West Germany, on the other hand, the East Germans and Soviet military missions in West Germany provided a steady stream of anti-American propaganda.

24. Carol Anderson, "From Hope to Disillusion: African Americans, the United Nations, and the Struggle for Human Rights, 1944–47," *Diplomatic History* 20.4 (Fall 1996): 531–63, 557.

25. Ibid.

26. The references here are to Mississippi senator Theodore G. Bilbo and Mississippi congressman John E. Rankin. See Dudziak, *Cold War*, 45. See also Anderson, "From Hope," 559.

27. President's Committee, *To Secure These Rights*, 101–2.

28. Lee Nichols, *Breakthrough on the Color Front* (New York: Random House, 1954), 173.

29. Cited in Borstelmann, *The Cold War*, 76.

30. James Ivy, "American Negro Problem in the European Press," *Crisis*, July 1950, 413–18.

31. See chapter 1, p. 18. See also Plummer, *Rising Wind*; von Eschen, *Race against Empire*; Anderson, *Eyes Off the Prize*; Glenda Gilmore, *Defying Dixie: The Radical Roots of Civil Rights, 1919–1950* (New York: W. W. Norton, 2008).

32. Editorials, "Democracy Defined at Moscow," *Crisis*, April 1947, 105. See also editorials, "Democratic Elections–In Poland," *Crisis*, March 1947, 73.

33. Langston Hughes, "US Likes Nazis and Franco Better Than Its Own Negroes," *Chicago Defender*, October 30, 1948.

34. Report of Trends in the Negro Press April 15, 1946 (Week ending April 15, 1946), 2, War Dept General Staff Decimale File, RG 165, Box 262, NARA.

35. Editorial, "Democracy Defined at Moscow," *Crisis*, April 1947, 105.

36. Report of Trends in the Negro Press, January 16, 1946 (Week ending January 9, 1946), 2, War Dept. General Staff Decimale File, RG 165, Box 261, NARA.

37. Roi Ottley, *No Green Pastures* (New York: Charles Scribner's Sons, 1951), 159.

38. Walter White, "What Negro GIs Are Doing in Germany," *Chicago Defender*, October 23, 1948, 7. See also "Bishop Walls Praises Negro Troops in Germany," *Chicago Defender*, August 23, 1947.

39. Lee Finkle, *Forum for Protest* (Rutherford: Fairleigh Dickinson University Press, 1975), 85.

40. Frank L. Stanley, President Negro Newspaper Publishers Association, "Report of the Negro Newspaper Publishers Association to the Honorable Secretary of War, Judge Robert P. Patterson on Troops and Conditions in Europe," July 18, 1946, RG 319, Box 175, NARA.

41. "Prattis Tells General Clay: Jim Crow Blights Army in Germany," *Pittsburgh Courier*, April 9, 1948.

42. Reddick, "The Negro Policy," 202–3. See also "The Forrestal Record," *Crisis*, July 1949.

43. "Editors' Confidential Army Report," *Chicago Defender*, April 17, 1948.

44. Editorial, *Philadelphia Tribune*, June 5, 1948. An editorial in the *Amsterdam News* on the same day also condemned the Jim Crow army but praised the fact that such an investigation, unlike in the Soviet Union, was possible. See also "Work of Occupation Troops in Germany Affected by Lack of Officers, Racial Bars," *Baltimore Afro-American*, June 22, 1948, on the effect of Germans' awareness of the Jim Crow army.

45. David Dempsey. "American Dilemma, Army Model," *New York Times*, September 5, 1948, book review section, 6.

46. "American Officers Abroad Propagating Race Hatred," *Pittsburgh Courier*, June 8, 1946. See also Joseph Starr, *Fraternization with the Germans in WWII, 1945–46*, Occupation Forces in Europe Series (Frankfurt: Office of the Chief Historian, 1946), 153.

47. Robert Engler, "The Individual Soldier and the Occupation," *Annals of the American Academy of Political and Social Science*, 244 (1948): 85.

48. White, "What Negro GIs Are Doing in Germany."

49. Walter White, Secretary NAACP, "Segregation in the Army," *New York Times*, August 17, 1948, 20.

50. Cited in Nichols, *Breakthrough on the Color Front*, 180.

51. McGregor, *Integrating the Army*, 410.

52. "Report from Professor Eli Ginzberg from Columbia University," 6, RG 338 Historical Division USAREUR, 314.7, NARA. These records were stored in moving boxes.

53. Letter from Javits to Secretary of Defense, Louis Johnson, December 22, 1949, RG 330, Box 591, NARA. See also his Press Release, RG 330, Box 591, NARA.

54. Alexander would later play a very important role in the civil rights movement, advising Thurgood Marshall, when he argued the 1954 *Brown v. Board of Education* case before the Supreme Court.

55. Letter of Raymond Pace Alexander to George Marshall, Secretary of Defense, October 3, 1950, RG 330, Box 591, NARA.

56. Ibid., 17–18.

57. Ibid., 10.

58. Ibid.

59. Ibid.

60. Ibid., 14–15.

61. Ottley, *No Green Pastures*, 159.

62. David Posner, "Afro-America in West German Perspective, 1945–1966," PhD diss. (Yale University, 1997), 139.

63. Ibid., 141.

64. Ibid., 141.

65. Discrimination in the U.S. Armed Forces, Part 9, Series A, reel 11, NAACP Records at Schomburg Archive.

66. Letter from Javits to Secretary of Defense, Louis Johnson, December 22, 1949, RG 330, Box 591, NARA. See also his Press Release, RG 330, Box 591, NARA.

67. "Yanks Hear Dr. Ferebee in Germany, " *Chicago Defender*, May 19, 1951.

68. Sampson's letter cited in Posner, "Afro-America," 60. On Sampson, see Helen Laville and Scott Lucas, "The American Way: Edith Sampson, the NAACP, and African American Identity in the Cold War," *Diplomatic History* 20.4 (Fall 1996): 565–90.

69. Nichols, *Breakthrough on the Color Front*, 179.

70. Bill Smith, "Average European Visualizes U.S. as Being a 'Land of Terror,' " *PC*, January 26, 1952.

71. Dudziak, *Cold War: Civil Rights*, esp. 47–78.

72. Posner, "Afro-America," 150.

73. "For Negroes It's a New Army Now," 112.

74. Ibid. Reuben Horner commented on how bad the situation was around many military bases in the United States. See Reuben Horner, "Fighting against My White Superiors," interview by Maggi Morehouse, Tucson, AZ, 1998. On how integration was undertaken in the United States and Germany, see ibid., as well as Felix Goodwin, "I Didn't Care Whether Their Daddy Was the Head of the Ku Klux Klan," interview by Maggi Morehouse, Tucson, AZ, 1998, both available at www. aacvr-germany.org/oralhistory.

75. "Service Abolish All-Negro Units," *New York Times*, October 31, 1954, 23.
76. "For Negroes It's a New Army Now," 112.
77. "Wives of Negro GIs Still Draw Stares in Germany," *Chicago Defender*, July 16, 1955.
78. "The New Germany and Negro Soldiers: The Tan Yanks Still Popular with Germans Although Chocolate Bars No Longer Buy Friends as in Early Occupation Days," *Ebony*, January 1952.
79. Jesse J. Johnson, *Ebony Brass* ([S.I.]: Carver, 1976), 99.
80. Goodwin, "I Didn't Care."
81. Colin Powell, *My American Journey* (New York: Random House, 1995), 53. For Powell's overall experience in Germany, see ibid., 45–55, 317–328; Karen DeYoung, *Soldier: The Life of Colin Powell* (New York: Vintage Books, 2007), 35–39, 144–47; as well as www.aacvr-germany.org/powell. See also Charles Moskos, *The American Enlisted Man: The Rank and File in Today's Military* (New York: Russell Sage Foundation, 1970), 126.
82. Joe McPhee, interview by Maria Höhn, Poughkeepsie, NY, 2010, www.aacvr-germany.org/oralhistory.
83. Medgar Evers, Aaron Henry, and Amzie Moore were among the most prominent civil rights leaders in the Mississippi Delta. See John Dittmer, *Local People: The Struggle for Civil Rights in Mississippi* (Urbana: University of Illinois Press, 1994); Charles M. Payne, *I've Got the Light of Freedom: The Organizing Tradition and the Mississippi Freedom Struggle* (Berkeley: University of California Press, 1995). The famous civil rights photographer Matt Herron presented a talk at Vassar College in October 2009, in which he stressed the crucial role of Southern World War II veterans in leading the civil rights movement at the time. See also Joseph Hairston, "We Structured the March on Washington Like an Army Formation," interview by Maggi Morehouse, Washington, DC, 1998, www.aacvr-germany.org/oralhistory. For biographies of Evers and Henry, see, e.g., Medgar Wiley Evers, Myrlie Evers-Williams, and Manning Marable, eds., *The Autobiography of Medgar Evers: A Hero's Life and Legacy Revealed through His Writings, Letters, and Speeches* (New York: Basic Civitas Books, 2005); and Aaron Henry and Constance Curry, *Aaron Henry: The Fire Ever Burning* (Jackson: University Press of Mississippi, 2000).
84. "The Digg's Report," 331, reprinted in *Blacks in the U.S. Armed Forces: Basic Documents*, vol. 13, ed. Morris J. MacGregor and Bernard Nalty (Wilmington: Scholarly Resources, Inc., 1977); "The President's Committee on Equality of Opportunity in the Armed Forces," 5–6.
85. "President's Committee on Equality," 7. See also MacGregor, *Integration*, 479.
86. MacGregor, *Integration*, 479 and 552.
87. Alan L. Gropman, *The Air Force Integrates, 1945–1964* (Washington, DC: Office of Air Force History, U.S. Air Force, 1985), 167.
88. Land Relations Officer, October 4, 1956, RG 338, NARA. The military made three black-only bars in Mainz off-limits to its troops.
89. See "Committee on Interracial Relations," September 22, 1953, RG 338, NARA, for an acknowledgment by the military that racial conflict occurred almost exclusively off base. See also Moskos, *The American Enlisted Man*, 122; Gropman, *The Air Force Integrates*, 166–67; Mershon and Schlossman, eds., *Foxholes and Color Lines*, 278.
90. "Baumholder: Wer ist das nächste Opfer dieser Willkür?—Jeder farbige amerikanische Soldat trägt ein Messer mit sich. Wirken sich die Vorfälle an der Uni Alabama bis nach Baumholder aus?" *Rheinzeitung (RZ)*, March 9, 1956.
91. "Steinstraßabsperrung mit militärischer Pünktlichkeit," *Pfälzische Volkszeitung (PV)*, September 9, 1957, has some descriptions of racial violence during the Little Rock crisis.

92. According to German police reports, during the 1950s, all communities observed a noticeable increase in violence and destruction of property, "mostly caused by occupation soldiers (US Army)." The great majority of these incidents did not affect Germans, however, but "occurred between white and black soldiers because of the increased racial conflicts caused by the ongoing integration of the military as well as the emerging civil rights struggle in the United States." See *Geschichte der Polizei des Birkenfelder Landes* (Birkenfeld: Kreisverwaltung, 1987), 374.

93. "Rassenhass und Schlägermethoden bei der Militärpolizei?" *PV*, December 19, 1958. For another protest about imposed American segregation, see the November 12, 1954, letter from Sgt. Hely R. Harrell to Congressman Adam Clayton Powell, Jr., forwarded to the Army Liaison Officer on December 7, 1954, RG 407, Box 129, NARA.

94. In 1962, 24 percent of military bases in the United States still had segregated schools, 34 percent had segregated restaurants, and 31 percent segregated theaters in their surrounding communities. See, "The President's Committee," 45; and Richard J. Stillman, *Integration of the Negro in the U.S. Armed Forces* (New York: Frederick Praeger, 1968), 90.

95. For McNamara's self-criticism, see Alan M. Osur, "Black White Relations in the U.S. Military 1940–1972," *Air University Review*, 33 (November/December 1981): 69–78, 75.

5   Bringing Civil Rights to East and West: Dr. Martin Luther King Jr. in Cold War Berlin

1. Alcyone Scott, interview by Martin Klimke, Sturgeon Bay, WI, June 8, 2009, available at www.aacvr-germany.org/oralhistory.

2. In addition to foreign correspondents, German emigrants to the United States and journalists who had studied there provided this coverage. See, e.g., Manfred George, "Die sanfte Gewalt der dunklen Menschen," *Die Zeit*, 16, April 19, 1956, 27–28; Theo Sommer, "Aufruhr in Arkansas," *Die Zeit*, 37, September 12, 1957, 3. See also Robert Sackett, "Press Coverage and Analysis in West Germany, 1949–1967" (Paper presented at the conference African American Civil Rights and Germany in the Twentieth Century, Vassar College, Poughkeepsie, NY, October 1–4, 2009).

3. For early reports on the situation of African Americans, see, e.g., Henri Pavre, "Comeback in Afrika," *konkret* 4 (April 1962): 12–13; Francis and Laura Randall, "Tagebuch einer Bürgerrechts-Fahrt," *Frankfurter Hefte* 9 (1961): 747–56; Francis B. Randall, "Der Kampf um Rassengleichheit in Amerika I," *Frankfurter Hefte* 6 (1962): 369–76; idem, "Der Kampf um Rassengleichheit in Amerika II," *Frankfurter Hefte* 7 (1962): 467–74; Martin Luther King, "Onkel Tom's Snackbar," *konkret* (June 1963): 7–9, 17; S. W. Wahrhaftig, "Die unbewältigte Vergangenheit der Amerikaner—Das Rassenproblem in den USA," *Frankfurter Hefte* 11 (1963): 746–57; Robert Scipion, "Black & White Blues, Von Greenwich Village bis Birmingham," *konkret* (November 1963): 11–14.

4. Sabina Lietzmann, "Nächstes Mal das Feuer," *Frankfurter Allgemeine Zeitung* (hereafter *FAZ*), June 1, 1963, "Bilder und Zeiten," Supplement 126.

5. Sabina Lietzmann, "Das Jahr der Neger," *FAZ*, January 11, 1964, "Ereignisse und Gestalten," Supplement 9.

6. See, e.g., Rolf Zundel, "Die Neger wollen nicht länger warten," *Die Zeit*, September 25, 1964, 9.

7. Wolfgang Kraushaar, ed., *Frankfurter Schule und Studentenbewegung: Von der Flaschenpost zum Molotowcocktail, 1946–1995*, 3 vols. (Frankfurt am Main: Rogner & Bernhard, 1998), 1:201. For the larger context of international migration to both East and West Germany during the 1960s, see, e.g., Patrice Poutrus, "An den Grenzen des proletarischen Internationalismus: Algerische Flüchtlinge in der DDR," *Zeitschrift für Geschichtswissenschaft* 2 (2007): 162–78; Quinn Slobodian, "Dissident Guests: Afro-Asian Students and Transnational Activism in the West German Protest Movement," in *Migration and Activism in Europe since 1945*, ed. Wendy Pojmann (New York: Palgrave, 2008), 33–56.

8. Willy Brandt, *Begegnungen und Einsichten: Die Jahre 1960–1975* (Hamburg: Hoffmann und Campe, 1976), 87. See also Program, Americans for Democratic Action, 17th Annual Convention, The Statler Hotel, Washington, DC, May 15–17, 1964, pp. 12–13 in: 125:7, Americans for Democratic Action, May 1964, Papers of Dr. Martin Luther King, Jr., KCA; Willy Brandt, Datebook, May 16, 1964, A1 53, p. 145; Seating List, Americans for Democratic Action, 17th Annual Convention, May 16, 1964, A 6, 99, both in Willy Brandt Archive in the Archives of Social Democracy of the Friedrich Ebert Foundation, Bonn. The abbreviated passage in the English edition of Brandt's biography misdates this encounter to 1961. See Willy Brandt, *My Life in Politics* (New York: Viking, 1992), 362.

9. Stenographical Minutes, Press Conference with Willy Brandt, West Berlin, May 21, 1964, 13–14, B Rep. 002, Nr. 3169, Landesarchiv Berlin.

10. Heinrich Grüber to Robert F. Kennedy, July 15, 1963, VI HA, 485, 32, Papers of Heinrich Grüber, Geheimes Staatsarchiv Preußischer Kulturbesitz, Berlin (hereafter GStA PK). See also Heinrich Grüber, *Erinnerungen aus sieben Jahrzehnten* (Cologne: Kiepenheuer & Witsch, 1968); idem, *Bevollmächtigt zum Brückenbau: Heinrich Grüber, Judenfreund und Trümmerpropst. Erinnerungen, Predigten, Berichte, Briefe* (Leipzig: Evangelische Verlagsanstalt, 1991), 264f.; Hartmut Ludwig, *An der Seite der Entrechteten und Schwachen. Zur Geschichte des "Büro Pfarrer Grüber" (1938 bis 1940) und der Ev. Hilfsstelle für ehemals Rasseverfolgte nach 1945* (Berlin: Logos-Verlag, 2009).

11. Heinrich Grüber to Dr. Martin Luther King, July 15, 1963, VI HA, 485, 42, Papers of Heinrich Grüber, GStA PK.

12. See also Dr. Martin Luther King to Heinrich Grüber, October 7, 1963; Heinrich Grüber to Dr. Martin Luther King, December 16, 1963, both VI HA, 485, 1, 36, Papers of Heinrich Grüber, GStA PK.

13. Dr. Martin Luther King to Heinrich Grüber, May 1, 1964, VI HA, 485, 2, Papers of Heinrich Grüber, GStA PK.

14. King's visit also coincided with the publication of the German translation of his book *Why We Can't Wait* in the first weeks of September 1964. See Martin Luther King, *Warum wir nicht warten können*, translated by Hans Lamm (Vienna: Düsseldorf, 1964). At the beginning of the year, another translation of his writings had already appeared in German: Idem, *Freiheit: Aufbruch der Neger Nordamerikas. Bericht über den Busstreik in Montgomery*, trans. Ruth Ristick and Alfred Schmidt (Kassel: Oncken, 1964).

15. Dr. Martin Luther King to Von Selchow, Deputy Chief of Protocol, Telegram, September 2, 1964, Papers of Dr. Martin Luther King, Jr., 4:23, KCA; "Dr. King Arrives in West Berlin," *Washington Post*, September 13, 1964, A20.

16. See Veronika Liebau and Andreas Daum, *The Freedom Bell in Berlin* (Berlin: Jaron, 2000).

17. The choirs were from Berlin's St. Hedwig's Cathedral, "Le petits chanteurs a la croix de bois" from Paris, the choir of the Abbey Grottaferrata from Rome, as well as the choir of the "Black Nativity Play" from New York. See, e.g., "Würdiger Start der Festwochen—Sehnsucht nach Freiheit," *B.Z.*, September 14, 1964, 8;

Margarete Roemer, "Die Afrikaner haben das Wort—Die Eröffnung galt dem Andenken John F. Kennedys," *Bild*, September 14, 1964, 8.

18. For the role of Berlin during the Cold War and the context of Kennedy's visit, see Andreas Daum, *Kennedy in Berlin* (New York: Cambridge University Press, 2008).

19. Willy Brandt, "Rede zur Eröffnung der Berliner Festwochen," *Pressedienst des Landes Berlin*, 180 (September 14, 1964): 2.

20. Martin Luther King Jr., "Comments on John F. Kennedy at the Berlin Festival," September 13, 1964, 1, 6, Papers of Dr. Martin Luther King, Jr., KCA. See also Martin Luther King Jr., "John F. Kennedy," *Transition* 15 (1964): 27–28. While acknowledging the political significance of the opening ceremony, some criticized the lack of harmony and coherence engendered by the cultural focus of the festival, e.g., S. M., "Eine Stunde mit politischer Bedeutung," *Der Tagesspiegel*, September 15, 1964, 4.

21. "Rioting Seen by Dr. King If GOP Wins," *Los Angeles Times*, September 13, 1964, 4. See also "Dr. King Foresees 'Social Disruption' If Goldwater Wins," *New York Times*, September 13, 1964, 66; "King Compares Goldwaterism to Hitlerism," *Daily Defender*, September 14, 1964, 2; "Dr. King Arrives in West Berlin," *Washington Post*, September 13, 1964, A20.

22. Uwe Siemon-Netto, "Wir sprachen mit dem Negerführer Dr. Luther King," *Welt am Sonntag*, September 13, 1964, 4 (translated from the German). For editorial and reader responses critical of King, see "An Unfortunate Remark," *Washington Post*, September 15, 1964, A16; Munroe Howard, "King's Words," *Los Angeles Times*, September 16, 1964, A4. On the anti-Goldwater campaign, see also Manfred Berg, *"The Ticket to Freedom": The NAACP and the Struggle for Black Political Integration* (Gainesville: University Press of Florida, 2005), 209–11.

23. "Berlin ehrte Martin Luther King," *Der Tagesspiegel*, September 15, 1964, 2; "King: 'Die Menschen schreien nach Gemeinschaft,'" *Der Abend*, September 14, 1964, 2; "Kirchliche Nachrichten—Waldbühne diesmal mit Martin Luther King," *Pressestelle der evangelischen Kirchenleitung—Kirchliche Nachrichten*, September 4, 1964, 1; "Martin Luther King beim 'Tag der Kirche,'" *Morgenpost*, August 11, 1964, 3; "Martin Luther King in der Waldbühne," *Welt am Sonntag*, September 6, 1964, 29.

24. Martin Luther King Jr., "East or West—God's Children," Sermon, September 13, 1964, 4f., Papers of Dr. Martin Luther King, Jr., KCA.

25. Ibid., 2.

26. Ibid., 16.

27. "Dibelius: Die Mauer muss weg—Kundgebung in der Waldbühne mit Dr. Martin Luther King," *Die Welt*, September 14, 1964, 2; "Waldbühne: Zwanzigtausend hörten Matin Luther King," *Der Kurier*, September 14, 1964, 6; "Berliners Promise Support to Dr. King," *New York Times*, September 14, 1964, 36.

28. "Ehrendoktortitel für Martin Luther King," *Pressestelle der evangelischen Kirchenleitung*, September 11, 1964, 1. See also "Dr. King in Berlin mit dem Theologischen Ehrendoktor ausgezeichnet," *Evangelischer Pressedienst*, Nr. 210, September 12, 1964, 1.

29. For detailed descriptions of the incident, see "Es ging um das Leben eines jungen Menschen," *Berliner Kurier*, September 14, 1964, 6; "West Berlin Police Fire on East German Guards," *Chicago Tribune*, September 13, 1964, 1; "40-Minute Gun Battle Rages at the Berlin Wall," *Victoria Advocate*, September 14, 1964, 1, 7; Stefan Appelius, "Martin Luther King in Ost-Berlin," *Der Tagesspiegel online*, September 6, 2009, http://www.tagesspiegel.de/zeitung/Sonntag-Geschichte-DDR-Martin-Luther-King-Sonntag;art2566,2891732; "Durch einen Kugelhagel in die Freiheit," *B.Z. online*, October 4, 2009, http://www.bz-berlin.de/aktuell/

mauerfall/durch-einen-kugelhagel-in-die-freiheit-article603493.html (both accessed December 4, 2009).

30. "Rev. Martin Luther King in West Berlin," *Chicago Daily Defender*, September 14, 1964; "Dr. King: 'Unfaßbar!' " *Telegraf*, September 15, 1964, 1; "Berlin ehrte Martin Luther King," *Der Tagesspiegel*, September 15, 1964, 2.

31. "Dr. Luther King: Um Berlin dreht sich heute die Weltgeschichte," *Bild*, September 14, 1964, 3; Siemon-Netto, "Wir sprachen mit dem Negerführer Dr. Luther King."

32. Heinrich Grüber, afterword to *Freiheit: Aufbruch der Neger Nordamerikas. Bericht über den Busstreik in Montgomery*, by Martin Luther King Jr. (Kassel: Oncken, 1964), 203–5. Grüber's great admiration for King's work is also evident in his inclusion of King in the dedication of his memoirs. Heinrich Grüber, *Erinnerungen aus sieben Jahrzehnten* (Cologne, Berlin: Kiepenheuer & Witsch, 1968), 9.

33. "Martin Luther King in Berlin," *Der Tagesspiegel*, September 13, 1964, 1.

34. "2 Berlins to Hear King," *Washington Post*, September 12, 1964, B9; AP, "Martin Luther King to Preach in East Berlin," *Cedar Rapids Gazette*, September 12, 1964, 1; "Martin Luther King to Preach to Reds," *Victoria Advocate*, September 12, 1964, 1.

35. "Andrang zu Kings Predigt," *Spandauer Volksblatt*, September 15, 1964, 3; "Alle wollten King hören—Kirchen in Ost-Berlin waren überfüllt," *Morgenpost*, September 15, 1964, 2.

36. Ministry for State Security, Main Office for Passport Control and Searches, Friedrich Street/Zimmer Street, Berlin, September 13, 1964, HAXXAP, 20721/92, 2–3, Behörde der Bundesbeauftragten für die Unterlagen des Staatssicherheitsdienstes der ehemaligen DDR (hereafter BStU). See also "No Passport, But King Goes to E. Berlin," *Kokomo Morning Times*, September 14, 1964, 1.

37. "Red Berlin Admits Popular Rights Leader Without Pass," *Ebony*, November 1964, 44.

38. Alcyone Scott, interview by Martin Klimke, Sturgeon Bay, WI, June 8, 2009, available at www.aacvr-germany.org/oralhistory.

39. Arnold was arrested in the fall of 1963 and was released to the West after Germany paid a large sum. He was also not allowed to reenter East Germany. See Roland Stolte, "Dr. Martin Luther King in 1964 in Berlin" (Paper presented at the conference African American Civil Rights and Germany in the Twentieth Century, Vassar College, Poughkeepsie, NY, October 1–4, 2009).

40. Stefan Appelius points out that the East German secret police had several informants watching Schmitt. See Stefan Appelius, "My Dear Christian Friends in East Berlin," *Chrismon Plus*, September 2009, http://www.chrismon.de/4698.php. On Gerhart Schmitt's role in this visit, as well as his reminiscences about it, see Armin Fuhrer and Thomas Tumovec, "Das Geheimnis um den Onkel," *Focus* 26 (2010): 22–27; and www.aacvr-germany.org/king.

41. Quoted in Appelius, "My Dear Christian Friends," online version.

42. Martin Luther King Jr., Sermon in St. Mary's Church, Transcript, September 13, 1964, www.aacvr-germany.org/king.

43. Dieter Hildebrandt, "Auf jeder Seite der Mauer Gottes Kinder," *FAZ*, September 15, 1964, 7.

44. Alcyone Scott, interview by Martin Klimke, Sturgeon Bay, WI, June 8, 2009, available at www.aacvr-germany.org/oralhistory.

45. "Alle wollten King hören—Kirchen in Ost-Berlin waren überfüllt." Writing for the *FAZ*, Dieter Hildebrandt seconded this by stating "The wish...to encounter a man who united revolution and humanity, a leader who dispensed with violence as well as ideology, a legendary human being, was palpable." Dieter

Hildebrandt, "Auf jeder Seite der Mauer Gottes Kinder," *FAZ*, September 15, 1964, 8.

46. "Red Berlin Admits Popular Rights Leader without Pass."

47. The few exceptions include "Kurz und knapp: Martin Luther King kommt," *B.Z. am Abend*, September 12, 1964, 2; "Dr. Martin Luther King in der DDR-Hauptstadt," *B.Z. am Abend*, September 14, 1964, 1; "Martin Luther King in der Marienkirche," *Neues Deutschland*, September 14, 1964, 2; " 'Wir werden eines Tages frei sein,' " *Neue Zeit*, September 15, 1964, 1, 7; "Westberliner Unbehagen," *Neue Zeit*, September 17, 1964, 2; "Aus den Kräften des Glaubens," *Die Kirche*, September 27, 1964, 1–2.

48. Christian Ostermann, "Die USA und die DDR," in *Die DDR und der Westen. Transnationale Beziehungen 1949–1989*, ed. Ulrich Pfeil (Berlin: Links, 2001), 165–83. For a comprehensive study of East Germany's foreign policy, see Hermann Wentker, *Außenpolitik in engen Grenzen: Die DDR im internationalen System, 1949–1989* (Munich: Oldenbourg, 2007).

49. Ina Merkel, "Eine andere Welt. Vorstellungen von Nordamerika in der DDR der fünfziger Jahre," in *Amerikanisierung. Traum und Alptraum im Deutschland des 20. Jahrhunderts*, ed. Alf Lüdtke, Inge Marßolek, and Adelheid von Saldern (Stuttgart: Steiner, 1996), 245–56; Heinrich Bortfeldt, "In the Shadow of the Federal Republic: Cultural Relations Between the GDR and the United States—Cultural Relations Before Diplomatic Recognition," in *The United States and Germany in the Era of the Cold War, 1945–1990: A Handbook*, vol. 2, ed. Detlef Junker (New York: Cambridge University Press, 2004), 305–11.

50. See Robert Goeckel, "Neue Akteure, neue Prioritäten: Die Beziehungen zwischen den Kirchen," in *Die USA und Deutschland im Zeitalter des Kalten Krieges 1945–1990*, ed. Detlef Junker (Stuttgart: Deutsche Verlags-Anstalt, 2001), 696–707; Hedwig Richter, " 'Wir spürten den Herzschlag brüderlicher Liebe': Vom transnationalen Austausch der Herrnhüter Brudergemeinde im Kalten Krieg," in *Umworbener Klassenfeind: Das Verhältnis der DDR zu den USA*, ed. Uta Balbier and Christiane Rösch (Berlin: Links, 2006), 96–122.

51. Rainer Schnoor, "The Good and the Bad America," in *The United States and Germany*, vol. 2, ed. Junker, 618–26. Research on the ambivalent relationship between the GDR and the United States, especially concerning its cultural dimension, is still in its infancy. For an overview of the historiography and a future research agenda, see Uta Balbier und Christiane Rösch, "Mehr als eine Fußnote: Das Verhältnis zwischen der DDR und den Vereinigten Staaten von Amerika," in *Umworbener Klassenfeind*, ed. Balbier and Rösch, 11–23. For contextualization of this relationship into the larger debate about the "other" in East Germany, see Jan Behrends, Thomas Lindenberger, and Patrice Poutrus, *Fremde und Fremd-Sein in der DDR* (Berlin: Metropol, 2003).

52. Quoted in Stolte, *Dr. Martin Luther King 1964 in Berlin*, 4.

53. Günter Wirth, East German CDU political and chief editor of the state-owned Union publishing house from 1964 to 1970, argues that despite secret admiration for King among some East German leaders, his nonviolent approach was seen as a "feeblish form of pacifism" that stood in stark contrast to the communist class ideology of East Germany. See Günter Wirth, " 'Die neue Richtung unseres Zeitalters—Martin Luther Kings Traum von Gerechtigkeit, Gleichheit und Gewaltlosigkeit': Martin Luther King und seine Bedeutung für uns heute," January 15, 1999, Martin-Luther-King-Zentrum, Werdau, e.V., http://www.king-zentrum.de/.

54. Emil Fuchs, afterword in *Warum wir nicht warten können*, by Martin Luther King, trans. Hans Lamm, 2nd ed. (1965; Berlin: Union Verlag, 1967), 195–96, 196. The publication of King's texts undoubtedly had an "affirmative character" in the eyes of East German officials, who were trying to demonstrate the

country's global solidarity and openness. See Günter Wirth, memoir, unpublished manuscript, December 2008, 59. For the series of publications, most of which Günter Wirth facilitated in various ways, see Martin Luther King, "Mein Weg zur Gewaltlosigkeit," *Zeichen der Zeit* 19 (1965): 41–47; Martin Luther King, *Die neue Richtung unseres Zeitalters: Nobelpreisrede in der Aula der Universität Oslo am 11. Dez. 1964* (Berlin: Union Verlag, 1965/1966); King, *Warum wir nicht warten können*; Günter Wirth, *Martin Luther King*, Christ in der Welt 5 (Berlin: Union Verlag, 1965; 8th ed., 1989); Theo Lehmann, *Blues and Trouble*, with a preface by Martin Luther King (Berlin: Henschel Verlag, 1966); Anneliese Vahl, *Martin Luther King: Stationen auf dem Wege. Berichte und Selbstzeugnisse* (Berlin: Evangelische Verlagsanstalt, 1968); Coretta Scott King, *Mein Leben mit Martin Luther King*, trans. Christa Wegen (Berlin: Union Verlag, 1971); Stanislav N. Kondraschow, *Martin Luther King: Leben und Kampf eines amerikanischen Negerführers* (Berlin: VEB Deutscher Verlag der Wissenschaften, 1972).

55. See, e.g., the case of Gregor Meusel: Gregor Meusel, "Träumer und schöpferischer Extremist: Martin Luther King und dessen Ausstrahlung auf die Friedens- und Bürgerrechtsbewegung in der DDR," Martin-Luther-King-Zentrum, Werdau, e.V., http://www.king-zentrum.de/. See also Deutscher Bundestag, ed., *Materialien der Enquete-Kommission "Aufarbeitung von Geschichte und Folgen der SED-Diktatur in Deutschland,"* vol. 1 (Baden-Baden: Nomos, 1995), 1, 221ff.; Erhart Neubert, *Geschichte der Opposition in der DDR 1949–1989*, 2nd ed. (Berlin: Links, 1997), 193, 393. For King's influence on Joachim Gauck, East German civil rights activist and first Federal Commissioner for the Stasi Archives (1990–2000), see Norbert Robers, *Joachim Gauck. Die Biografie einer Institution* (Berlin: Henschel, 2000); 71f.; Joachim Gauck, *Winter im Sommer—Frühling im Herbst: Erinnerungen* (Munich: Siedler, 2009), 210f.; Joachim Gauck, "Freiheit—Verantwortung—Gemeinsinn: Wir in unserem Staat," Speech, Deutsches Theater Berlin, June 22, 2010, available at www.joachim-gauck.de

56. Apart from the texts cited above, the following publications make reference to King's visit: Lerone Bennett, *What Manner of Man: A Biography of Martin Luther King, Jr.*, 3rd rev. ed. (Chicago: Johnson, 1968), 224; Helmut Giese, "Steine der Hoffnung vom Berg der Verzweiflung," *Berliner Sonntagsblatt*, April 2, 1978, 5; David Lewis, *King: A Biography*, 2nd ed. (Urbana: University of Illinois Press, 1978), 254; Georg Meusel, "Mit Kreditkarte über die Mauer," *Der Freitag*, September 24, 2004, 18; Kanishk Tharoor, "Martin Luther King in Berlin: Marienkirche or the Brandenburg Gate?" http://*www.opendemocracy.net*, April 8, 2008; Jane Dailey, "Obama's Omission," *Chicago Tribune*, July 30, 2008, 19; Stefan Appelius, "Let My People Go," *einestages/SPIEGEL online*, September 13, 2009, http://einestages.spiegel.de/page/Home.html.

57. Although speculations already abounded during King's time in Berlin that he might be honored by the Nobel committee, the decision was announced only a month later, in October 1964. See Ernst Luuk, "Ist die Bank der Gerechtigkeit bankrott?" *Berliner Stimme*, September 12, 1964, 3.

58. "Red Berlin Admits Popular Rights Leader without Pass."

59. Martin Luther King, Jr., to Günter Wirth, facsimile, in King, *Warum wir nicht warten können*, 2nd ed., 197.

60. "Noble Prize Winner's Triumph in Europe," *Ebony*, November 1964, 6.

61. "Germans Acted Different on King's Visit," *New York Amsterdam News*, November 21, 1964, 39.

62. Siemon-Netto, "Wir sprachen mit dem Negerführer Dr. Luther King."

63. "Speaking of Walls," *Baltimore Afro-American*, October 13, 1964, 4. Already in the summer, King had received an invitation from a graduate of Morris Brown College who was the Post Quartermaster of the Seventh Army Training Center at

Grafenwöhr in Bavaria to come and visit, noting that the base had "several Negro officers here with key and responsible positions." Referring to his obligations in the United States and the need to keep his visit to Germany brief, King, however, regretfully declined to visit the base. See Captain Thomas J. Holman to Dr. Martin Luther King Jr., June 1, 1964; Dr. Martin Luther King Jr. to Captain Thomas J. Holman, August 10, Papers of Dr. Martin Luther King, Jr., 59:16, KCA.

64. Quoted in William Weart, "Dr. King Assails Policy at Girard," *New York Times*, August 4, 1968, 19. This "kind of Berlin wall to keep the colored children of God out" (King's words) was finally removed in 1968 when the Supreme Court ordered the desegregation of the school, thereby upholding previous rulings that deemed the exclusion of African American students a violation of the Fourteenth Amendment; the first black and Asian students were admitted to Girard College in the fall semester. See Jesse Lewis, "King Supports NAACP in Girard College Drive," *Washington Post*, August 4, 1965, A6; *Commonwealth of Pennsylvania v. Revelle W. Brown*, U.S. Court of Appeals Third Circuit, 392 F.2d 120, Decided March 7, 1968.

65. Early examples were the conclusions King drew from his visits to Ghana in 1957 and to India in 1959. See, e.g., Nikihil Pal Singh, *Black Is a Country: Race and the Unfinished Struggle for Democracy* (Cambridge, MA: Harvard University Press, 2005), 176f., 185; Kevin K. Gaines, "The Civil Rights Movement in World Perspective," in *America on the World Stage: A Global Approach to U.S. History/ The Organization of American Historians*, ed. Gary W. Reichard and Ted Dickson (Urbana and Chicago: University of Illinois Press, 2008), 197–98.

66. For Dr. King's Nobel lecture, see http://nobelprize.org/nobel_prizes/peace/ laureates/1964/king-lecture.html.

67. Quoted in Taylor Branch, "Globalizing King's Legacy," *New York Times*, January 16, 2006, A15. For other examples of King's global consciousness, see Thomas Borstelmann, *The Cold War and the Color Line. American Race Relations in the Global Arena* (Cambridge, MA: Harvard University Press, 2001), 110, 160, 167; Mary L. Dudziak, *Cold War Civil Rights* (Princeton: Princeton University Press, 2000), 254.

6 Revolutionary Alliances: The Rise of Black Power

1. SDS Westberlin und Internationales Nachrichten- und Forschungsinstitut (INFI), ed., *Der Kampf des vietnamesischen Volkes und die Globalstrategie des Imperialismus: Internationaler Vietnam-Kongress 17./18. Februar 1968 Westberlin* (Berlin: SDS, 1968), 139f.

2. Rudi Dutschke, *Internationaler Emanzipationskampf*, 123.

3. Carol Anderson, "From Hope to Disillusion: African Americans, the United Nations, and the Struggle for Human Rights, 1944–1947," *Diplomatic History* 20.4 (Fall 1996): 531–63; idem, *Eyes Off the Prize: The United Nations and the African American Struggle for Human Rights, 1944–1955* (Cambridge: Cambridge University Press, 2003). See also Gerald Horne, *Black and Red: W. E. B. Du Bois and the Afro-American Response to the Cold War, 1944–1963* (Albany: State University of New York Press, 1986); Penny von Eschen, *Race against Empire: Black Americans and Anticolonialism, 1937–1957* (Ithaca: Cornell University Press, 1997); Mary Dudziak, *Cold War Civil Rights: Race and the Image of American Democracy* (Princeton: Princeton University Press, 2000), 61ff.; James Meriwether, *Proudly We Can Be Africans: Black Americans and Africa, 1935–1961*

(Chapel Hill: University of North Carolina Press, 2002); Nikihil Pal Singh, *Black Is a Country: Race and the Unfinished Struggle for Democracy* (Cambridge, MA: Harvard University Press, 2005), 134–84; Manfred Berg, "Black Civil Rights and Liberal Anticommunism: The NAACP in the Early Cold War," *Journal of American History* 94.1 (2007): 75–96; Glenda Gilmore, *Defying Dixie: The Radical Roots of Civil Rights, 1919–1950* (New York: W. W. Norton, 2008); Carol Anderson, "International Conscience, the Cold War, and Apartheid: The NAACP's Alliance with the Reverend Michael Scott for South West Africa's Liberation, 1946–1951," *Journal of World History* 19.3 (September 2008): 297–325.

4. See, e.g., Singh, *Black Is a Country*, 184–93; Besenia Rodriguez, "'Long Live Third World Unity! Long Live Internationalism!' Huey P. Newton's Revolutionary Intercommunalism," in *Transnational Blackness: Navigating the Global Color Line*, ed. Manning Marable and Vanessa Agard-Jones (New York: Palgrave Macmillan, 2008), 149–73; Robyn Spencer, "Merely One Link in the Worldwide Revolution: Internationalism, State Repression, and the Black Panther Party, 1966–1972," in *From Toussaint to Tupac: The Black International since the Age of Revolution*, ed. Michael West, William Martin, and Fanon Che Wilkins (Chapel Hill: University of North Carolina Press, 2009), 215–31. For the growing literature on the internationalist streak of the African American civil rights movement, see endnote 12 in the introduction above.

5. Günter Amendt, "Die Studentenrevolte in Berkeley," *neue kritik* 28 (February 1965): 5–7, 7.

6. Joachim Schwelien, "Nach der Freiheit die Gleichheit," *Die Zeit*, October 22, 1965, 32. See also Imanuel Geiss, "Freisein im Lande der Freiheit: Zur Geschichte der Bürgerrechtsbewegung in den USA," *Atomzeitalter* 5/6 (June/July 1965) 190–96.

7. "The political scene in the South will change. A candidate who promises his (white) voters that he will fight until he drops to retain segregation will no longer have a chance of getting elected." Quoted in Hanns Krammer, "Das Negerelend bleibt Amerikas Bürde," *Süddeutsche Zeitung* (hereafter *SZ*), August 17, 1965, 3.

8. Joachim Schwelien, "Weiße Übermacht—schwarze Macht," *Die Zeit*, August 19, 1966, 3.

9. "Der Rassenkampf wird zum Bürgerkrieg…," *SZ*, July 26, 1967, 3.

10. Herbert von Borch, "Als Schwarzer in Vietnam streben?" *SZ*, June 21, 1966, 9; Manfred Riedel, "Die 'Schwarze Macht' pocht auf ihr Recht," *Die Welt*, June 28, 1966, 5.

11. "Was und warum," *Der Spiegel*, August 7, 1967, 67–73, 73.

12. Philipp Gassert, "Blick über den Atlantik: DIE ZEIT und Amerika in den 1960er Jahren," in Christian Haase und Axel Schildt, eds., *DIE ZEIT und die Bonner Republik. Eine meinungsbildende Wochenzeitung zwischen Wiederbewaffnung und Wiedervereinigung* (Göttingen: Wallstein, 2008), 65–83.

13. Philipp Gassert and Alan Steinweis, eds., *Coping with the Nazi Past: West German Debates on Nazism and Generational Conflict, 1955–1975* (New York: Berghahn Books, 2006).

14. Karl Jaspers, *Wohin treibt die Bundersrepublik? Tatsachen, Gefahren, Chancen* (Munich: Piper, 1966); idem, *The Future of Germany* (Chicago: University of Chicago Press, 1967).

15. For a detailed discussion, see Martin Klimke, *The Other Alliance: Student Protest in West Germany & the United States in the Global Sixties* (Princeton: Princeton University Press, 2010).

16. Karl Dietrich Wolff, "'Amis' and 'Naner': With Americans in Hesse since 1945," in *Amerikaner in Hessen: Eine besondere Beziehung im Wandel der Zeit*, ed. Gundula Bavendamm (Hanau: Cocon-Verlag, 2008), 127–46, online version at www.aacvr-germany.org/online_publications.

17. The text of the flyer "Von diesem Gespräch haben wir nichts zu erwarten"—created by a group around Rudi Dutschke during conflicts about university reform at the Free University—was, e.g., inspired by a speech by Stokely Carmichael. See Siegward Lönnendonker, Bernd Rabehl, and Jochen Staadt, *Die antiautoritäre Revolte: der Sozialistische Deutsche Studentenbund nach der Trennung von der SPD* (Wiesbaden: Westdeutscher Verlag, 2002), 164.

18. Gerhardt Amendt, "Das Elend der amerikanischen Neger," *Frankfurter Rundschau* (hereafter *FR*), January 27, 1968, Supplement *Zeit und Bild*, 1.

19. "Die XXII. Ordentliche Delegiertenkonferenz des SDS (Resolutionen und Beschlüsse)," 26, in Papers of Ronny Loewy, vol. 1 (SDS 1966–1970), Hamburger Institut für Sozialforschung, Hamburg (hereafter HIS).

20. See also the German publication of his speech in Stokely Carmichael, "Black Power," *Kursbuch* 16 (March 1969): 111–30.

21. Bernward Vesper, *Die Reise* (Reinbek: Rowohlt, 1989), 588f.

22. See, e.g., Bernward Vesper, ed., *Black Power. Ursachen des Guerilla-Kampfes in den Vereinigten Staaten*, Voltaire Flugschriften 14 (Berlin: Voltaire, 1967); Michael Schneider, ed., *Malcolm X: Schwarze Gewalt. Reden* (Frankfurt: Edition Voltaire, 1968); Stokely Carmichael, *Die Dritte Welt, unsere Welt. Thesen zur Schwarzen Revolution*, Voltaire Flugschriften 29 (Berlin: Voltaire, 1969); Robert F. Williams and Robert B. Bigg, *Großstadtguerilla*, Voltaire Flugschriften 24 (Berlin: Voltaire, 1969).

23. Vesper, ed., *Black Power*, 3.

24. Ekkehart Krippendorff, "Über Martin Luther King," *Berliner Extra-Dienst* 29/11, April 10, 1968, 10.

25. Quoted in " 'Eine Krankheit ist ausgebrochen,' " *Bild am Sonntag*, April 14, 1968, 6. With respect to the attack on Dutschke and the murder of King, for members of the Kommune I, a West Berlin countercultural group influenced by Situationism, this strategy of polarization and provocation of violence was regrettably true. See Aribert Reimann, *Dieter Kunzelmann: Avantgardist, Protestler, Radikaler* (Göttingen: Vandenhoeck & Ruprecht, 2009), 188–90.

26. "Testimony of Karl-Dietrich Wolff. Hearings before the Subcommittee to Investigate the Administration of the Internal Security Act and other Security Laws of the Committee on the Judiciary," U.S. Senate, 91st Cong., 1st Sess., March 14 and 18, 1969 (Washington, DC: U.S. Government Printing Office, 1969), 7.

27. Ibid., 15f.

28. For the international dimension of the Black Panther Party, see Jennifer B. Smith, *An International History of the Black Panther Party* (New York: Garland, 1999); Michael L. Clemons and Charles E. Jones, "Global Solidarity: The Black Panther Party in the International Arena," in *Liberation, Imagination, and the Black Panther Party: A New Look at the Panthers and Their Legacy*, ed. Kathleen Cleaver and George Katsiaficas (New York: Routledge, 2001), 20–39; Besenia Rodriguez, " 'Long Live Third World Unity! Long Live Internationalism!' Huey P. Newton's Revolutionary Intercommunalism"; Robyn Spencer, "Merely One Link in the Worldwide Revolution."

29. Black Panther Solidaritätskomitee, "Solidaritätskomitee für die Black-Panther-Partei," *Sozialistische Correspondenz-Info* 24, December 6, 1969, 11. See also Maria Höhn, "The Black Panther Solidarity Committee and the Trial of the Ramstein 2," in *Changing the World, Changing the Self: Political Protest and Collective Identities in 1960/70s West Germany and the United States*, ed. Belinda Davis, Wilfried Mausbach, Martin Klimke, and Carla MacDougall (New York: Berghahn Books, 2010), 215–39.

30. Bobby Seale, *Der Prozeß gegen Bobby Seale: Rassismus und politische Justiz in den USA* (Frankfurt: Roter Stern, 1970); Eldridge Cleaver, *Zur Klassenanalyse der*

Black Panther Partei: Erziehung und Revolution (Frankfurt: Roter Stern, 1970); Michael Tabor, *Harlem: Kapitalismus & Heroin = Völkermord* (Frankfurt: Roter Stern, 1970); Huey Newton, *Selbstverteidigung* (Frankfurt: Roter Stern, 1971). See also the series of articles by Helmut Reinicke on revolutionary movements in the United States: Helmut Reinicke, "berichte aus ameriKKKa (1)," *Sozialistische Correspondenz-Info* 34/35, February 28, 1970, 29–34; idem, "berichte aus ameriKKKa (2)," *Sozialistische Correspondenz-Info* 37, March 14, 1970, 23–25. A reader with this title also emerged from the Verlag Roter Stern, eds., *LERNEN: subversive. AmeriKKKa: ein Lese-Bilder-Buch* (Frankfurt: Verlag Roter Stern, 1974). For the financial calculations of the committee, see Karl Dietrich Wolff, "Überlegungen zur Internationalismusfrage," *Sozialistische Correspondenz-Info* 34/35, February 28, 1970, 26–28, 27.

31. See Uta Poiger, *Jazz, Rock and Rebels: Cold War Politics and American Culture in a Divided Germany* (Berkeley: University of California Press, 2000).

32. Bommi Baumann, "God bless America: Die USA als Vorbild für die 68er," in *Radikales Amerika. Wie die amerikanische Protestbewegung Deutschland veränderte*, ed. Bommi Baumann and Till Meyer (Berlin: Rotbuch Verlag, 2007), 9–36, 15.

33. Ibid., 15. For the increasing comparison of the Vietnam conflict to Auschwitz in the West German antiwar movement, see also Wilfried Mausbach, "Auschwitz and Vietnam: West German Protest against America's War during the 1960s," in *America, the Vietnam War and the World: Comparative and International Perspectives*, ed. Andreas Daum, Lloyd Gardner, and Wilfried Mausbach (New York: Cambridge University Press, 2003), 279–98. For the significance of the Nazi past, see also Hans Kundnani, *Utopia or Auschwitz: Germany's 1968 Generation and the Holocaust* (New York: Columbia University Press, 2009); Wolfgang Kraushaar, "Hitler's Children? The German 1968 Movement in the Shadow of the Nazi Past," in *Memories of 1968: International Perspectives*, ed. Ingo Cornils and Sarah Waters (Bern: Peter Lang, 2010), 79–101.

34. Summoned to the board of the Rotary Club the next day, Wolff recalls his reaction after being asked by the club's president how, after the Holocaust, he, as a German, could make such a remark: "At the time, I found the question outrageous—the older I get, the more important I find it, and it has stayed with me throughout my entire life." Wolff, *"Amis" and "Naner,"* online version.

35. From 1963 to 1972, Schultz studied and worked in the United States and became active in the civil rights movement. In September 1965, she took up a teaching position at a black college in Mississippi (Rust College in Holly Springs), where she got involved with the Mississippi Freedom Democratic Party (MFDP).

36. Dagmar Schultz, "Seltsam schönes Land—Land der Ungerechtigkeit," *Frankfurter Hefte* 9 (1966): 627–34, 633.

37. Ibid., 634. See also Dagmar Schultz, "Witnessing whiteness—ein persönliches Zeugnis," in *Mythen, Masken und Subjekte: kritische Weissseinsforschung in Deutschland*, ed. Maureen Maisha Eggers, Grada Kilomba, Peggy Piesche, and Susan Arndt (Münster: Unrast, 2005), 514–29.

38. May Ayim, Katharina Oguntoye, and Dagmar Schultz, eds., *Farbe bekennen: Afrodeutsche Frauen auf den Spuren ihrer Geschichte* (Berlin: Orlanda Frauenverlag, 1986). For the English version, see idem, *Showing Our Colors: Afro-German Women Speak Out* (Amherst: University of Massachusetts Press, 1992). See also the conclusion of this book.

39. Klaus Harpprecht, "Der schwarze Tribun," *Christ und Welt*, August 5, 1966, 28; N. B., "Schwarze Demagogie," *FAZ*, July 13, 1968, "Ereignisse und Gestalten," Supplement 160. On this issue, see also Sabine Broeck, "The Erotics of African-American Endurance, Or: On the Right Side of History? White (West)-German

Public Sentiment between Pornotroping and Civil Rights Solidarity," in *German and African American Crossovers: Two Centuries of Contact*, ed. Larry Greene and Anke Ortlepp (Jackson: University of Mississippi Press, forthcoming).

40. Hans Steinitz, "Wie krank ist Amerika?" *Rheinischer Merkur*, August 4, 1967, 24; N. B., *Schwarze Demagogie*.

41. Joachim E. Berendt, "Den Schwarzen der USA fehlen die Politiker," *Frankfurter Hefte 5* (1970): 339–42, 340.

42. See Black Panther Solidaritätskommitee, "Solidaritätsveranstaltung mit der Black Panther Partei: Connie Matthews," Flyer, April 18, 1970, in USA BPP, Black Panther Party, Box, German SDS Papers, APO-Archive, Free University of Berlin, Berlin (hereafter APOB); Brigitte Heinrich, "Die Unterstützung des US-Imperialismus durch die BRD und die Auswirkungen im Innern," in *Am Beispiel Angela Davis: Der Kongreß in Frankfurt*, ed. Angela Davis Solidaritätskomitee (Frankfurt: Fischer, 1972), 159–69, esp. 164.

43. RAF, "Die Rote Armee aufbauen!" *agit 883* 62, June 5, 1970, 6. See also Michael Hahn, "Land der Superpigs: Wie *agit 883* mit Black Panthers und Weathermen die 'zweite Front in den Metropolen eröffnete," in *agit 883: Bewegung, Revolte, Underground in Westberlin, 1969–1972*, ed. Rotaprint 25 (Hamburg: Assoziation A, 2006), 141–55.

44. RAF, "Das Konzept Stadtguerilla," in *Rote Armee Fraktion: Texte und Materialien zur Geschichte der RAF*, ed. ID-Verlag (Berlin: ID-Verlag, 1997), 35.

45. RAF, "Über den bewaffneten Kampf in Westeuropa," in *RAF: Texte und Materialien*, 71.

46. Moritz Ege, *Schwarz werden: "Afroamerikanophilie" in den 1960er und 1970er Jahren* (Bielefeld: Transcript, 2007); Detlef Siegfried, "White Negroes: The Fascination of the Authentic in the West German Counterculture of the 1960s," in *Changing the World*, ed. Davis et al., 191–214.

47. Angela Davis, *An Autobiography* (New York: Random House, 1974), 133–45.

48. See Detlev Claussen, "Zur Verhaftung von Angela Davis," *Sozialistische Correspondenz-Info* 56/57 (November 11, 1970): 18–20. For the early reception in West Germany, see Jürgen Leinemann, "Sind schwarze Häftlinge in USA Kriegsgefangene?" *Frankfurter Rundschau am Abend*, August 20, 1970.

49. Herbert Marcuse, "Helft Angela," *Neues Forum* 17 (November 1970): 1020, quoted in Wolfgang Kraushaar, *Frankfurter Schule und Studentenbewegung: Von der Flaschenpost zum Molotowcocktail 1946–1995*, vol. 2 (Frankfurt: Rogner & Bernhard, 1998), 727f.

50. Black Panther Solidaritätskomitee, "Zum Prozeß gegen die Soledad Brothers," "Letter to the Government of FRG." Letter, 1970, 10/22, 5–8, in USA BPP, Black Panther Party, Box, German SDS Papers, APOB.

51. As the distributed paper declared, "The Soledad Brothers will only find justice in the court of Salinas if we, by our actions, make it impossible for the state to execute them." Quoted in ibid., 8.

52. "Solidarität mit Angela Davis," *FR*, December 22, 1970.

53. Oskar Negt, "Der Fall Angela Davis," *konkret*, January 28, 1971, 52–54, quoted in Kraushaar, *Frankfurter Schule und Studentenbewegung*, vol. 2, 732.

54. Angela Davis Solidaritätskomitee, ed., *Am Beispiel Angela Davis: Der Kongreß in Frankfurt* (Frankfurt: Fischer, 1972), 2. The committee was founded by Manfred Clemenz, Lothar Menne, Oskar Negt, Claudio Pozzoli, and Klaus Vack.

55. "Angela Davis women and children solidarity demonstration," Flyer, 1971, 03/13, in USA BPP, Black Panther Party, Box, German SDS Papers, APOB; see also Kraushaar, *Frankfurter Schule und Studentenbewegung*, vol. 1, 506.

56. Angela Davis Solidaritätskomitee, "Freiheit für Angela Davis!" Wall Paper, 1971, 11, in USA BPP, Black Panther Party, Box, German SDS Papers, APOB.

57. Initiativgruppe Angela Davis am John F. Kennedy Institut, "[Call for solidar-
    ity with Angela Davis]," Flyer, undated, in USA BPP, Black Panther Party, Box,
    German SDS papers, APOB.
58. Herbert Marcuse, Speech during an Angela Davis Rally at Berkeley, October 24,
    1969, in Stadt- und Universitätsbibliothek Frankfurt/Main, Herbert-Marcuse-
    Archiv, quoted in Kraushaar, *Frankfurter Schule und Studentenbewegung*, vol.
    2, 689. On the role of women in the civil rights and black power movements, see
    most recently Dayo F. Gore, Jeanne Theoharis, and Komozi Woodard, eds., *Want
    to Start a Revolution?: Radical Women in the Black Freedom Struggle* (New York:
    NYU Press, 2009).

7 Heroes of the Other America: East German
Solidarity with the African American
Freedom Struggle

1. For the history of the GDR, see Mary Fulbrook, *Anatomy of a Dictatorship:
   Inside the GDR, 1949–1989* (New York: Oxford University Press, 1995); Konrad
   Jarausch, ed., *Dictatorship as Experience: Towards a Socio-Cultural History of
   the GDR* (New York: Berghahn Books, 1999); Mary Fulbrook, *The People's State:
   East German Society from Hitler to Honecker* (New Haven: Yale University Press,
   2005); Andrew Port, *Conflict and Stability in the German Democratic Republic*
   (Cambridge: Cambridge University Press, 2007).
2. Constitution of East Germany, October 7, 1949, Article 6, paragraph 2, in
   *Dokumente des Geteilten Deutschland: Quellentexte zur Rechtslage des Deutschen
   Reiches, der Bundesrepublik Deutschland und der Deutschen Demokratischen
   Republik*, ed. Ingo von Münch (Stuttgart: Kröner, 1976), 301–23, 302.
3. Klaus Bollinger, *Freedom Now—Freiheit sofort! Die Negerbevölkerung der USA
   im Kampf um Demokratie* (Berlin: Staatsverlag der Deutschen Demokratischen
   Republik, 1968), 4f.
4. Kongress für Bürgerliche Rechte, New York 1951, *Rassenmord! Wir klagen
   an!: Petition an die Vereinten Nationen zum Schutze der Negerbevölkerung in
   den Vereinigten Staaten von Amerika*, translated by Hermann Stürmer (Berlin:
   Rütten & Loening, 1953). The citation for the original English petition is William
   Patterson, ed., *We Charge Genocide: The Historic Petition to the United Nations
   for Relief from a Crime of the United States Government against the Negro People*
   (New York: Civil Rights Congress, 1951). For the Civil Rights Congress and the
   1951 petition, see Gerald Horne, *Communist Front? The Civil Rights Congress,
   1946–1956* (Rutherford, NJ: Fairleigh Dickinson University Press, 1987); Charles
   Martin, "Internationalizing 'The American Dilemma': The Civil Rights Congress
   and the 1951 Genocide Petition to the United Nations," *Journal of American
   Ethnic History* 16.4 (Summer 1997): 35–61.
5. Kongress für Bürgerliche Rechte, *Rassenmord*, 8ff.
6. Emphasis original. Bollinger, *Freedom Now*, 5. See also Ministry of Foreign Affairs
   of the German Democratic Republic, ed., *The Anti-Imperialist Liberation Struggle
   of the Afro-Asian and Latin American Peoples and the German Democratic
   Republic* (Dresden: Verlag Zeit im Bild, 1964).
7. Bollinger, *Freedom Now*, 4.
8. See Gerald Horne, *Black and Red: W. E .B. Du Bois and the Afro-American
   Response to the Cold War, 1944–1963* (Albany: State University of New York
   Press, 1986); David Levering Lewis, *W. E. B. Du Bois: The Fight for Equality and
   the American Century: 1919–1963* (New York: Holt, 2001), 496–553; Patricia

Sullivan, *Lift Every Voice: The NAACP and the Making of the Civil Rights Movement* (New York: New Press, 2009), 367–70.

9. He also visited Germany in 1923 and 1926. For his time in Nazi Germany, see Werner Sollors, "W. E. B. Du Bois in Nazi Germany, 1936," *Amerikastudien/ American Studies* 44 (1999): 207–22; Harold Brackman, "'A Calamity Almost beyond Comprehension': Nazi Anti-Semitism and the Holocaust in the Thought of W. E. B. Du Bois," *American Jewish History* 88 (2000): 53–93; David Levering Lewis, *W. E. B. Du Bois: The Fight for Equality and the American Century: 1919–1963* (New York: Holt, 2001), 308–405; Christina Oppel, "W. E. B. Du Bois, Nazi Germany, and the Black Atlantic," *GHI Bulletin Supplement* 5 (2008): 99–120. For an image gallery, source materials, and further information about the 1958 visit and Du Bois's general relationship to Germany, see www.aacvr-germany. org/dubois.

10. Honorary Degree Certificate, Faculty of Economics, Humboldt University, November 3, 1958, in Ehrenpromotion, W. E. B. Du Bois, Humboldt University Archive, Berlin (hereafter HUAB). See also W. E. B. Du Bois, *The Autobiography of W. E. B. Du Bois: A Soliloquy of Viewing My Life from the Last Decade of Its First Century* (New York: International, 1968), 23.

11. Heinz Mohrmann to Wilhelm Girnus, East German Minister for Higher Education, Explanation for the Award of Honorary Degree to W. E. B. Du Bois, October 28, 1958, in Ehrenpromotion, W. E. B. Du Bois, HUAB. See also "Ansprache des Dekans der Wirtschaftswissenschaftlichen Fakultät der Humboldt Universität zu Berlin Professor Dr. rer. pol. (hab.) Heinz Mohrmann, anlässlich der Ehrenpromotion von Prof. Dr. Dr. Du Bois, New York," *Wissenschaftliche Zeitschrift der Humboldt-Universität zu Berlin* 8.1 (1958/59): 111–13.

12. The birthday delegation included Deputy Foreign Minister Otto Winzer, the head of the African desk at the East German Foreign Ministry Gottfried Lessing, and Karl-Heinz Kern, acting chairman of the GDR's trade office in Ghana. Condolences were offered by Georg Heiderrich, head of the East German trade delegation in Ghana in August 1963, and a wreath was laid at Du Bois's grave by Gerald Götting in December 1963. For the visits to Ghana and East German obituaries, as well as the perception of Du Bois in East Germany and the details of his visit in 1958, see Hamilton Beck, "Censoring Your Ally: W. E. B. Du Bois in the German Democratic Republic," in *Crosscurrents: African Americans, Africa, and Germany in the Modern World*, ed. David McBride, Leroy Hopkins, and Carol Blackshire-Belay (Columbia, SC: Camden House, 1998), 197–232, esp. 221.

13. See Oliver Harrington, *Bootsie and Others: A Selection of Cartoons* (New York: Dodd, 1958); Oliver Harrington, *Soul Shots: Political Cartoons by Ollie Harrington* (New York: Longview, 1972); Oliver Harrington, *Why I Left America and Other Essays* (Jackson: University Press of Mississippi, 1993); M. Thomas Inge, ed., *Dark Laughter: The Satiric Art of Oliver W. Harrington* (Jackson: University Press of Mississippi, 1993). See also Chapter 3.

14. Regrettably, Oliver Harrington has not yet found the attention of a biographer. On Harrington's friendship to Paul Robeson, see Ollie Harrington, "In einem schwarzen Ghetto," *Das Magazin* 7, July 1971, 23–28. See also Aribert Schroeder, "Ollie Harrington: His Portrait Drawn on the Basis of East German (GDR) Secret Service Files," in *German and African American Crossovers: Two Centuries of Contact*, ed. Larry Greene and Anke Ortlepp (Jackson: University Press of Mississippi, forthcoming). For his 1972 visit to the offices of the *Chicago Daily Defender*, see Robert McClory, "Ollie Harrington: Bootsie Artist Visits U.S.," *Chicago Daily Defender*, October 21, 1972, 1. For examples of his artwork, an image gallery, as well as further information about Oliver Harrington, see www. aacvr-germany.org/harrington.

15. "Deserteure: Verdammt in alle Ewigkeit," *Der Spiegel*, May 26, 1954, 8–11; Victor Grossman, *Crossing the River: A Memoir of the American Left, the Cold War, and Life in East Germany* (Amherst: University of Massachusetts Press, 2003), 116–35; idem, "Prologue: African Americans in the GDR," in *German and African American Crossovers, ed.* Greene and Ortlepp. The accounts of Grossman, himself a U.S. soldier who fled to East Germany in 1952 and has lived there ever since, shed an extremely illuminating light on life in East Germany from the perspective of an American communist.

16. Jack Anderson, "US Misfits Train as Red Spies," *Washington Post*, June 13, 1964, 39. See also Arna Vogel and Christian Blees, "Der Cowboy im Sozialismus: US-Amerikaner in der DDR," Westdeutscher Rundfunk, Cologne, October 5, 2005.

17. Lucas, however, seemed to have suffered from emotional problems or from difficulties adjusting because his German was poor. In June 1956, only a few months after getting married, he committed suicide. On Lucas, see "Red Report Defection," *New York Times*, December 9, 1952, 9; Grossman, *Crossing the River*, 106f.; Peter Köpf, "Charles Lucas' Big Mistake," *Atlantic Times*, September 2009, 20–21.

18. "Langes Gedächtnis," *Der Spiegel*, April 10, 1995, 96f.; Victor Grossman, "African Americans in the GDR," in *German and African American Crossovers, ed.* Greene and Ortlepp.

19. Regina Kerner, "Mit Blueberry Hill kam der eine bis nach Taschkent," *Berliner Zeitung*, April 25, 1995, 3.

20. Ministerium des Inneren, Staatsekretariat für Innere Angelegenheiten, "Geheime Verschlusssache B14–6898/54," April 22, 1954, in BArch DO 1/17056, Bundesarchiv, Berlin-Lichterfelde (hereafter BArch-Berlin).

21. Max Zimmering, *Im herben Morgenwind: Ausgewählte Gedichte aus zwei Jahrzehnten* (Berlin: Dietz, 1953), 56–58.

22. Anna Seghers, *Der erste Schritt* (Berlin: Aufbau-Verlag, 1953, edition 1957), 26–32, 28.

23. For an overview of these works, see Ursula Dibbern and Horst Ihde, "Das Echo der Kultur und des Freiheitskampfes der nordamerikanischen Neger in der DDR, 1945–1969," *Zeitschrift für Anglistik und Amerikanistik* 3.20 (1972): 429–42; Daisy Wessel, *Bild und Gegenbild: Die USA in der Belletristik der DDR (bis 1987)* (Opladen: Leske & Budrich, 1989), 104–18.

24. The seminal work on this issue is Uta Poiger, *Jazz, Rock, and Rebels: Cold War Politics and American Culture in a Divided Germany* (Berkeley: University of California Press, 2000).

25. For a detailed discussion, see ibid., 150–67.

26. Friedensrat der Deutschen Demokratischen Republik, *Days with Paul Robeson* (Berlin: Deutscher Friedensrat, 1961), 8. This is a translated version of the German original: Friedensrat der Deutschen Demokratischen Republik, *Tage mit Paul Robeson: Paul Robeson im Oktober 1960 in der Deutschen Demokratischen Republik* (Berlin: Deutscher Friedensrat, 1961).

27. Friedensrat, *Days with Paul Robeson*, 14; Martin Duberman, *Paul Robeson* (New York: New Press, 1989), 738; Paul Robeson Jr., *The Undiscovered Paul Robeson: Quest for Freedom, 1939–1976* (Hoboken: Wiley, 2010), 301. For Du Bois's and Robeson's stance toward the Soviet Union, see also Kate A. Baldwin, *Beyond the Color Line and the Iron Curtain: Reading Encounters between Black and Red, 1922–1963* (Durham, NC: Duke University Press, 2002), 149–252.

28. Friedensrat, *Days with Paul Robeson*, 21, 16–30; Duberman, *Paul Robeson*, 486–87. According to Robeson Jr., Paul Robeson also visited East Berlin on June 15, 1960, to participate in a festival sponsored by an East German communist

newspaper. For the complete genesis of and correspondence related to the visit, see Ministerium für Kultur, Kulturpolitische Beziehungen zu den USA, Bd. 1, BArch DR 1/19183, BArch-Berlin. See also Robeson Jr., *The Undiscovered Paul Robeson,* 305. For other related publications, see Viktor Gorokhov, *Ich singe Amerika: Ein Lebensbild Paul Robesons,* trans. Herbert Schirrmacher (Berlin: Verlag Neues Leben, 1955); Paul Robeson, *Mein Lied—meine Waffe,* trans. Georg Friedrich Alexander (Berlin: Kongress-Verlag, 1958); Paul-Robeson-Komitee der Deutschen Demokratischen Republik, ed., *Paul Robeson. Ausstellung zu Ehren seines 70. Geburtstages am 9. April 1968. Internationales Ausstellungszentrum Berlin, 8.–28. April (Katalog)* (Berlin: Deutsche Akademie der Künste, 1968).

29. Friedensrat, *Days with Paul Robeson,* 17. See also Albert Norden, "Umlauf-Vorlage für das Politbüro, Beschlussvorschlag 'Stern der Völkerfreundschaft' für Paul Robeson," October 4, 1960, in SAPMO-BArch DY 30, IV, 2/2.028, 5, Stiftung Archiv der Parteien und Massenorganisationen der DDR im Bundesarchiv, Berlin (hereafter SAPMO).

30. Paul Robeson, "Interview with Press Berlin, German Democratic Republic," October 1960, in *Paul Robeson Speaks: Writings, Speeches, Interviews, 1918–1974,* ed. Philip Sheldon Foner (New York: Brunner/Mazel, 1978), 464–67, 466.

31. Duberman, *Paul Robeson,* 514–21. During his 1963 visit, he met with his old friend Oliver Harrington, among others. See also Paul and Eslanda Robeson, "For the Celebration of the 15th Anniversary of the Founding of the GDR," Mermaid Theatre, London, October 25, 1964, in *Paul Robeson Speaks,* ed. Foner, 473.

32. Brigitte Bögelsack, ed., *Symposium: Paul Robeson and the Struggle of the Working Class and the Afro-American People of the USA against Imperialism, Held in Berlin, April 13 and 14, 1971* (Berlin: German Academy of Art, 1972). See also Brigitte Bögelsack, ed., *Paul Robeson, April 9, 1898—January 23, 1976: For his 80th Birthday* (Berlin: Academy of Arts of the German Democratic Republic, 1978).

33. Albert Norden, "Dem schwarzen Vorkämpfer der Menschheit," in *Symposium: Paul Robeson and the Struggle of the Working Class,* ed. Bögelsack, 6.

34. For the organization of the symposium, see Box 5751–5752, Paul Robeson Archive, Academy of Arts, Berlin (PRA); Jürgen Große, *Amerikapolitik und Amerikabild der DDR 1974–1989* (Bonn: Bouvier, 1999), 212.

35. "Abernathy Leaves for Moscow," *Chicago Tribune,* September 20, 1971, A15.

36. Dr. Ralph Abernathy to Rev. Edwin Brandt, September 1, 1964, Papers of Dr. Martin Luther King, Jr., 71:42; KCA.

37. "Reverend Abernathy in Berlin begrüßt," *Neues Deutschland,* September 28, 1971, 1; "Herzliches Willkommen für Ralph Abernathy," *B.Z. am Abend,* September 28, 1971, 2; "Echte Freunde in der DDR," *Neue Zeit,* September 29, 1971, 1. For a full report of his visit, see also Friedensrat der Deutschen Demokratischen Republik, *"Every Cloud Has a Silver Lining ... " Pastor Ralph D. Abernathy, President of the Southern Christian Leadership Conference Visits the German Democratic Republic, September 27–29, 1971* (Dresden: Peace Council of the German Democratic Republic, 1971).

38. "Brüderliche Solidarität," *Neue Zeit,* September 30, 1971, 1, 2; "Vereinter Ruf nach Freiheit für Angela," *Junge Welt,* September 29, 1971, 1.

39. Ralph Albernathy, Sermon in St. Mary's Church, Transcript, September 28, 1971, www.aacvr-germany.org/abernathy.

40. For the details and evaluation of Abernathy's visit by East German officials, see Friedensrat der DDR, Sekretariat, "Information für die Genossen des Politbüros über den Aufenthalt Dr. Ralph D. Abernathys und seiner Begleitung vom 27.-29.9.1971 in der Hauptstadt der DDR, Berlin," in SAPMO-BArch DY 30/J IV, 2/2J, 3676, SAPMO.

41. The list included, among others, Gerald Götting (chairman of the conservative Christian satellite party in East Germany), Dr. Günther Drefahl (President of the German Peace Council), Werner Kirchhoff (Vice President of the National Council of the National Front), Dr. Heinrich Toeplitz (President of the Supreme Court of the GDR), Bishop Albrecht Schönherr.

42. "Friedensmedaille für Ralph Abernathy," *Neues Deutschland*, September 29, 1971, 1, 2.

43. Albin Krebs, "Notes on People," *New York Times*, September 30, 1971, 61; "Peace Medal for Abernathy," *Washington Post*, September 30, 1971, B5; "Friedensmedaille für Ralph Abernathy," *Neues Deutschland*, September 29, 1971, 2.

44. Viktor Schless, "R. Abernathy: 'Eng verbunden mit der DDR,'" *Berliner Zeitung*, September 30, 1971, 1, 2; Ralph Albernathy, Sermon in St. Mary's Church, Transcript, September 28, 1971, www.aacvr-germany.org/abernathy. Abernathy returned to East Germany at least twice during the 1970s, and in 1974 he received another honor, the "Ehrennadel der Liga für Völkerfreundschaft in Gold." See *Neue Zeit*, September 15, 1974, 1.

45. William Buckley, Jr., "On Political Salesmanship—Two Parables," *Los Angeles Times*, December 31, 1972, B3.

46. "Grüße an Angela nach San Rafael," *Junge Welt*, September 25, 1971, 1, 4, 4. See also "Berliner Jugend: Freiheit für Angela," *Berliner Zeitung*, September 25, 1971, 1; Eckhard Galler, "Fest verbunden mit den Verfolgten des Nixon-Regimes," *Neues Deutschland*, September 25, 1971, 8. For an extensive image gallery of Angela Davis solidarity events and her visits to East Germany, as well as further information about her general relationship to Germany, see www.aacvr-germany.org/davis.

47. Nationalrat der Nationalen Front, Büro des Sekretariats, Solidaritätskundgebung "Freiheit für Angela Davis!" in Berlin, Kongreßhalle, January 26, 1971, in SAPMO-BArch DY 6, Vorl. 3017, SAPMO; Nationalrat der Nationalen Front des demokratischen Deutschland, ed., *Kämpft Angela Davis frei* (Suhl: Freies Wort, 1971), 37–38.

48. The campaign supposedly emerged during a delegate conference at the local FDJ branch at the clock factory Ruhla (VEB Uhrenwerke Ruhla) on January 15 in the presence of Günter Jahn, First Secretary of the Central Committee of the FDJ. Put forward by Angelika Löffler, the idea spread quickly and was popularized by the FDJ daily *Junge Welt*. See "1000000 Rosen für Angela," *Junge Welt*, January 16/17, 1971, 1; Lothar Winkler, "Die Zeit läuft für uns!," *Junge Welt*, January 18, 1971, 3; "Eine Million Rosen für Angela," *Junge Welt*, January 19, 1971, 1, 6. For further details about this campaign, see www.aacvr-germany.org/davis. For the ongoing FDJ efforts on Davis's behalf, see FDJ Central Committee (ZR-FDJ), Minutes, 40th Secretarial Meeting, March 30, 1972, SAPMO-BArch DY 24/8466, SAPMO; Sozialistische Einheitspartei Deutschlands, *Protokoll der Verhandlungen des VIII. Parteitages der Sozialistischen Einheitspartei Deutschlands: 15. bis 19. Juni 1971 in der Werner-Seelenbinder-Halle zu Berlin* (Berlin: Dietz Verlag, 1971).

49. "The peoples have branded the torture chambers of the Gestapo and the genocide committed by the SS as symptoms of an ignominious period and a blemish in the history of the German people. The nations of the world also see the crimes of the murderers of Son My as an indelible symbol of the shame of America." In "Save Angela Davis!," Berlin, February 12, 1972, SED, ZK Institut für die Geschichte der Arbeiterbewegung, Zentrales Parteiarchiv, Internationale Verbindungen, SAPMO-BArch DY 30/IV, B 2/20, 227, SAPMO. Signatories included composer Paul Dessau, actress Gisela May, writer Anna Seghers, and figure skater Gabriele Seyfert, among others. See also Peace Council of the GDR, "United States versus

Angela Davis: Open letter addressed by Attorney Professor Dr. Friedrich Karl Kaul to Judge Richard E. Arnason," Berlin, February 14, 1972, ibid.

50. Sekretariat des Zentralkomitee (ZK) der SED, Reinschriftenprotokoll Nr. 44, October 21, 1971, in SAPMO-BArch DY 30/J IV 2/3, 1798, SAPMO. For the perspective of an American youth visiting East Germany in the summer of 1971, see Steven Kelman, *Behind the Berlin Wall: An Encounter in East Germany* (Boston: Houghton Mifflin, 1972).

51. Sekretariat des ZK, Reinschriftenprotokoll Nr. 31, September 23, 1971, in SAPMO-BArch, DY 30/J IV 2/3, 1785, SAPMO; Paul Markowski, Abteilung Internationale Verbindungen beim ZK der SED, to Werner Kirchhoff, Sekretariat des Nationalrates der Nationalen Front, January 11, 1972, SED, ZK Institut für die Geschichte der Arbeiterbewegung, Zentrales Parteiarchiv, Internationale Verbindungen, SAPMO-BArch-DY 29 IV, B 2/20, 227, SAPMO. For internal tensions about the "correct" coverage of the Angela Davis trial and alleged "objectivist tendencies" by the journalist Walter Kaufmann, see Paul Markowski, Abteilung Internationale Verbindungen beim ZK der SED, to Hans Modrow, Abteilung Agitation des ZK der SED, February 3, 1972 and May 25, 1972, in ibid.

52. For example, the regime tried to convince them to influence George McGovern's position on East Germany via the CPUSA; see "Vermerk über ein Gespräch des Genossen Axen, Mitglied des Politbüros und Sekretär des ZK der SED, mit James E. Jackson, Mitglied des Nationalen Exekutivkomitees der KP der USA, am 22. Juni 1972," June 25, 1972, 3. See also Minutes, "Gespräch mit Mrs. Libby Frank, USA, Direktor des Bergen County Peace Center, New Jersey (Friedenszentrum von Bergen) am 15. Februar 1972," February 16, 1972; Friedel Malter, Chairman, DDR-Komitee für Menschenrechte, "Kurze Information über den Besuch des Genossen Henry Winston im DDR-Komitee für Menschenrechte am 4. Mai 1972," May 8, 1972; "Programm für den Aufenthalt des Genossen Claude Lightfoot mit Gattin und Sohn in der DDR vom 5.–9.9.72," all SED, ZK Institut für die Geschichte der Arbeiterbewegung, Zentrales Parteiarchiv, Internationale Verbindungen, SAPMO-BArch DY 30/IV, B 2/20, 227, SAPMO.

53. For the work of this correspondent, Klaus Steininger, see Klaus Steiniger, "Weltsolidarität beschirmt Angela," *Neues Deutschland*, September 24, 1971, 6; idem, *Free Angela Davis. Hero of the Other America* (Berlin: National Council of the National Front of the GDR, 1972); "Personalie," *Der Spiegel*, March 13, 1972, 186; Klaus Steiniger, *Bei Winston und Cunhal. Reporter auf vier Kontinenten* (Berlin: Edition Ost, 2004), 8–13, 137–139. For the increase of solidarity events, see, e.g., Sekretariat des ZK, Reinschriftenprotokoll Nr. 11, February 1, 1972, in SAPMO-BArch DY 30/J IV 2/3, 1834, SAPMO. Examples of related publications include Maximilian Scheer, *Der Weg nach San Rafael. Für Angela Davis. Ein Hörspiel* (Berlin: Verlag der Nation, 1971); idem, *Liebste Angela—Erste unter Gleichen: Gefängnisbriefe von George Jackson* (Berlin: Verlag der Nation, 1971); Werner Lehmann, *Schwarze Rose aus Alabama* (Berlin: Neues Leben, 1972); Walter Kaufmann, *Unterwegs zu Angela. Amerikanische Impressionen* (Berlin: Verlag der Nation, 1973). Angela Davis was also the topic of East Germany's chief TV propagandist, Karl-Eduard von Schnitzler: see Karl-Eduard von Schnitzler, Der Schwarze Kanal, "Die 'ganz neuen USA,'" No. 620, February 28, 1972, in E001-00-01/0002/159, Deutsches Rundfunkarchiv, Frankfurt (http://sk.dra.de).

54. "East Germany: St. Angela," *Time*, April 3, 1972, 46.

55. See, e.g., "Freiheit für Angela Davis! Solidaritätstelegramm der 3. Tagung des Zentralrats der FDJ an das United National Committee to Angela Davis," *Junge Welt*, October 1, 1971, 1. Readymade postcard samples could be found in Nationalrat der Nationalen Front des demokratischen Deutschland, ed., *Kämpft Angela Davis frei*, 45f.

56. Karsten Fritz, "Bilder eines ganz normalen Lebens in einem ganz normalen Film," in *Dreizehn deutsche Geschichten: Erzähltes Leben aus Ost und West*, ed. Winfried Ripp and Wendelin Szalai (Hamburg: Edition Körber-Stiftung, 1998), 360–85, 369f.

57. Erich Honecker, First Secretary of the Central Committee of the SED, to Angela Davis, telegram, June 5, 1972, SED, ZK Institut für die Geschichte der Arbeiterbewegung, Zentrales Parteiarchiv, Internationale Verbindungen, SAPMO-BArch DY 30/IV, B 2/20, 227, SAPMO.

58. Quoted in *Peace Friendship Solidarity: Angela Davis in the GDR* (Dresden: Verlag Zeit im Bild, 1973), 6.

59. Ibid., 8f.

60. Ibid., 10.

61. Ibid., 15.

62. For the meticulous planning, exact program, and reception of the visit, see, e.g., Sekretariat des ZK, Reinschriftenprotokoll Nr. 87, August 30, 1972, in SAPMO-BArch DY 30/J IV 2/3, 1910; Sekretariat des ZK, Reinschriftenprotokoll Nr. 88, August 31, 1972, in SAPMO-BArch DY 30/J IV 2/3, 1910; Sitzung des Politbüros des Zentralkomitees, Protokoll Nr. 36/72, September 5, 1972, in SAPMO-BArch DY 30/J IV 2/2, 1410; FDJ, Zentralrat, Sekretariatsprotokolle, September 21, 1972, in SAPMO-BArch DY 24/8487; FDJ, Kundgebung mit Angela Davis, September 11, 1972, Friedrichsstadt-Palast, in SAPMO-BArch DY 24, 112328, all SAPMO. For reports from across the country, see Nationalrat der Nationalen Front, Sektor Information, Eingehende Informationsberichte aus dem Bezirk Neubrandenburg, February-December 1972, 5, in SAPMO-BArch DY 6/4732; idem, Eingehende Informationsberichte aus dem Bezirk Rostock, 1972, 4, in SAPMO-BArch DY 6/4684, both SAPMO.

63. Sekretariat des ZK, Reinschriftenprotokoll Nr. 104, October 16, 1972, Anlage 1, 14–16, in SAPMO-BArch DY 30/J IV 2/3, 1927, SAPMO. See also Große, *Amerikapolitik und Amerikabild der DDR*, 213–14. For the postcard, see Andreas Ludwig, *Fortschritt, Norm und Eigensinn: Erkundungen im Alltag der DDR* (Berlin: Links, 1999), 263.

64. Quoted in Stefan Wolle, *Der Traum von der Revolte: Die DDR 1968* (Berlin: Links, 2008), 237. On the world youth festival, see also Marc Dietrich Ohse, *Jugend nach dem Mauerbau. Anpassung, Protest und Eigensinn (DDR 1961–1974)* (Berlin: Links, 2003), 339–56.

65. On the extensive efforts to gain international recognition, see Philip Matthes, "Der Anerkennungslobbyismus der DDR in den USA von 1964 bis 1974," in *Umworbener Klassenfeind: Das Verhältnis der DDR zu den USA*, ed. Uta Balbier and Christiane Rösch (Berlin: Links, 2006), 40–58.

66. See Stefan Wolle, *Die heile Welt der Diktatur: Alltag und Herrschaft in der DDR 1971–1989* (Berlin: Links, 1998), 164–66.

67. U.S. Mission Berlin to Secretary of State, "World Youth Festival Wrap-Up," Telegram, August 7, 1973, in RG 59, Department of State Records, NARA.

68. SED, ZK, Büro Werner Lamberz, Report on Press Conference on August 2, 1973, 277–278, in SAPMO-BArch DY 30/IV 2/2.033, 57, SAPMO; "Angela Davis Leaves E. Berlin," *Washington Post*, August 11, 1973, D3.

69. Axel Bachmann, "Die Beziehungen der DDR zu den angelsächsischen Ländern," in *Die Westpolitik der DDR: Beziehungen der DDR zu ausgewählten westlichen Industriestaaten in den 70er und 80er Jahren*, ed. Peter Weilemann (Melle: E. Knoth, 1989), 69–131, 79ff. In an interview in 1986, Davis still considered the GDR one of the countries that best served its citizens. See Leroy Woodson Jr., "So Says Angela Davis," *Los Angeles Times*, March 2, 1986, X28ff. See also her preface to Klaus Steiniger, *Angela Davis: Eine Frau schreibt Geschichte* (Berlin:

Neues Leben, 2010), 9–13, as well as "Wiedersehen mit Angela Davis," *Neues Deutschland*, June 17, 2010, 3.

70. Große, *Amerikapolitik und Amerikabild der DDR*, 214–15. Benjamin Chavis was part of a group of civil rights activists in Wilmington, North Carolina, convicted of arson and conspiracy in 1976 for their role in the riots that erupted in the city in February 1971 after African American students boycotted the local schools and a grocery store was firebombed. The "Wilmington Ten" were sentenced to a combined 282 years in prison, but a federal appeals court overturned the conviction in 1980.

71. Art Carter, "East Germans Seek Peace, Friendship," *Washington Afro-American*, August 5, 1975.

72. See, e.g., Klaus Steiniger, "Das Flagschiff: USA-Redakteur beim 'Neuen Deutschland,'" in *Amerikanistik in der DDR: Geschichte-Analysen-Zeitzeugenberichte*, ed. Rainer Schnoor (Berlin: Trafo Verlag, 1999), 229–35.

73. See Dorothee Wierling, "Amerikabilder in der DDR," in *Umworbener Klassenfeind*, ed. Balbier and Rösch, 32–38, 37; Rainer Schnoor, "Between Private Opinion and Official Pronouncement: Images of America in the German Democratic Republic, 1971–1990," in *The United States and Germany in the Era of the Cold War, 1945–1990: A Handbook*, vol. 2, ed. Junker (New York: Cambridge University Press, 2004), 519–26; Louis Helbig, "The Myth of the 'Other' America in East German Popular Consciousness," *Journal of Popular Culture* 10.4 (March 5, 2004): 797–807. See also chapter 5, note 49.

74. For these historical connections and the xenophobic waves of the 1990s, see Jan Behrends, Thomas Lindenberger, and Patrice Poutrus, eds., *Fremde und Fremd-Sein in der DDR: Zu den historischen Ursachen der Fremdenfeindlichkeit in Ostdeutschland* (Berlin: Metropol, 2003). See especially in this volume Jürgen Danyel, "Spätfolgen? Der ostdeutsche Rechtsextremismus als Hypothek der DDR-Vergangenheitspolitik und Erinnerungskultur," 23–40.

75. See, e.g., Marianne Krüger-Potratz, *Anderssein gab es nicht: Ausländer und Minderheiten in der DDR* (Münster: Waxmann, 1991); Andrea Schmelz, "Bildungsmigration und Interkulturalität: Ausländische Studierende aus afrikanischen und asiatischen Ländern in Ostdeutschland vor und nach 1989," *Deutschlandarchiv* 38.1 (2005): 84–92, 90.

76. Aubrey Panky, Letter to Gerhart Eisler, Staatliches Rundfunkkomitee, April 19, 1959, 128, in Büro Kurella, SAPMO-BArch DY 30/IV 2–2.026, 105, SAPMO.

77. Alfred Kurella, Kommission für Fragen der Kultur beim Kulturbüro, Letter to Aubrey Pankey, May 2, 1959, 125, in Büro Kurella, SAPMO-BArch DY 30/IV 2–2.026, 105, SAPMO.

78. Alfred Kurella, Letter to Albert Norden, May 2, 1959, 126, in Büro Kurella, SAPMO-BArch DY 30/IV 2–2.026, 105, SAPMO.

79. "Interview with Oliver Harrington," *Visa*, Immigrantenpolitisches Forum e.V. (IPF) (February 1991): 19–22, 21–22. See also Grossman, *Crossing the River*, 175.

8   A Call for Justice: The Racial Crisis in the Military and the GI Movement

1. "Race Relations: A New Military Mission for the New American Revolution," 92nd Cong., 1st Sess., *Congressional Record* 117 (March 9, 1971): H 5650–52.

2. William Hauser, *America's Army in Crisis: A Study in Civil-Military Relations* (Baltimore: Johns Hopkins University Press, 1973).

3. Lawrence Fellows, "U.S. 7th Army in Germany Acts to Lift Sagging Morale," *International Herald Tribune*, December 6, 1971, 7.

4. Davison, cited in Haynes Johnson and George Wilson, *Army in Anguish*, Washington Post National Report (New York: Pocket Book, 1972), 20.
5. Congressional Record, 92nd Cong., 1st Sess., July 16, 1971, 25543.
6. Johnson and Wilson, *Army in Anguish*; Hauser, *America's Army in Crisis*; and Daniel Nelson, *Defenders or Intruders? The Dilemmas of U.S. Forces in Germany* (Boulder: Westview, 1987), 102–8. For a German depiction of events, see Adalbert Weinstein, "Die Siebte Armee erholt sich von Vietnam," *FAZ*, August 25, 1972, 6; "Wir mußten die Siebte Armee ruinieren," *Der Spiegel*, April 17, 1972, 64–81, 65; Dietrich Staritz, "Die Armee schafft sich immer neue Neger. *Spiegel* Interview mit den desertierten US-Soldaten Ronald Bolden und Samuel Robertson," *Der Spiegel*, June 21, 1971, 32–33. See also Maria Höhn, " 'I Prefer Panthers to Pigs': The Black Panther Solidarity Committee, the *Voice of the Lumpen* and the Trial of the Ramstein 2," in *Changing the World, Changing The Self: Political Protest and Collective Identities in 1960/70s West Germany and the United States*, ed. Belinda Davis, Wilfried Mausbach, Martin Klimke, Carla McDougall (New York: Berghahn Books, 2010), 215–39; and idem, "The Black Panther Solidarity Committees and the *Voice of the Lumpen*," *German Studies Review* 31.1 (February 2008): 133–54.
7. "Wir mussten die Siebte Armee ruinieren," 81.
8. Ibid., 72. For a detailed description of the crisis, see Alexander Vazansky, "An Army in Crisis: Social Conflict in the United States Army Europe and 7th Army, 1968–1975," PhD diss. (University of Heidelberg, 2009); Dieter Brünn, ed., *Widerstand in der US-Armee: GI Bewegung in den siebziger Jahren* (Berlin: Harald Kater Verlag, 1986); and David Cortright, *Soldiers in Revolt: The American Military Today* (Chicago: Haymarket Books, 1975; new edition, 2005).
9. "Wir mussten die Siebte Armee ruinieren," 65. Johnson and Wilson, *Army in Anguish*, 26.
10. On the drug problems in the military, see "Orientierungsbericht Deutsche Botschaft, August 10, 1971, Drogenmissbrauch in der US-Armee," B 31/346, Archiv des Auswärtigen Amtes (hereafter AAA); "Die Siebte Armee erholt sich von Vietnam," *FAZ*, August 25, 1972, 6; "Wir mussten die Siebte Armee ruinieren," 65; Staritz, "Die Armee schafft sich immer neue Neger," 32–33. See also Vazansky, "Army in Crisis."
11. Nelson, *Defenders or Intruders*, 108; and "Die Siebte Armee erholt sich von Vietnam," 6.
12. NAACP, *The Search for Military Justice: Report of an NAACP Inquiry into the Problems of the Negro Servicemen in West Germany* (New York: NAACP, 1971); and Department of Defense, U.S. Assistant Secretary of Defense, Manpower and Reserve Affairs, Memorandum for the Secretary of Defense, "U.S. Military Race Relations in Europe—September 1970" (hereafter Render Report); Paul Delaney, "U.S. to Study Race Issues Among Troops in Europe," *New York Times*, August 31, 1970, 3; Horst Szwitalski, "Ku-Klux-Klan in Deutschland," October 11, 1970, *Der Stern*, 68–72; "Brennendes Kreuz vor der Kaserne—Militärpolizei ermittelt," *Mannheimer Morgen*, September 15, 1970, 4. See also "Wir mussten die Siebte Armee ruinieren"; and "Die Armee schafft sich immer neue Neger." For detailed depictions of the racial strife in the U.S. press, see Hauser, *America's Army in Crisis*; and Johnson and Wilson, *Army in Anguish*.
13. Adalbert Weinstein, "Die Siebte Armee erholt sich von Vietnam. Kampfbereit trotz Haschisch und Rassenspannungen/Besuch beim V. Korps (II)," *FAZ*, 6. Brünn, ed., *Widerstand in der US-Armee*, 90.
14. Thomas Johnson, " 'I'll Bleed for Myself,' Says Black U.S. Soldier in Europe," *New York Times*, October 11, 1970, 1 and 8.

15. NAACP, *The Search for Military Justice*. See also "Race Relations," 5650–51; and "The United States and NATO: Troop Reductions–VIII," 92nd Cong., 1st Sess., *Congressional Record* 117 (July 16, 1971): S 25542–43.
16. "Wir mussten die Siebte Armee ruinieren," 65.
17. Hauser, *America's Army in Crisis*, 47, 78.
18. George Wilson and Haynes Johnson, "GI Crime, Violence Climb Overseas: Race, Drugs, Idleness Mix Together in Explosive Combination," *Washington Post*, September 13, 1971, 1, 4.
19. "Die XXII. Ordentliche Delegiertenkonferenz des SDS (Resolutionen und Beschlüsse), 27, in Papers of Ronny Loewy, vol. 1 (SDS 1966–1970), HIS.
20. "Fluchthelfer: Raketen über West-Berlin," *konkret* 12 (December 1967): 49–50; "Geheimgehalten: 'Raketen' gegen US-Hauptquartier in Westberlin," *Berliner Extra-Dienst* 46 (October 1967): 1.
21. Manbey to Department of State, "October 21 Demonstrations," Telegram, Priority 2942, American Consulate Frankfurt, October 22, 1967, in RG 59, Central Foreign Policy Files, 1967–1969, POL 13–2, GER W, 1/1/67, Box 2125, NA.
22. AStA Mannheim, "The Afro-American." Booklet, 1967, in U.S. GIs, German SDS Papers, APOB.
23. "Aufruf zum Teach-In und Demonstration," *Sozialistische Correspondenz-Info* (hereafter *SCI*), May 9, 1970.
24. "Racism in the Military," 92nd Cong., 2nd Sess., *Congressional Record* 118 (October 13–14, 1972), 36588. There was widespread coverage in the *New York Times* and the *Washington Post* on the troubles in West Germany. See, e.g., Thomas Johnson, "Black GI Activists in Germany Will Boycott Pentagon Inquiry," *New York Times*, September 28, 1970, 4; idem, "'I'll Bleed for Myself,' Says Black U.S. Soldier in Europe," October 11, 1970, 1, 8; idem, "GI's in Germany: Black Is Bitter," *New York Times*, November 23, 1970, 1, 26; as well as Johnson's "Pentagon Aide Calls for Fight on Racism," *New York Times*, November 24, 1970, 2. See also Johnson's "Military Race Relations Held 'Explosive,'" *New York Times*, November 18, 1971, 18; and his "Organized Servicemen Abroad Intensify Drive Against Racism," *New York Times*, November 19, 1971, 14; Paul Delaney, "U.S. to Study Race Issues Among Troops in Europe," *New York Times*, August 31, 1970, 3; as well as the extensive article by Hazel Guild,"GI Race War in Germany," *Sepia* 20 (1971): 56–61; and the Web site African American Involvement in Vietnam, Tensions in the Military, http://www.aavw.org/served/homepage_racetensions_racismandresistance.html.
25. "Die Armee schafft sich immer neue Neger," 31–32; and "Höherer Grad," *Der Spiegel*, June 21, 1971, 33.
26. "Cite 'Frustrations, Anger' of Black Troops in Europe," *Chicago Defender*, December 19, 1970, 1. That statement was first reported in the Render Report, 8, and was subsequently reprinted in German publications. "Wir mussten die Siebte Armee ruinieren", 72. See also "Schwarze Frustration," *Der Spiegel*, January 25, 1971, 18; "Wie Coca Cola," *Der Spiegel*, August 12, 1971, 56; and "Die Armee schafft sich immer neue Neger." The transcript of the interview with Bolden and Roberts is at the Archive for Soldiers' Rights, e. V., Berlin.
27. "'I'll Bleed for Myself'," 1 and 8.
28. The problem of "cultural" nationalism bedeviled the collaboration from the beginning. See, e.g., the flyer from the SDS and AStA of Mannheim University, which invited black GIs to a demonstration to express solidarity with the struggle of black Americans. The clumsily worded flyer expressed hope that the GIs ignore the "suggestion by black power leaders not to join any action organized by whities" by assuring them that the "part of German youth sympathizing with black power

is much more radical as [sic] those at home in the States." See flyer entitled "Black GIs," Black Panther Folder, APO Archive.

29. KD Wolff, interview by Maria Höhn; Elizabeth Pfeifer, "Public Demonstrations of the 1960s: Participatory Democracy or Leftist Fascism?" in *Coping with the Nazi Past: West German Debates on Nazism and Generational Conflict, 1955–1975,* ed. Philipp Gassert and Alan Steinweis (New York: Berghahn Books, 2006), 199, makes this case for student protestors in general.

30. "GIs," SDS Nachlass, APOB. See Moritz Ege, *Schwarz Werden. "Afroamerikanophilie" in den 1960er und 1970er Jahren* (Bielefeld: Transcript, 2007), for a thoughtful discussion of these problems.

31. *Voice of the Lumpen* (hereafter *VOL*), May/June 1971. The first issue of November 1970 has an extensive overview of how the *VOL* sees its role in the revolutionary struggle. The Archiv für Soldatenrecht, e.V., in Berlin has copies of the paper. The copies are not always identified by date.

32. KD Wolff, interview by Maria Höhn.

33. Bundesarchiv Koblenz (BArch-Koblenz), B 106/39985, contains numerous reports by the *Bundesministerium für Verfassungsschutz* and the *Innenministerium* on the pro–Black Panther meetings that took place all over West Germany in December 1969 and January 1970. Up to 1,000 people took part in each of these teach-ins at German universities.

34. Bernd Armbruster, "Schwarze GIs: 'Wir wollen Freiheit jetzt,'" *Heidelberger Tageblatt,* July 6, 1970, 11. See also "700 farbige US-Soldaten in der neuen Aula," *Rhein-Neckar-Zeitung,* July 6, 1970, 3; Szwitalski, "Ku-Klux-Klan in Deutschland"; B.N., "Einmischung," *Die Welt,* July 7, 1970, 4; Th.,"Treten farbige GI's in Aktion?" *Rhein-Neckar Zeitung,* June 27, 1970, 3; Rmc., "Rassenstreit der Amerikaner in Europa," *FAZ,* September 7, 1970, 3.

35. Th., "Treten Farbige GI's in Aktion?"

36. Ibid.

37. For an overview of activities in Frankfurt, see Kraushaar, *Frankfurter Schule und Studentenbewegung,* 1:474–92.

38. Akte Fruchthalle Vermietung, Kulturamt, Stadtarchiv Kaiserslautern. See also Sammlung Wolff, "Black Panther Info," booklet published by the Solidarity Committee Kaiserslautern (1971), 16, HIS; Bundesminister der Justiz report of February 15, 1971, to Auswärtiges Amt, "Black Panther," B 31/346, AAA.

39. There were actually three men in the car, but the third Black Panther activist was able to flee. Former leading members of the German SDS took him to East Germany, from where he left for Algiers in December 1970. Jochen Staadt, "Ein Schwarzer Panther auf der Flucht," *Frankfurter Allgemeine Sonntagszeitung,* September 7, 2008, 10.

40. For media coverage of the trial, see Wolfgang Müller, "Küßchen, Zigaretten und Lange Pausen" *Rheinpfalz,* July 2, 1971, 16; "Black Panther Prozess mit Zwischenfällen," *Rheinpfalz* June 17/18, 1971, 14; "Schwarze Hinne" *Der Spiegel,* June 21, 1971, 73–74; and "Die heile juristische Welt kam doch in Unordnung," *FR,* June 28, 1971, 3. For a more detailed description of how the trial of the Ramstein 2 prompted German debates about racism and the Nazi past, see Höhn, "I Prefer Panthers."

41. For the extensive trial records, see Oberstaatsanwalt Zweibrücken. For the GIs' and the students' perspective of the trial, see *VOL,* May 1971; and "Political Prisoners in West Germany," *VOL,* May/June 1971. See also "Freiheit für die Ramstein 2," *Antiimperialistischer Kampf 2/3 Materialien & Diskussion, Ramstein 2 Prozess,* Black Panther folder, APOB.

42. "The Trial of the Ramstein 2 Begins," *VOL,* 6th ed.

43. *VOL,* May/June 1971, and *VOL,* 6th ed.

44. *Antiimperialistischer Kampf 2/3 Materialien & Diskussion*, Ramstein 2 Prozess, 34.

45. Thomas A. Johnson, "Black GI Activists in Germany Will Boycott Pentagon Inquiry," *New York Times*, September 28, 1970, 4; and " 'I'll Bleed for Myself,' " 1 and 8.

46. Müller, "Küßchen, Zigaretten und Lange Pausen," 16.

47. Armbruster, "Schwarze GIs."

48. Wolff tried to save his organization after the break-up of the Black Panther Party in the United States by insisting that the Solidarity Committee had never identified with the Black Panther Party unconditionally but saw its main purpose in creating solidarity with the struggle of the Black Panthers in the United States and Germany. See *Antiimperialistischer Kampf*, 1.

49. "Rassenstreit der Amerikaner in Europe" credits the July 4, 1970, meeting of Black Panthers at Heidelberg University with having set in motion the investigation of the U.S. government over discrimination in the Armed Forces.

50. Record groups B 86/1425, B86/1392 and B 106/80798 at the AAA show how concerned German government officials were that the increasing anger of black GIs over German racism would undermine their morale and thus threaten German security. For responses to the crisis at the state level, see Staatskanzlei, 502–7425–26, Hauptstaatsarchiv Hessen. For newspaper coverage on initiatives set in motion by the protests, see "Farbige fühlen sich ausgeschlossen. Gespräche mit amerikanischen Soldaten in Deutschland," *FR*, February 13, 1971, and "US Neger in Deutschland beklagen Diskriminierung," *General Anzeiger*, June 6, 1971. For American debates, see "Race Relations," 25442–43.

51. "Black Explosions in West Germany," *Time*, September 21, 1970, accessed at http://www.time.com/time/magazine/article/0,9171,942275,00.html.

52. Box 2704 folder 9, NAACP Part 5, Library of Congress (NAACP, Part 5 hereafter).

53. Memorandum, Box 2704 folder 8, NAACP Part 5.

54. Alarmed that no substantial changes were forthcoming a year after those investigations had been conducted, the CBC gathered its findings from the November 1971 hearings and entered them into the Congressional Record in October 1972. See "Racism in the Military," 36596.

55. "Racism in the Military," 36584.

56. Box 2704 folder 9, 37, NAACP Part 5.

57. Box 2704 folder 9, 18, NAACP Part 5; and *The Search for Military Justice*, 19.

58. Johnson and Wilson, *Army in Anguish*, 26.

59. Box 2704 folder 9, 18, NAACP Part 5; and *The Search for Military Justice*, 19.

60. "Racism in the Military," 36583; and "Race Relations," 5651.

61. Box 2704 folder 9, 26–28, NAACP Part 5.

62. Box 2705 folder 11, NAACP Part 5.

63. Box 2705 folder 7, NAACP Part 5.

64. Wilson and Johnson, "GI Crime, Violence Climb Overseas," 14.

65. "Racism in the Military," 36584–86. Out of 136 JAGs, only three were black (see ibid., 36594). See also NAACP, *The Search for Military Justice*, 13.

66. "Racism in the Military," 36583, 36584, 36594; and Trip Report, 20, Box 2704 folder 9, NAACP Part 5.

67. "Racism in the Military," 36584, 36586.

68. Box 2704 folder 9, 30, NAACP Part 5.

69. For German coverage of racism in the U.S. military, see Monica Moebius and Lotha Jene, " 'Schwierigkeiten' im Militärgefängnis eine Folge von Rassenhass und Schikanen?" *Mannheimer Morgen*, August 15, 1970, 4; and Szwitalski, "Ku-Klux-Klan in Deutschland."

70. NAACP, *The Search for Military Justice*.

71. Render Report, 10.
72. Box 2704 folder 9, 33, NAACP Part 5; and "Panther Sprung nach Europa," *SZ*, December 18, 1970. See also Szwitalski, "Ku-Klux-Klan in Deutschland."
73. Box 2705 folder 11, NAACP Part 5.
74. Box 2705 folder 11, 6, NAACP Part 5.
75. Larry Philipps, "Military Racism Cited by Caucus," *Air Force Times*, December 8, 1971, 63.
76. Box 2704 folder 9, NAACP Part 5; "Racism in the Military," 36594.
77. Box 2704 folder 9, 28, NAACP Part 5.
78. "Racism in the Military," 36582.
79. Trip Report, 20, Box 2704 folder 9, NAACP Part 5.
80. "Racism in the Military," 36589–90.
81. Johnson and Wilson, *Army in Anguish*, 20.
82. Box 2703 folder 7, NAACP Part 5.
83. Speech by General Michael Davison given on November 10, 1971, at the Equal Opportunity Conference in Berchtesgaden. Staatskanzlei 502–7426, 105–109, Hessisches Hauptstaatsarchiv, Wiesbaden.
84. "Investigation: USAREUR Equal Opportunity/Human Relations Conference 10 November 1971," Box 2703 folder 7, NAACP Part 5.
85. Vazansky, "An Army in Crisis," 135.
86. For a detailed discussion on these reforms, see Vazansky, "An Army in Crisis," 89–96.
87. Guild, "GI Race War in Germany," 56–61.
88. Hans Massaquoi, "A Battle the Army Can't Afford to Lose," *Ebony*, February 1974, 116–23, 117.
89. Ibid., 120. Original emphasis.
90. Charles Moskos, *The American Enlisted Man: The Rank and File in Today's Military* (New York: Russell Sage Foundation, 1970), 126. The President's Committee on Equal Opportunity in the Armed Forces, "Final Report: Military Personnel Stationed Overseas," 1964, in *Blacks in the United States Armed Forces: Basic Documents*, vol. 13, ed. Morris MacGregor and Bernhard Nalty (Wilmington: Scholarly Resources, 1997), 125–152; also available at www.aacvr-germany.org/gesellreport.
91. Box 2704 folder 9, 31, NAACP Part 5.
92. Sam Washington, "Negroes Face Race Bias in Germany," *Daily Defender*, April 17, 1967, 5.
93. *Heute*, May 24, 1971. See B 86/1425, AAA.
94. Maria Höhn, "'Ein Atemzug der Freiheit': Afro-amerikanische GIs, deutsche Frauen, und die Grenzen der Demokratie (1945–1968)," in *Demokratiewunder. Transatlantische Mittler und die kulturelle Öffnung Westdeutschlands, 1945–1970*, ed. Arnd Bauerkämpfer, Konrad H. Jarausch und Marcus Payk (Göttingen: Vandenhoeck & Ruprecht, 2005), 104–28.
95. Tyler Stoval, *Paris Noir: African Americans in the City of Light* (New York: Mariner Books, 1998), 217, makes the same case for the African American expatriate community in Paris, which was much more critical of France by the second half of the 1960s. On this shift, see also William Gardner Smith, *Return to Black America* (New York: Prentice Hall, 1970), 242–66.
96. "A Battle the Army Can't Afford to Lose," 122.
97. Ibid.
98. Ibid.
99. Box 2704 folder 9, 20–21, 31, NAACP Part 5.
100. Letter to Auswärtiges Amt, March 2, 1971, Department of the Army, B 86/1425, AAA.

101. "US Neger in Deutschland beklagen Diskriminierung." See also Gerhard Specht, "Die ungeliebten GIs: Unsere Beschützer brauchen Hilfe," *Vorwärts*, November 18, 1971, 1. See also "Schwarze Frustration."

102. Wolfgang Bormann, "Rassendiskriminierung in der Bundesrepublik. Ein Farbiger Captain klagt deutsche Vermieter an," *Stuttgarter Zeitung*, March 31, 1971, 3.

103. Letter from Congressional Black Caucus to President Nixon, July 22, 1971, Box 2704 folder 9, NAACP Part 5.

104. B 86/1425, AAA.

105. HQ USAREUR, December 2, 1971, Equal Opportunity and Human Relations, B 86/1425, AAA. See also "Deutsche Botschaft, Miltärattachéstab, June 15, 1971 letter to Bundesminister der Verteidigung," Staatskanzlei 502/7425–26, Hessisches Hauptstaaatsarchiv.

106. Letter of Bundesminister der Verteidigung, November 16, 1971, Staatskanzlei 502/7425, Hessisches Hauptstaaatsarchiv.

107. For Brandt's speech of March 21, 1971, see B 86/1425, AAA.

108. That initiative helped those soldiers who, because of their low military rank, were not eligible for command-sponsored tours. The extra housing built for command-sponsored GIs alleviated the pressure on the tight housing market.

109. Record groups B 86/1425, B86/1392, and B 106/80798 at the AAA show the extensive programs that were initiated.

110. Letter of Ministry of Defense to Prime Minister of Baden Württemberg, November 16, 1971, B86/1425, AAA.

111. The 1963/64 Gesell Report was intended to do away with widespread racism in the military, but the Pentagon grew too occupied with the war in Vietnam to effectively follow through with the antidiscrimination directives it had issued.

Conclusion

1. Office of the Press Secretary, The White House, "Remarks by President Obama, German Chancellor Merkel, and Elie Wiesel at Buchenwald Concentration Camp," Weimar, Germany, June 5, 2009, www.whitehouse.gov.

2. Barack Obama, interview with Tom Brokaw, Dresden, Germany, June 5, 2009, http://www.msnbc.msn.com/id/21134540/vp/31120874#31120874.

3. See Ron E. Armstead, "Veteran in the Fight for Equal Rights: From the Civil War to Today," in *Trotter Review*, (Autumn 2008/Winter 2009), 92–105. Although only a few of the following cultural and academic projects focus on the connection to the civil rights movement, they explore the African American experience in the European and Asian theater during World War II. For Italy: *Miracle at St. Anna* (2008), dir. Spike Lee, based on James McBride, *Miracle at St. Anna* (New York: Riverhead Books, 2002). Detailing the story of the segregated African American unit fighting in World War II, the 92nd Infantry Division, and its actions in Italy is the movie: *Inside Buffalo* (2009), dir. Fred Kudjo Kuworno. For the UK, see Graham Smith, *When Jim Crow Met John Bull: Black American Soldiers in World War II Britain* (New York: St. Martin's Press, 1988); Neil A. Wynn, "'Race War': Black American GIs and West Indians in Britain during the Second World War," *Immigrants & Minorities* 24.3 (2006): 324–46; or the documentary *Choc'late Soldiers from the USA* (2009), dir. Sonny Izon and Gregory Cooke. For Korea and Japan, see Maria Höhn and Seungsook Moon, eds., *"Over There": Living with the U.S. Military Empire* (Durham: Duke University Press, 2010). For a general history, see *For Love of Liberty: The Story of America's Black Patriots*, dir. Frank Martin (Encino, CA: Eleventh Day Entertainment, 2010).

4. House of Representatives, Concurrent Resolution 238, February 26, 2010, 111th Cong., 2nd Sess.
5. David Brion Davis, "The Americanized Mannheim of 1945–1946," in *American Places: Encounters With History. A Celebration of Sheldon Meyer*, ed. William E. Leuchtenburg (Oxford: Oxford University Press, 2000), 79–91, 91.
6. May Ayim, Katharina Oguntoye, and Dagmar Schultz, eds., *Farbe bekennen: Afrodeutsche Frauen auf den Spuren ihrer Geschichte* (Berlin: Orlanda Frauenverlag, 1986). For the English version, see idem, *Showing Our Colors: Afro-German Women Speak Out* (Amherst: University of Massachusetts Press, 1992). Over time, the term has come to include not only blacks with German citizenship but also blacks residing in the country. Both terms were meant to counter degrading expressions such as "mixed-breed" (*Mischling*), "mulatto" (*Mulatte*), or "colored people" (*Farbige*).
7. "Adefra" is Amharic for "the woman who shows courage." For more information on both organizations, please visit http://www.adefra.org and http://www.isdonline.de
8. See, e.g., the professional organization Black Artists in German Film established in 2006 (http://www.sfd-net.com) or "der braune mob," a media-watch organization founded in 2001 (http://www.derbraunemob.info).
9. For descendents of African Americans and Germans, see Doris McMillon, *Mixed Blessing* (New York: St. Martin's Press, 1985); Jimmy Hartwig, *'Ich möcht' noch so viel tun': Meine Kindheit, meine Karriere, meine Krankheit* (Bergisch Gladbach: Bastei Lübbe, 1994); Harald Gerunde, *Eine von uns: Als Schwarze in Deutschland geboren* (Wuppertal: Peter Hammer, 2000); Thomas Usleber, *Die Farben unter meiner Haut: Autobiographische Aufzeichnungen* (Frankfurt: Brandes & Apsel, 2002); Günther Kaufmann and Gabriele Droste, *Der weiße Neger vom Hasenbergl* (Munich: Diana, 2004); Ika Hügel-Marshall, *Invisible Woman: Growing Up Black in Germany* (New York: Continuum, 2001; rev. and annot. ed.: New York: Peter Lang, 2008); Steffi Jones, *Der Kick des Lebens. Wie ich den Weg nach oben schaffte* (Frankfurt: Fischer, 2007). For others, see Chima Oji, *Unter die Deutschen gefallen: Erfahrungen eines Afrikaners* (Wuppertal: Hammer, 1992); May Ayim, *Grenzenlos und unverschämt* (Berlin: Orlanda, 1997; Frankfurt: Fischer, 2002); Abini Zöllner, *Schokoladenkind. Meine Familie und andere Wunder* (Reinbek: Rowohlt, 2003); Charles Huber, *Ein Niederbayer im Senegal. Mein Leben zwischen zwei Welten* (Frankfurt: Scherz, 2004); Lucia Ngombe, *Kind Nr. 95. Meine deutsch-afrikanische Odyssee* (Berlin: Ullstein, 2004); Eva Massingue, *Sichtbar anders: Aus dem Leben afrodeutscher Kinder und Jugendlicher* (Frankfurt: Brandes & Apsel, 2005); Marie Nejar, *Mach nicht so traurige Augen, weil du ein Negerlein bist: Meine Jugend im Dritten Reich* (Reinbek: Rowohlt, 2007); Manuela Ritz, *Die Farbe meiner Haut: Die Antirassismustrainerin erzählt* (Freiburg: Herder, 2009); Samy Deluxe, *Dis wo ich herkomm: Deutschland Deluxe* (Reinbek: Rowohlt, 2009).
10. Hans Massaquoi, *Destined to Witness: Growing Up Black in Nazi Germany* (New York: William Morrow, 1999); Hans Massaquoi, *Hänschen klein, ging allein … Mein Weg in die Neue Welt* (Frankfurt: Scherz, 2004; Frankfurt: Fischer, 2005); *"Neger, Neger, Schornsteinfeger": Ein Leben in Deutschland*, dir. Jörg Grünler (2006).
11. For more information on the Black German Cultural Society, please visit http://www.blackgermans.us. For a personal story, see also Rosemarie Peña, "Staatenlos," in BlogHer, April 10, 2008, http://www.blogher.com/staatenlos. For an organization exclusively dedicated to tracing American GI fathers and their families, please see http://www.gitrace.org

12. The movie *Schwarz auf Weiss: Eine Reise durch Deutschland* (2009), dir. Günter Wallraff, is also accompanied by a book: Günter Wallraff, *Aus der schönen neuen Welt. Expeditionen ins Landesinnere* (Cologne: Kiepenheuer & Witsch, 2009). For the ensuing debate, see Henning Hoff, "Blackface Filmmaker Sparks a Race Debate in Germany," *Time*, November 18, 2009, online, http://www.time.com/time/world/article/0,8599,1940290,00.html; "Es geht nicht um Schwarze. Es geht um Weiße," interview with Carol Campbell, Yonas Endrias, and Günter Wallraff, *ZEITmagazin*, December 17, 2009, 24–28.

13. Susan Arndt, ed., *AfrikaBilder: Studien zu Rassismus in Deutschland* (Münster: Unrast, 2001/2006); Noah Snow, *Deutschland Schwarz Weiss: Der alltägliche Rassismus* (Munich: Bertelsmann, 2008). See also *Roots Germania* (2007), dir. Mo Asumang. For a transatlantic historical perspective, see also Norbert Finzsch and Dietmar Schirmer, eds., *Identity and Intolerance: Nationalism, Racism, and Xenophobia in Germany and the United States* (Cambridge: Cambridge University Press, 1998).

14. Sander Gilman, *On Blackness Without Blacks: Essays on the Image of the Black in Germany* (Boston: G. K. Hall, 1982); Ayim, Oguntoye, and Schultz, *Farbe bekennen*; Carol Blackshire-Belay, ed., *The African-German Experience: Critical Essays* (Westport: Praeger, 1996); David McBride, Leroy Hopkins, and Carol Blackshire-Belay, eds., *Crosscurrents: African Americans, Africa, and Germany in the Modern World* (Columbia, SC: Camden House, 1998); Katharina Oguntoye, *Eine afro-deutsche Geschichte: Zur Lebenssituation von Afrikanern und Afro-Deutschen in Deutschland von 1884 bis 1950* (Berlin: Hoho Verlag, 1997); Tina Campt, Pascal Grosse, and Yara-Colette Lemke-Muniz de Faria, "Blacks, Germans, and the Politics of Imperialist Imagination, 1920–1960," in *The Imperialist Imagination: German Colonialism and Its Legacy*, ed. Sara Friedrichsmeyer, Sara Lennox, and Susanne Zantop (Ann Arbor: University of Michigan Press, 1998), 205–29; Fatima El-Tayeb, *Schwarze Deutsche: Der Diskurs um "Rasse" und Nationale Identität 1890–1933* (Frankfurt: Campus, 2001); Peter Martin, *Schwarze Teufel, edle Mohren: Afrikaner in Geschichte und Bewusstsein der Deutschen* (Hamburg: Hamburger Edition, 2001); Peggy Piesche, "Black and German? East German Adolescents Before 1989: A Retrospective View of a 'Non-Existent Issue' in the GDR," in *The Cultural After-Life of East Germany: New Transnational Perspectives*, ed. Leslie A. Adelson (Washington, DC: AICGS, 2002), 37–59; Michelle M. Wright and Tina M. Campt, eds., "Reading the Black German Experience," special issue, *Callaloo: A Journal of African Diaspora Arts and Letters* 26.2 (2003); Peter Martin and Christine Alonzo, *Zwischen Charleston und Stechschritt: Schwarze im Nationalsozialismus* (Hamburg: Dölling und Galitz, 2004); Maureen Maisha Eggers, Grada Kilomba, Peggy Piesche, Susan Arndt, eds., *Mythen, Masken und Subjekte: Kritische Weissseinsforschung in Deutschland* (Münster: Unrast, 2005); Patricia Mazón and Reinhild Steingröver, eds., *Not So Plain as Black and White: Afro-German Culture and History, 1890–2000* (Rochester: University of Rochester Press, 2005); Volker Langbehn, ed., *German Colonialism, Visual Culture, and Modern Memory* (New York: Routledge, 2010); Volker Langbehn and Mohammad Salama, eds., *German Colonialism: Race, the Holocaust, and Postwar Germany* (New York: Columbia University Press, forthcoming); Maria Diedrich and Jürgen Heinrichs, eds., *From Black to Schwarz: Cultural Crossovers between African America and Germany* (Münster: LIT-Verlag, forthcoming); Larry Greene and Anke Ortlepp, eds., *German and African American Crossovers: Two Centuries of Contact* (Jackson: University of Mississippi Press, forthcoming); Mischa Honeck, Martin Klimke, and Anne Kuhlmann-Smirnov, eds., *Blacks and Germans, German Blacks: Germany and the Black Diaspora, 1450–1914* (forthcoming).

15. For Nazi Germany, see Clarence Lusane, *Hitler's Black Victims: The Historical Experiences of Afro-Germans, European Blacks, Africans, and African Americans in the Nazi Era* (New York: Routledge, 2003); Tina Campt, *Other Germans: Black Germans and the Politics of Race, Gender, and Memory in the Third Reich* (Ann Arbor: University of Michigan, 2004); Raffael Scheck, *Hitler's African Victims: The German Army Massacres of Black French Soldiers in 1940* (Cambridge: Cambridge University Press, 2006). For the postwar period, see Johannes Kleinschmidt, *Do Not Fraternize. Die schwierigen Anfänge deutsch-amerikanischer Freundschaft, 1944–1949* (Trier: WVT Wissenschaftler Verlag, 1997); Georg Schmundt-Thomas, "America's Germany: National Self and Cultural Other After World War II," PhD diss. (Northwestern University, 1992); Maria Höhn, *GIs and Fräuleins: The German-American Encounter in 1950s West Germany* (Chapel Hill: University of North Carolina Press, 2002); Petra Goedde, *GIs and Germans: Culture, Gender and Foreign Relations, 1945–1949* (New Haven: Yale University Press, 2003); Heide Fehrenbach, *Race after Hitler: Black Occupation Children in Postwar Germany and America* (Princeton: Princeton University Press, 2005); Annette Brauerhoch, *Fräuleins und GIs: Geschichte und Filmgeschichte* (Frankfurt: Stroemfeld, 2006); Timothy Schroer, *Recasting Race after World War II: Germans and African Americans in American-Occupied Germany* (Boulder: University Press of Colorado, 2007). For the European dimension, see Maria Diedrich, Theron Cook, and Flip Lindo, eds., *Crossing Boundaries: African American Inner City and European Migrant Youth* (Münster: LIT-Verlag, 2004); Heike Raphael-Hernandez, ed., *Blackening Europe: The African American Presence* (New York: Routledge, 2004); Rita Chin, Heide Fehrenbach, Geoff Eley, and Atina Grossmann, eds., *After the Nazi Racial State: Difference and Democracy in Germany and Europe* (Ann Arbor: University of Michigan Press, 2009); Darlene Clark Hine, Trica Danielle Keaton, and Stephen Small, eds., *Black Europe and the African Diaspora* (Urbana: University of Illinois Press, 2009).
16. Among others, the contributions of Berndt Ostendorf, Maria Diedrich, Friederike Hajek, Werner Sollors, Elisabeth Schäfer-Wünsche, Sieglinde Lemke, Sabine Broeck, and Manfred Berg stand out in this regard.
17. Sabine Sielke, "Theorizing American Studies: German Interventions into an Ongoing Debate," *European Journal of American Studies*, EJAS 2006, article 7, put online January, 12, 2006 at http://ejas.revues.org/document470.html. See also Simon Wendt, "Transnational Perspectives on the History of Racism in America," *Amerikastudien/American Studies* 54.3 (2009): 473–98; Eva Boesenberg, "Reconstructing 'America': The Development of African American Studies in the Federal Republic of Germany," in *German and African American Crossovers*, ed. Greene and Ortlepp, forthcoming.
18. Colin L. Powell, "Guest Speaker Address," November 6, 1986, 18, 18th USAREUR Equal Opportunity Conference "The Value of 'EO' in Today's Army," November 3–7, 1986, AFRC Garmisch, in HQ USAREUR Archive, Heidelberg. See also Colin Powell, *My American Journey* (New York: Random House, 1995), 107f.
19. Powell, "Guest Speaker Address," 19.
20. Ibid.

Bibliography

Archival Collections

United States

Congressional Record, Washington, DC

91st Cong., 1st sess., 1969. March 14 and 18. "Testimony of Karl-Dietrich Wolff. Hearings before the Subcommittee to Investigate the Administration of the Internal Security Act and other Security Laws of the Committee on the Judiciary."

92nd Cong., 1st sess., 1971. Vol. 117, H 5650–52. "Race Relations: A New Military Mission for the New American Revolution."

92nd Cong., 1st sess., 1971. Vol. 117, S 25540–43. "The United States and NATO: Troop Reductions–VIII."

92nd Cong., 2nd sess., 1972. Vol. 118, 6739–6746. "Institutional Racism in the Military."

92nd Cong., 2nd sess., 1972. Vol. 118, 36582–36596. "Racism in the Military."

Meader, George. *The Meader Report.* Confidential Report to the Special Senate Committee Investigating the National Defense Program on the Preliminary Investigation in the Occupied Areas of Europe, November 22, 1946, in special committee hearing.

Render, Frank. *The Render Report.* Department of Defense, U.S. Assistant Secretary of Defense, Manpower and Reserve Affairs, Memorandum for the Secretary of Defense, "U.S. Military Race Relations in Europe—September 1970."

King Center, Atlanta, GA (KCA)
 Papers of Dr. Martin Luther King Jr.
Library of Congress, Washington, DC
 NAACP Records
Schomburg Center for Research in Black Culture, New York
 Clipping File William Gardner Smith
 NAACP, Discrimination in the United States Armed Forces 1918–1955
U.S. Army Military History Institute, Carlisle, PA
U.S. National Archives, College Park, Maryland (NARA)
 Central Foreign Policy Files, 1967–69
 Department of State Records
 Records of the Adjutant General's Office
 Records of the Army Staff
 Records of the Office of the Secretary of Defense
 Records of the Office of the Secretary of War
 Records of the U.S. Army Commands

Records of the U.S. Theater of War, World War II
Records of U.S. Army Operational, Tactical, and Support Organizations
Records of the War Department General and Special Staff

Germany

Archiv "APO und soziale Bewegungen," Free University of Berlin (APOB)
    Papers of the German SDS
Archiv der sozialen Demokratie der Friedrich-Ebert-Stiftung, Bonn (Archives of Social
    Democracy of the Friedrich Ebert Foundation, Bonn)
    Willy- Brandt Archiv
Archiv für Soldatenrechte, Berlin (Archive for Soldiers' Rights)
    Voice of the Lumpen (VOL)
Behörde der Bundesbeauftragten für die Unterlagen des Staatssicherheitsdienstes der
    ehemaligen DDR, Berlin (Office of the Federal Commissioner for the Files of the
    State Security Service of the Former GDR) (BStU)
    Ministry for State Security, Main Office for Passport Control and Searches
Bundesarchiv, Berlin-Lichterfelde (BArch-Berlin)
    Ministerium des Inneren, Staatsekretariat für Innere Angelegenheiten
Bundesarchiv, Koblenz (BArch-Koblenz)
Geheimes Staatsarchiv Preußischer Kulturbesitz, Berlin (Secret State Archive,
    Foundation for Prussian Cultural Heritage) (GStA PK)
    Papers of Heinrich Grüber, GStA
Hamburger Institut für Sozialforschung (Institute for Social Research, Hamburg)
    (HIS)
    Papers of Ronny Loewy
    Sammlung Wolff (K.-D. Wolff Collection)
Herbert-Marcuse-Archiv, Stadt- und-Universitätsbibliothek, Frankfurt am Main
Hessisches Hauptstaatsarchiv, Wiesbaden (Main State Archive of Hessen)
    Staatskanzlei (State Chancellery)
HQ USAREUR Archive, Heidelberg
    AFRC Garmisch
    Historical Division
    U.S. Army
Humboldt-Universität zu Berlin, Universitätsarchiv, Berlin (HUAB)
    Ehrenpromotion, W. E. B. Du Bois
Interdisziplinärer Arbeitskreis für Nordamerikastudien, Johannes-Gutenberg-
    Universität (Interdisciplinary Work Group for North American Studies), Mainz
    IANAS Video Collection
Paul-Robeson Archiv (PRA), Academy of Arts, Berlin
Politisches Archiv des Auswärtigen Amtes, Berlin (Political Archive of the Foreign
    Ministry) (AAA)
    Stationierung ausländischer Truppen (1951–1972)
Stiftung Archiv der Parteien und Massenorganisationen der DDR im Bundesarchiv,
    Berlin (SAPMO) (Foundation Archives of Parties and Mass Organisations of the
    GDR in the Federal Archives)
    Büro Kurella
    FDJ, Zentralrat
    Nationalrat der Nationalen Front, Büro des Sekretariats
    Nationalrat der Nationalen Front, Sektor Information
    SED, Zentralkomitee, Büro Werner Lamberz
    Sekretariat des Zentralkomitees der SED

Sitzungen des Politbüros des Zentralkomitees
Oberstaatsanwalt Zweibrücken

Newspapers and Periodicals

Der Abend
agit 883
Air Force Times
Annals of the American Academy of Political and Social Science
Atlantic Monthly
Atlantic Times
Atomzeitalter
Baltimore Afro-American
Berliner Extra-Dienst
Berliner Kurier
Berliner Sonntagsblatt
Berliner Stimme
Berliner Zeitung
Bild
Bild am Sonntag
B. Z. (Berliner Zeitung)
B. Z. am Abend
B. Z. online
Cedar Rapids Gazette
Chicago Daily Defender
Chicago Defender
Crisis, The
Daily Worker
Ebony
Evangelischer Pressedienst
Frankfurter Allgemeine Sonntagszeitung
Frankfurter Allgemeine Zeitung
Frankfurter Hefte
Frankfurter Rundschau
Frankfurter Rundschau am Abend
Generalanzeiger
Heidelberger Tageblatt
International Herald Tribune
Journal of Negro Education
Journal of Negro History
Junge Welt
Die Kirche
Kokomo Morning Times
konkret
Der Kurier
Kursbuch
Los Angeles Times
Das Magazin
Mannheimer Morgen
Morgenpost
Nation
Negro Digest

neue kritik
Neue Zeit
Neues Deutschland
New Republic
New York Amsterdam News
New York Herald Tribune
New York Post
New York Times
Newsweek
Norfolk Journal and Guide
Opportunity: Journal for Negro Life
Pittsburgh Courier
Pfälzische Volkszeitung
Philadelphia Tribune
PM (Picture Magazine)
Pressedienst des Landes Berlin
Pressestelle der evangelischen Kirchenleitung
Rheinischer Merkur
Rhein-Neckar-Zeitung
Rheinpfalz
Rheinzeitung
Sepia
Social Forces
Sozialistische Correspondenz-Info
Spandauer Volksblatt
Der Spiegel
Stars and Stripes
Der Stern
Stuttgarter Zeitung
Süddeutsche Zeitung
Survey
Der Tagesspiegel
Telegraf
Time
Transition
Victoria Advocate
Visa, IPF
Voice of the Lumpen
Vorwärts
Washington Afro-American
Washington Post
Die Welt
Welt am Sonntag
Wissenschaftliche Zeitschrift der Humboldt-Universität zu Berlin
Zeichen der Zeit
Die Zeit

Select Bibliography

Apart from crucial primary sources (monographs and collected volumes), we list here principally the secondary literature—monographs, contributions to edited collections, and articles in academic journals—as well as some recent (post-2000) newspaper articles and web sites, consulted in writing this book. A complete list of primary sources, including not only contemporary newspaper and periodical articles, but also films and oral history interviews, can be found online at www.breathoffreedom.org.

Amana, Harry. "The Art of Propaganda: Charles Alston's World War II Editorial Cartoons for the Office of War Information and the Black Press." *American Journalism* 21.2 (2004): 79–111.

Anderson, Carol. *Eyes Off the Prize: The United Nations and the African American Struggle for Human Rights, 1944–1955.* Cambridge: Cambridge University Press, 2003.

———. "From Hope to Disillusion: African Americans, the United Nations, and the Struggle for Human Rights, 1944–47." *Diplomatic History* 20, no. 4 (Fall 1996): 531–63.

———. "International Conscience, the Cold War, and Apartheid: The NAACP's Alliance with the Reverend Michael Scott for South West Africa's Liberation, 1946–1951." *Journal of World History* 19.3 (September 2008): 297–325.

Angela Davis Solidaritätskomitee, ed. *Am Beispiel Angela Davis: Der Kongreß in Frankfurt.* Frankfurt: Fischer, 1972.

Appelius, Stefan. "Let My People Go." *einestages/SPIEGEL online*, September 13, 2009. http://einestages.spiegel.de/page/Home.html.

———. "Martin Luther King in Ost-Berlin." *Der Tagesspiegel*, September 6, 2009. http://www.tagesspiegel.de/zeitung/Sonntag-Geschichte-DDR-Martin-Luther-King-Sonntag;art2566,2891732.

———. "My Dear Christian Friends in East Berlin." *Chrismon Plus*, September 2009. http://www.chrismon.de/4698.php.

Armstead, Ronald E. "Veterans in the Fight for Equal Rights: From the Civil War to Today." *Trotter Review* (2008/2009): 92–105.

Arndt, Susan, ed. *AfrikaBilder: Studien zu Rassismus in Deutschland.* Münster: Unrast, 2001/2006.

Ayim, May. *Grenzenlos und unverschämt.* Berlin: Orlanda, 1997; Frankfurt: Fischer, 2002.

Ayim, May, Katharina Oguntoye, and Dagmar Schultz, eds. *Farbe bekennen: Afro-deutsche Frauen auf den Spuren ihrer Geschichte.* Berlin: Orlanda Frauenverlag, 1986.

———, eds. *Showing Our Colors: Afro-German Women Speak Out.* Amherst: University of Massachusetts Press, 1992.

Bachmann, Axel. "Die Beziehungen der DDR zu den angelsächsischen Ländern." In *Die Westpolitik der DDR: Beziehungen der DDR zu ausgewählten westlichen Industriestaaten in den 70er und 80er Jahren*, ed. Peter Weilemann, 69–131. Melle: E. Knoth, 1989.

Baker, William J. *Jesse Owens: An American Life.* Urbana: University of Illinois Press, 2006.

Balbier, Uta, and Christiane Rösch. "Mehr als eine Fußnote: Das Verhältnis zwischen der DDR und den Vereinigten Staaten von Amerika." In *Umworbener Klassenfeind*, ed. Balbier and Rösch, 11–23.

———, eds. *Umworbener Klassenfeind: Das Verhältnis der DDR zu den USA.* Berlin: Links, 2006.

Baldwin, Kate A. *Beyond the Color Line and the Iron Curtain: Reading Encounters between Black and Red, 1922–1963.* Durham, NC: Duke University Press, 2002.

Barbeau, Arthur, and Florette Henri. *The Unknown Soldiers: African American Troops in World War I.* Philadelphia: Temple University, 1974.

Barkin, Kenneth. " 'Berlin Days,' 1892–1894: W.E.B. DuBois and German Political Economy." *boundary 2* 27, no. 3 (2000): 79–101.

Bass, Leon, and Pam Sporn. "'I Saw The Walking Dead': A Black Sergeant Remembers Buchenwald." Interview segment of the documentary "Blacks and Jews: Are They Really Sworn Enemies?" Educational Video Center. http://historymatters.gmu.edu/d/142, undated.

Bauerkämpfer, Arnd, Konrad H. Jarausch, and Marcus Payk, eds. *Demokratiewunder. Transatlantische Mittler und die kulturelle Öffnung Westdeutschlands, 1945–1970.* Göttingen: Vandenhoeck & Ruprecht, 2005.

Baumann, Bommi. "God bless America: Die USA als Vorbild für die 68er." In *Radikales Amerika. Wie die amerikanische Protestbewegung Deutschland veränderte,* ed. Bommi Baumann and Till Meyer, 9–36. Berlin: Rotbuch Verlag, 2007.

Beck, Hamilton. "Censoring Your Ally: W. E. B. Du Bois in the German Democratic Republic." In *Crosscurrents: African Americans, Africa, and Germany in the Modern World,* ed. David McBride, Leroy Hopkins, and Carol Blackshire-Belay, 197–232.

———. "W. E. B. Du Bois as a Study Abroad Student in Germany, 1892–1894." *Frontiers: The Interdisciplinary Journal of Study Abroad* 2 (Fall 1996), www.frontiersjournal.com/issues/vol2/vol2–03_beck.htm.

Behrends, Jan, Thomas Lindenberger, and Patrice Poutrus, eds. *Fremde und Fremd-Sein in der DDR: Zu den historischen Ursachen der Fremdenfeindlichkeit in Ostdeutschland.* Berlin: Metropol, 2003.

Bender, Thomas. *A Nation among Nations: America's Place in World History.* New York: Hill and Wang, 2006.

Bennett, Lerone. *What Manner of Man: A Biography of Martin Luther King, Jr.,* 3rd rev. ed. Chicago: Johnson, 1968.

Berg, Manfred. "American Wars and the Black Struggle for Freedom and Equality." In *The American Experience of War,* ed. Georg Schild, 133–54. Paderborn: Ferdinand Schöningh, 2010.

———. "Black Civil Rights and Liberal Anticommunism: The NAACP in the Early Cold War." *Journal of American History* 94, no. 1 (2007): 75–96.

———. *"The Ticket to Freedom": The NAACP and the Struggle for Black Political Integration.* Gainesville: University Press of Florida, 2005.

Blackshire-Belay, Carol, ed. *The African-German Experience: Critical Essays.* Westport: Praeger, 1996.

Boesenberg, Eva. "Reconstructing 'America': The Development of African American Studies in the Federal Republic of Germany." In *German and African American Crossovers,* ed. Greene and Ortlepp, forthcoming.

Bögelsack, Brigitte, ed. *Paul Robeson, April 9, 1898—January 23, 1976: For his 80th Birthday.* Berlin: Academy of Arts of the German Democratic Republic, 1978.

———, ed. *Symposium: Paul Robeson and the Struggle of the Working Class and the Afro-American People of the USA against Imperialism, Held in Berlin, April 13 and 14, 1971.* Berlin: German Academy of Art, 1972.

Bollinger, Klaus. *Freedom now—Freiheit sofort! Die Negerbevölkerung der USA im Kampf um Demokratie.* Berlin: Staatsverlag der Deutschen Demokratischen Republik, 1968.

Bolté, Charles G., and Louis Harris. *Our Negro Veterans.* Public Affairs Pamphlet No. 128. New York: Public Affairs Committee, 1947.

Borstelmann, Thomas. *The Cold War and the Color Line: American Race Relations in the Global Arena.* Cambridge, MA: Harvard University Press, 2001.

Bortfeldt, Heinrich. "In the Shadow of the Federal Republic: Cultural Relations Between the GDR and the United States—Cultural Relations Before Diplomatic Recognition." In *The United States and Germany,* vol. 2, ed. Junker, 305–11.

Brackman, Harold. "'A Calamity Almost beyond Comprehension': Nazi Anti-Semitism and the Holocaust in the Thought of W. E. B. Du Bois." *American Jewish History* 88 (2000): 53–93.

Branch, Taylor. "Globalizing King's Legacy." *New York Times*, January 16, 2006, A15.

Brandt, Willy. *Begegnungen und Einsichten: Die Jahre 1960–1975*. Hamburg: Hoffmann und Campe, 1976.

———. *My Life in Politics*. New York: Viking, 1992.

Brauerhoch, Annette. *Fräuleins und GIs: Geschichte und Filmgeschichte*. Frankfurt: Stroemfeld, 2006.

Broeck, Sabine. "The Erotics of African-American Endurance, Or: On the Right Side of History? White (West)-German Public Sentiment between Pornotroping and Civil Rights Solidarity." In *German and African American Crossovers*, ed. Greene and Ortlepp, forthcoming.

Brown, Nikki. *Private Politics and Public Voices: Black Women's Activism from World War I to the New Deal*. Bloomington: Indiana University Press, 2006.

Brown, Sterling A. "Count Us In." In *What the Negro Wants*, ed. Logan, 308–44.

Brünn, Dieter, ed. *Widerstand in der US-Armee: GI Bewegung in den siebziger Jahren*. Berlin: Harald Kater Verlag, 1986.

Campt, Tina. *Other Germans: Black Germans and the Politics of Race, Gender, and Memory in the Third Reich*. Ann Arbor: University of Michigan, 2004.

Campt, Tina, Pascal Grosse, and Yara-Colette Lemke-Muniz de Faria. "Blacks, Germans, and the Politics of Imperialist Imagination, 1920–1960." In *The Imperialist Imagination: German Colonialism and Its Legacy*, ed. Sara Friedrichsmeyer, Sara Lennox, and Susanne Zantop, 205–29. Ann Arbor: University of Michigan Press, 1998.

Carmichael, Stokely. *Die Dritte Welt, unsere Welt. Thesen zur Schwarzen Revolution*. Voltaire Flugschriften 29. Berlin: Voltaire, 1969.

Carson, Clayborne, David J. Garrow, Bill Kovach, and Carol Polsgrove, eds. *Reporting Civil Rights, Part One: American Journalism 1941–1963*. New York: Library of America, 2003.

Chafe, William H., ed. *The Achievement of American Liberalism: The New Deal and Its Legacies*. New York: Columbia University Press, 2003.

Chin, Rita, Heide Fehrenbach, Geoff Eley, and Atina Grossmann, eds. *After the Nazi Racial State: Difference and Democracy in Germany and Europe*. Ann Arbor: University of Michigan Press, 2009.

Cleaver, Eldridge. *Zur Klassenanalyse der Black Panther Partei: Erziehung und Revolution*. Frankfurt: Roter Stern, 1970.

Clemons, Michael L., and Charles E. Jones. "Global Solidarity: The Black Panther Party in the International Arena." In *Liberation, Imagination, and the Black Panther Party: A New Look at the Panthers and their Legacy*, ed. Kathleen Cleaver and George Katsiaficas, 20–39. New York: Routledge, 2001.

Cobb, James. "World War II and the Mind of the Modern South." In *Remaking Dixie*, ed. McMillen, 3–20.

Cortright, David. *Soldiers in Revolt: The American Military Today*. Chicago: Haymarket Books, 1975; new edition, 2005.

Dailey, Jane. "Obama's Omission." *Chicago Tribune*, July 30, 2008, 19.

Danyel, Jürgen. "Spätfolgen? Der ostdeutsche Rechtsextremismus als Hypothek der DDR-Vergangenheitspolitik und Erinnerungskultur." In *Fremde und Fremd-Sein in der DDR*, ed. Behrends et al., 23–40.

Daum, Andreas. *Kennedy in Berlin*. New York: Cambridge University Press, 2008.

Davis, Angela. *An Autobiography*. New York: Random House, 1974.

Davis, Belinda, Wilfried Mausbach, Martin Klimke, and Carla McDougall, eds. *Changing the World, Changing Oneself: Political Protest and Collective Identities in 1960/70s West Germany and the United States*. New York: Berghahn Books, 2010.

Davis, David Brion. "The Americanized Mannheim of 1945–1946." In *American Places: Encounters With History—A Celebration of Sheldon Meyer*, ed. Leuchtenburg, 79–91.

Deluxe, Samy. *Dis wo ich herkomm: Deutschland Deluxe*. Reinbek: Rowohlt, 2009.

Deutscher Bundestag, ed. *Materialien der Enquete-Kommission "Aufarbeitung von Geschichte und Folgen der SED-Diktatur in Deutschland,"* vol. 7.1. Baden-Baden: Nomos, 1995.

DeYoung, Karen. *Soldier: The Life of Colin Powell*. New York: Vintage Books, 2007.

Dibbern, Ursula, and Horst Ihde. "Das Echo der Kultur und des Freiheitskampfes der nordamerikanischen Neger in der DDR, 1945–1969." *Zeitschrift für Anglistik und Amerikanistik* 3, no. 20 (1972): 429–42.

Diedrich, Maria, and Jürgen Heinrichs, eds. *From Black to Schwarz: Cultural Crossovers between African America and Germany*. Münster: LIT-Verlag, forthcoming.

Diedrich, Maria, Theron Cook, and Flip Lindo, eds. *Crossing Boundaries: African American Inner City and European Migrant Youth*. Münster: LIT-Verlag, 2004.

Dittmer, John. *Local People: The Struggle for Civil Rights in Mississippi*. Urbana: University of Illinois Press, 1994.

Dobie, Kathryn S., and Eleanor Lang, eds. *Her War: American Women in WWII*. New York: Universe, 2003.

Du Bois, W. E. B. *The Autobiography of W. E. B. Du Bois: A Soliloquy of Viewing My Life from the Last Decade of Its First Century*. New York: International, 1968.

———. *Dusk of Dawn: An Essay toward an Autobiography of a Race Concept*. 1940; New York: Oxford University Press, 2007.

Duberman, Martin. *Paul Robeson*. New York: New Press, 1989.

Dudziak, Mary. *Cold War Civil Rights: Race and the Image of American Democracy*. Princeton: Princeton University Press, 2000.

———. *Exporting American Dreams: Thurgood Marshall's African Journey*. Oxford: Oxford University Press, 2008.

Dutschke, Rudi. "Die geschichtlichen Bedingungen für den internationalen Emanzipationskampf." In *Der Kampf des vietnamesischen Volkes und die Globalstrategie des Imperialismus, Internationaler Vietnam-Kongress 17./18. Februar 1968, Westberlin*, ed. SDS Westberlin und Internationales Nachrichten und Forschungsinstitut, INFI, 107–24. Berlin: Peter von Maikowski, 1968.

Earley, Charity Adams. *One Woman's Army: A Black Officer Remembers the WAC*. College Station: Texas A & M University Press, 1996.

Edgcomb, Gabrielle Simone. *From Swastika to Jim Crow: Refugee Scholars at Black Colleges*. Malabar, FL: Krieger, 1993.

Edwards, Brent Hayes. *The Practice of Diaspora: Literature, Translation, and the Rise of Black Internationalism*. Cambridge, MA: Harvard University Press, 2003.

Ege, Moritz. *Schwarz werden: "Afroamerikanophilie" in den 1960er und 1970er Jahren*. Bielefeld: Transcript, 2007.

Eggers, Maureen Maisha, Grada Kilomba, Peggy Piesche, Susan Arndt, eds. *Mythen, Masken und Subjekte: Kritische Weissseinsforschung in Deutschland*. Münster: Unrast, 2005.

El-Tayeb, Fatima. *Schwarze Deutsche: Der Diskurs um 'Rasse' und Nationale Identität 1890–1933*. Frankfurt: Campus, 2001.

Endrias, Yonas, and Günter Wallraff. "Es geht nicht um Schwarze. Es geht um Weiße." Interview with Carol Campbell. *ZEITmagazin*, December 17, 2009, 24–28.

Engler, Robert. "The Individual Soldier and the Occupation." *Annals of the American Academy of Political and Social Science* 244 (1948): 77–86.

Erenberg, Lewis A. *The Greatest Fight of Our Generation: Louis vs. Schmeling*. New York: Oxford University Press, 2006.

Erenberg, Lewis A., and Susan E. Hirsch, eds. *The War in American Culture: Society and Consciousness During World War II.* Chicago: University of Chicago Press, 1996.

Eschen, Penny von. *Race against Empire: Black Americans and Anticolonialism, 1937–1957.* Ithaca: Cornell University Press, 1997.

Estes, Steve. *I am a Man! Race, Manhood, and the Civil Rights Movement.* Chapel Hill: University of North Carolina Press, 2005.

Evangelischer Pressedienst. "Dr. King in Berlin mit dem Theologischen Ehrendoktor ausgezeichnet." Nr. 210, September 12, 1964, 1.

Evers, Medgar Wiley, Myrlie Evers-Williams, and Manning Marable, eds. *The Autobiography of Medgar Evers: A Hero's Life and Legacy Revealed through His Writings, Letters, and Speeches.* New York: Basic Civitas Books, 2005.

Fairclough, Adam. *Race and Democracy: The Civil Rights Struggle in Louisiana, 1915–1972,* 2nd ed. Athens, GA: University of Georgia Press, 2008.

Fehrenbach, Heide. *Race After Hitler: Black Occupation Children in Postwar Germany and America.* Princeton: Princeton University Press, 2005.

Feimster, Crystal N. *Southern Horrors: Women and the Politics of Rape and Lynching.* Cambridge, MA: Harvard University Press, 2009.

Finkle, Lee. *Forum For Protest: The Black Press during World War II.* Rutherford, NJ: Fairleigh Dickinson University Press, 1975.

Finzsch, Norbert, and Dietmar Schirmer, eds. *Identity and Intolerance: Nationalism, Racism, and Xenophobia in Germany and the United States.* Cambridge: Cambridge University Press, 1998.

Foner, Philip Sheldon, ed. *Paul Robeson Speaks: Writings, Speeches, Interviews, 1918–1974.* New York: Brunner/Mazel, 1978.

Friedensrat der Deutschen Demokratischen Republik. *Days with Paul Robeson.* Berlin: Deutscher Friedensrat, 1961.

———. *"Every Cloud Has a Silver Lining ..." Pastor Ralph D. Abernathy, President of the Southern Christian Leadership Conference Visits the German Democratic Republic, September 27–29, 1971.* Dresden: Peace Council of the German Democratic Republic, 1971.

———. *Tage mit Paul Robeson: Paul Robeson im Oktober 1960 in der Deutschen Demokratischen Republik.* Berlin: Deutscher Friedensrat, 1961.

Fritz, Karsten. "Bilder eines ganz normalen Lebens in einem ganz normalen Film." In *Dreizehn deutsche Geschichten: Erzähltes Leben aus Ost und West,* ed. Winfried Ripp and Wendelin Szalai, 360–85. Hamburg: Edition Körber-Stiftung, 1998.

Fuchs, Emil. Afterword in *Warum wir nicht warten können,* by Martin Luther King, trans. Hans Lamm, 2nd ed., 195–96. 1965; Berlin: Union Verlag, 1967.

Fuhrer, Armin, and Thomas Tumovec. "Das Geheimnis um den Onkel." *Focus* 26 (2010): 22–27.

Fulbrook, Mary. *Anatomy of a Dictatorship: Inside the GDR, 1949–1989.* New York: Oxford University Press, 1995.

———. *The People's State: East German Society from Hitler to Honecker.* New Haven: Yale University Press, 2005.

Gaines, Kevin K. "The Civil Rights Movement in World Perspective." In *America on the World Stage: A Global Approach to U.S. History/The Organization of American Historians,* ed. Gary W. Reichard and Ted Dickson, 189–207. Urbana and Chicago: University of Illinois Press, 2008.

———. *American Africans in Ghana: Black Expatriates and the Civil Rights Era.* Chapel Hill, University of North Carolina Press, 2006.

Gassert, Philipp. "Blick ueber den Atlantik: DIE ZEIT und Amerika in den 1960er Jahren." In *DIE ZEIT und die Bonner Republik. Eine meinungsbildende*

Wochenzeitung zwischen Wiederbewaffnung und Wiedervereinigung, ed. Christian Haase und Axel Schildt, 65–83. Göttingen: Wallstein, 2008.

Gassert, Philipp, and Alan Steinweis, eds. *Coping with the Nazi Past: West German Debates on Nazism and Generational Conflict, 1955–1975*. New York: Berghahn Books, 2006.

Gauck, Joachim. "Freiheit—Verantwortung—Gemeinsinn: Wir in unserem Staat." Speech, Deutsches Theater Berlin, June 22, 2010, available at www.joachim-gauck.de.

———. *Winter im Sommer—Frühling im Herbst: Erinnerungen*. Munich: Siedler, 2009.

Geis, Margaret. *Morale and Discipline in the European Command 1945–49*. Occupation Forces in Europe Series. Karlsruhe, Germany: Historical Division, European Command, 1952.

Gerunde, Harald. *Eine von uns: Als Schwarze in Deutschland geboren*. Wuppertal: Peter Hammer, 2000.

Geschichte der Polizei des Birkenfelder Landes. Birkenfeld: Kreisverwaltung, 1987.

Geselbracht, Raymond H., ed. *The Civil Rights Legacy of Harry S. Truman*. Kirksville, MO: Truman State University Press, 2007.

Gilman, Sander. *On Blackness without Blacks: Essays on the Image of the Black in Germany*. Boston: G. K. Hall, 1982.

Gilmore, Glenda Elizabeth. *Defying Dixie: The Radical Roots of Civil Rights, 1919–1950*. New York: W. W. Norton, 2008.

Gilroy, Paul. *The Black Atlantic: Modernity and Double Consciousness*. Cambridge, MA: Harvard University Press, 1993.

Goeckel, Robert. "Neue Akteure, neue Prioritäten: Die Beziehungen zwischen den Kirchen." In *Die USA und Deutschland im Zeitalter des Kalten Krieges 1945–1990*, ed. Junker, 696–707.

Goedde, Petra. *GIs and Germans: Culture, Gender and Foreign Relations, 1945–1949*. New Haven: Yale University Press, 2003.

Gore, Dayo F., Jeanne Theoharis, and Komozi Woodard, eds. *Want to Start a Revolution?: Radical Women in the Black Freedom Struggle*. New York: NYU Press, 2009.

Gorokhov, Viktor. *Ich singe Amerika: Ein Lebensbild Paul Robesons*. Transl. Herbert Schirrmacher. Berlin: Verlag Neues Leben, 1955.

Graham, Herman. *The Brothers' Vietnam War. Black Power, Manhood, and the Military Experience*. Gainesville: University Press of Florida, 2003.

Greene, Larry, and Anke Ortlepp, eds. *German and African American Crossovers: Two Centuries of Contact*. Jackson: University of Mississippi Press, forthcoming.

Grill, Johnpeter Horst. "The American South and Nazi Racism." In *The Impact of Nazism: New Perspectives on the Third Reich and Its Legacy*, ed. Alan E. Steinweis and Daniel E. Rogers. Lincoln: University of Nebraska Press, 2003.

Gropman, Alan L. *The Air Force Integrates 1945–1964*. Washington, DC: Office of Air Force History, U.S. Air Force, 1985.

Große, Jürgen. *Amerikapolitik und Amerikabild der DDR 1974–1989*. Bonn: Bouvier, 1999.

Grossman, Victor. *Crossing the River: A Memoir of the American Left, the Cold War, and Life in East Germany*. Amherst: University of Massachusetts Press, 2003.

———. "Prologue: African Americans in the GDR." In *German and African American Crossovers*, ed. Greene and Ortlepp, forthcoming.

Grüber, Heinrich. Afterword in *Freiheit: Aufbruch der Neger Nordamerikas. Bericht über den Busstreik in Montgomery*, by Martin Luther King Jr., 203–205. Kassel: Oncken, 1964.

————. *Bevollmächtigt zum Brückenbau: Heinrich Grüber, Judenfreund und Trümmerpropst. Erinnerungen, Predigten, Berichte, Briefe.* Leipzig: Evangelische Verlagsanstalt, 1991.

————. *Erinnerungen aus sieben Jahrzehnten.* Cologne: Kiepenheuer & Witsch, 1968.

Guglielmo, Thomas A. " 'Red Cross, Double Cross': Race and America's World War II–Era Blood Donor Service." *Journal of American History* 97.1 (June 2010): 63–90.

Hahn, Michael. "Land der Superpigs: Wie *Agit 883* mit Black Panthers und Weathermen die 'zweite Front in den Metropolen eröffnete." In *agit 883: Bewegung, Revolte, Underground in Westberlin, 1969–1972,* ed. Rotaprint 25, 141–55. Hamburg: Assoziation A, 2006.

Halsell, Grace. *Black/White Sex.* New York: W. Morrow, 1972.

Harpprecht, Klaus. "Der schwarze Tribun." *Christ und Welt,* August 5, 1966, 28.

Harrington, Oliver. *Bootsie and Others: A Selection of Cartoons.* New York: Dodd, 1958.

————. *Soul Shots: Political Cartoons by Ollie Harrington.* New York: Longview, 1972.

————. *Why I Left America and Other Essays.* Jackson: University Press of Mississippi, 1993.

Harris, Stephen. *Harlem's Hell Fighters—The African American 369th Infantry in World War I.* Dulles: Potomac Books, 2002.

Hartwig, Jimmy. *'Ich möcht' noch so viel tun': Meine Kindheit, meine Karriere, meine Krankheit.* Bergisch Gladbach: Bastei Lübbe, 1994.

Hauser, William. *America's Army in Crisis: A Study in Civil-Military Relations.* Baltimore: Johns Hopkins University Press, 1973.

Heinrich, Brigitte. "Die Unterstützung des US-Imperialismus durch die BRD und die Auswirkungen im Innern." In *Am Beispiel Angela Davis: Der Kongreß in Frankfurt,* ed. Angela Davis Solidaritätskomitee, 159–69.

Helbig, Louis. "The Myth of the 'Other' America in East German Popular Consciousness." *Journal of Popular Culture* 10, no. 4 (March 5, 2004): 797–807.

Henry, Aaron, and Constance Curry. *Aaron Henry: The Fire Ever Burning.* Jackson: University Press of Mississippi, 2000.

Hine, Darlene Clark, Trica Danielle Keaton, and Stephen Small, eds. *Black Europe and the African Diaspora.* Urbana: University of Illinois Press, 2009.

Hodes, Martha, ed. *Sex, Love, Race: Crossing Boundaries in North American History.* New York, NYU Press, 1999.

Hoff, Henning. "Blackface Filmmaker Sparks a Race Debate in Germany." *Time,* November 18, 2009. http://www.time.com/time/world/article/0,8599,1940290,00.html.

Höhn, Maria. " 'Ein Atemzug der Freiheit.' Afro-amerikanische GIs, deutsche Frauen, und die Grenzen der Demokratie (1945–1968)." In *Demokratiewunder. Transatlantische Mittler und die kulturelle Öffnung Westdeutschlands, 1945–1970,* ed. Bauerkämpfer, Jarausch, and Payk, 104–28.

————. "The Black Panther Solidarity Committees and the *Voice of the Lumpen.*" *German Studies Review* 31, no. 1 (February 2008): 133–54.

————. *GIs and Fräuleins: The German-American Encounter in 1950s West Germany.* Chapel Hill: University of North Carolina Press, 2002.

————. " 'I Prefer Panthers to Pigs': The Black Panther Solidarity Committee, the *Voice of the Lumpen* and the Trial of the Ramstein 2." In *Changing the World,* ed. Davis et al., 215–39.

————. " 'We Will Never Go Back to the Old Way Again': Germany in the African American Debate on Civil Rights." *Central European History* 41, no. 4 (December 2008): 605–37.

————. " 'When Negro Soldiers Bring Home White Brides': Deutsche und amerikanische Debatten über die 'Mischehe' (1945–1967)." In *Amerikaner in Rheinland-Pfalz. Alltagskulturelle Begegnungen*, ed. Kremp and Tumalis, 147–64.

————, and Seungsook Moon, eds. *"Over There": Living with the U.S. Military Empire*. Durham: Duke University Press, 2010.

Honeck, Mischa, Martin Klimke, and Anne Kuhlmann-Smirnov, eds. *Blacks and Germans, German Blacks: Germany and the Black Diaspora, 1450–1914*, forthcoming.

Horne, Gerald. *Black and Brown: African Americans and the Mexican Revolution*. New York: NYU Press, 2005.

————. *Black and Red: W. E. B. Du Bois and the Afro-American Response to the Cold War, 1944–1963*. Albany: State University of New York Press, 1986.

————. *Communist Front? The Civil Rights Congress, 1946–1956*. Rutherford, NJ: Fairleigh Dickinson University Press, 1987.

————. *The End of Empires: African Americans and India*. Philadelphia: Temple University Press, 2009.

————. *Red Seas: Ferdinand Smith and Radical Black Sailors in the United States and Jamaica*. New York: NYU Press, 2009.

————. "Toward a Transnational Research Agenda for African American History in the 21st Century." *Journal of African American History* 91, no. 3 (2006): 288–303.

Huber, Charles. *Ein Niederbayer im Senegal. Mein Leben zwischen zwei Welten*. Frankfurt: Scherz, 2004.

Hügel-Marshall, Ika. *Invisible Woman: Growing Up Black in Germany*. New York: Continuum, 2001, rev. and annot. ed.: New York: Peter Lang, 2008.

Hughes, Langston. "My America." In *What the Negro Wants*, ed. Logan, 299–307. Chapel Hill: University of North Carolina Press, 1944.

Hutton, Bud, and Andy Rooney. *Conqueror's Peace: A Report to the American Stockholder*. New York: Double Day, 1947.

ID-Verlag, ed. *Rote Armee Fraktion: Texte und Materialien zur Geschichte der RAF*. Berlin: ID-Verlag, 1997.

Iggers, Wilma and Georg. *Two Lives in Uncertain Times: Facing the Challenges of the 20th Century as Scholars & Citizens*. New York: Berghahn Books, 2006.

Inge, M. Thomas, ed. *Dark Laughter: The Satiric Art of Oliver W. Harrington*. Jackson: University Press of Mississippi, 1993.

Jarausch, Konrad, ed. *Dictatorship as Experience: Towards a Socio-Cultural History of the GDR*. New York: Berghahn Books, 1999.

Jaspers, Karl. *The Future of Germany*. Chicago: University of Chicago Press, 1967.

————. *Wohin treibt die Bundesrepublik? Tatsachen, Gefahren, Chancen*. Munich: Piper, 1966.

Johnson, Haynes, and George Wilson. *Army in Anguish*. Washington Post National Report. New York: Pocket Book, 1972.

Johnson, Jesse J. *Ebony Brass*. [S.I.]: Carver, 1976.

Johnson, Kevin. *Mixed Race America and the Law*. New York: New York University, 2003.

Jones, Steffi. *Der Kick des Lebens. Wie ich den Weg nach oben schaffte*. Frankfurt: Fischer, 2007.

Junker, Detlef, ed. *The United States and Germany in the Era of the Cold War, 1945–1990: A Handbook*, vol. 2. New York: Cambridge University Press, 2004.

Kaufmann, Günther, and Gabriele Droste. *Der weiße Neger vom Hasenbergl*. Munich: Diana, 2004.

Kaufmann, Walter. *Unterwegs zu Angela. Amerikanische Impressionen*. Berlin: Verlag der Nation, 1973.

Keene, Jennifer. "W. E. B. Du Bois and the Wounded World: Seeking Meaning in the First World War for African-Americans." *Peace & Change* 26, no. 2 (April 2001): 135–52.

Kellogg, Peter J. "Civil Rights Consciousness in the 1940s." *Historian* 42, no. 1 (1979): 18–41.

Kelman, Steven. *Behind the Berlin Wall: An Encounter in East Germany.* Boston: Houghton Mifflin, 1972.

Kerner, Regina. "Mit Blueberry Hill kam der eine bis nach Taschkent." *Berliner Zeitung*, April 25, 1995, 3.

King, Coretta Scott. *Mein Leben mit Martin Luther King.* Transl. Christa Wegen. Berlin: Union Verlag, 1971.

King, Martin Luther. *Freiheit: Aufbruch der Neger Nordamerikas. Bericht über den Busstreik in Montgomery.* Transl. Ruth Ristick and Alfred Schmidt. Kassel: Oncken, 1964.

———. *Die neue Richtung unseres Zeitalters: Nobelpreisrede in der Aula der Universität Oslo am 11. Dez. 1964.* Berlin: Union Verlag, 1965/1966.

———. *Warum wir nicht warten können.* Transl. Hans Lamm. Vienna: Düsseldorf, 1964.

Kleinschmidt, Johannes. *"Do not fraternize." Die schwierigen Anfänge deutsch-amerikanischer Freundschaft, 1944–1949.* Trier: WVT Wissenschaftler Verlag, 1997.

Klimke, Martin. *The Other Alliance: Student Protest in West Germany & the United States in the Global Sixties.* Princeton: Princeton University Press, 2010.

Klotman, Phyllis R. "Military Rights and Wrongs: African Americans in the U.S. Armed Forces." In *The Black Studies Reader,* ed. by Jacqueline Bobo, Cynthia Hudley, and Claudine Michel, 113–37. New York: Routledge, 2004.

Kondraschow, Stanislav N. *Martin Luther King: Leben und Kampf eines amerikanischen Negerführers.* Berlin: VEB Deutscher Verlag der Wissenschaften, 1972.

Kongress für Bürgerliche Rechte New York 1951. *Rassenmord! Wir klagen an!: Petition an die Vereinten Nationen zum Schutze der Negerbevölkerung in den Vereinigten Staaten von Amerika.* Transl. Hermann Sturmer. Berlin: Rütten & Loening, 1953.

Köpf, Peter. "Charles Lucas' Big Mistake." *Atlantic Times*, September 2009, 20–21.

Kraushaar, Wolfgang, ed. *Frankfurter Schule und Studentenbewegung: Von der Flaschenpost zum Molotowcocktail, 1946–1995,* 3 vols. Frankfurt am Main: Rogner & Bernhard, 1998.

Kraushaar, Wolfgang. "Hitler's Children? The German 1968 Movement in the Shadow of the Nazi Past." In *Memories of 1968: International Perspectives,* ed. Ingo Cornils and Sarah Waters, 79–101. Bern: Peter Lang, 2010.

Kremp, Werner, and Martina Tumalis, eds. *Amerikaner in Rheinland-Pfalz. Alltagskulturelle Begegnungen.* Trier: WVT Wissenschaftlicher Verlag, 2008.

Krüger-Potratz, Marianne. *Anderssein gab es nicht: Ausländer und Minderheiten in der DDR.* Münster: Waxmann, 1991.

Kryder, Daniel. *Divided Arsenal: Race and the American State During WWII.* New York: Cambridge University Press, 2000.

Kundnani, Hans. *Utopia or Auschwitz: Germany's 1968 Generation and the Holocaust.* New York: Columbia University Press, 2009.

Lake, Marilyn. *Drawing the Global Colour Line: White Men's Countries and the International Challenge of Racial Equality.* New York: Cambridge University Press, 2008.

Lawson, Steven F., ed. *Running for Freedom: Civil Rights and Black Politics in America Since 1941,* 3rd ed. Malden, MA: Wiley-Blackwell, 2009.

———. *To Secure These Rights: The Report of Harry S. Truman's Committee on Civil Rights.* Boston: Bedford/St. Martin's, 2004.

Langbehn, Volker, ed. *German Colonialism, Visual Culture, and Modern Memory*. New York: Routledge, 2010.

Langbehn, Volker, and Mohammad Salama, eds. *German Colonialism: Race, the Holocaust, and Postwar Germany*. New York: Columbia University Press, forthcoming.

Laville, Helen, and Scott Lucas. "The American Way: Edith Sampson, the NAACP, and African American Identity in the Cold War." *Diplomatic History* 20, no. 4 (Fall 1996): 565–90.

Layton, Azza Salama. *International Politics and Civil Rights Policies in the United States, 1941–1960*. Cambridge, UK: Cambridge University Press, 2000.

Lee, Ulysses Grant. *The Employment of Negro Troops*. Washington, DC: Office of the Chief of Military History, U.S. Army, 1966.

Lehmann, Theo. *Blues and Trouble*. Berlin: Henschel Verlag, 1966.

Lehmann, Werner. *Schwarze Rose aus Alabama*. Berlin: Neues Leben, 1972.

Lemire, Elise. *'Miscegenation': Making Race in America*. Philadelphia: University of Pennsylvania Press, 2002.

Lemke Muniz de Faria, Yara-Collette. *Zwischen Fürsorge und Ausgrenzung. Afrodeutsche "Besatzungskinder" im Nachkriegsdeutschland*. Berlin: Metropol, 2002.

Lemke, Sieglinde. "Berlin and Boundaries: *sollen* versus *geschehen*." *boundary 2*, 27, no. 3 (2000): 45–78.

Lentz-Smith, Adriane. *Freedom Struggles: African Americans and World War I*. Cambridge, MA: Harvard University Press, 2009.

Lester, Rosemarie. *Trivialneger: Das Bild des Schwarzen im westdeutschen Illustriertenroman*. Stuttgart: Akademischer Verlag H.-D. Heinz, 1982.

Leuchtenburg, William E., ed. *American Places: Encounters With History—A Celebration of Sheldon Meyer*. Oxford and New York: Oxford University Press, 2000.

Lewis, David Levering. *King: A Biography*, 2nd ed. Urbana: University of Illinois Press, 1978.

———. *W. E. B. Du Bois: The Fight for Equality and the American Century: 1919–1963*. New York: Holt, 2001.

Liebau, Veronika, and Andreas Daum. *The Freedom Bell in Berlin*. Berlin: Jaron, 2000.

Lilly, J. Robert. "Dirty Details: Executing U.S. Soldiers During WWII." *Crime & Delinquency* 42.4 (1996): 491–516.

Lilly, J. Robert, and J. Michael Thomson. "Executing U.S. Soldiers in England during WWII: The Power of Command Influence and Sexual Racism." *British Journal of Criminology* 37.2 (Spring 1997): 262–88.

Little, Monroe H., Jr. "The Black Military Experience in Germany: From the First World War to the Present." In *Crosscurrents: African-Americans, Africa, and Germany in the Modern World*, ed. McBride, Hopkins, and Blackshire-Belay, 177–96.

Logan, Rayford W., ed. *What the Negro Wants*. Chapel Hill: University of North Carolina Press, 1944.

Lönnendonker, Siegward, Bernd Rabehl, and Jochen Staadt. *Die antiautoritäre Revolte: der Sozialistische Deutsche Studentenbund nach der Trennung von der SPD*. Wiesbaden: Westdeutscher Verlag, 2002.

Ludwig, Andreas. *Fortschritt, Norm und Eigensinn: Erkundungen im Alltag der DDR*. Berlin: Links, 1999.

Ludwig, Hartmut. *An der Seite der Entrechteten und Schwachen zur Geschichte des "Büro Pfarrer Grüber" (1938 bis 1940) und der Ev. Hilfsstelle für ehemals Rasseverfolgte nach 1945*. Berlin: Logos-Verlag, 2009.

Lusane, Clarence. *Hitler's Black Victims: The Historical Experiences of Afro-Germans, European Blacks, Africans, and African Americans in the Nazi Era.* New York: Routledge, 2003.

Macdonald, Dwight, and Nancy Macdonald. *The War's Greatest Scandal! The Story of Jim Crow in Uniform.* [New York]: March on Washington Movement [1943].

MacGregor, Morris J. *Integration of the Armed Forces 1940–1965.* Washington, DC: Center for Military History, 1981.

MacGregor, Morris J., and Bernard Nalty, eds. *Blacks in the U.S. Armed Forces: Basic Documents,* vols. 12–13. Wilmington: Scholarly Resources, 1977.

Marable, Manning, and Vanessa Agard-Jones, eds. *Transnational Blackness: Navigating the Global Color Line.* New York: Palgrave Macmillan, 2008.

Margolick, David. *Beyond Glory: Joe Louis vs. Max Schmeling and a World on the Brink.* New York: Knopf, 2005.

Martin, Charles. "Internationalizing 'The American Dilemma': The Civil Rights Congress and the 1951 Genocide Petition to the United Nations." *Journal of American Ethnic History* 16, no. 4 (Summer 1997): 35–61.

Martin, Peter. *Schwarze Teufel, edle Mohren: Afrikaner in Geschichte und Bewusstsein der Deutschen.* Hamburg: Hamburger Edition, 2001.

Martin, Peter, and Christine Alonzo, eds. *Zwischen Charleston und Stechschritt: Schwarze im Nationalsozialismus.* Hamburg: Dölling und Galitz, 2004.

Massaquoi, Hans. *Destined to Witness: Growing Up Black in Nazi Germany.* New York: W. Morrow, 1999.

———. *Hänschen klein, ging allein … Mein Weg in die Neue Welt.* Frankfurt: Scherz, 2004; Frankfurt: Fischer, 2005.

Massingue, Eva. *Sichtbar anders: Aus dem Leben afrodeutscher Kinder und Jugendlicher.* Frankfurt: Brandes & Apsel, 2005.

Matthes, Philip. "Der Anerkennungslobbyismus der DDR in den USA von 1964 bis 1974." In *Umworbener Klassenfeind,* ed. Balbier und Rösch, 40–58.

Mausbach, Wilfried. "Auschwitz and Vietnam: West German Protest against America's War during the 1960s." In *America, the Vietnam War and the World: Comparative and International Perspectives,* ed. Andreas Daum, Lloyd Gardner, and Wilfried Mausbach, 279–98. New York: Cambridge University Press, 2003.

Mazón, Patricia, and Reinhild Steingröver, eds. *Not So Plain as Black and White: Afro-German Culture and History, 1890–2000.* Rochester: University of Rochester Press, 2005.

McBride, David, Leroy Hopkins, and C. Aisha Blackshire-Belay. *Crosscurrents: African-Americans, Africa, and Germany in the Modern World.* Columbia, SC: Camden House, 1998.

McBride, James. *Miracle at St. Anna.* New York: Riverhead Books, 2002.

McMillen, Neil. *Dark Journey: Black Mississippians in the Age of Jim Crow.* Urbana: University of Illinois Press, 1990.

———. "Fighting for What We Didn't Have: How Mississippi's Black Veterans Remember World War II." In *Remaking Dixie,* ed. McMillen, 93–110.

McMillen, Neil, ed. *Remaking Dixie. The Impact of World War II on the American South.* Jackson: University Press of Mississippi, 1997.

McMillon, Doris. *Mixed Blessing.* New York: St. Martin's Press, 1985.

McPherson, Tara. *Reconstructing Dixie: Race, Gender, and Nostalgia in the Imagined South.* Durham: Duke University Press, 2003.

McRae, Donald. *Heroes without a Country: America's Betrayal of Joe Louis and Jesse Owens.* New York: Ecco, 2002.

Meriwether, James. *Proudly We Can Be Africans: Black Americans and Africa, 1935–1961.* Chapel Hill: University of North Carolina Press, 2002.

Merkel, Ina. "Eine andere Welt. Vorstellungen von Nordamerika in der DDR der fünfziger Jahre." In *Amerikanisierung. Traum und Alptraum im Deutschland des 20. Jahrhunderts,* ed. Alf Lüdtke, Inge Marßolek, and Adelheid von Saldern, 245–56. Stuttgart: Steiner, 1996.

Mershon, Sherie R., and Steven Schlossman. *Foxholes and Color Lines: Desegregating the U.S. Armed Forces.* Baltimore: Johns Hopkins University Press, 1998.

Mettler, Suzanne. *Soldiers to Citizens: The G.I. Bill and the Making of the Greatest Generation.* Oxford: Oxford University Press, 2005.

Meusel, Georg. "Mit Kreditkarte über die Mauer." *Der Freitag,* September 24, 2004, 18.

———. "Träumer und schöpferischer Extremist: Martin Luther King und dessen Ausstrahlung auf die Friedens- und Bürgerrechtsbewegung in der DDR." Martin-Luther-King-Zentrum, Werdau, e.V. http://www.king-zentrum.de/, undated.

Ministry of Foreign Affairs of the German Democratic Republic, ed. *The Anti-Imperialist Liberation Struggle of the Afro-Asian and Latin American Peoples and the German Democratic Republic.* Dresden: Verlag Zeit im Bild, 1964.

Moore, Brenda L. *To Serve My Country, To Serve My Race: The Story of the Only African American WACs Stationed Overseas during World War II.* New York: NYU Press, 1996.

Moore, Michaela Hoenicke. *Know Your Enemy: The American Debate on Nazism, 1933–1945.* New York: Cambridge University Press, 2010.

Morehouse, Maggi M. *Fighting in a Jim Crow Army: Black Men and Women Remember World War II.* Lanham, MD: Rowman and Littlefield, 2000.

Moskos, Charles. *The American Enlisted Man: The Rank and File in Today's Military.* New York: Russell Sage Foundation, 1970.

Moye, Todd J. *Freedom Flyers: The Tuskegee Airmen of World War II.* New York: Oxford University Press, 2010.

Münch, Ingo von, ed. *Dokumente des Geteilten Deutschland: Quellentexte zur Rechtslage des Deutschen Reiches, der Bundesrepublik Deutschland und der Deutschen Demokratischen Republik.* Stuttgart: Kröner, 1976.

Myrdal, Gunnar. *An American Dilemma: The Negro Problem and Modern Democracy.* New York: Harper, 1944.

NAACP. *The Search for Military Justice: Report of an NAACP Inquiry Into the Problems of the Negro Servicemen in West Germany.* New York: NAACP Special Contribution Fund, 1971.

Nalty, Bernard C. *Strength for the Fight: A History of Black Americans in the Military.* New York: Free Press, 1989.

Nalty, Bernard C., and Morris J. MacGregor, eds. *Blacks in the Military: Essential Documents.* Wilmington: Scholarly Resources, 1981.

Nationalrat der Nationalen Front des demokratischen Deutschland, ed. *Kämpft Angela Davis frei.* Suhl: Freies Wort, 1971.

Nejar, Marie. *Mach nicht so traurige Augen, weil du ein Negerlein bist: Meine Jugend im Dritten Reich.* Reinbek: Rowohlt, 2007.

Nelson, Daniel. *Defenders or Intruders? The Dilemmas of U.S. Forces in Germany.* Boulder: Westview, 1987.

Neubert, Erhart. *Geschichte der Opposition in der DDR 1949–1989,* 2nd ed. Berlin: Links, 1997.

Newton, Huey. *Selbstverteidigung.* Frankfurt: Roter Stern, 1971.

Ngombe, Lucia. *Kind Nr. 95. Meine deutsch-afrikanische Odyssee.* Berlin: Ullstein, 2004.

Nichols, Lee. *Breakthrough on the Color Front.* New York: Random House, 1954.

Ninkovich, Frank, and Liping Bu, eds. *The Cultural Turn: Essays in the History of Foreign Relations.* Chicago: Imprint, 2001.

Obama, Barack. Campaign speech in Berlin on July 24, 2008. Organizing for America. http://my.barackobama.com/page/content/berlinvideo.

———. Interview with Tom Brokaw, Dresden, Germany, June 5, 2009. MSNBC. http://www.msnbc.msn.com/id/21134540/vp/31120874#31120874.

Office of the Press Secretary, The White House. "Remarks by President Obama, German Chancellor Merkel, and Elie Wiesel at Buchenwald Concentration Camp." Weimar, Germany, June 5, 2009. The White House. www.whitehouse.gov.

Oguntoye, Katharina. *Eine afro-deutsche Geschichte: Zur Lebenssituation von Afrikanern und Afro-Deutschen in Deutschland von 1884 bis 1950*. Berlin: Hoho Verlag, 1997.

Ohse, Marc Dietrich. *Jugend nach dem Mauerbau. Anpassung, Protest und Eigensinn (DDR 1961–1974)*. Berlin: Links, 2003.

Oji, Chima. *Unter die Deutschen gefallen: Erfahrungen eines Afrikaners*. Wuppertal: Hammer, 1992.

Onkst, David H. "'First a Negro…Incidentally a Veteran': Black World War Two Veterans and the G.I. Bill in the Deep South, 1944–1948." *Journal of Social History* 31 (Spring, 1998): 517–44.

Oppel, Christina. "W. E. B. Du Bois, Nazi Germany, and the Black Atlantic." *GHI Bulletin Supplement* 5 (2008): 99–120.

Ostendorf, Berndt. "Forschungsreise in die Dämmerung: The Strange Transatlantic Career of Julius Lips between Howard University and Leipzig University." In *Transatlantic Cultural Contexts: Essays in Honor of Eberhard Brüning*, ed. Hartmut Keil, 115–27. Tübingen: Stauffenburg, 2005.

Ostermann, Christian. "Die USA und die DDR." In *Die DDR und der Westen. Transnationale Beziehungen 1949–1989*, ed. Ulrich Pfeil, 165–83. Berlin: Links, 2001.

Osur, Alan M. "Black White Relations in the U.S. Military 1940–1972." *Air University Review* 33 (November/December 1981): 69–78.

Ottley, Roi. *New World A-Coming*. New York: Houghton, Mifflin, 1943.

———. *No Green Pastures*. New York: Charles Scribner's Sons, 1951.

Ovington, Mary White. *The Walls Came Tumbling Down*. New York: Harcourt, Brace, 1947.

Parker, Jason C. "'Made-in-America Revolutions'? The 'Black University' and the American Role in the Decolonization of the Black Atlantic." *Journal of American History* 96, no. 3 (December 2009): 727–50.

Pascoe, Peggy. *What Comes Naturally: Miscegenation Law and the Making of Race in America*. Oxford: Oxford University Press, 2009.

Patterson, William, ed. *We Charge Genocide: The Historic Petition to the United Nations for Relief from a Crime of the United States Government against the Negro People*. New York: Civil Rights Congress, 1951.

Paul-Robeson-Komitee der Deutschen Demokratischen Republik, ed. *Paul Robeson. Ausstellung zu Ehren seines 70. Geburtstages am 9. April 1968. Internationales Ausstellungszentrum Berlin, 8.–28. April (Katalog)*. Berlin: Deutsche Akademie der Künste, 1968.

Payne, Charles M. *I've Got the Light of Freedom: The Organizing Tradition and the Mississippi Freedom Struggle*. Berkeley: University of California Press, 1995.

Peña, Rosemarie. "Staatenlos." BlogHer, April 10, 2008. http://www.blogher.com/staatenlos.

Pennybacker, Susan D. *From Scottsboro to Munich: Race and Political Culture in 1930s Britain*. Princeton: Princeton University Press, 2009.

Pfeifer, Elizabeth L. B. "Public Demonstrations of the 1960s: Participatory Democracy or Leftist Fascism?" In *Coping with the Nazi Past*, ed. Gassert and Steinweis, 194–209.

Piesche, Peggy. "Black and German? East German Adolescents Before 1989: A Retrospective View of a 'Non-Existent Issue' in the GDR." In *The Cultural After-Life of East Germany: New Transnational Perspectives*, ed. Leslie A. Adelson, 37–59. Washington, DC: AICGS, 2002.

Plummer, Brenda Gayle. *Rising Wind: Black Americans and U.S. Foreign Affairs, 1935–1960.* Chapel Hill: University of North Carolina Press, 1996.

Poiger, Uta. *Jazz, Rock and Rebels: Cold War Politics and American Culture in a Divided Germany.* Berkeley: University of California Press, 2000.

Pollack, Jack. "Literacy Tests" (1947), reprinted in *Reporting Civil Rights, Part One: American Journalism 1941–1963*, ed. Carson, Garrow, Kovach, and Polsgrove, 85–91.

Port, Andrew. *Conflict and Stability in the German Democratic Republic.* Cambridge: Cambridge University Press, 2007.

Posner, David. "Afro-America in West German Perspective, 1945–1966." PhD diss., Yale University, 1997.

Potter, Lou, William Miles, and Nina Rosenblum. *Liberators: Fighting on Two Fronts in World War II.* New York: Houghton Mifflin Harcourt, 1992.

Poutrus, Patrice. "An den Grenzen des proletarischen Internationalismus: Algerische Flüchtlinge in der DDR." *Zeitschrift für Geschichtswissenschaft* 2 (2007): 162–78.

Powell, Colin. *My American Journey.* New York: Random House, 1995.

Putney, Martha S. *When the Nation Was in Need: Blacks in the Women's Army Corps During World War II.* Metuchen, NJ: Scarecrow, 1992.

Randall, Francis B. "Der Kampf um Rassengleichheit in Amerika I." *Frankfurter Hefte* 6 (1962): 369–76.

———. "Der Kampf um Rassengleichheit in Amerika II." *Frankfurter Hefte* 7 (1962): 467–74.

Randall, Francis B., and Laura Randall. "Tagebuch einer Bürgerrechts-Fahrt." *Frankfurter Hefte* 9 (1961): 747–56.

Raphael-Hernandez, Heike, ed. *Blackening Europe: The African American Presence.* New York: Routledge, 2004.

Reimann, Aribert. *Dieter Kunzelmann: Avantgardist, Protestler, Radikaler.* Göttingen: Vandenhoeck & Ruprecht, 2009.

Richter, Hedwig. " 'Wir spürten den Herzschlag brüderlicher Liebe': Vom transnationalen Austausch der Herrnhüter Brudergemeinde im Kalten Krieg." In *Umworbener Klassenfeind*, ed. Balbier and Rösch, 96–122.

Ritz, Manuela. *Die Farbe meiner Haut: Die Antirassismustrainerin erzählt.* Freiburg: Herder, 2009.

Robers, Norbert. *Joachim Gauck. Die Biografie einer Institution.* Berlin: Henschel, 2000.

Roberts, Randy. *Joe Louis: Hard Times Man.* New Haven: Yale University Press, forthcoming.

Robeson, Paul. *Mein Lied—meine Waffe.* Transl. Georg Friedrich Alexander. Berlin: Kongress-Verlag, 1958.

Robeson, Paul, Jr. *The Undiscovered Paul Robeson: Quest for Freedom, 1939–1976.* Hoboken: Wiley, 2010.

Rodriguez, Besenia. " 'Long Live Third World Unity! Long Live Internationalism!' Huey P. Newton's Revolutionary Intercommunalism." In *Transnational Blackness,* ed. Marable and Agard-Jones, 149–73.

Roeder, George H., Jr. "Censoring Disorder: American Visual Imagery of World War II." In *The War in American Culture*, ed. Erenberg and Hirsch, 46–70.

Romano, Renee. *Race Mixing: Black-White Marriage in Postwar America.* Cambridge, MA: Harvard University Press, 2003.

Rosen, Hannah. *Terror in the Heart of Freedom: Citizenship, Sexual Violence, and the Meaning of Race in the Postemancipation South.* Chapel Hill: University of North Carolina Press, 2009.

Rosenberg, Jonathan Seth. *How Far the Promised Land? World Affairs and the American Civil Rights Movement from the First World War to Vietnam.* Princeton: Princeton University Press, 2006.

———. " 'Sounds Suspiciously Like Miami': Nazism and the U.S. Civil Rights Movement, 1933–1941." In *The Cultural Turn: Essays in the History of U.S. Foreign Relations,* ed. Ninkovich and Bu, 105–30.

Sackett, Robert. "Press Coverage and Analysis in West Germany, 1949–1967." Paper presented at the conference African American Civil Rights and Germany in the Twentieth Century, Vassar College, Poughkeepsie, New York, October 1–4, 2009.

Schaap, Jeremy. *Triumph: The Untold Story of Jesse Owens and Hitler's Olympics.* Boston: Houghton Mifflin, 2007.

Scheck, Raffael. *Hitler's African Victims: The German Army Massacres of Black French Soldiers in 1940.* Cambridge: Cambridge University Press, 2006.

Scheer, Maximilian. *Liebste Angela—Erste unter Gleichen: Gefängnisbriefe von George Jackson.* Berlin: Verlag der Nation, 1971.

———. *Der Weg nach San Rafael. Für Angela Davis. Ein Hörspiel.* Berlin: Verlag der Nation, 1971.

Schmelz, Andrea. "Bildungsmigration und Interkulturalität: Ausländische Studierende aus afrikanischen und asiatischen Ländern in Ostdeutschland vor und nach 1989." *Deutschlandarchiv* 38, no. 1 (2005): 84–92.

Schmidt, Oliver. "African American Troops in World War II: Transnational Perspectives on the 'Race War.' " *European Journal of Transnational Studies* 1.2 (Autumn 2009): 5–24.

Schmundt-Thomas, Georg. "America's Germany: National Self and Cultural Other After World War II." PhD diss., Northwestern University, 1992.

Schneider, Michael, ed. *Malcolm X: Schwarze Gewalt. Reden.* Frankfurt: Edition Voltaire, 1968.

Schnoor, Rainer. "Between Private Opinion and Official Pronouncement: Images of America in the German Democratic Republic, 1971–1990." In *The United States and Germany,* vol. 2, ed. Junker, 519–26.

———. "The Good and the Bad America." In *The United States and Germany,* vol. 2, ed. Junker, 618–26.

Schroeder, Aribert. "Ollie Harrington: His Portrait Drawn on the Basis if East German (GDR) Secret Service Files." In *German and African American Crossovers: Two Centuries of Contact,* ed. Greene and Ortlepp, forthcoming.

Schroer, Timothy L. *Recasting Race after World War II: Germans and African Americans in American-Occupied Germany.* Boulder: University Press of Colorado, 2007.

Schultz, Dagmar. "Witnessing whiteness—ein persönliches Zeugnis." In *Mythen, Masken und Subjekte: kritische Weissseinsforschung in Deutschland,* ed. Eggers et al., 514–29.

Scott, Lawrence P., and William M. Womack. *Double V: The Civil Rights Struggle of the Tuskegee Airmen.* East Lansing: Michigan State University Press, 1994.

Scott, William A., III. "World War II Veteran Remembers the Horror of the Holocaust." Illustrated pamphlet, ca. 1991. The Civil Rights Struggle, African American GIs, and Civil Rights. http://www.aacvr-germany.org/scott.

SDS Westberlin und Internationales Nachrichten- und Forschungsinstitut (INFI), ed. *Der Kampf des vietnamesischen Volkes und die Globalstrategie des*

Imperialismus: Internationaler Vietnam-Kongress 17./18. Februar 1968 Westberlin. Berlin: SDS, 1968.

Seale, Bobby. *Der Prozeß gegen Bobby Seale: Rassismus und politische Justiz in den USA.* Frankfurt: Roter Stern, 1970.

Seghers, Anna. *Der erste Schritt.* Berlin: Aufbau-Verlag, 1953, edition 1957.

Siegfried, Detlef. "White Negroes: The Fascination of the Authentic in the West German Counterculture of the 1960s." In *Changing the World*, ed. Davis et al., 191–214.

Sielke, Sabine. "Theorizing American Studies: German Interventions into an Ongoing Debate." *European Journal of American Studies*, January, 12, 2006. EJAS 2006, article 7. http://ejas.revues.org/document470.html.

Singh, Nikihil Pal. *Black Is a Country: Race and the Unfinished Struggle for Democracy.* Cambridge, MA: Harvard University Press, 2005.

Sitkoff, Harvard. "African Americans, American Jews, and the Holocaust." In *The Achievement of American Liberalism*, ed. Chafe, 181–204.

———. "Harry Truman and the Election of 1948: The Coming of Age of Civil Rights in American Politics." *Journal of Southern History* 37 (November 1971): 597–616.

———. *A New Deal for Blacks: The Emergence of Civil Rights as an Issue.* New York: Oxford University Press, 1978.

Slobodian, Quinn. "Dissident Guests: Afro-Asian Students and Transnational Activism in the West German Protest Movement." In *Migration and Activism in Europe since 1945*, ed. Wendy Pojmann, 33–56. New York: Palgrave, 2008.

Smith, Graham. *When Jim Crow Met John Bull: Black American Soldiers in World War II Britain.* New York: St. Martin's Press, 1987.

Smith, Jennifer B. *An International History of the Black Panther Party.* New York: Garland, 1999.

Smith, William Gardner. *Last of the Conquerors.* New York: Farrar, Straus, 1948.

———. *Return to Black America: A Negro Reporter's Impressions after 16 Years of Self-Exile.* Englewood Cliffs: Prentice Hall, 1970.

Snow, Noah. *Deutschland Schwarz Weiss: Der alltägliche Rassismus.* Munich: Bertelsmann, 2008.

Sollors, Werner. *Interracialism: Black-White Intermarriage in American History, Literature, and Law.* Oxford: Oxford University Press, 2000.

———. "W. E. B. Du Bois in Nazi Germany, 1936." *Amerikastudien/American Studies* 44 (1999): 207–22.

Sozialistische Einheitspartei Deutschlands. *Protokoll der Verhandlungen des VIII. Parteitages der Sozialistischen Einheitspartei Deutschlands: 15. bis 19. Juni 1971 in der Werner-Seelenbinder-Halle zu Berlin.* Berlin: Dietz Verlag, 1971.

Spencer, Robyn. "Merely One Link in the Worldwide Revolution: Internationalism, State Repression, and the Black Panther Party, 1966–1972." In *From Toussaint to Tupac*, ed. West et al., 215–31.

Spickard, Paul. *Mixed Blood: Intermarriage and Ethnic Identity in Twentieth-Century America.* Madison: University of Wisconsin, 1989.

Starr, Joseph [United States Army]. *Fraternization with the Germans in World War II, 1945–46*, Occupation Forces in Europe Series. Frankfurt: Office of the Chief Historian, European Command, 1947.

Steiniger, Klaus. *Angela Davis: Eine Frau schreibt Geschichte.* Berlin: Neues Leben, 2010.

———. "Das Flagschiff: USA-Redakteur beim 'Neuen Deutschland.'" In *Amerikanistik in der DDR: Geschichte-Analysen-Zeitzeugenberichte*, ed. Rainer Schnoor, 229–35. Berlin: Trafo Verlag, 1999.

———. *Free Angela Davis: Hero of the Other America.* Berlin: National Council of the National Front of the GDR, 1972.

———. *Bei Winston und Cunhal. Reporter auf vier Kontinenten.* Berlin: Edition Ost, 2004.

Stillman, Richard J. *Integration of the Negro in the U.S. Armed Forces.* New York: Frederick Praeger, 1968.

Stolte, Roland. "Dr. Martin Luther King in 1964 in Berlin." Paper presented at the conference African American Civil Rights and Germany in the Twentieth Century, Vassar College, Poughkeepsie, New York, October 1–4, 2009.

Stovall, Tyler. *Paris Noir: African Americans in the City of Light.* New York: Mariner Books, 1998.

Sugrue, Thomas J. *Sweet Land of Liberty: The Forgotten Struggle for Civil Rights in the North.* New York: Random House, 2008.

Sullivan, Patricia. *Days of Hope: Race and Democracy in the New Deal Era.* Chapel Hill: University of North Carolina Press, 1996.

———. *Lift Every Voice: The NAACP and the Making of the Civil Rights Movement.* New York: New Press, 2009.

Tabor, Michael. *Harlem: Kapitalismus & Heroin = Völkermord.* Frankfurt: Roter Stern, 1970.

Tharoor, Kanishk. "Martin Luther King in Berlin: Marienkirche or the Brandenburg Gate?" Open Democracy, August 4, 2008, http://www.opendemocracy.net.

Torrence, Ridgely. *The Story of John Hope.* New York: Macmillan, 1948.

Tyrrell, Ian. *Transnational Nation: United States History in Global Perspective since 1789.* Basingstoke: Palgrave Macmillan, 2007.

U.S. War Department. *Command of Negro Troops: War Department, 29 February 1944,* Pamphlet No. 20–26. Washington, DC: US Government Printing Office, 1944.

Usleber, Thomas. *Die Farben unter meiner Haut: Autobiographische Aufzeichnungen.* Frankfurt: Brandes & Apsel, 2002.

Vahl, Anneliese. *Martin Luther King: Stationen auf dem Wege. Berichte und Selbstzeugnisse.* Berlin: Evangelische Verlagsanstalt, 1968.

Vazansky, Alexander. "An Army in Crisis: Social Conflict in the United States Army Europe and 7th Army, 1968–1975." PhD diss., University of Heidelberg, 2009.

Verlag Roter Stern, eds. *LERNEN: subversive. AmeriKKKa: ein Lese-Bilder-Buch.* Frankfurt: Verlag Roter Stern, 1974.

Verlag Zeit im Bild, ed. *Peace, Friendship, Solidarity: Angela Davis in the GDR.* Dresden: Verlag Zeit im Bild, 1973.

Vesper, Bernward, ed. *Black Power. Ursachen des Guerilla-Kampfes in den Vereinigten Staaten.* Voltaire Flugschriften 14. Berlin: Voltaire, 1967.

———. *Die Reise.* Reinbek: Rowohlt, 1989.

Vogel, Arna, and Christian Blees. "Der Cowboy im Sozialismus: US-Amerikaner in der DDR." Westdeutscher Rundfunk, Cologne, October 5, 2005.

Wallraff, Günter. *Aus der schönen neuen Welt. Expeditionen ins Landesinnere.* Cologne: Kiepenheuer & Witsch, 2009.

Washburn, Patrick. *A Question of Sedition: The Federal Government's Investigation of the Black Press.* New York and Oxford: Oxford University Press, 1986.

Weatherford, Doris. *American Women During World War II: An Encyclopedia.* New York: Routledge, 2010.

Wendt, Simon. *The Spirit and the Shotgun: Armed Resistance and the Struggle for Civil Rights: New Perspectives on the History of the South.* Gainesville: University Press of Florida, 2007.

———. "Transnational Perspectives on the History of Racism in America." *Amerikastudien/American Studies* 54.3 (2009): 473–98.

Wentker, Hermann. *Außenpolitik in engen Grenzen: Die DDR im internationalen System, 1949–1989.* Munich: Oldenbourg, 2007.

Wessel, Daisy. *Bild und Gegenbild: Die USA in der Belletristik der DDR (bis 1987)*. Opladen: Leske & Budrich, 1989.

West, Michael, William Martin, and Fanon Che Wilkins, eds. *From Toussaint to Tupac: The Black International Since the Age of Revolution*. Chapel Hill: University of North Carolina Press, 2009.

White, Walter Francis. *A Rising Wind*. Garden City: Doubleday, Doran, 1945.

Wierling, Dorothee. "Amerikabilder in der DDR." In *Umworbener Klassenfeind*, ed. Balbier and Rösch, 32–38.

Williams, Robert F., and Robert B. Bigg. *Großstadtguerilla*. Voltaire Flugschriften 24. Berlin: Voltaire, 1969.

Willoughby, John. *Remaking the Conquering Heroes: The Postwar American Occupation of Germany*. New York: Palgrave Macmillan, 2001.

Wirth, Günter. *Martin Luther King*. Christ in der Welt 5. Berlin: Union Verlag, 1965; 8th ed., 1989.

———. " 'Die neue Richtung unseres Zeitalters—Martin Luther Kings Traum von Gerechtigkeit, Gleichheit und Gewaltlosigkeit': Martin Luther King und seine Bedeutung für uns heute." January 15, 1999, Martin-Luther-King-Zentrum, Werdau, e.V. http://www.king-zentrum.de/.

Wolff, Karl Dietrich. " 'Amis' and 'Naner': With Americans in Hesse since 1945." In *Amerikaner in Hessen: Eine besondere Beziehung im Wandel der Zeit*, ed. Gundula Bavendamm, 127–400. Hanau: Cocon-Verlag, 2008. Available at www.aacvr-germany.org/online_publications.

Wolle, Stefan. *Die heile Welt der Diktatur: Alltag und Herrschaft in der DDR 1971–1989*. Berlin: Links, 1998.

———. *Der Traum von der Revolte: Die DDR 1968*. Berlin: Links, 2008.

Wormser, Richard. *The Rise and Fall of Jim Crow*. New York: St. Martin's Press, 2003.

Wright, Michelle. M. *Becoming Black: Creating Identity in the African Diaspora*. Durham: Duke University Press, 2004.

Wright, Michelle M., and Tina M. Campt, eds. "Reading the Black German Experience." Special issue, *Callaloo: A Journal of African Diaspora Arts and Letters* 26, no. 2 (2003): 288–94.

Wynn, Neil A. " 'Race War': Black American GIs and West Indians in Britain during the Second World War." *Immigrants & Minorities* 24, no. 3 (2006): 324–46.

Zhang, Junfu. "Black-White Relations: The American Dilemma." *Perspectives* 1, no. 4 (February 29, 2000). http://www.oycf.org/oycfold/httpdocs/Perspectives2/4_022900/black_white.htm.

Zimmering, Max. *Im herben Morgenwind: Ausgewählte Gedichte aus zwei Jahrzehnten*. Berlin: Dietz, 1953.

Zimmermann, Andrew. *Alabama in Africa: Booker T. Washington, the German Empire, and the Globalization of the New South*. Princeton: Princeton University Press, 2010.

Zöllner, Abini. *Schokoladenkind. Meine Familie und andere Wunder*. Reinbek: Rowohlt, 2003.

Index